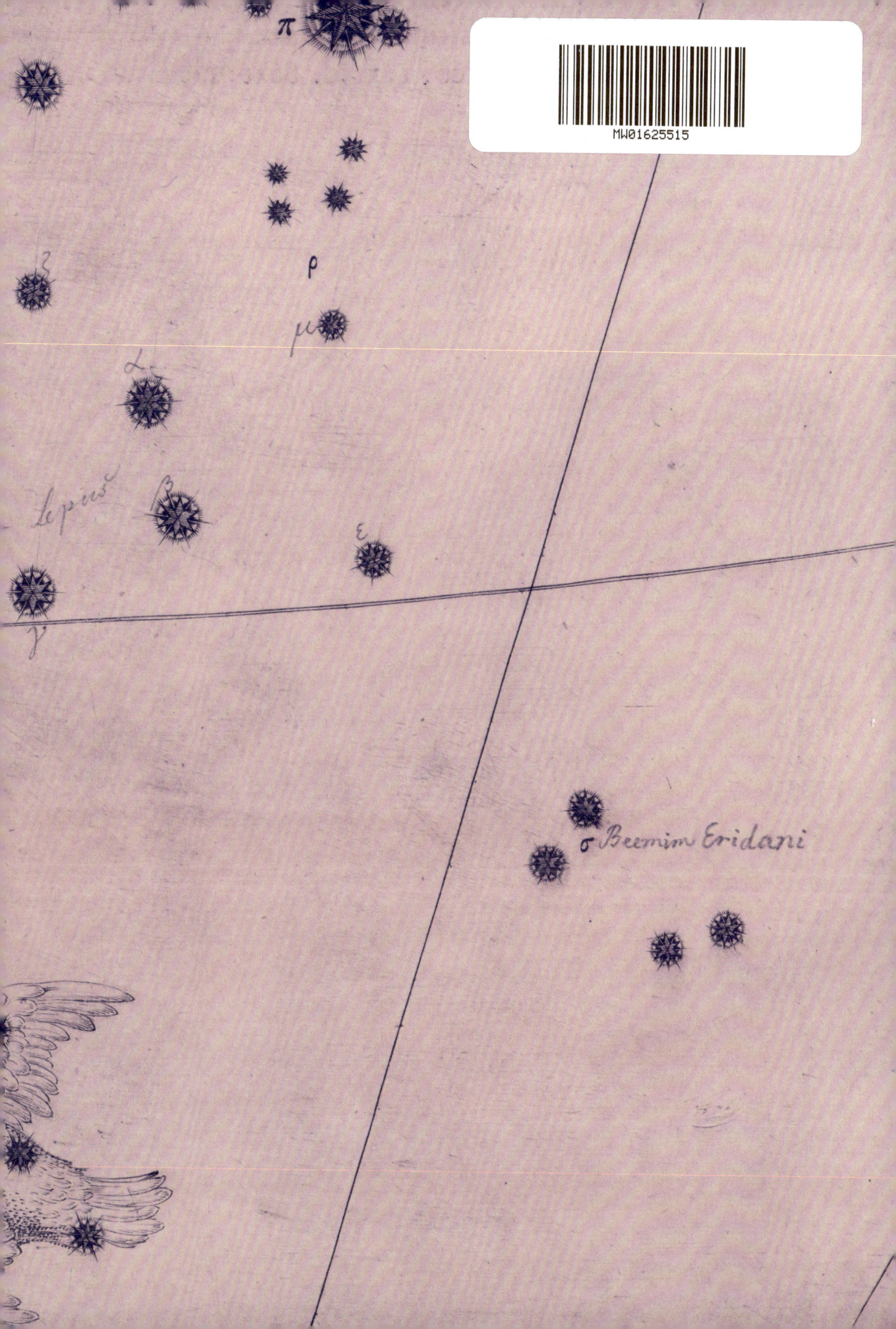
π
ρ
μ
Lepus
β
ε
γ
σ Beemim Eridani
MW01625515

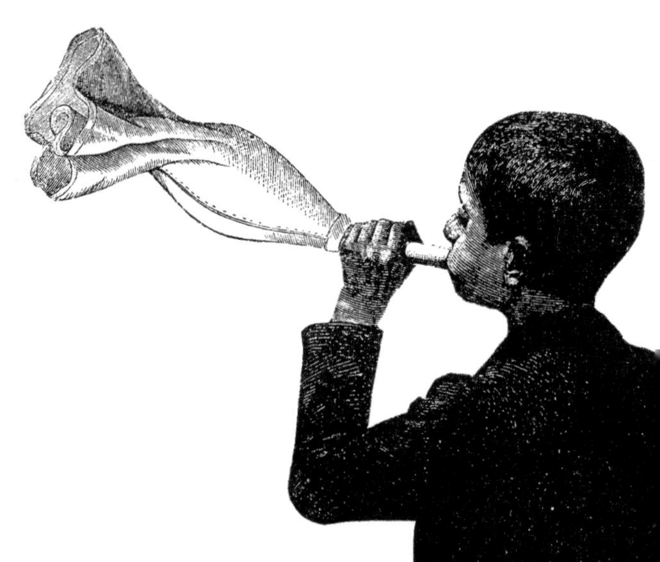

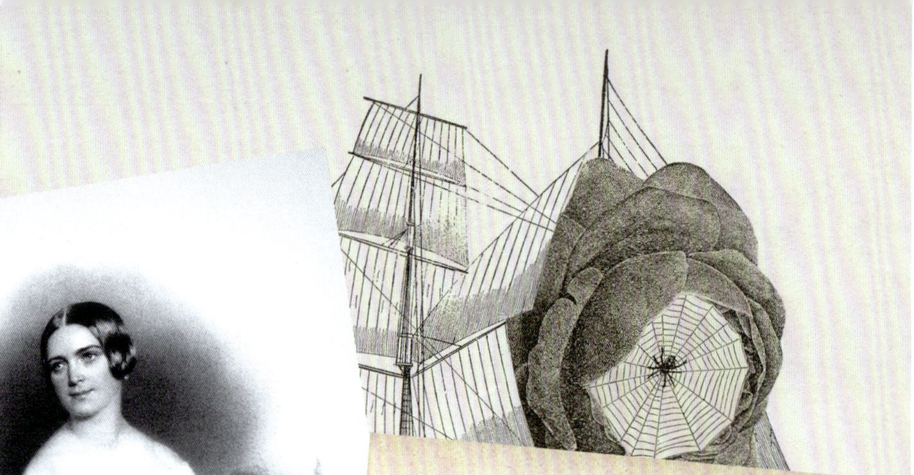

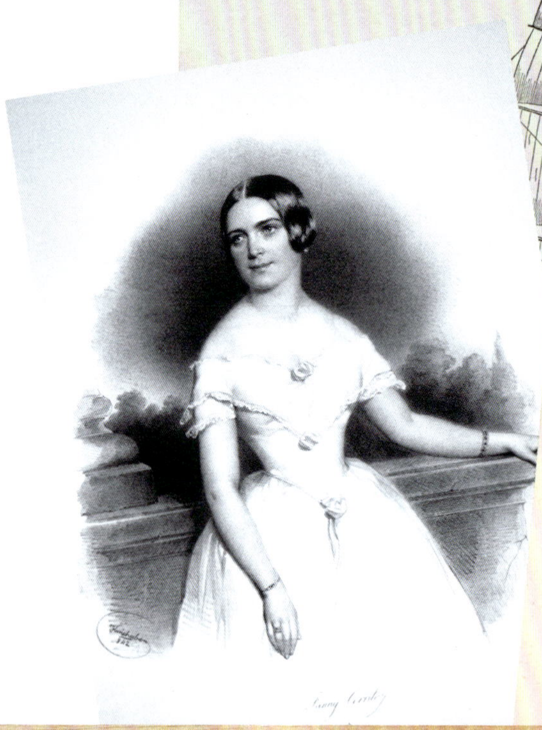

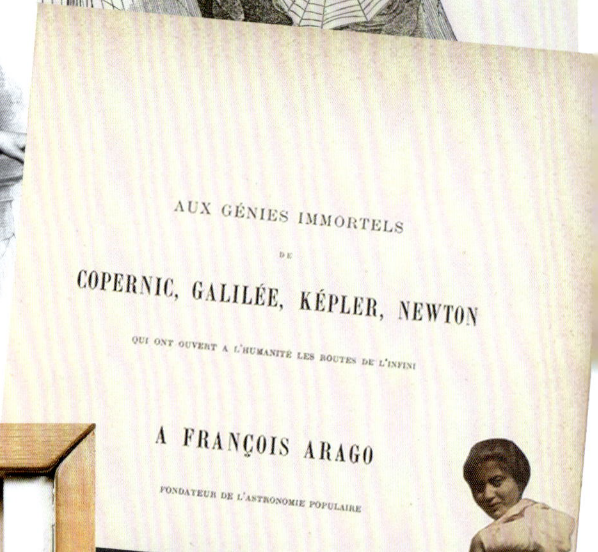

AUX GÉNIES IMMORTELS

DE

COPERNIC, GALILÉE, KÉPLER, NEWTON

QUI ONT OUVERT A L'HUMANITÉ LES ROUTES DE L'INFINI

A FRANÇOIS ARAGO

FONDATEUR DE L'ASTRONOMIE POPULAIRE

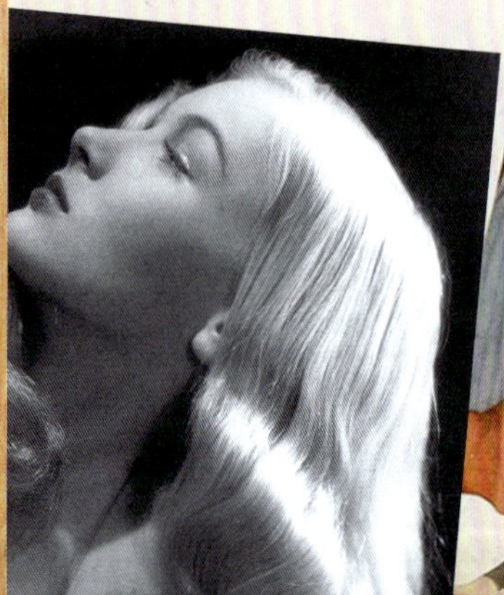

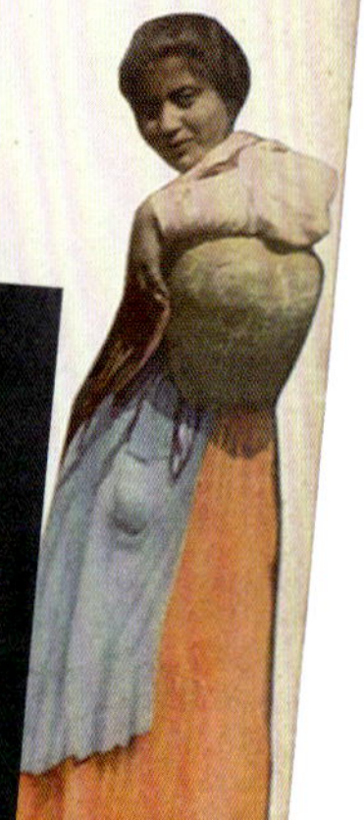

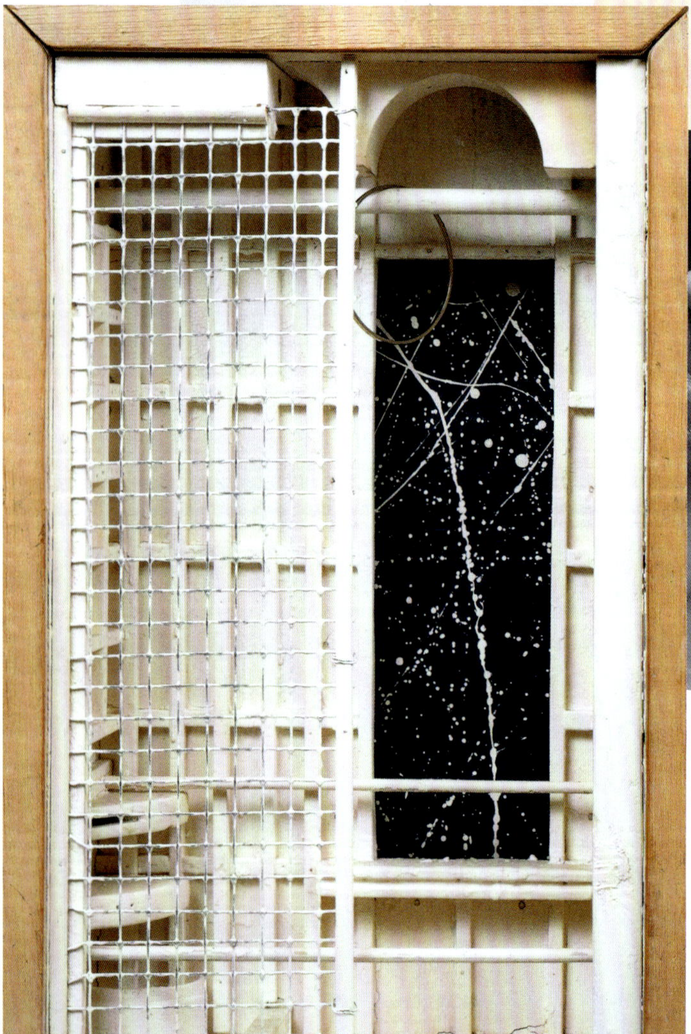

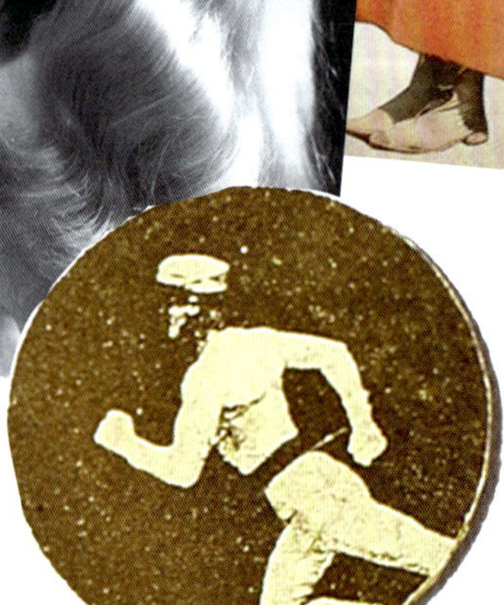

ENCHANTMENTS

Joseph Cornell and American Modernism

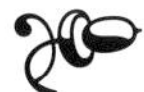

Marci Kwon

PRINCETON UNIVERSITY PRESS
PRINCETON AND OXFORD

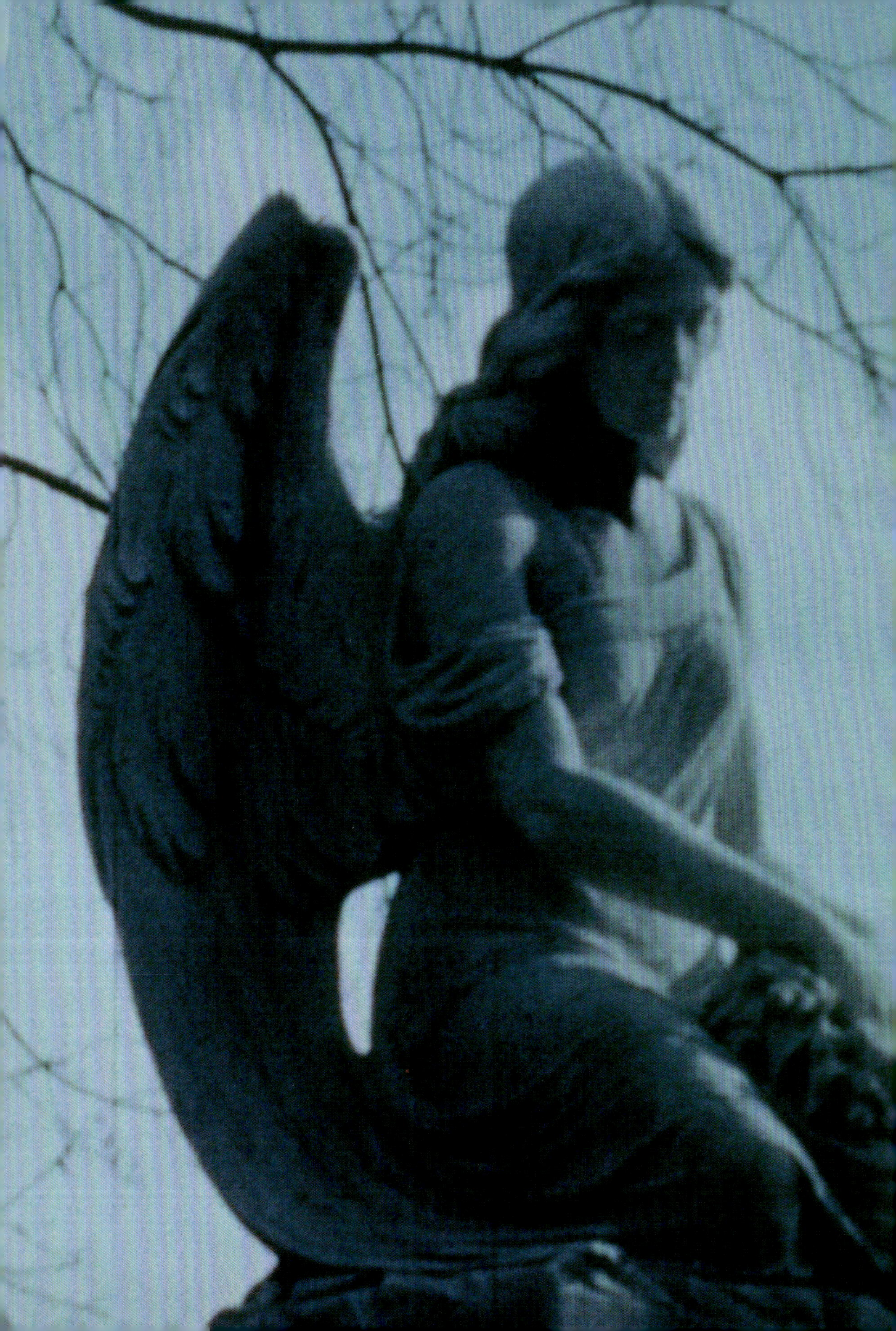

For David, *my imagination*

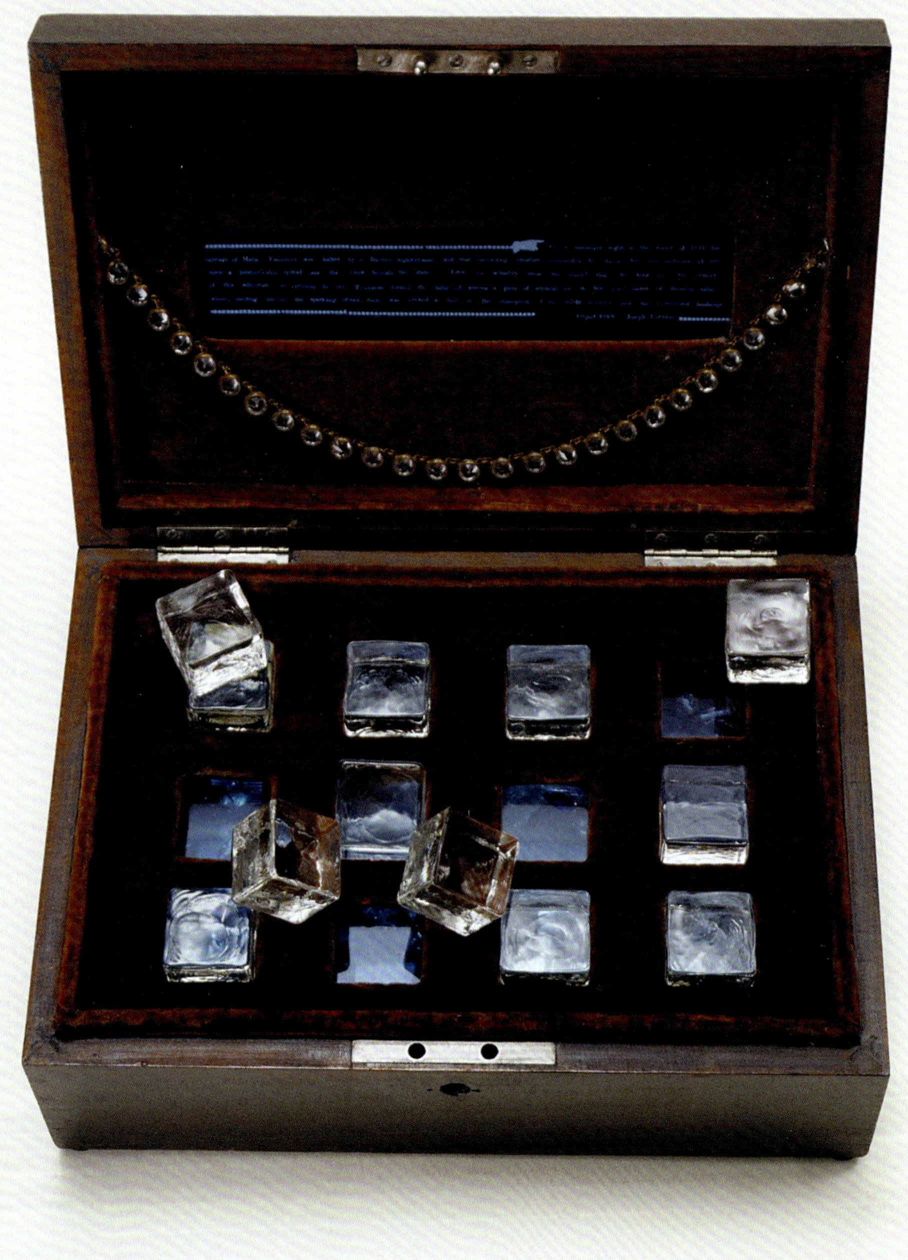

FIG. P.1 Joseph Cornell, *Taglioni's Jewel Casket*, 1940. Velvet-lined wooden box containing glass necklace, jewelry fragments, glass chips, and glass cubes resting in slots on glass, $4\frac{3}{4} \times 11\frac{7}{8} \times 8\frac{1}{4}$ inches. Museum of Modern Art, New York.

PREFACE The Great and the Small

"How very beautiful these gems are!" said Dorothea, under a new current of feeling, as sudden as the gleam. "It is strange how deeply colours seem to penetrate one, like scent. I suppose this is the reason why gems are used as spiritual emblems in the Revelation of St John. They look like fragments of heaven." **George Eliot, *Middlemarch: A Study of Provincial Life***

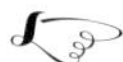

I remember the first time I encountered Joseph Cornell. It was 2004, a few months into my sophomore year of college, and the Museum of Modern Art had just reopened in a gleaming building on Fifty-Third Street. Ascending the ziggurat of escalators to the fifth floor, I wandered past paintings by Cézanne, Picasso, and Matisse before arriving at the gallery dedicated to Surrealism. Cornell's *Taglioni's Jewel Casket* from 1940 was installed in the corner of a large plexiglass vitrine (figs. P.1, P.2). Just twelve inches wide, this modest box holds a world. Glass cubes shine like diamonds, like the paste necklace draped across the box's lid, whose rhinestones form an arc of sparkle below a block of blue text. This text tells the tale of the famed nineteenth-century ballet dancer Marie Taglioni (fig. P.3). While traveling on a Russian highway one snowy night in 1835, Taglioni's carriage was stopped by a bandit. Unfurling a panther's skin on the icy ground, she proceeded to dance so beautifully that the robber allowed her to leave unmolested, her jewels still in her possession. The story concludes: "From this actuality arose the legend that to keep alive the memory of this adventure so precious to her, TAGLIONI formed the habit of placing a piece of artificial ice in her jewel casket or dressing table where, melting among the sparkling stones, there was evoked a hint of the atmosphere of the starlit heavens over the ice-covered landscape."

At this moment, Cornell's work seemed to capture everything I loved about art: its ability to call forth places and times other than my own, its unabashed investment in the magic of the aesthetic encounter. Unlike the painters and sculptors who preceded him in MoMA's galleries, Cornell eschewed the hallowed mediums of paint, marble, and bronze in favor of altogether more modest materials. Before my eyes, chunks of glass were transformed into gleaming repositories of history and memory, precious as the diamonds they mimic.

Yet I could not help but notice that Cornell's work seemed at odds with its companions in the Surrealism gallery, to say nothing of the preceding parade of ambitious paintings and sculptures. The brutality of André Masson's bloody fishes, battling amongst haphazard passages of sand and gesso; the startling juxtaposition of taxidermy parrot and mannequin leg in Joan Miró's *Object* (1936): these works seemed more concerned with shattering illusions than creating them.[1]

I was not the first to observe Cornell's incongruity with canonical narratives of Modern art. Deborah Solomon's popular biography presents Cornell as a hermitic figure who, despite his engagement with New York City culture, remained ensconced in his mother's basement, lost in dreams.[2] When I returned to the artist years later, I found scholars had done much to complicate this stubborn caricature. Their books have detailed Cornell's engagement with subjects such as astronomy, cinema, childhood, travel, and Surrealism to establish his place in modernity.[3] While sympathetic to the aims of these interpreters, I could not help but notice that these accounts remained structured by the dualistic oppositions—between belief and disbelief, ideal and real—that Cornell seemed determined to overcome. *Taglioni's Jewel Casket* is after all an expression of the artist's belief in the incantatory power of the aesthetic

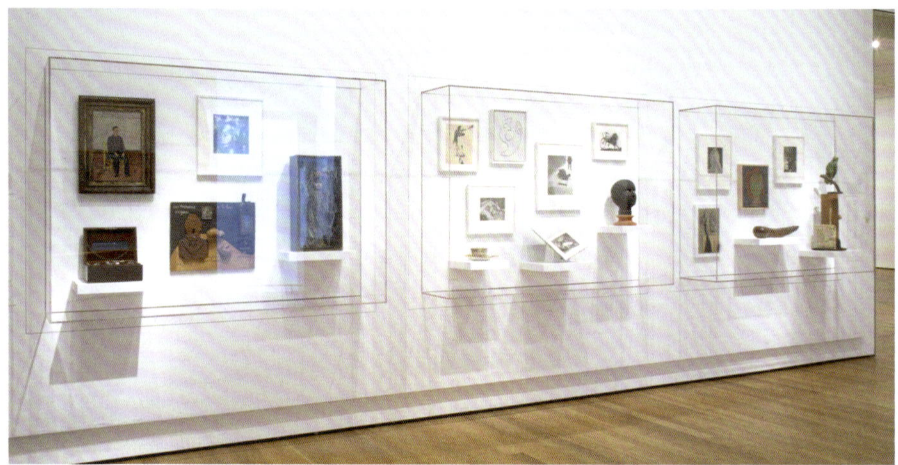

FIG. P.2 Installation view of the exhibition *Painting and Sculpture: Inaugural Installation*, November 20, 2004–December 31, 2005, with Joseph Cornell's *Taglioni's Jewel Casket* at bottom left. Museum of Modern Art, New York.

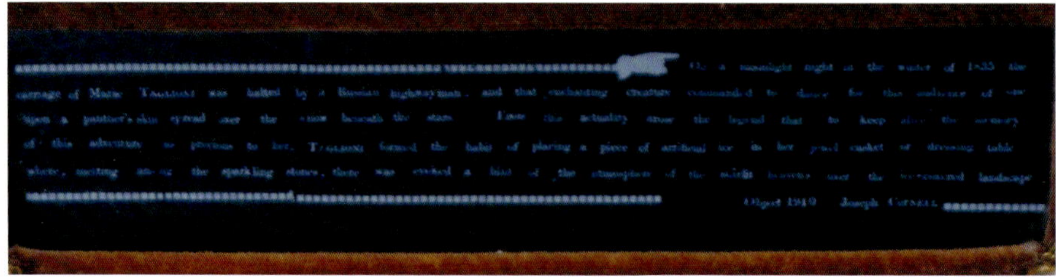

FIG. P.3 Detail of *Taglioni's Jewel Casket*.

encounter. Cornell was also a lifelong practitioner of Christian Science, a religion devoted to mending what its followers perceive as the false divide between the material and the divine. Why, I wondered, was the price of Cornell's modernity the abnegation of his most deeply held principles? How did belief become antithetical to intelligence and seriousness?

To answer these questions, this book examines Cornell's work alongside narratives of enchantment in twentieth-century American art. My title is drawn from Max Weber's infamous description of modernity as the "disenchantment of the world" in his 1918 speech "Science as Vocation."[4] Weber defines disenchantment as modernity's loss of a higher unifying power, religious or otherwise. An impoverished rationalism arose in its place, wrenching the world into distinct spheres governed by their own internal logic rather than divine law. Weber's disenchantment thesis describes this loss of faith as the defining condition of modernity. As a believer, both in Christian Science and in nineteenth-century artistic movements that struggled against the world's perceived disenchantment, Cornell's work offers a vantage onto the fraught history of enchantment in twentieth-century America.[5]

Weber's understanding of modernity as the negation of enchantment has had significant consequences for the way art historians understand the history and ethical stakes of twentieth-century art, for the structural paradox I discerned within the literature on Cornell also describes the epistemic grounding of many art historical accounts of Modernism. Writing in *Farewell to an Idea*, T. J. Clark states that Weber's disenchantment thesis "still seems to me to sum up this side of modernity best."[6] Rosalind Krauss likewise relies on this model when describing the options open to twentieth-century artists: "Given the absolute rift that had opened between the sacred and the secular," she asserts, "the modern artist was obviously faced with the necessity to choose between one mode of expression and the other." Now, Krauss continues, "We find it indescribably embarrassing to mention *art* and *spirit* in the same sentence."[7] Although distinct in aim and approach, Clark and Krauss's foundational texts share a confidence in disenchantment as a synonym for modernity. In their telling, Modernism was either a doomed struggle against the pernicious contingencies imposed by capitalism, or it gave rise to an avant-garde that sought to demystify modernity's most unbearable fictions: the subject, the commodity, the sign, and the very idea of "art" itself.

Within such narratives, Cornell's enchantment can only be understood as escapist and antimodern. Despite the best efforts of Cornell scholars, this view of the artist remains stubborn, as evidenced by a 2015 review of the sensitive exhibition *Joseph Cornell: Wanderlust*, titled "Joseph Cornell: How the Reclusive Artist Conquered the Art World—from His Mum's Basement."[8] Cornell's distress at this pervasive misprision was such that he ended a close friendship with Robert Motherwell over the painter's description of him as "withdrawn."[9] And in the late 1960s, Cornell noted acidly, "The preoccupation with my seclusion in the mass media and critiques is based on misconceptions, repeated parrot-like by those who should know better—until it has acquired the semblance of fact."[10] This dogged misconception, and its continued purchase into the present moment, suggests that a new approach is needed. What is required is an investigation of the epistemological structures undergirding the very concept of modernity, and the facile dismissal of belief as a mere evasion of the real.

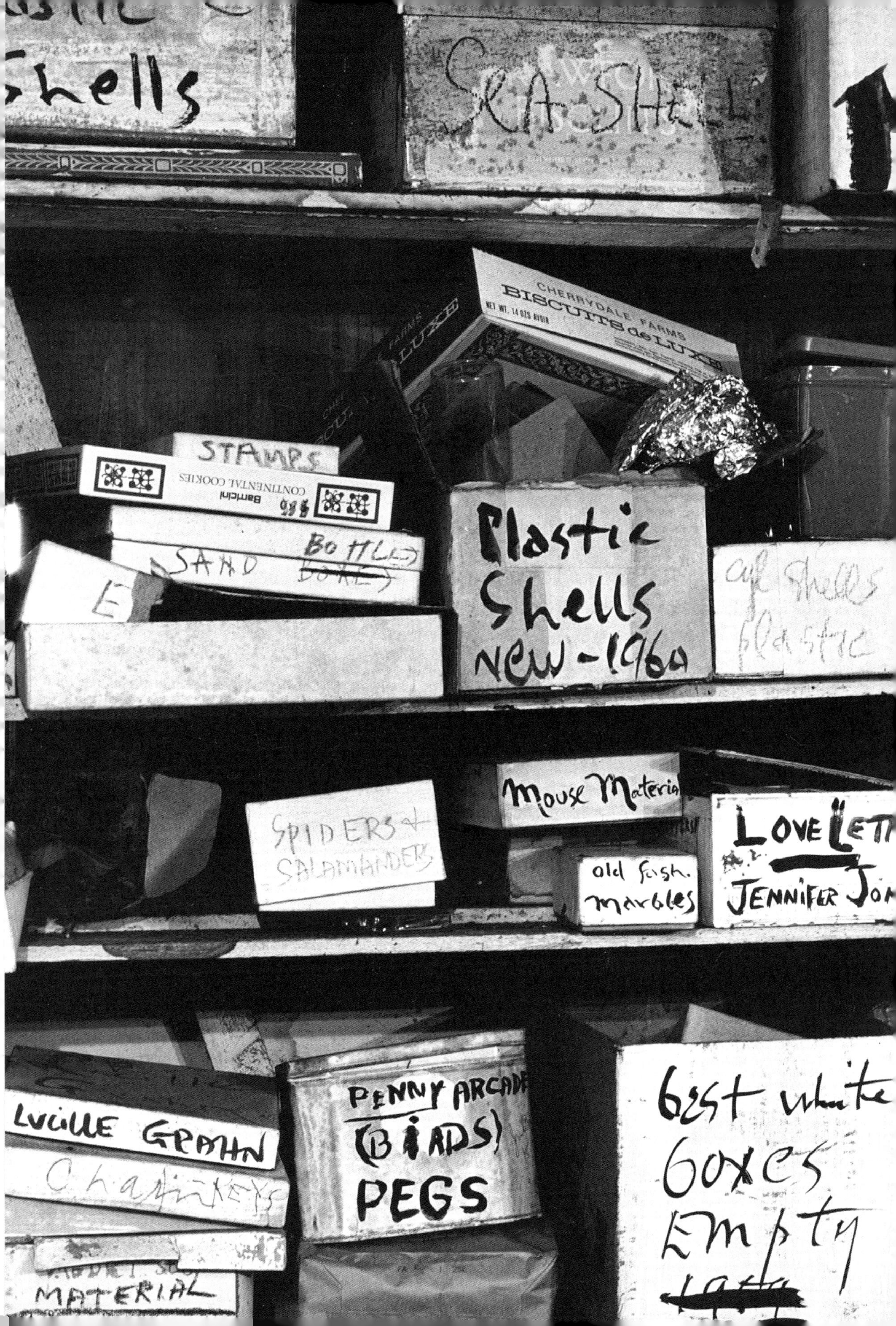

Shells
STAMPS
CHERRYDALE FARMS
BISCUITS de LUXE
NET WT. 14 OZS AVDP
Barbini
CONTINENTAL COOKIES
SAND
BOTTLES
BOXES
Plastic
Shells
NEW-1960
SPIDERS +
SALAMANDERS
Mouse Materia
old fash.
marbles
JENNIFER
LUCILLE GRAHN
PENNY ARCADE
(BIRDS)
PEGS
best white
boxes
Empty
MATERIAL

ACKNOWLEDGMENTS

This book was written in New York; Washington, DC; and California, and was shaped by communities of scholars and friends in each place. At the Institute of Fine Arts at NYU, I am especially grateful to Robert Slifkin and Jennifer Raab. Rob helped me see the myriad ways language and art mean, and therefore matter. Jenny's friendship and profound sensitivity to the literary and the visual enriched my life and work in countless ways. I am also grateful to Jonathan Hay, Pepe Karmel, Rob Lubar, Alex Nagel, Kenneth Silver, and Barry Flood, whose proseminar "Beyond Representation" first prompted me to think about the limitations of Enlightenment rationality. When I told Thomas Crow I wanted to write a dissertation on Cornell, he said to me, "This means you will be writing about small things. But small things are often the most important." These words reverberate throughout the book. Tom taught me the ethical stakes of what we do as art historians, and his wisdom and generosity have shaped my thinking in countless ways, great and small.

At Stanford, I am grateful to my colleagues and students for creating a warm, encouraging, and intellectually adventurous environment. I am especially thankful to my chair and mentor, Alex Nemerov, whose sage advice and way of being in the world helped me find the courage to say what I mean. Richard Meyer's passionate commitment to the overlooked and underestimated remains a guiding light for my work. Alex, Richard, Scott Bukatman, Karla Oeler, and Shelly Fisher Fishkin participated in an enormously productive Manuscript Review Workshop at the Stanford Humanities Center, which was also attended by Jennifer Jane Marshall and Richard Cándida-Smith. I am grateful for the countless insights and suggestions offered by these scholars, as well as to Caroline Winterer and Kelda Jamison for organizing the workshop. Thanks also to Jennifer Brody, Gordon Chang, and Michelle and Harry Elam for their generosity and mentorship. And to my students, especially Sara Carrillo, Indie Choudhury, Laura Feigen, Irene Hsu, Alexis Lefft, Viv Liu, Roshii Kyra Montano, Isabella Shey Robbins,

Emily Wang, Kristin Wilson, Jennie Yoon, and those in my graduate seminars "Folk/Self-Taught/Outsider" and "American Mystics," thank you for helping me understand what it means to look, feel, and write at times like this. You are my teachers.

This project has benefited from conversations with numerous scholars across fields. I am especially indebted to the pathbreaking scholarship of Cornell scholar Lynda Hartigan, who generously offered feedback on the project during its earliest stages, and to Pat Barrett of Palo Alto's Christian Science Reading Room. My thinking was also shaped by conversations with Matthew Affron, Ian Alteveer, Jeremy Braddock, Julia Bryan-Wilson, Lynne Cooke, Susan Dackerman, Rachael DeLue, Don Duco, Eleanor Harvey, Jennifer Homans, Nicholas Jenkins, Lauren Kroiz, Joshua Landy, Karen Lemmey, Nick Mauss, Mary Clare McKinley, Laura Messinger, Angela Miller, Anne Morra, Sally Promey, Rebecca Rabinow, Bruce Robertson, Marvin Taylor, Jason Weems, and Cécile Whiting. And I am especially grateful to Florence Grant, who offered incisive editorial feedback at a moment when the manuscript needed it the most.

Thanks also to the staffs of the Archives of American Art, the Art Institute of Chicago, Anthology Film Archives, the Jerome Robbins Dance Division at New York Public Library, the Beinecke Rare Book and Manuscript Library, the Dedalus Foundation, the Getty Research Institute, the Philadelphia Museum of Art, the Wadsworth Atheneum, the Menil Collection, the Institute of Fine Arts, Fales Library, the Museum of Modern Art, and especially the Smithsonian American Art Museum, where Betsy Anderson and Richard Sorenson facilitated access to Cornell's work and papers. Anna Rimel of SAAM's Joseph Cornell Study Center generously shared her important discoveries and photographed work for this book. At Stanford, I am indebted to the staff of Special Collections, the David Rumsey Map Center, and Bowes Art Library, particularly Peter Blank, Andrea Hattendorf, Vanessa Kam, and Amber Ruiz, and especially Elis Imboden and the staff of the Art and Art History Department. At Princeton University Press, Michelle Komie championed this book from the earliest stages. I am grateful for her belief in me, as well as her compassion and guidance through the publication process. Thanks are also due to the staff of PUP, and especially Kenneth Guay, Beth Gianfagna, Terri O'Prey, and the two anonymous readers, whose incisive feedback improved the book immeasurably. Throughout the editing and publication process I was ably assisted by my undergraduate research assistants Carlos Valladares and Ekalan Hou. Finally, I owe a particular debt of gratitude to my graduate research assistant Yechen Zhao, who worked with me on this book for three years. His keen eye, sharp theoretical mind, and unflappable calm contributed to the work in countless ways.

The research, writing, and production of this book were generously supported by grants from the ACLS/Luce Foundation, the Getty Research Institute, the Mellon Foundation, Stanford's Pauline Brown Fund for Advanced Study in American Art, Yale's Center for the Study of Material and Visual Cultures of Religion, The Stanford Art & Art History Department's Publication Fund, Princeton University Press's Global Equity Grant, and the Smithsonian American Art Museum. SAAM's predoctoral fellowship program not only allowed me to spend a year with the Joseph Cornell Study Center but also provided the ideal place to complete my dissertation. I am particularly grateful to Amelia Goerlitz for facilitating my time there, as well as my fellow fellows, especially Caitlin Beach, Layla Bermeo, Ruthie Dibble, and Tobias Wofford. In 2015, I spent a transformative summer at the School of Criticism and Theory at Cornell University, sponsored by NYU's Graduate School of Arts and Sciences, where my work with Eli Friedlander allowed me to deepen the philosophical roots of this project. I also benefited from the generosity and feedback of audiences at the annual conferences of the College Art Association and the Modernist Studies Association, as well as at the Bruce Museum, the China Art Academy in Hangzhou, the Contemporary Art Museum, St. Louis, the Detroit Institute of Arts, the Metropolitan Museum of Art, and NYU's Center for Ballet Arts, where I presented portions of this work. Parts of chapter 2 were published in the volumes *Complementary Modernisms in China and the United States* and *Establishing the Modern: MoMA and the Modern Experiment 1929–1949* and benefited from feedback by Austin Porter and Sandra Zalman.

This project would not have been possible without my friends, who supported and nourished me in myriad ways. In New York, I am particularly grateful to Max Belkin, Bobby Brennan, Grace Chuang, Kara Fiedorek, Nellie Killian, Thomas Lax, Brett Lazer, Michael Lieberman, Elyse Nelson, Sean Nesselrode, Antonia Pocock, Holly Shen, Christopher Taylor, and Jeffrey Uslip. In California, Aleesa Alexander, Michael Bronstein and Chris Grobe, Angèle Christin and Andre Pesic, Karin and Shane Denson, Joseph Gallucci and Brett Armendinger, A-lan Holt, Jesse Howell, Usha Iyer and Cyril Sebastian, Emanuele Lugli and Michal Sokolowski, Jody Maxmin, David Pedulla and Matt Sainsbury, Iván Ramos, Aileen Robinson, and Hentyle Yapp and Alec Holmes offered profound and sustaining friendships. Most of my dissertation was written under the harsh fluorescent lights of Bobst Library, where I met weekly for a year with Gillian Young, Leon Hilton, and Jamie Parra. Their emotional honesty, humor, and brilliance remains a model of the pleasures of intellectual exchange. I am especially indebted to Leon Hilton, whose incisive feedback and unparalleled critical mind sharpened the arguments and stakes of this project. Finally, I barely have words to express my gratitude to Shawon Kinew and Jamie Parra. Shawon taught me many things about Michelangelo and Aby Warburg, about movement and stillness, about seeing and feeling, but above all she makes me feel seen. And Jamie and I have been traveling this road together for so long that this book feels like ours, rather than mine alone. He read every word of this book multiple times, and his suggestions augmented its precision and wisdom. He taught me how to be a scholar and continues to teach me about language, art, love, courage, and above all friendship.

My greatest debt is to my family. My grandparents, Pearl and Tom Kim, have been an unfailing source of support, as have Larry, Ginny, and Kate Reilly. My mother, Micki, my sister, Casey, and I have weathered many difficult things together over these past years. They are the most courageous people I know, and I hope I have made them proud. And finally, my partner, David Reilly is present in every word of this book. Our love shaped its convictions, for there is no enchantment without love. His being gives meaning to my life. This book is for him.

INTRODUCTION

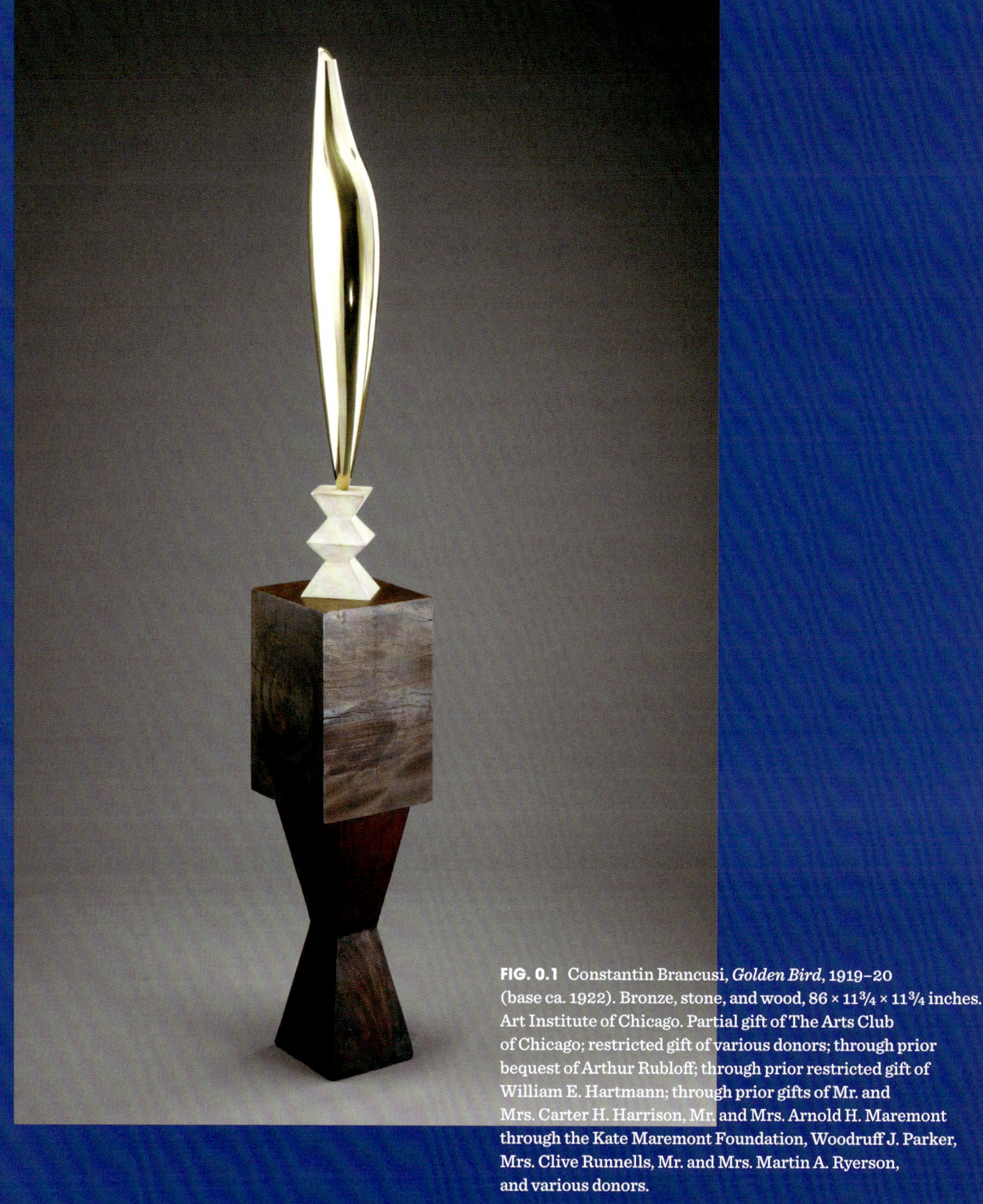

FIG. 0.1 Constantin Brancusi, *Golden Bird*, 1919–20 (base ca. 1922). Bronze, stone, and wood, 86 × 11¾ × 11¾ inches. Art Institute of Chicago. Partial gift of The Arts Club of Chicago; restricted gift of various donors; through prior bequest of Arthur Rubloff; through prior restricted gift of William E. Hartmann; through prior gifts of Mr. and Mrs. Carter H. Harrison, Mr. and Mrs. Arnold H. Maremont through the Kate Maremont Foundation, Woodruff J. Parker, Mrs. Clive Runnells, Mr. and Mrs. Martin A. Ryerson, and various donors.

Enchantments

Only for the sake of the hopeless ones
have we been given hope.

Walter Benjamin, "Goethe's Elective Affinities"

In 1947, Joseph Cornell jotted down a memory from some twenty years earlier. At once impressionistic and precise, his diary entry describes an autumn afternoon in New York City. The year is 1927, four years before Cornell made his first documented work of art. On this day, he took a seat on a trolley car, paging through a book of poetry by Walt Whitman and a compendium of Christian Science psalms as Broadway whizzed by. Then, he looked up:

> Aug 9–1947 * C.S.
> a persistent image—
> about 1927—riding down B'way on the
> old trolley-cars. A warm satisfaction reading
> W. Whitman's (selections little blue bks
> pocket size) also Psalms -
> the "~~discovery~~" of the Brass Knob
> (What a revelation it was)
> of the motorman—conductor shined
> to a equiv. of Brancusi "golden Bird"
> from constant manip. of gloved hands
> all of the above 20 yrs. later seemingly indelible
> the original glow of exhilaration +
> nuances of detail—"the context"
> sense of past traveling on trolley
>   on B'way
> probably autumnal weather.[1]

At this moment, Cornell discovered an equivalence between the trolley car's brass knob and Constantin Brancusi's iconic *Golden Bird* (1920, base ca. 1922), which he had seen a year earlier at the Brummer Gallery (figs. 0.1, 0.2).[2] Both bronze and brass had been polished to a golden gleam by the labor of their respective makers. And although one was a sculpture and the other a common implement burnished by rote motion, Cornell experienced a "glow of exhilaration" in both. The glide of trolley wheels over iron and wood tracks, the experience of reading Whitman and the Psalms, the autumnal weather and light—for Cornell these "nuances of detail" were far from inconsequential. Rather, they formed an inextricable part of experience, as interconnected as knob and sculpture. Upon seeing the motorman's knob and linking it to Brancusi's sculpture, literature, art, city, and life became one. "What a revelation it was," the artist marveled.

Cornell sought to give form to this revelation. For him, enchantment was located not in some distant firmament but in the world around him. From his vantage, anything—a fragment of driftwood, a found photograph, a trapeze trick—holds the numinous power traditionally seen as the exclusive purview of religion or fine art. Cornell's protean artistic output, which included collage, film, and graphic design, as well as his famed box constructions, were attempts to capture the magic he experienced in the world around him.

Consider Cornell's austere box construction *Untitled (Homage to Blériot)* (fig. 0.3), from 1956. A metal coil protrudes from the box's back panel. Slim white bars hold the spiral steady. Mounted at an angle, this delicate structure traces the space of the box, a space parceled out

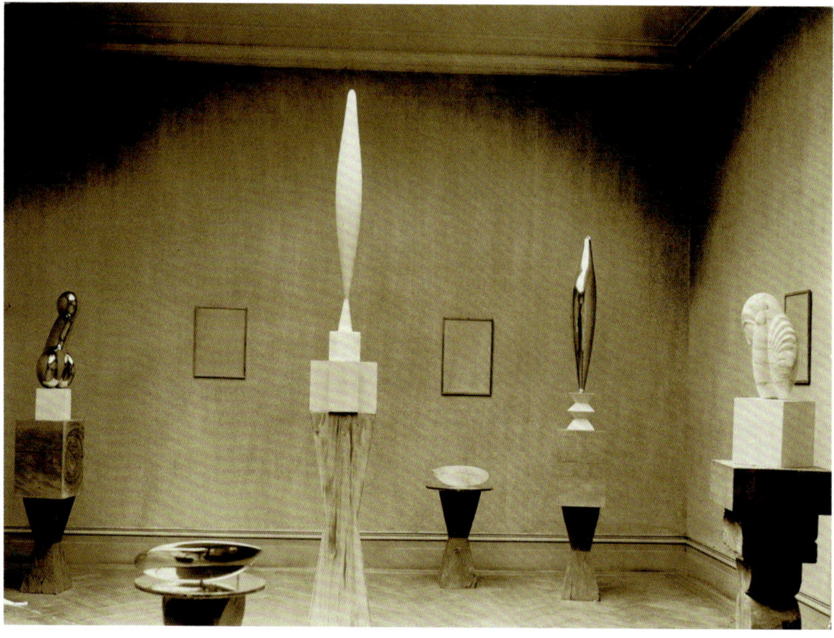

FIG. 0.2 Installation view of the Brancusi exhibition at the Brummer Gallery, New York, 1926. Photographic Archives, Museum of Modern Art, New York.

from the world by a pane of glass and five walls of wood, tinted blue. With this wash of color, the wood grain begins to ripple like the surface of the ocean, like a whisper of clouds blown across the sky. The box forms an appropriate tribute to the daring French pilot Louis Blériot, who in 1909 became the first person to cross the English Channel in an airplane.[3] Just as the trolley knob became Brancusi's golden bird, here a few lines of metal and a wooden frame suggest the lateral spread of airplane wings soaring across a blue sky, over a blue sea. "It is as though he were telling us that in this small space infinity and eternity are contained," wrote the painter Fairfield Porter, in one of the few descriptions of his work that Cornell approved of.[4]

FIG. 0.3 Joseph Cornell, *Untitled (Homage to Blériot)*, 1956. Box construction, 18½ × 11¼ × 4¾ inches. Art Institute of Chicago, Lindy and Edwin Bergman Joseph Cornell Collection.

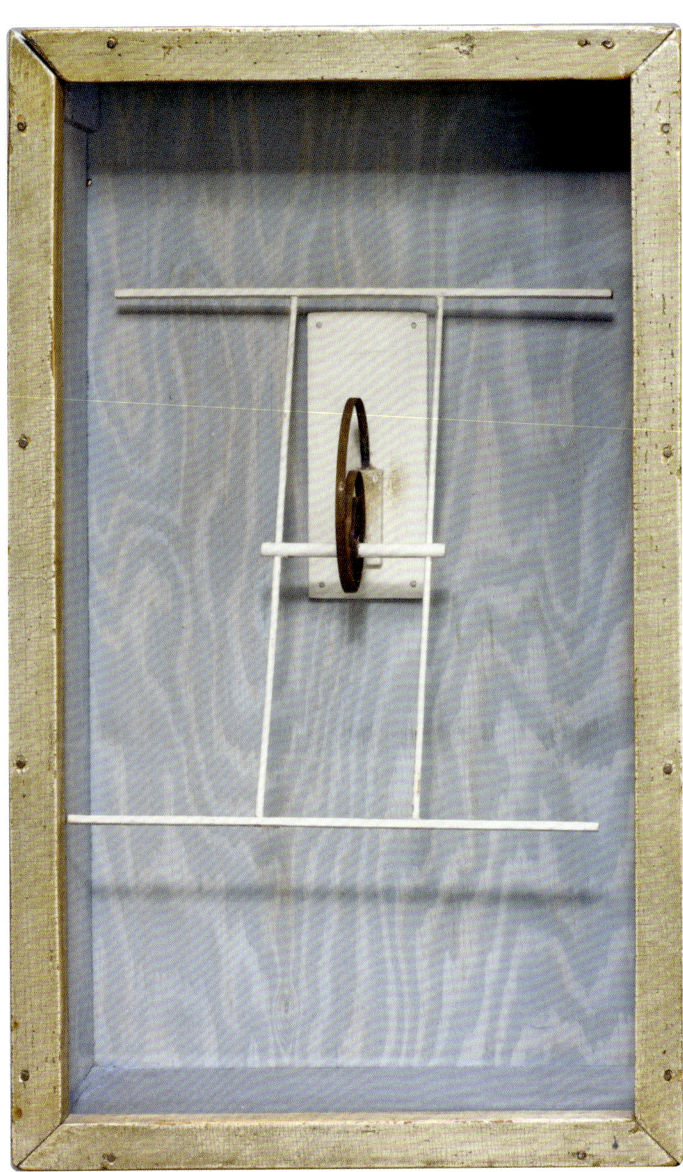

In this box, a hovering spring embodies the miracle of flight; the wood grain captures the liquid expanse of sky and sea. Even the humblest of things contain great significance—provided we are attentive enough to feel it.

Enchantment is deceptively complex. In the broadest sense, it is a force that exceeds rational comprehension, encompassing the divine, the metaphysical, the ideal, and the occult. Colloquially, enchantment conjures images of magic, beauty, and charm. Together with its synonyms, fantasy, imagination, and wonder, it is often used to describe the effects of poetry and art. Enchantment thus cuts across discrete historical periods, appearing—in vastly different forms—within movements that sought an alternative to Enlightenment rationalism, such as Transcendentalism, Romanticism, Symbolism, and Surrealism. As such, in this book I approach enchantment and its antonym, disenchantment, as contingent and contested epistemological constructs rather than ontological certainties.

To be enchanted is to enter a state that defies explanation by rational thought, leading to enchantment's underbelly: its association with trickery, sorcery, and delusion.[5] Shakespeare's Hecate describes the "fire burn and cauldron bubble" of her coven as "enchanting all you put in," capturing the occult power of the witches' brew.[6] Enchantment is a plunge into a realm beyond everyday life; beyond the material world. Thus, to be enchanted would seem to risk losing touch with the "real" world. Because of its associations with mysterious and ungovernable realms and forces, enchantment is ineluctably entangled with power: how is it characterized, where it is it located, and who controls it.[7]

Midcentury American art was shaped by disputes over the meaning and political stakes of enchantment's perceived power. I examine Cornell's work from 1920 to 1960 in the context of these struggles. Although this chronological scope covers the majority of Cornell's career, this book is not a comprehensive account of the artist's practice. Rather, by tracking Cornell's peregrinations through a number of overlapping cultural spheres, I shed light on the ways debates about enchantment and disenchantment were mobilized in period conversations about art's relationship to the public, to popular culture, and its potential for moral authority. While enchantment (via Symbolism and Surrealism) was understood as a demotic, critical artistic ethos in the 1920s and '30s, the rise of totalitarianism in the 1940s led enchantment to be denigrated as a means of social control and propaganda, leading to the rationalist, materialist narratives of autonomy and demystification that continue to shape accounts of Modernism and postwar art. As this history suggests, enchantment is neither inherently emancipatory nor inherently authoritarian but rather can be put to a variety of uses.[8]

Cornell lay at an oblique angle to artistic movements such as Surrealism, Symbolism, and Abstract Expressionism, at moments appearing to align directly with them (as in his relationship to Surrealism in the early 1930s) and at other times chaffing against their strictures. Although his work and reception were shaped by these movements, his own approach to enchantment emerged from deeply personal and idiosyncratic passions and religious beliefs rather than a predetermined philosophical program. To this point, in the last year of his life the artist described religion's importance to his work as an "imponderable area."[9]

Rather than describing Cornell's beliefs as "eccentric" or "escapist," in this book I am interested in how and why such descriptions became attached to Cornell's work—and to enchantment itself. When speaking about the beliefs of artists, art historians would do well to keep in mind William James's pragmatic assertion that "our own more 'rational' beliefs are based on evidence exactly similar in nature to that which mystics quote for theirs."[10] Instead of approaching mystical experiences as delusions, James reminds rational moderns that "our senses, namely, have assured us of certain states of fact; but mystical experiences are as direct perceptions of fact for those who have them as any sensations ever were for us."[11] Moreover, as literary theorist Branka Arsić has noted in her trenchant reading of Henry David Thoreau, the modern ability to grasp the reality of imagination is limited by the "dogmatic and critical epistemologies of the West . . . predicated on the idealistic understanding of truth as noncontradictory."[12] Within these epistemologies, fantasy, imagination, and the real cannot be reconciled precisely because they offer contradictory approaches to truth.[13]

Twentieth-century American art is rife with so-called eccentrics, such as Gertrude Abercrombie (a practicing Christian Scientist like Cornell), Wallace Berman, Helen Lundeberg, and Agnes Pelton, to name but a few. Cornell's example elucidates the epistemological barriers to taking seriously the beliefs, religious or otherwise, of these artists. Yet historical accuracy depends on our ability to do so.[14] As Arsić notes, "To an antebellum American the divide between fantastic and real was less distinct that it is to us postmoderns, which imposes the requirement that the faithful historian of ideas respect this blur."[15]

Cornell worked in this blur between fantastic and real, and his example suggests the difficulty of maintaining this contradictory position. In his work, Cornell attempted to capture his experience of enchantment in material form and to communicate it to others. As Michael Moon has perceptively observed, his practice can be understood as a "two-sided, never resolved dialogue between a set of (in Freud's terms) apparently 'brief, meagre, and laconic' contents and the torrents of thinking, reading, writing, and conversation they absorbed and could, with effort, release."[16] This "never resolved dialogue" between ephemeral, expansive *experiences* of enchantment and their consolidation into discrete objects, images, and works of art structured Cornell's practice. The artist's enchantment did not remain constant but wobbled in and out of focus like the shimmering image of a thaumatrope, or a quivering reflection on a pane of glass.

Cornell struggled to articulate the character of the world's intangible power, to convey it in material form, and to maintain his belief amidst the horrific conflagrations of the twentieth century. These questions were not circumscribed to the realm of fine art. Rather, they were deeply felt inquiries about the relationship between art, imagination, and the real; the pain and impossibility of desire and creation; the ethical stakes of making art in the midst of violence and suffering; and the possibility of what has been described as human fullness, or a sense of meaning and purpose beyond instrumental rationality.[17] Although I am not religious, these questions resonate deeply with me. To paraphrase the epigraph to this introduction, Cornell sought hope in an increasingly hopeless world. I can think of no more consequential question to consider at this moment.

THE ENCHANTMENT OF JOSEPH CORNELL

The remainder of this introduction tracks three distinct yet related registers of enchantment. First, I examine Cornell's enchantment, and the relevance of his Christian Science beliefs to his artistic practice.[18] I then move to a broad consideration of enchantment's contested definition in a range of scholarly discourses including art history, religious studies, and literary studies. Finally, I offer an overview of enchantment's historical relevance to twentieth-century American art, culture, and society. In considering these biographical, genealogical, and historical registers of enchantment, I hope to clarify their distinctiveness while also elucidating their connections.[19]

Cornell's enchantment was rooted in his experience of the world.[20] Quotidian events such as browsing the secondhand shops of New York City, riding his bike through Queens, or watching a film engendered evanescent moments of beauty, peace, and spirituality in the artist. In his diary, Cornell occasionally used the word "enchantment" to describe such experiences. More often, he marked these moments with an asterisk or the notation "C.S." (for "Christian Science"), suggesting the difficulty of capturing these revelations in language. The artist's extensive diary entries and vast collection of books, clippings, and assorted materials attest to his desire to preserve moments of enchantment. Such revelations—Cornell's religious term for his 1927 trolley car ride—helped him understand that there was more to life than simply waking up, commuting, and working.

Cornell arrived at these convictions following an unusual trajectory for an American Modernist. He spent no time in Paris at the feet of Gertrude Stein, nor did he study at New York's numerous art academies.[21] Joseph Cornell was born in 1903 on Christmas Eve, the oldest son of an upper-middle-class family. His idyllic childhood in Nyack, New York, was cut short by the death of his father in 1917. At age fourteen, Joseph became the head of a household that included his mother, two sisters, and a younger brother, Robert, who had cerebral palsy. To prepare him for this responsibility, his father's employer helped send him to the venerable prep school Phillips Andover, where he enrolled as a scholarship student.[22] Unlike his wealthier classmates, Cornell spent his summers working at a textile mill to support his family and did not attend university after graduating.[23] Instead, he sought employment in his father's field, working as a textile salesman at William Whitman Company from 1921 to 1929.[24]

To reach Whitman's offices in the Garment District, Cornell took the train from his family home in Flushing to Grand Central Station. Once in Manhattan, he traversed the city making sales calls to downtown manufacturers, which he later described as the "nightmare alley of Lower Broadway."[25] Like the beleaguered John Sims in King Vidor's 1928 film *The Crowd*, he felt himself a mere cog in city's great machine of industry and capitalism. And like Sims, who at the film's end found solace in New York's vaudeville theaters, Cornell turned to the city's vibrant cultural offerings to ameliorate the arduousness of his daily routine and his burdensome responsibility to provide for his aging mother and younger brother.

When I began work on this project, I spent months poring over the annotated books at the Smithsonian's Joseph Cornell Study Center. Among the volumes I examined was *Prose Works*, by Mary Baker Eddy, the founder of Christian Science. Next to Eddy's description of Christian Science as "right thinking and right acting, physical and moral harmony . . . supplying the universal need of better health and better men," a single word is written in graphite: "art."[26] While this inscription seemed to be the smoking gun that all researchers dream of, the rounded letters did not look like the familiar slanted script of Cornell's hand, nor his sister's fluid cursive. After years of research, I finally realized that the handwriting belonged not to Joseph, but to Robert.

Joseph's faith was inseparable from his love for Robert. The Cornell brothers converted to Christian Science after early visits to the church seemed to alleviate Robert's symptoms.[27] Among Christian Science's foundational beliefs is the idea that any illness might be cured simply by acknowledging the human body as a manifestation of God's perfection, and therefore incapable of being ill. Christian Scientists believe that one might banish physical malady simply by understanding the impossibility of sickness in a perfect world. Rather than dismissing such beliefs, consider this: many visitors to the Cornell home on Utopia Parkway assumed Robert's physical disabilities meant diminished mental capabilities. As the annotation in *Prose Works* suggests, this could not have been further from the truth. For Joseph, living with Robert was a constant reminder that appearances do not constitute reality. The "better health" Robert connected to "art" was more than relief from physical illness, but from the impoverished understanding of the world as reducible to its outward appearance.

Christian Science teachings formed the core of Cornell's enchantment. The artist converted to Christian Science in 1929 and remained a practitioner for the rest of his life. Founded by Eddy in the late nineteenth century, Christian Science sought to transform the modern understanding of ontology, which she described as "the science of real being" in *Science and Health with Key to the Scriptures*.[28] Christian Scientists reject the idea of God as a personified, corporeal figure; rather they believe "God is Love . . . God is Intelligence."[29] This abstract point is explicated in Eddy's glossary, which includes the following synonyms for "God": "Principle; Mind; Soul; Spirit; Life; Truth; Love; all substance; intelligence."[30] Within Christian Science ontology, God is synonymous with the world itself ("all substance"), and palpably present in all its manifestations. The world is not a mere *reflection* of God, in a Platonic sense; it *is* God. "The divine Mind maintains all identities, from a blade of grass to a star, as distinct and eternal," writes Eddy.[31] This is what is meant when Christian Scientists invoke the primacy of the divine Spirit. As William James noted of all "mind cure" religions, Christian Science included, theirs is a theology of immanence, or a "doctrine of the oneness of our life with God's life."[32]

In other words, at its core Christian Science ontology is concerned with conquering disenchantment, or "magic's [and God's] exit from the henceforth law-governed world."[33] In *Science and Health with Key to the Scriptures*, Eddy proffers frequent warnings about the danger of ascribing the workings of the world to materialist scientific processes.[34] For Christian Scientists, the description of a flower as a collection of cells produced through pollination and photosynthesis fails to apprehend its true nature as a manifestation of the divine. The central aim of Christian Science theology is to correct the idolatrous belief that matter is reducible only to itself. In understanding the divine as immanent in the material world, Christian Science ontology contests one of modernity's foundational epistemological constructs: the irreconcilable divide between the ideal and the real.

While Christian Science provided the guideposts for Cornell's artistic ambitions, it also erected a set of challenges for him to negotiate in his work. Strikingly, Cornell does not mention "Jesus," or "Christ" in any of his diary entries, signaling his divergence from Christian Science orthodoxy. Eddy's warnings against the veneration of materialism raises a potential danger for artists in particular: idolatry. As numerous scholars have shown, fear of idolatry—the improper assignment of power to the worldly rather than the spiritual—was one of the primary drivers of disenchantment in the history of art. "Protestant iconoclasm," writes Joseph Leo Koerner, "sought disenchantment—mere wood and nothing else."[35] Iconoclasm diagnoses idolatry as a category mistake: by locating divine power in the material world, idolaters fail to apprehend its true nature. Extending this inquiry into postwar period, Thomas Crow has described the problem of idolatry as central to the "missing theology" of modern art. Artists such as Mark Rothko, Colin McCahon, and James Turrell turned to abstraction to convey the metaphysical's "inability to be expressed," picturing the paradox in order to transcend it.[36]

Christian Science's understanding of the divine as immanent in "all substance" allowed Cornell to approach the problem of idolatry in a different way. For Christian Scientists, idolatry's "posture of submission to a merely material object" is not a misplaced veneration of the material but rather the misunderstanding of the material as *merely* material. Unlike Protestant iconoclasts or Expressionist painters, Cornell did not need to abnegate images or the material world to convey divine force but located this force within the world. Unlike Wassily Kandinsky, Hilma af Klint, or Arthur Dove, he did not require abstraction to depict the undepictable. Christian Science's doctrine of immanence instead offered Cornell a model for conveying enchantment not by transcending the material world but by engaging it.

There is another danger that must be vanquished within Christian Science: the ascription of power to matter itself, as in fetishism.[37] This idea helps distinguish Cornell's version of enchantment from prominent period conversations about theosophy and occultism.[38] Eddy explicitly denies that such power can be found in the material world, writing of occultism, "As light destroys darkness and in the place of darkness all is light, so (in absolute Science), Soul, or God, is the only truth giver to man."[39] Her use of the metaphor of darkness and light to distinguish Christian Science ontology from occultist thought has important consequences for understanding Cornell's practice, for as I discuss in chapter 2, Cornell sought to distance himself from the Surrealists by describing their procedures as "black magic" and his own as "white magic." Yet the white magic of divine power easily slips into darker registers. The black magic of fetishism and occultism, with their attribution of power to non-divine sources, remains the shadow of Cornell's enchantment. White and black magic are not so easily separated, and to this point, the epilogue of this book considers the racialized dimensions of this constructed dichotomy. Although Cornell abjured black magic, his work often inadvertently blurred the line between these categories. All that Cornell tried to suppress would come to fore in the generation of artists who took up his work in the 1950s and '60s.

Cornell's experiences of enchantment were agonizingly brief.[40] He was plagued by his inability to preserve such moments, to capture them in physical form. As he told artist Carolee Schneemann, "A box may resolve frustrations but it is not an equation to the experiences which prompt it."[41] Cornell's art is characterized by this interplay of belief and doubt. As literary theorist Erich Auerbach wrote of Jean-Jacques Rousseau in 1932, the philosopher was "the first who, despite a thoroughly Christian constitution, was no longer able to be a Christian."[42] Auerbach understands Rousseau's work as attempting to find grace in a fallen world, and Cornell too was "beset by this fate."[43] His perpetual oscillation between faith and doubt, between his conviction that there is more to the world than can be explained by scientific positivism and rational thought, and his acknowledgment of his limitations to convey this force, offers a richer description of what it meant to be an artist in twentieth-century America than any abstract concept ever could.

AS IF

How might one capture enchantment in material form? Let us return to Cornell's transformative trolley car ride. The artist's invocation of Brancusi's "golden bird" forges a link not only to the sculpture but also to Mina Loy's 1922 poem "Brancusi's Golden Bird," first published in Schofield Thayer's influential Modernist little magazine *The Dial* (fig. 0.4).[44] Loy, who shared Cornell's Christian Science faith, was also the mother-in-law of his first dealer, Julien Levy. Like the artist's trolley knob as sculpture, Loy's opening stanza addresses the elevation of a humble thing.

> The toy
> become the aesthetic archetype
> As if
> some patient peasant God
> had rubbed and rubbed
> the Alpha and Omega
> of Form
> into a lump of metal

BRANCUSI'S GOLDEN BIRD

BY MINA LOY

The toy
become the aesthetic archetype

As if
some patient peasant God
had rubbed and rubbed
the Alpha and Omega
of Form
into a lump of metal

A naked orientation
unwinged unplumed
—the ultimate rhythm
has lopped the extremities
of crest and claw
from
the nucleus of flight

The absolute act
of art
conformed
to continent sculpture
—bare as the brow of Osiris—
this breast of revelation

an incandescent curve
licked by chromatic flames
in labyrinths of reflections

This gong
of polished hyperaesthesia
shrills with brass

FIG. 0.4 Mina Loy, "Brancusi's Golden Bird," *The Dial* 73 (November 1922).

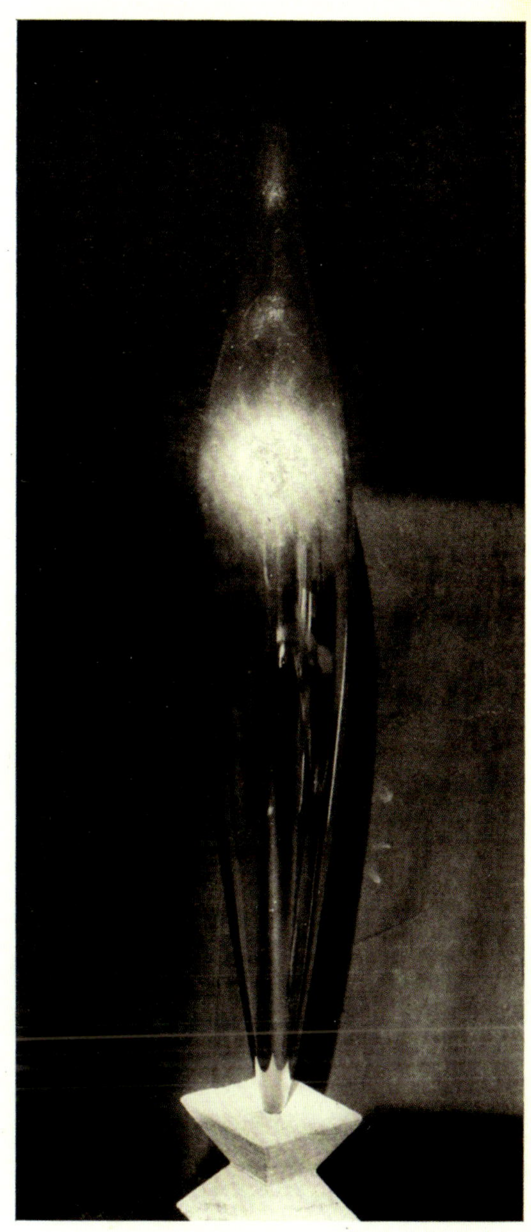

Courtesy of John Quinn

THE GOLDEN BIRD. BY CONSTANTIN BRANCUSI

Alpha and Omega, beginning and end, are "rubbed and rubbed," recalling the trolley knob "shined . . . from constant manipulation of gloved hands." The chiastic structure of the poem transforms its central simile into a strategy of equivalence. The toy's momentary transformation into archetype, in the upper portion of the poem, is mirrored in the lower portion by ideal Form's transformation back into a "lump of metal." Loy's offset "As if" functions as a chiastic mirror, reversing the transformation at top and suggesting the equivalence of these processes.[45] Chiasmus also structures the poem's layout. Art historian Ashley Lazevnick has perceptively noted that the offset "As if" mimics the point where Brancusi's bronze bird meets its base, transforming the text into an upside-down rendering of the sculpture.[46] The chiasmus generated by Loy's "As if" thus extends to the poem's rendering of metal in language. Loy posits poem and sculpture as reflections, mirror images, and thus ontological equivalents. Her poem is more than an ekphrasis of Brancusi's sculpture, just as for Cornell, the motorman's knob was more than an evocation of Brancusi's sculpture. Rather, Loy's poem *is* the *Golden Bird,* paralleling Cornell's memory, in which the knob momentarily *becomes* this same sculpture. Loy's placement of "As if" just outside the column of text highlights its distinctiveness and locates it in the margin, forming a hinge—a moment of separation and continuity—between the poem and the world beyond.[47] For Cornell and Loy, figuration was more than a linguistic flourish, but a means of connection and transformation.

Yet by the end of the stanza, ideal "Form" has turned back into a common "lump of metal." The moment of the toy's elevation has passed as quickly as it took to read these eight lines. Like experiences slipping from Cornell's grasp, like the fugitive figuration connoted by Loy's "As if," enchantment slips away.[48]

Figuration lay at the heart of Cornell's attempt to capture enchantment. Drawing on the work of Paul de Man, Robert Slifkin has argued that figuration connotes more than morphological resemblance, but "forg[es] associative chains of reference and analogy" in order to "create a structure of meaning."[49] In *Taglioni's Jewel Casket* figuration is the means by which glass cubes become ice; paste diamonds metamorphose into precious gems; and a wooden box lined with velvet comes to stand for a nineteenth-century fairy tale. Such analogies rely on the "binary logic" of semiotics, in which the figurative substitutes for the figured, a logic whose arbitrariness would seem to exclude a power exterior to the figurative structure. But approached differently, figuration can also hold spiritual connotations.[50]

Auerbach elucidates figuration's spiritual capacities in his 1929 book, *Dante: Poet of the Secular World,* published at the very moment Cornell began to think of himself as an artist. He describes Dante's attempts to reconcile the concrete reality of the world with "the physical, ethical, and political unity of the Scholastic Christian cosmos at a time when it was beginning to lose its ideological integrity."[51] Figuration was the means by which Dante achieved this. For the Italian poet, figuration "establish[es] a connection between two events or persons in such a way that the first signifies not only itself, but also the second, while the second involves and fulfills the first."[52] The deeper kinship among these ostensibly unlike entities can only be apprehended through "the *intellectus spiritualis*," for as Auerbach notes, "their interdependence is a spiritual act."[53] Here, the relationship between figure and figured is neither arbitrary nor supplemental, but motivated by a higher force. *The Divine Comedy*'s poetic form presented a "figural interpretation of reality" in which divine power is immanent, or "revealed and true reality is present at all times, or timelessly."[54] An earthly event embodies the "divine order which encompasses it," rather than being a pale shadow of truth, as the Neoplatonists would have it.[55] In Dante's figuration, there is no gap between the real world and spiritual power, for they are one and the same. "But actually there is no choice between historical and hidden meaning; both are present," Auerbach writes. "The figural structure preserves the historical event while interpreting it as revelation; and must preserve it in order to interpret it."[56] Figuration maintains the particularity of an earthly event while also reading it as a sign of something else, calling into question the hard divide between representation and the so-called real world. Figuration was the means by which Dante was able to convey the perfect unity of the earthly and the spiritual, and thus allow the earthly to take on higher connotations, or "the figure of perfection on earth . . . a vision of the unity of earthly manifestation and eternal archetype."[57]

Auerbach's insight clarifies the centrality of figuration to Cornell's enchantment. For the artist, glittering panes of glass, wispy feathers, grains of sand, and shards of wood were more than merely themselves, just as for a poet, words are more than instrumental units of communication. As Fairfield Porter noted of Cornell's boxes: "They allude not so much to volume and space as to the kind of emotions and memories that are a material of poetry. Instead of illustrating poetry, they compete with it."[58] To this point, the artist maintained friendships with poets, including Loy and Marianne Moore, and drew inspiration from the poems of Emily Dickinson and Stéphane Mallarmé. Just as Loy's "As if" transforms humble toy into Ideal, language into sculpture, Cornell sought to transform common ephemera into experiences of enchantment. His boxes are poems, their contents arranged as precisely as the syllables of a sonnet. In the chapters that follow, I consider specific formal strategies such as montage, fragmentation, the box format, and plays of scale to explore how Cornell transformed common materials into figurative objects, which bring far places near, make the past present, and give form to experiences of enchantment.

A BRIEF HISTORY OF ENCHANTMENT

To grasp the broader implications of enchantment for American Modernism requires a digression into the genealogy of the term. Much of the scholarly literature on enchantment takes Weber's linkage of disenchantment and modernity as a starting point. But what exactly did Weber mean by disenchantment? Delivered to a hall of students at Munich University just three years before his death from influenza, "Wissenschaft als Beruf" addresses the higher purpose of scholarly inquiry. Thus, the common English translation of *Beruf* as "vocation," a term that connotes religious calling, is apt. In an oft-quoted phrase, Weber describes the triumph of "intellectual rationalization," or the assumption that "there are no mysterious incalculable forces that come into play, but rather that one can, in principle, master all things by calculation." He continues, "This means that the world is disenchanted," or *entzauberung*, literally "de-magic-ing."[59] A disenchanted world is a world that can only be described through intellectual rationalization, a world in which all "mysterious and incalculable forces" have been banished. Weber mourned this condition. In the second half of his speech, he investigates the insufficiency of intellectual rationalization to answer the "why" implied by "vocation."[60]

Weber makes clear the equivalence between intellectual rationalization and modernity. Less apparent is that which has been suppressed by disenchantment's presumed triumph. How might one draw a definition of enchantment from a text whose subject is its antonym? Within the scholarly literature, enchantment is alternately described as the agency of supposedly inert materials; the feeling of wonder as one considers nature; the desire Pygmalion felt when he gazed upon Galatea; the imaginary words conjured by fantasy literature; paganism; and the continued purchase of Christianity. This broad range of examples extends from the capaciousness of Weber's initial thesis. For Weber, enchantment connotes both pagan "spirits" and a Christian God.[61] In short, while enchantment is often conflated with religious belief, and disenchantment with its negation, the term encompasses more than a single religious doctrine. As such, enchantment is often deployed as a catch-all to describe that which exceeds rational explanation. What unites these disparate considerations is their shared sense that enchantment is Enlightenment rationality's other.

A number of scholars, in a variety of fields, have challenged the absolutism of Weber's alignment of modernity and disenchantment (and by extension, enchantment's exclusion from modernity).[62] Scholars of "re-enchantment" such as Joshua Landy and Michael Saler explore secular replacements for a lost divine unity.[63] Their prefix encapsulates the basic tenets of this line of thought. "Re-enchantment" assumes the fundamental truth of Weber's disenchantment thesis, taking as a given his description of modernity as fallen. In this narrative, poets, artists, philosophers, and occultists seek compensatory offerings in the face of Enlightenment rationality. Religious studies take a more agnostic approach to the presumed triumph of disenchantment, challenging the dominance of what Sally Promey describes as the "secularization thesis," or "the idea that the secular and religion will not coexist in the modern world, that religion represents a premodern vestige of superstition."[64] Philosopher Charles Taylor writes against this "substitution model" in his monumental *A Secular Age*. In Taylor's account, "[t]hose attuned to religious belief and experience . . . are pulled toward openings to transcendence, while others feel the pull of the 'closure of immanence.' "[65] For him, the hyphen that binds "re-enchantment" is not a loss but a dialectic between belief and disbelief.[66] Taylor's account hews closest to my sense of Cornell's enchantment. Although the artist was a believer, he did not live in a state of perpetual enchantment but struggled to hold on to those fleeting moments of presence and grace. "I'd better get this down before it evaporates," he wrote after one particularly potent experience.[67]

Religious studies scholar David Morgan proposes that enchantment persists in modernity's continued "recognition of the power of things."[68] Morgan's work draws on Bruno

Latour's influential *We Have Never Been Modern,* which details the continual "blending" of "natural mechanisms and human passions" to critique modernity's sense of its own exceptionalism.[69] By recognizing the agency and animacy of those materials and objects that scientific inquiry would deem lifeless, new materialism offers an implicit critique of intellectual rationalization's anthropocentrism.[70] New materialism thus draws some of its ethical frisson from postcolonial theory's insight that Western thought enacts violent distinctions between the rational Western subject and the supposedly primitive other (although the extent to which new materialism's practitioners recognize this aim remains an open question).[71] Perhaps because of these associations, new materialism tends to abjure any consideration of spiritual power, Christian or otherwise.

In this book, I am less interested in determining whether or not "we have ever been disenchanted" than I am in thinking about the historical effects of narratives of enchantment and disenchantment.[72] As such, I move away from the ontological questions ("What is enchantment?" "Is the world enchanted?" "Is modernity disenchanted?" "What are the various categories of enchantment?") that have preoccupied the aforementioned scholars, to think instead about how the contested discourses of enchantment and disenchantment shaped Cornell's work—and the course of twentieth-century American art.

Art has always been bound up with questions of enchantment; thus art history offers a crucial perspective on these discussions.[73] "Insofar as modern souls possess a religion," writes anthropologist Alfred Gell, "that religion is the religion of art."[74] By this Gell means that the very idea of art, and the "auratic" power bestowed upon it by modern ideas of originality, authorship, and taste can be understood as the sole bastion of sacred values within a predominantly secular world. Hans Belting's influential discussion of the supplanting of "cult" by "art" likewise traces disenchantment to the emergence of Renaissance humanism, which sought to replace the cultic power of relics and icons with a self-reflexive, man-made category of objects called "art."[75]

At stake in these discussions is the oft-discussed concept of art's aura and its relationship to theories of enchantment. As Jeffrey Hamburger has noted, Belting's work can be understood as "part of a larger set of historical narratives attempting to cope with secularization, and, in particular, Weber's concept of disenchantment."[76] Hamburger aligns Belting's project with Walter Benjamin's famed "Work of Art" essay and specifically the German philosopher's understanding of aura as originating "in the service of rituals—first magical, then religious."[77] Aura connotes originality and singularity; it is the residue of enchantment that remains after the purported onset of secularization. Mechanically reproduced media such as photography is "useful for the formulation of revolutionary demands in the politics of art," because of its challenge to aura, or its capacity to "emancipat[e] the work of art from its parasitical subservience to ritual."[78] The basic contours of this argument are familiar enough: art's aura is complicit with ideologies of social distinction; thus a truly revolutionary art must be freed from ritual.[79] Like Weber before him, Benjamin combines ritual, religion, and aura into a single pernicious force, mentioning neither denominational distinctions nor divisions between institutional and vernacular religious practices. I hope that the historical account provided by this book will nuance this narrative. Enchantment is not a monolithic force; it appeared in different forms in Cornell's work and in the movements he engaged. The midcentury turn toward disenchantment has led art historians to likewise combine occultism, institutional and alternative forms of religion and spirituality, and the aesthetic power of art and poetry into a single force. This consolidation has overshadowed the many *uses* to which various forms of enchantment were put before its dismissal as dangerous irrationality, and occluded enchantment's capacity to offer trenchant critiques of modernity.

ENCHANTMENT AND ITS DISCONTENTS

If Modernism in its broadest sense can be understood as the multiple and heterogeneous cultural responses to modernity, then it also presents an opportunity to consider enchantment's changing role in the twentieth century.[80] Conversely, unsettling the epistemological alignment of disenchantment and modernity offers a new way of understanding the capaciousness of Modernism. And yet, a whiff of indescribable embarrassment (*pace* Krauss) lingers around questions of belief and enchantment in art historical considerations of Modernism. As Lisa Florman writes in her book on Kandinsky and Hegel, "I don't want to deny the significance of [theosophy and Eastern mysticism and the occult] to the development of Kandinsky's thinking and writing about art—or, rather, even though I *want* to deny their significance, I find I can't entirely."[81] Florman's admirably self-reflexive admission of her *desire* to abnegate belief and to return Kandinsky to the bosom of Western philosophy (and save him from the taint of Eastern mysticism) is related to the historical narrative I put forth in this book. Her tacit admission that she cannot fully disregard the mystical aspects of Kandinsky's practice speaks to the way enchantment continues to haunt Modernism.

Enchantment's purchase for Modernism was due to its implicit critique of modernity. To this point, consider Jennifer Roberts's salient gloss on poststructuralist readings of Robert Smithson: "[This scholarship] has demonstrated the challenges that Smithson's work posed to the totalizing impulses associated with high modernism by detailing his unabashed contamination of idealistic aesthetics with materiality, contingency, and physical labor; his dislocation of the traditional sites of artistic production; his complication of the authorial function; and his violation of disciplinary boundaries."[82] With little alteration, Roberts could be describing Cornell's practice. Her discussion of Smithson's engagement with Catholicism is germane. As Roberts shows, in Catholicism Smithson found an alternative model of temporality and history, complicating the description of his practice as a turn to base materialism.

For art historians steeped in the lessons of poststructuralism, Modernist values of authenticity, originality, and authorship—and their complicity with capitalism and possessive individualism—are precisely that which artists such as Smithson sought to critique. These scholars uphold disenchantment, or in critical theory parlance, demystification, as the primary goal of advanced twentieth-century art.[83] I do not (for how could I?) dispute the ethical commitments undergirding this stance: so much violence has been done in the name of supposedly "universal" ideas such as a Christian God, or "Man."[84] And yet, despite their commitment to critiquing the idea of individual artistic genius, many such accounts reinscribe the rational, agentive subject as the sole agent of intelligence, ethics, and criticality, while overlooking the challenges belief itself might pose to modernity's fetishization of rationality. Contra such accounts, this book shows how discourses of Modernist autonomy and poststructuralist critique share a fear of enchantment and have worked together to smooth over the complexities and ambivalences of many twentieth-century artists. As Roberts writes, Smithson felt a "need to pre-figure a transcendent, eternal condition beyond the limitations of that history. This condition was not to be metaphysical but rather, in his terms, 'infraphysical,' a condition to be located within rather than without the material."[85] Even Smithson hoped to find something else in a meaningless world, even if that something else was simply the very same world.

Because of its presumed opposition to Enlightenment rationality, early-twentieth-century American artists and writers understood enchantment not as an escape from, but as an alternative to, capitalist accumulation and individuality. As I discuss in chapters 1 and 2, during the 1920s and 1930s, enchantment (filtered through the discourses of Transcendentalism and Surrealism) appeared to offer a critique of Gilded Age excesses, a challenge to fine art's perceived elitism, and a potential site of social cohesion in the face of the Great Depression. With the rise of totalitarianism, enchantment instead came to be viewed as a potential tool of mass delusion and violence, appearing to align with the effects of propaganda. This historical trajectory speaks to one of this book's themes: the centrality of narratives of enchantment and disenchantment to midcentury debates over the relationship between fine art and popular or vernacular culture. This line of argument was famously consolidated in Clement Greenberg's 1939 essay, "Avant-Garde and Kitsch,"[86] which attempted to secure art as a site of integrity beyond the dangerous enchantments of kitsch and propaganda.[87]

Greenberg's Kantian formalism is a prime example of what literary critic Mark Greif has described as a midcentury ethos of "re-Enlightenment," or a return to Enlightenment ideals of progress, reason, and the autonomous subject.[88] Theodor Adorno and Max Horkheimer took an altogether more skeptical view of these ideals in the *Dialectic of the Enlightenment*, written in the aftermath of the Second World War and published in German 1947. They diagnose Enlightenment rationality and its unshakeable faith in historical progress as modernity's most dangerous myth. For Adorno and Horkheimer, the danger of the Enlightenment was not its advocacy of reason but its mythic narrative of progress.[89] Accordingly, they maintained a hostility to "irrational" fictions such as myth, belief, and the so-called culture industry.

Such convictions were deeply felt. Adorno elaborated the stakes of this argument in his 1950 book, *The Authoritarian Personality*, written in response to the Holocaust. Drawing on recent anthropological theories of personality, Adorno describes the "authoritarian type" as "combin[ing] the ideas and skills which are typical of a highly industrialized society with irrational or antirational beliefs." An individual's irrationality, Adorno argues, renders her susceptible to the pernicious and false promises of propaganda. Only the self-reflexive negation of myth, or a disenchanting "disclos[ure] of each image as script," can protect against this danger.[90] In the book's preface, Horkheimer praises "the impact of Cartesian rationalism" for laying bare the "roots of delusion," thereby discrediting early modern superstition and witchcraft. "Once this scientifically untenable dogma was eliminated," he explains, "the foundations of the belief in magic were destroyed."[91] This brief historiographic summary helps elucidate disenchantment's centrality to midcentury debates about art's moral authority. Totalitarianism's cynical deployment of enchantment cloaked it in nostalgia, delusion, and escapism, securing disenchantment as a critique of modernity's violence.

Revisiting midcentury debates about totalitarianism at this moment is a sobering exercise. The force and clarity of *The Authoritarian Personality* has only grown in salience with the global rightward turn. And yet, I continue to be troubled by the question of *who* is denigrated by the wholesale dismissal of belief as "delusion." The midcentury suspicion of belief, myth, Romanticism, and magic were an understandable reaction to totalitarianism's reliance on what Émile Durkheim described as "collective effervescence."[92] Yet throughout this book, I also track how the elevation of disenchantment as the sole bastion of ethics in art was—like all hierarchies of taste—a form of social ordering. How does this narrative consolidate heterogeneous forms of enchantment into mere delusion, and secure rationality as the sole site of intelligence? Who is expelled from serious consideration when enchantment can only be understood as complicit with conservative social forces?

As these questions suggest, the historical denigration of enchantment has ramifications for thinking through art history's continued reliance on Euro-American epistemologies.[93] To this point, scholars of Asian, Islamic, and Byzantine art have turned to issues of animacy and agency as a methodological alternative to the Western rationalism. Genealogical accounts of the idol and the fetish have shown how the failure to recognize the life and power to supposedly "inanimate" objects lies at the heart of colonial violence.[94] As a straight, putatively asexual white man whose beliefs were grounded in Judeo-Christian tradition, Cornell's practice is far from a challenge to Western hegemony.[95] Moreover, the artist maintained an idealizing if objectifying view of women, the subject of chapter 4. Despite this, Cornell's work became a touchstone for several younger artists who held avowedly feminist, antiracist ambitions. Their example suggests enchantment's relevance to the artistic and social ambitions of postwar American art.

Although Cornell never directly engaged these critical debates, he experienced their effects. In a 1944 letter to Loy, he wrote of seeing a "smoked fish delivery truck" adorned with a painting of "fat pieces of meat surrounded by whole fish in colors that make one think it might at one time have been bright decalcomania, silvery whites and greys . . ." Cornell continued, "All of the above seems sometimes so evanescent and nebulous that I have never mentioned the trifle to anyone. . . . I have generally paid a pretty high price of the above kind of experience, however silly this might sound to some."[96]

And yet he continued to make art. In a 1969 statement titled "Notes on Art Work and 'Rationale,'" he writes, "Anyone who has shown concern, involv., my work and has not been moved or inspired to become involved somehow or other with the humanities in a down-to-earth context . . . has not understood its basic import. The heart of its message (of the work) has not come across."[97] Here, Cornell describes the true aim of his artistic project as generating connection, not just among materially distinct entities, but among people.

Consider the gleaming glass fronts of Cornell's boxes. These transparent planes are often described as devices of enclosure, sealing away the world within. And yet we can see through them. "Effect of box depends upon glass being kept shiny," Cornell wrote on the back of one work (fig. 0.5). Their pristine shine reflects the world around them. They are contingent planes that transform our presence into ephemeral flashes of light, shadow, and color. They at once acknowledge and transcend their own materiality, making continuous the space inside Cornell's boxes and the world around them. Cornell's work provides a fleeting experience of a realm in which appearances do not constitute reality, a realm that, despite its denigration, exists.

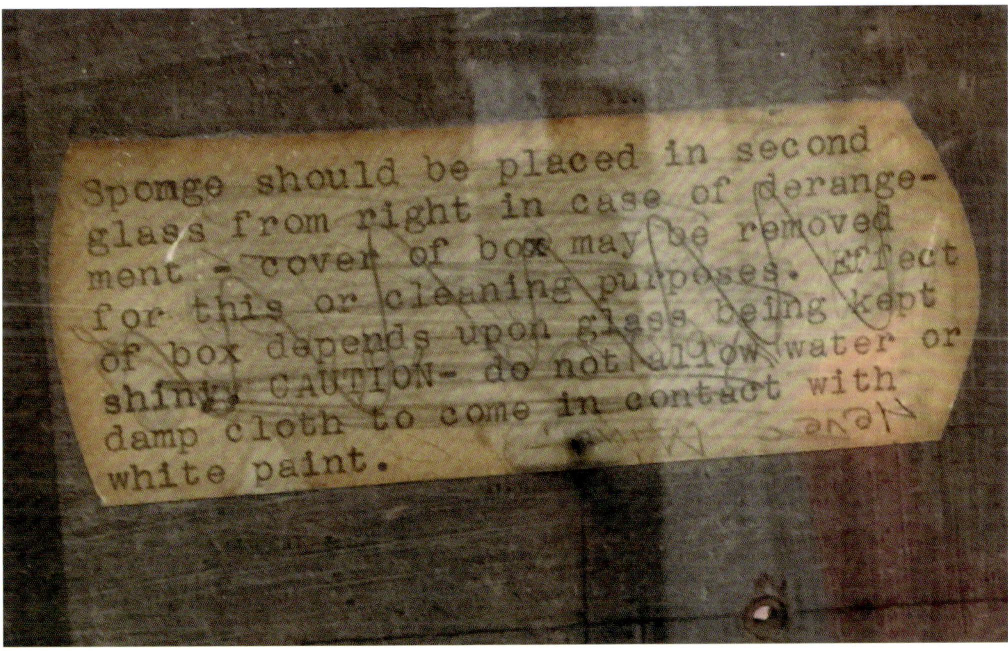

FIG. 0.5 Detail of Joseph Cornell, *Soap Bubble Set*, 1949–50, showing a note by Cornell with cleaning instructions. Smithsonian American Art Museum, Washington, DC.

CHAPTER ONE

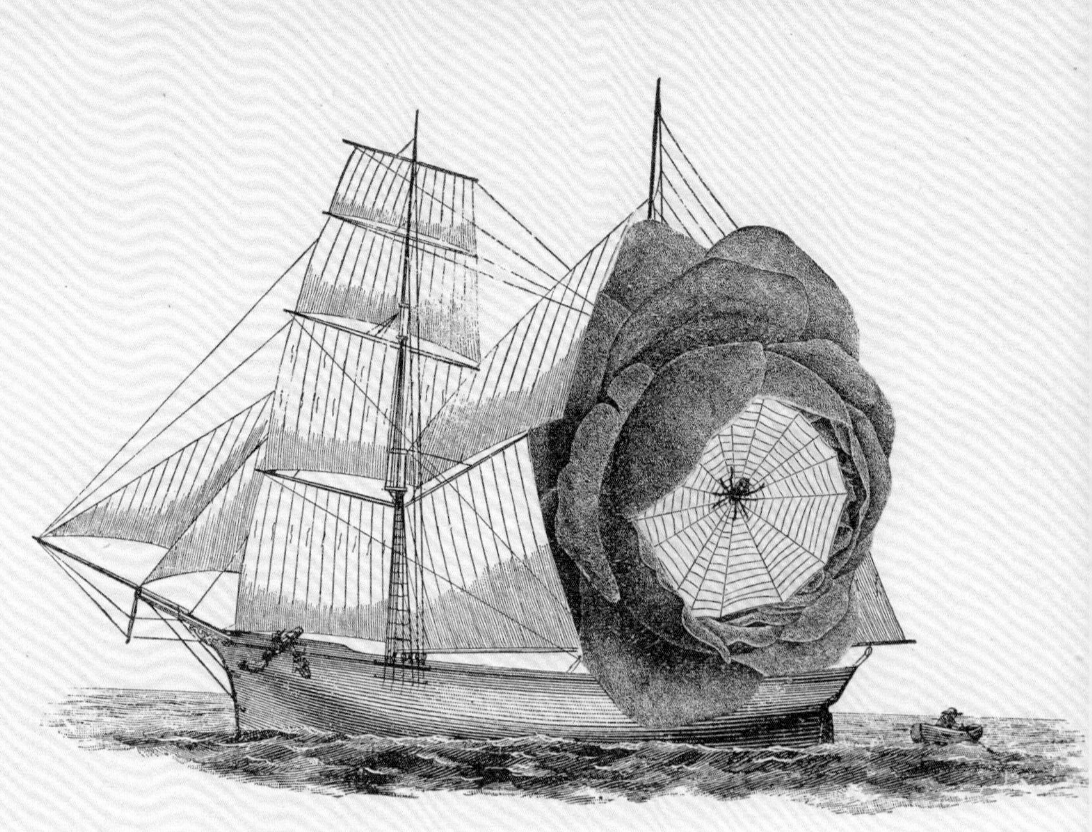

FIG. 1.1 Joseph Cornell, *Untitled (Schooner)*, 1931. Collage of photomechanical reproductions on paperboard mounted to paperboard, $4\frac{1}{4} \times 5\frac{13}{16}$ inches. Hirshhorn Museum and Sculpture Garden, Smithsonian Institution, Washington, DC.

Parts of a World

From the earth, as a shore, I look out into that silent sea. I seem to partake its rapid transformations: the active enchantment reaches my dust, and I dilate and conspire with the morning wind.

Ralph Waldo Emerson, "Nature"

Particularity is all-decisive.

Erich Auerbach, "On the Anniversary Celebration of Dante"

One November day in 1931, a young man walked into Julien Levy Gallery. Although he had likely visited the gallery before, during those previous trips he kept to himself. This time, however, he was not so timid. This time he had something to show the gallerist. In his memoirs, Levy recalled his astonishment as this "gray young man" produced a handful of collages from his coat pocket.[1] In material and composition, Joseph Cornell's collages bore a striking resemblance to the work of Max Ernst, a Surrealist whom Levy just happened to be featuring in an upcoming exhibition.[2] While Levy's written account compressed several visits by Cornell into a single narrative, at some point, the gallery purchased several works from the artist for display in the upcoming show, *Surréalisme,* only the second exhibition of Surrealism in the United States.

Untitled (Schooner) (1931, fig. 1.1), Cornell's first dated work of art, was likely among the collages purchased by Levy. Measuring just four by five inches, the little collage is pieced together from three distinct prints. The picture shows a schooner adrift on a black sea. Wind fills the ship's sails, pulling its riggings taut; yet only a hint of waves ruffle the ocean's surface. The rippling petals of the enormous rose blooming from the ship's stern lends the scene a drama the sea does not. The ship's delicate riggings twist, at the blossom's center, into the spiral of a spiderweb, whose architect is perched at its center. The work shows a world of spiders the size of men and flowers the size of ships—a world in which the conventional laws of nature do not apply, a world where dreams become reality.

Yet this reading, temptingly surreal as it may be, fails to capture the complexity of this little collage. For this we must look to Cornell's annotated copy of Walt Whitman's *Leaves of Grass,* which he acquired in the early 1920s. On page 399, he marks two consecutive poems with graphite checks (fig. 1.2):

Here, Sailor!
What ship, puzzled at sea, cons for the true reckoning?
Or, coming in, to avoid the bars, and follow the channel, a per-
fect pilot needs?
Here, sailor! Here, ship! take aboard the most perfect pilot,
Whom, in a little boat, putting off, and rowing, I, hailing you,
offer.

A Noiseless, Patient Spider
A noiseless, patient spider,
I mark'd, where, on a little promontory, it stood, isolated;
Mark'd how, to explore the vacant, vast surrounding,
It launch'd forth filament, filament, filament, out of itself;
Ever unreeling them—ever tirelessly speeding them.

And you, O my Soul, where you stand,
Surrounded, surrounded, in measureless oceans of space,
Carelessly musing, venturing, throwing,—seeking the spheres,
to connect them;
Till the bridge you will need, be form'd—till the ductile anchor
hold;
Till the gossamer thread you fling, catch somewhere, O my
Soul.[3]

As in Cornell's collage, Whitman places ship and spider alongside one another.[4] In the first poem, a maritime pilot hails a passing ship. His opening address asks the "puzzled" vessel if it might require a "reckoning," implying his ability to steer a true course.[5] He boasts of himself as a "perfect pilot." Only at the end of the poem do we realize that this "perfect" navigator is in fact "in a little boat, putting off, and rowing," casting his lofty ambitions in an ironic light. Whitman's description of the pilot's skiff draws our attention to the rowboat trailing behind Cornell's fantastical schooner. Cloaked in the shadow of the marvelous ship, the tiny boat is steered by a hunched figure, whose presence underscores the schooner's eerie emptiness.

"A Noiseless, Patient Spider" nuances the prior poem's desire for connection. The speaker watches a spider weave its web. Unlike the vocalized ambitions of the pilot in the prior poem, the spider is silent, for it seeks something altogether more ambiguous. When the time is right, it sends "filament, filament, filament," out of itself, throwing these shining ropes into "the vacant, vast surrounding." The speaker finds existential weight in these actions, likening the spider's spinning to her soul's search for a place in the "measureless oceans of space." She, too, flings her metaphorical threads into an unknown void, hoping for a connection, hoping something will catch.

Considered alongside Whitman's poems, Cornell's collage emerges as a meditation on creation as a means of connection, on the multitudes contained by tiny things. Just as Whitman's placement of these poems upon the same page transforms them into a single narrative, Cornell's collage unites ship and spider. The unexpected scalar relationships among ship, spider, and rose are mediated by his meticulous matching of their physical sizes. Cornell's canny play of size and scale, of actual and relational, infuses the fantastic scene with an air of organic continuity. Within the world of the work, the world created by Cornell, enchantment is rendered material, present.

This deceptively modest collage raises many questions about Cornell's early artistic practice. While it stands as his first documented work, it displays none of the tentativeness that usually characterizes an artist's youthful career. The formal economy with which it conveys the insight and force of Whitman's poetry instead suggests a confident, even mature artist.

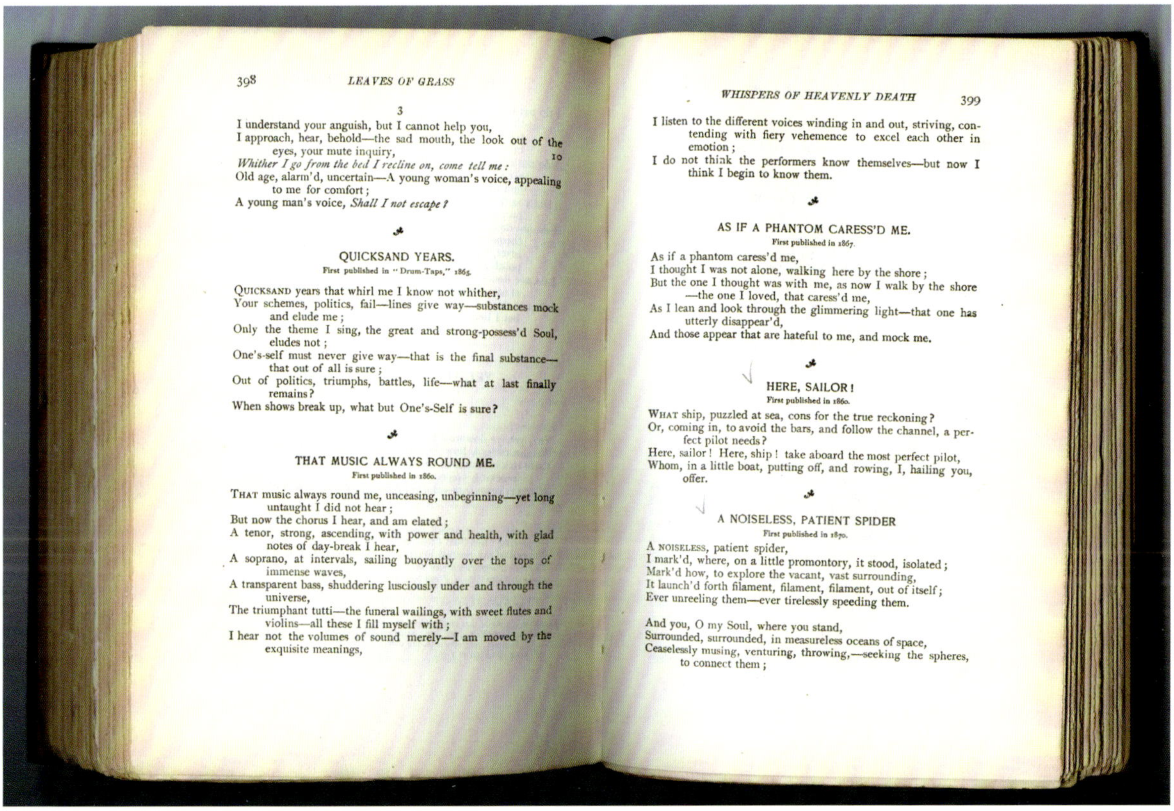

398 *LEAVES OF GRASS*

3

I understand your anguish, but I cannot help you,
I approach, hear, behold—the sad mouth, the look out of the eyes, your mute inquiry,
Whither I go from the bed I recline on, come tell me:
Old age, alarm'd, uncertain—A young woman's voice, appealing to me for comfort;
A young man's voice, *Shall I not escape?*

QUICKSAND YEARS.

First published in "Drum-Taps," 1865.

QUICKSAND years that whirl me I know not whither,
Your schemes, politics, fail—lines give way—substances mock and elude me;
Only the theme I sing, the great and strong-possess'd Soul, eludes not;
One's-self must never give way—that is the final substance—that out of all is sure;
Out of politics, triumphs, battles, life—what at last finally remains?
When shows break up, what but One's-Self is sure?

THAT MUSIC ALWAYS ROUND ME.

First published in 1860.

THAT music always round me, unceasing, unbeginning—yet long untaught I did not hear;
But now the chorus I hear, and am elated;
A tenor, strong, ascending, with power and health, with glad notes of day-break I hear,
A soprano, at intervals, sailing buoyantly over the tops of immense waves,
A transparent bass, shuddering lusciously under and through the universe,
The triumphant tutti—the funeral wailings, with sweet flutes and violins—all these I fill myself with;
I hear not the volumes of sound merely—I am moved by the exquisite meanings,

WHISPERS OF HEAVENLY DEATH 399

I listen to the different voices winding in and out, striving, contending with fiery vehemence to excel each other in emotion;
I do not think the performers know themselves—but now I think I begin to know them.

AS IF A PHANTOM CARESS'D ME.

First published in 1867.

As if a phantom caress'd me,
I thought I was not alone, walking here by the shore;
But the one I thought was with me, as now I walk by the shore—the one I loved, that caress'd me,
As I lean and look through the glimmering light—that one has utterly disappear'd,
And those appear that are hateful to me, and mock me.

HERE, SAILOR!

First published in 1860.

WHAT ship, puzzled at sea, cons for the true reckoning?
Or, coming in, to avoid the bars, and follow the channel, a perfect pilot needs?
Here, sailor! Here, ship! take aboard the most perfect pilot,
Whom, in a little boat, putting off, and rowing, I, hailing you, offer.

A NOISELESS, PATIENT SPIDER

First published in 1870.

A NOISELESS, patient spider,
I mark'd, where, on a little promontory, it stood, isolated;
Mark'd how, to explore the vacant, vast surrounding,
It launch'd forth filament, filament, filament, out of itself;
Ever unreeling them—ever tirelessly speeding them.

And you, O my Soul, where you stand,
Surrounded, surrounded, in measureless oceans of space,
Ceaselessly musing, venturing, throwing,—seeking the spheres, to connect them;

FIG. 1.2 Joseph Cornell's annotated copy of *Leaves of Grass* by Walt Whitman, pp. 398–99. Joseph Cornell Study Center, Smithsonian American Art Museum, Washington, DC.

Following Levy, scholars have discussed this little collage as evidence of Cornell's debt to Surrealism.[6] Yet the work's reference to Whitman suggests that at this early date, Cornell's artistic and intellectual interests extended beyond the European movement. Because of the absence of extant objects by Cornell before 1931, scholarship on the artist's life during the 1920s remains scant, a lacuna that has reinforced Levy's mythic story of Cornell's origins and contributed to the view of his practice as purely instinctive.[7]

By placing Cornell's recollections of the 1920s alongside later works of art, this chapter instead approaches Cornell's visit to Levy and engagement with Surrealism as the culmination of a decade of artistic and spiritual exploration. During the 1920s, Cornell began an intensive study of Romanticism, Symbolism, and Transcendentalism; converted to Christian Science; and began to amass a collection of objects and ephemera that would serve as the basis for his subsequent work. Romanticism, Symbolism, and Transcendentalism are cruxes of enchantment and disenchantment, seeking religion's numinous power in imagination, art, and nature rather than the divine. They are at once rejoinders to Enlightenment rationalism and attempts to express the metaphysical without recourse to an overtly religious power. Alfred Stieglitz's ironic description of himself as "a transcendentalist without God" encapsulates this idea, while also suggesting that Cornell was not alone in his preoccupations during the 1920s, although of course he did so from the position of a believer rather than a skeptic.[8] For Transcendentalist-inspired writers such as Waldo Frank and Paul Rosenfeld, enchantment was no solipsistic escape but a means to combat the Gilded Age's cult of individual achievement and material acquisition.

Although Cornell felt a deep kinship with these movements, he did not simply align himself with them. Rather, he wove their most salient lessons into a distinctive formal grammar of fragmentation, correspondence, and montage, which became the foundation for his nascent artistic practice. Cornell turned to these devices to condense his vast collections of material into discrete works of art, which in turn drew connections among an eclectic array objects, experiences, and historical moments. Cornell's deployment of these formal strategies made him particularly well-suited to Julien Levy's attempts to promote Surrealism in the United States. Conversely, Surrealism's engagement with Romanticism and Symbolism, as well its deployment of found objects, also offered the artist a ready-made discourse through which to present his work as fine art. Cornell's artistic formation, however, preceded his encounter with Surrealism.

COLLECTING

Writing in the 1960s, Cornell described his collecting during the 1920s as initiating a "life-long preoccupation with things."[9] Around the same time that Cornell wrote this entry, Hans Namuth photographed the artist's basement studio (figs. 1.3, 1.4). Namuth's pictures show the result of Cornell's four-decade "preoccupation with things": a room crammed with half-finished works and source materials, sorted into white boxes labeled with cerulean paint. If Namuth's famous photographs of Jackson Pollock visualized artmaking as a virile physical act (fig. 1.5), here artistic process is instead pictured as material accumulation. Any consideration

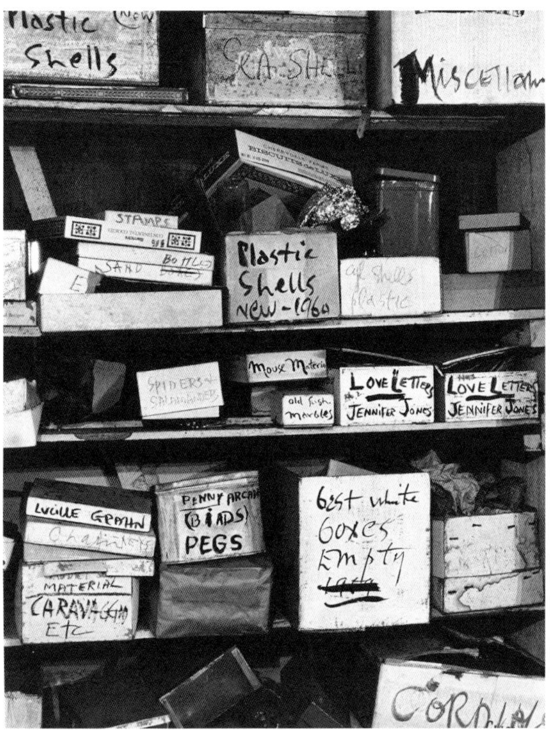

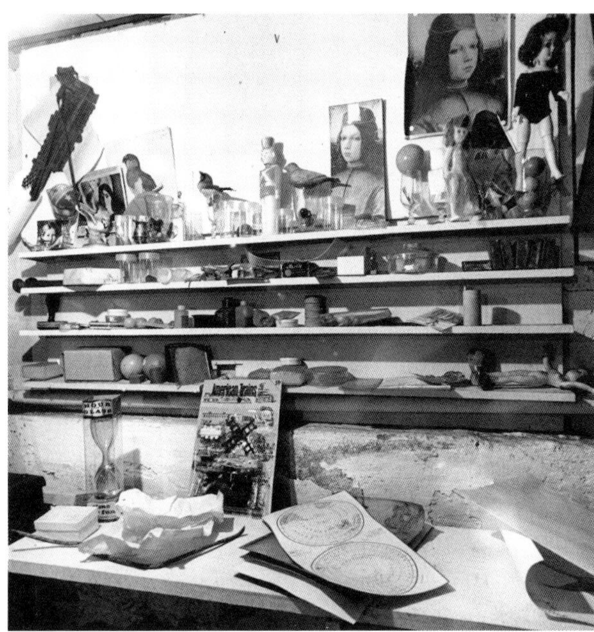

FIG. 1.3 *Cornell's Queens Studio*, 1969. Gelatin silver print. Center for Creative Photography, University of Arizona.

FIG. 1.4 *Cornell's Queens Studio*, 1969. Gelatin silver print. Center for Creative Photography, University of Arizona.

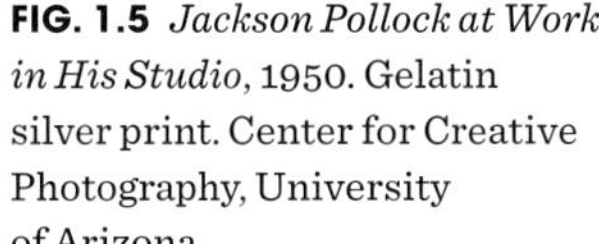

FIG. 1.5 *Jackson Pollock at Work in His Studio*, 1950. Gelatin silver print. Center for Creative Photography, University of Arizona.

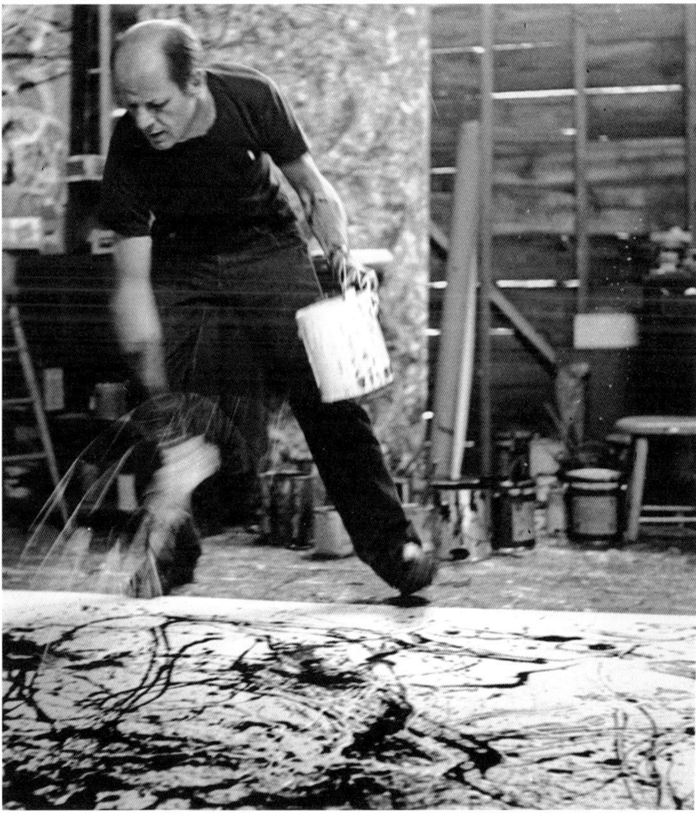

of enchantment in Cornell's work must grapple with the paradox presented by his collecting. While the characterization of Christian Science as strictly antimaterialist simplifies the religion's philosophy of immanence, a seeming mismatch remains between Cornell's religious convictions and this "preoccupation with things." Collecting was the first site where he explored this paradox.

A 1947 diary entry recalling the 1920s illuminates the convictions undergirding Cornell's early collecting. During this decade, he wrote that he felt "the world lived in of artistic appreciation made real thru applic. and in daily realization as experience vs. estheticism."[10] The distinctive ethos of New York's "Book Row," which Cornell later described as the "richest and most significant" source of materials for his collection, helps clarify the artist's statement (fig. 1.6).[11] Established in the 1890s, Book Row comprised dozens of shops scattered between Astor Place and Madison Square Park.[12] Among Cornell's favorite stores was The Sign of the Sparrow, located just two blocks from the offices of his employer, the wholesale textile firm William Whitman Company.[13] Cornell paints a vivid picture of the bookstore in a 1948 essay:

> To the end it remained a "hole in the wall." Purposely, and many were the well known authors, writers, theatrical people etc. who frequented it for its quiet charm. The proprietor had an honest disdain for commercialism, and an irrepressible habit of asking innocent customers who did not know him better questions about the most wild and absurdly ridiculous personages whose cognomens were manufactured impromptu. While preserving the "amateur standing" of the shop its dealer was actually tops in the first edition field, well recognized as such but not an easy mark for a sharper. He was as well the leading authority in his time on Walt Whitman, specializing too on Lewis Carroll and Ada Isaacs Menken. For documentary information, collected items etc.[14]

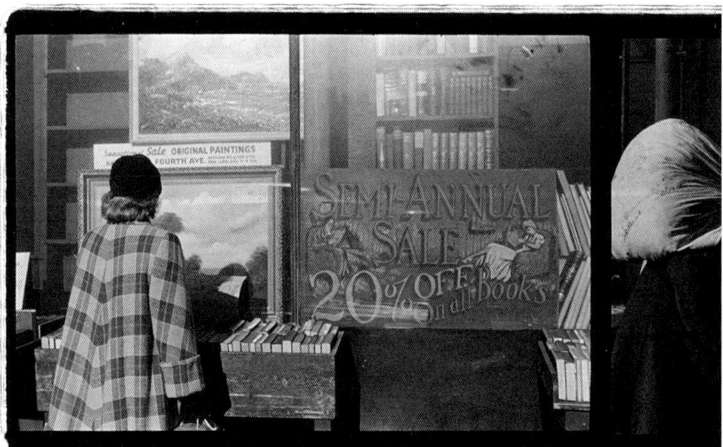

FIG. 1.6 *New York, NY*, 1940. Scan (1979) of extant 35-mm gelatin film negative. The Miriam and Ira D. Wallach Division of Art, Prints and Photographs: Photography Collection, New York Public Library.

Cornell delights in the contrast between The Sign of the Sparrow's "hole in the wall" appearance and the sophistication of its clientele and proprietor.[15] Edmund Wilson's 1926 essay "Book Galleries and Bookshops" confirms the artist's observation, describing Book Row as "at the service of the general public, selling all kinds of books to all kinds of people." Wilson saw Book Row's ethos of democratic intellectual inquiry as a rejoinder to what he described as the Gilded Age's first edition "fetish," in which wealthy collectors approached books as "articles of luxury rather than intellectual currency."[16] Cornell's collecting married Book Row's rejection of "estheticism" (the artist's term for aesthetic judgment based on financial value), with his burgeoning idealist convictions. Eschewing rare or valuable items, Cornell instead collected objects that evoked feelings of enchantment. For example, in 1921 he purchased a 1917 issue of the French periodical *Musica* because it included a photograph of Romantic composer Emmanuel Chabrier playing with his children, which likely recalled the artist's childhood home.[17] To Gilded Age "estheticism," Cornell opposed "experience." In another diary entry, from 1952, he describes the visceral enchantment he felt in the act of collecting: "Some vivid, strong reaction was felt, often a true inspiration of beauty and experience, in acquisition."[18] For the artist, the experience of encountering an object—rather than the object's monetary value—offered a moment of "artistic appreciation made real."

A scrapbook compiled in the 1920s suggests Cornell's early interest in theories of experience. The scrapbook included excerpts from specialist and popular publications, such as Scofield Thayer's Modernist magazine *The Dial* as well as the *Christian Science Monitor*.[19] Founded in 1908 by Mary Baker Eddy as an alternative to mainstream newspapers, the *Christian Science Monitor*'s stated mission was "to injure no man, but to bless all mankind."[20] This ethos was especially apparent in the main source of Cornell's clippings, the newspaper's Home Forum section, which published poetry and excerpts from art and literary criticism. The titles of the artist's selections from the paper, which included "Night Butterflies," "Magic Casements," and "Songs of Innocence," speak to the Home Forum's engagement with British Romantic poetry. Perhaps the section's editors found in that movement's emphasis on imagination and feeling a corollary to its stated aim of "bless[ing] all mankind."[21]

One clipping included in Cornell's scrapbook, "Insight into Poetry's Essential Nature," by poet and critic Henry Newbolt, encapsulates the tenor of the Home Forum's miscellany.[22] A poet, Newbolt writes, is "not by himself nor for himself alone—how could he, seeing that he is not a separate individual existence, but a member of a multitude, not all independent but interdependent, all receiving the best part of that which they have to give!"[23] Newbolt goes on to describe poetry as a form of connection, an act of both giving and receiving. A poet transforms her experience into aesthetic form, an act that in turn engenders experience in the reader, joining them together in a collective.

That Cornell held similar views is evident from a quotation he copied at the start of this scrapbook: "Nothing is ours to keep for ourselves. Money, talent, time, whatever it may be that we may possess, is only ours to use. This is the great law written everywhere. No one owns anything for himself alone, and no one can live to himself alone."[24] Although Cornell's

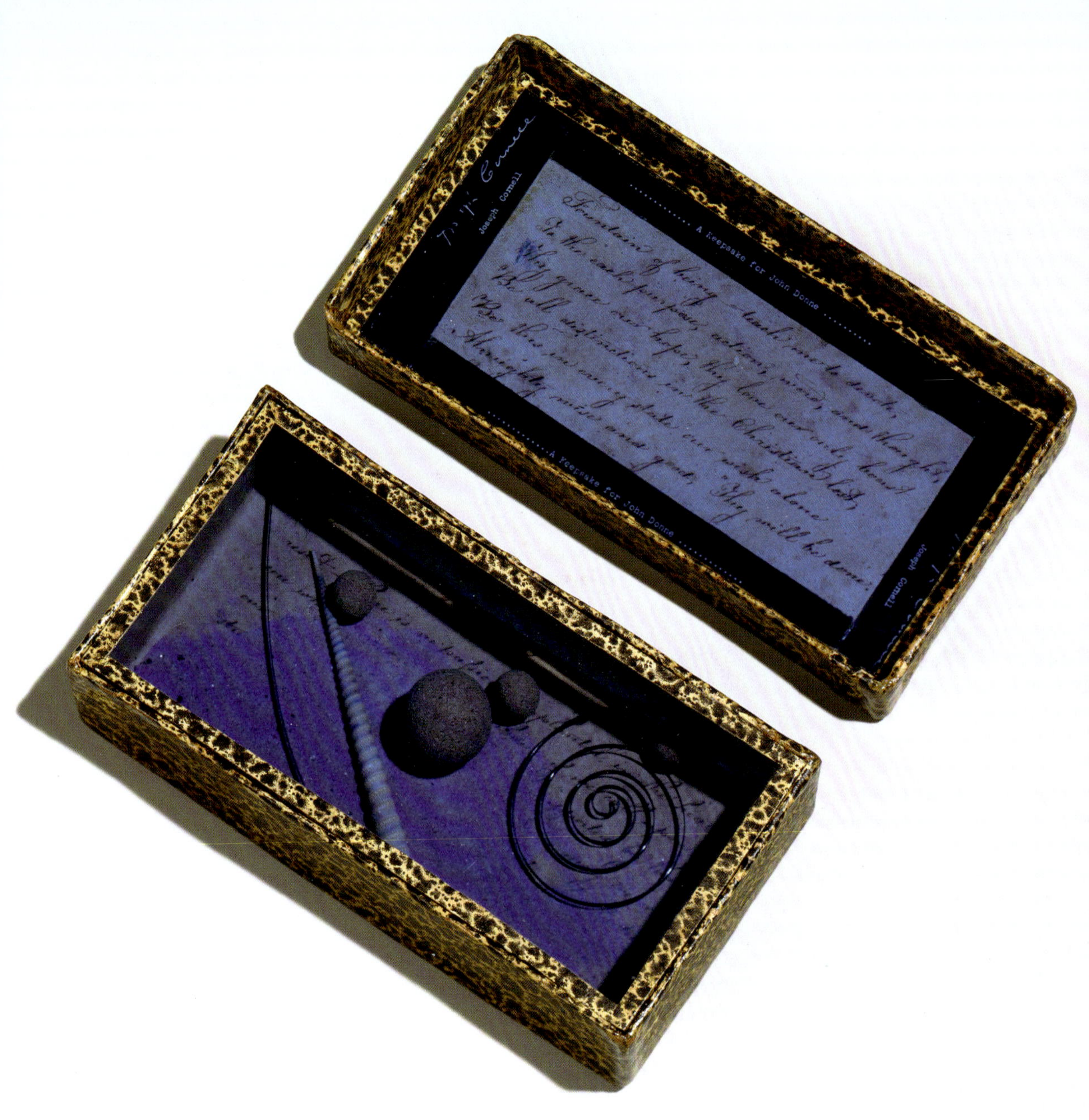

FIG. 1.7 Joseph Cornell, *A Keepsake for John Donne*, ca. 1938. Box construction with blue glass, 1½ × 5¾ × 3 inches, when closed. Private collection.

emphasis on personal experience accords with Susan Stewart's description of collecting as the "replacement of the narrative of history with the narrative of the individual subject," his approach also undercuts the idea of individual possession.[25] For the artist, collecting was more than ownership; it was an experience of connection to other times, places, and people. Like poetry, experience belongs to everyone, and therefore to no one. It is therefore apt that Cornell chose to express this crucial sentiment through a quotation—through the words of another.

ROMANTIC TIME

Much of Cornell's subsequent work takes the form of a collection. *A Keepsake for John Donne* (ca. 1938, fig. 1.7) is covered with black-and-tan speckled paper, recalling the marbled leaves of antiquarian books. Like Cornell's *Untitled* (*Marie Taglioni Letter Case*, ca. 1946–52, fig. 1.8), the work serves as a repository for a group of treasured letters, sanctified by their presence in Cornell's intricate receptacle. Two pages, written in the same florid hand, line the box's lid and base. The base also holds sand, glitter, three round stones, a white auger shell, and a single metal spiral, all loose. When the box is tilted, these objects move across the sparkling sand like flotsam floating on the sea's surface. The work's pelagic mood is augmented by the blue tint

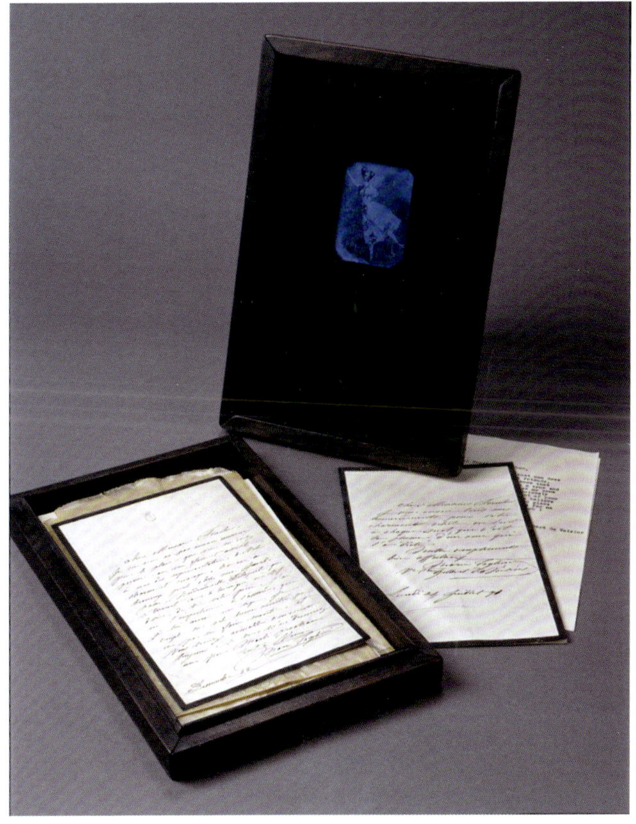

FIG. 1.8 Joseph Cornell, *Untitled (Marie Taglioni Letter Case)*, ca. 1946–52. Velvet on paperboard and wood, glass on paper, $1^{3}/_{4} \times 7^{1}/_{2} \times 11^{1}/_{2}$ inches. Smithsonian American Art Museum, Washington, DC., gift of Mr. and Mrs. John A. Benton.

imparted by the glass sealing the container. *A Keepsake for John Donne* fits oceanic expanse into a small space, allowing it open onto the infinite waters of the Romantic past.

Despite its dedication to a metaphysical, rather than a Romantic poet, *A Keepsake for John Donne* links Cornell's collecting with his study of Romanticism. According to art historian Dore Ashton, Cornell was convinced "that his natural and spiritual home was there, back in the reaches of Romantic history."[26] Romanticism and theories of enchantment and disenchantment are ineluctably entwined: as religious studies scholar David Morgan points out, Weber's phrase "disenchantment of the world" was likely drawn from the German Romantic poet Friedrich Schiller.[27] Morgan describes the Romantic valorization of individual imagination and concomitant championing of the artist as the "the lord of an aesthetic realm" as a compensation for disenchantment, encapsulating the modern suspicion of Romanticism as solipsistic individualism.[28] Cornell instead understood Romanticism as a theory of connection across time. During the 1920s, he was particularly taken by French Romantic writers Théophile Gautier and Gérard de Nerval (nom de plume of Gérard Labrunie), treasuring their unabashed revelry in the aesthetic encounter. For Cornell, to read their work was to experience the world as they did, allowing him to share in their experiences, and momentarily feel the past's presence.

Gautier's *A History of Romanticism*, which Cornell owned, details the author's encounter with a tattered folder of Nerval's effects several decades after the poet's suicide.[29] As the writer leaves through these pages, time unfolds in fits and starts, lurching from past to present. Upon reading a letter to Nerval from playwright Joseph Bouchardy, Gautier recalls, "The remembrance is as sweet as if it were but of yesterday; the feeling of enchantment still survives."[30] Yet just pages before, Gautier had lamented time's inexorable passing: "In 1857 that letter was but an autograph; now it may take its place as a relic in the green portfolio consecrated to the memory of my dead friend."[31] In the decades since Nerval's death, the letter has become a relic, an object that indexes the simultaneous presence and absence of its subject. Although the experience of enchantment remains vivid to Gautier, even this experience is transitory: "No doubt such a delight could not last," he writes.[32]

A Keepsake for John Donne likewise presents time as at once ephemeral and permanent, immediate and eternal. Preserved under blue amber, its handwritten letters are fixed, frozen, untouchable beneath their translucent shroud. Yet these letters also embody the *presence* of the departed figure, whose touch endures in the looping curves of the still-legible letters. The box's loose contents likewise figure the past's coincident presence and absence. Set in motion by the gentlest manipulation, sand courses across the box like grains flowing through an hourglass, or sands washed in and out to sea by the eternal repetition of littoral movement.[33] The delicate metal spiral, a constant Cornell motif, is the mainspring of a watch, that which provides its movement. To wind a watch is to tighten this coil, infusing it with potential energy until, released, it decompresses into the standard tick-tock rhythm of individual seconds. In Cornell's box, the unwound spiral disaggregates time from this instrumental march forward, following not the prescribed rhythms of a clock, but the movements of the box's handler. The mainspring is a time machine.

A Keepsake for John Donne embodies what literary critic Nicholas Halmi has described as the Romantic paradox of time, characterized by its "simultaneous inaccessibility and unavoidability."[34] This idea of time as both passed and eternal also has theological connotations, encapsulated by Erich Auerbach's distinction between horizontal and vertical time. Horizontal time flows forward. It is secular time, the time of the wound mainspring. Vertical time is instead governed by the higher logic of one for whom all time exists simultaneously. Within a vertical conception of time, Isaac's sacrifice of Jacob may be said to prefigure Christ's sacrifice on the cross, for to the divine eye, they are one and the same.[35]

Cornell's choice of letters for *A Keepsake for John Donne* shows the artist attempting to unite horizontal and vertical time. The letter affixed to the lid quotes *Search after Happiness: A Pastoral Drama,* by eighteenth-century British writer Hannah More. More's geographic proximity to Donne, as well her overt religiosity, makes her writing an apposite choice for a box dedicated to the metaphysical poet. Indeed, the quoted passage is a prayer, asking the divine "Fountain of being" to "Teach me to devote / To Thee each purpose, action, word, and thought."[36] Here, More asks how religious faith may be brought into contact with daily life, a question that also lies at the heart of both Cornell's work and Donne's poetry. In his famed poem "The Canonization," Donne addresses an unnamed lover:

> We'll build in sonnets pretty roomes;
> As well a well wrought urne becomes
> The greatest ashes, as halfe-acre tombes,
> And by these hymnes, all shall approve
> Us *Cannoniz'd* for Love:[37]

Poetry is the well-wrought urn, a purportedly trifling container that in fact "provides a finer memorial for one's ashes than does the pompous and grotesque monument," to quote midcentury literary critic Cleanth Brooks.[38] For Brooks, the paradox between the earthly and the spiritual—the paradox at the heart of enchantment—forms the core of poetic language: "It is the scientist whose truth requires a language purged of every trace of paradox; apparently the truth which the poet utters can be approached only in terms of paradox."[39] Cornell's box likewise takes the form of a paradox. Within it, time past and time present, the times of John Donne and Hannah More, and the time in which the viewer manipulates its contents, are present within a single material object. It is only through this paradox that the work can convey "a feeling that a particular moment of the past was transmuting the present moment with an unnamed but significant touch," as Cornell wrote.[40] Another of Cornell's Romantic touchstones, the German poet Novalis stated, "By endowing the commonplace with a higher meaning, the ordinary with mysterious respect, the known with the dignity of the unknown, the finite with the appearance of the infinite, I am making it Romantic."[41] Cornell's box is a well wrought urn, a material poem that renders horizontal and vertical time, past and present, one and the same. To achieve this paradoxical temporality is no small accomplishment.
In the chapter dedicated to Nerval, Gautier offers a pointed rejoinder to critics who derided

the poet as lazy: "On the contrary, the star-gazer, the butterfly hunter, the blower of soap-bubbles, the so-called idler led the most active intellectual life. Under his outward calm, he lived in the fiercest of mental effervescence."[42] There are few better descriptions or defenses of Cornell.

CORRESPONDENCES

If Romanticism shaped Cornell's understanding of temporality as malleable and recursive rather than linear, Symbolism offered him a model for engaging the material world. In his aptly titled memoir, *Tracking the Marvelous*, critic John Bernard Myers recalls a moment in which Cornell tried to show him how he saw the world:

> "Stand here," [Cornell] said at one spot, "and hold your hands to the right and left of your eyes so that you see only what is in front of you." In the distance was a small old-fashioned brick building, probably a pump house. By cutting off the surrounding environment, it became a Swiss chalet nesting among trees. It looked like the kind of romantic vista one sees in an old engraving. The next spot provided a spectacular view of New York, the whole of it stretched out and illuminated by the silvery gray light of the afternoon. I had never seen New York from such a vantage point. Its skyscrapers became minarets, it seemed to float on a low-lying mist. It was Baghdad.[43]

Cornell shows Myers how he excerpts fantastical views from a common landscape, much as he would pluck a dusty volume from a Fourth Avenue bookstall. This technique of fragmentation is also a method of figuration: a brick pump house becomes a chalet from a Romantic engraving; New York City becomes Baghdad. This strategy recalls the poetic theory of Symbolist Stéphane Mallarmé, another of Cornell's touchstones. Mallarmé understood language as containing two registers of meaning: utilitarian and evocative. He writes,

> Speaking only refers commercially to the reality of things: in literature, it is sufficient to make an allusion to them or to abstract their quality which will be embodied by some idea.
> On this condition, the song bounds forth, a joy unburdened.
> This aim I call Transposition—another I call Structure.[44]

Language's "commercial" function is signification: the word "rose" represents a specific kind of flower. Within the realm of literature, context, which Mallarmé calls "transposition," has the capacity to transform the literal meaning of this word into something entirely different.[45] Symbolist poets took this insight to its extreme, foregrounding language's sound, rhythm, and even the physical appearance of words on a page in order to divest words of their signifying function. These formal innovations allowed them instead to express the contingency of meaning and a poet's unrepresentable feelings or experiences. Mallarmé taught Cornell the potential of fragmentation. In excerpting language from its context, a word may be divested of its literal meaning and become the material of poetry.

Cornell was explicit about his debt to Symbolism. In addition to the Romantics, he consistently named the same cohort of Symbolist artists, critics, and musicians when describing his artistic formation. During the 1920s, Cornell read work by "latter-day Symbolists," including Marsden Hartley's *Adventures in the Arts* and Paul Rosenfeld's *Port of New York*, and also studied the European movement.[46] As Cornell recalled of the decade, "I was more influenced by the work of the modern French School in painting and music at least a dozen years before doing creative work. More particularly Redon and Debussy, and through the writings of the first man to write about the subject in America, James Huneker."[47]

One need look no further than the famed 1913 Armory Show to discern artistic Symbolism's importance to the formation of American Modernism. The exhibition featured work by Symbolists Odilon Redon, Paul Gauguin, and Puvis de Chavannes alongside examples of Cubism and Futurism.[48] While the formal audacity of the latter incensed critics and audiences, and continues to dominate scholarly considerations of the exhibition, Symbolism was among the best represented of all European avant-garde movements. Redon, a friend and collaborator of Mallarmé, was represented by over fifty paintings, pastels, and prints, of which he sold approximately thirty, including the show's first sale.[49] In contrast to Cubism's vitriolic reception, Redon's work proved popular in the press, with *The Sun* praising him as "a man of power and originality, a creator and a leader."[50] Walter Pach described Redon's relevance to young American artists as "help[ing] them reach to a finer aestheticism, and still more—to a higher ideal of significance."[51] This idea is echoed by Paul Rosenfeld in a 1933 essay: "Where [mysterious forces] appear and are felt and known," Rosenfeld writes, "there is no longer an 'I' and a 'thou.' There is only something wonderful working itself out in all men and things. There is only a 'we': and perhaps an "It.' "[52] In Rosenfeld's Transcendentalist-inflected account, the artist's sensitivity to enchantment, and his ability to convey it, is a means of defeating the individualistic "I" of modern life.

The lessons Cornell drew from Symbolism are apparent in a 1952 diary entry, in which he recalls reading a monograph on Redon by art historian André Mellerio.[53] Merely mentioning Mellerio's name, Cornell writes, "brings back the rich color sense of the artist he championed."[54] In this same diary entry, he writes of listening to a concerto by composer Ernest Chausson, marveling, "what a 'correspondence,' (Redon's word) . . . just inside the cabin looking out through 'doors' and 'windows' and with cooling breezes relieving the intense sun. . . . an 'extension' at least of the mood above, an unexpectedly delightful 'recapturing' . . ."[55]

"Correspondence," a key principle of Symbolist poetry, is a figurative connection between two distinct entities.[56] Redon famously used the term to describe a portfolio of engravings inspired by writers including Charles Baudelaire, Gustave Flaubert, and Edgar Allan Poe, which attempted to convey meaning of the poem without "illustrat[ing]" it. As Redon declared, "I have never used the defective word 'illustration.' You will not find it in my catalogues. The right term has not yet been coined. I can only think of transmission, of interpretation."[57]

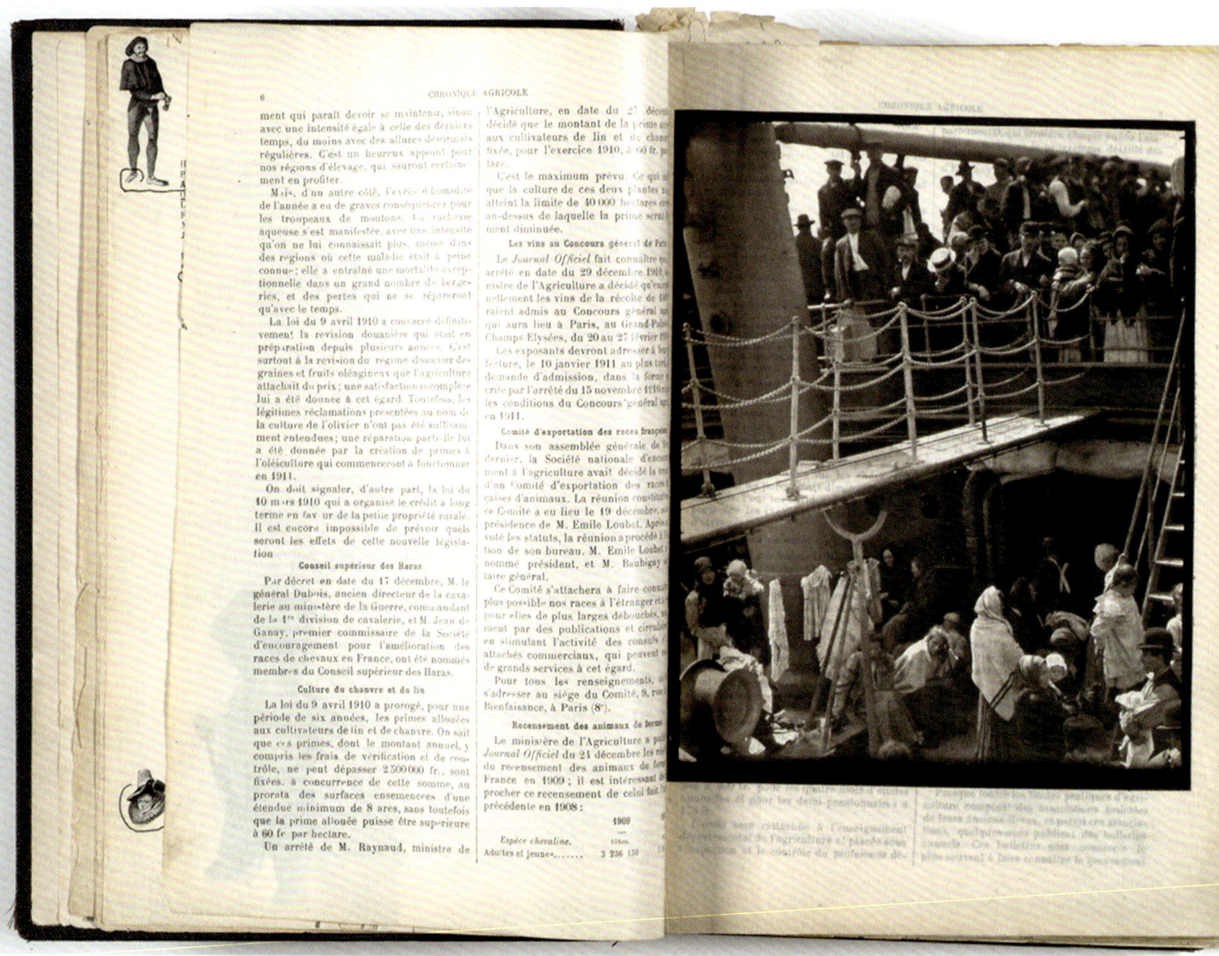

FIG. 1.13 Joseph Cornell, *Untitled Book Object (Journal d'Agriculture Pratique et Journal de L'Agriculture)*, p. 7, featuring Alfred Stieglitz's *The Steerage*.

Journal d'Agriculture Pratique also contains a photogravure of Stieglitz's famed *The Steerage*, which Cornell excised from an issue of *Camera Work* (fig. 1.13). Stieglitz's "prismatic fragment," to use artist Jason Francisco's apt phrase, refracts the common sight of people boarding a ship into a scene of aesthetic force.[59] The photograph's fractured and recombined forms puncture the dry French text of its support, transferring Stieglitz's transformative vision into an additional material register. The inclusion of this unaltered photograph near the beginning of the book signals Cornell's exploration of what film theorist Kaja Silverman has described as photography's "analogic function." As she writes, "When I say 'analogy' . . . I am talking about the authorless and untranscendable similarities that structure Being, or what I will be calling 'the world,' and that give everything the same ontological weight."[60] Silverman's observation clarifies how photography might figure enchantment. Photography points to the ontological equivalence of all things in the world—what Silverman calls "Being"—creating an image that exceeds representation's mimetic reproduction of visual incident.

Consider Stieglitz's famed *Equivalent* series, the photographer's most explicitly Symbolist statements.[61] A 1926 work from this series captures a sky dense with clouds (fig. 1.14). Their thick covering diffuses the glow of the sun, whose outline is barely visible. The nuanced, numinous quality of clouds is at once frozen into a rectangular image and intensified by the crisp detail of the gelatin silver print. Inspired by Symbolist poetry and Kandinsky's theory of forms, Stieglitz understood these photographs as equivalents to the vast unknowable and unquantifiable experience consolidated and captured, but not diminished, by the photographic apparatus.[62]

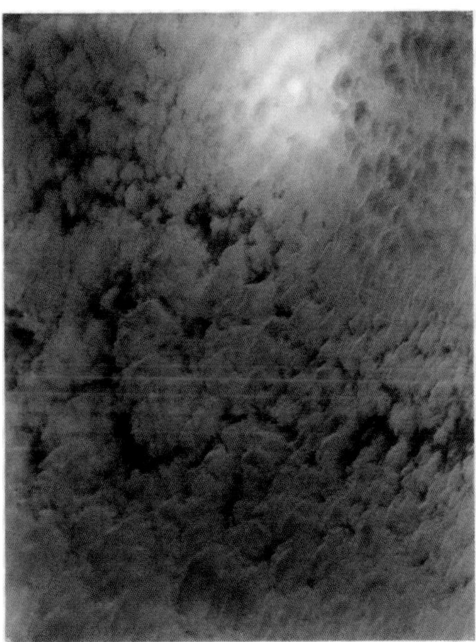

FIG. 1.14 Alfred Stieglitz, *Equivalent*, 1926. Gelatin silver print, 4¾ × 3¾ inches. Phillips Collection, Washington DC.

Cornell included his own equivalent within the pages of *Journal d'Agriculture Pratique*. A silhouette of a woman is incised into a page of "Correspondance" and backed by a fragment of sky (fig. 1.15). Turn the page, and the sky is revealed in all its glory, crowning a reproduction of Jacob van Ruysdale's 1670 painting *The Bleaching Grounds near Haarlem* (fig. 1.16). Ruysdale's lush, painterly clouds fill three-fourths of the composition, their pillowy curves forming a stark contrast with the geometric Dutch landscape dotted with tiny figures. Cornell plucks one of the minuscule female figures from the foreground of Ruysdale's painting and brings her closer, placing her silhouette over a passage in the painting where clouds meet the sky. Cloud

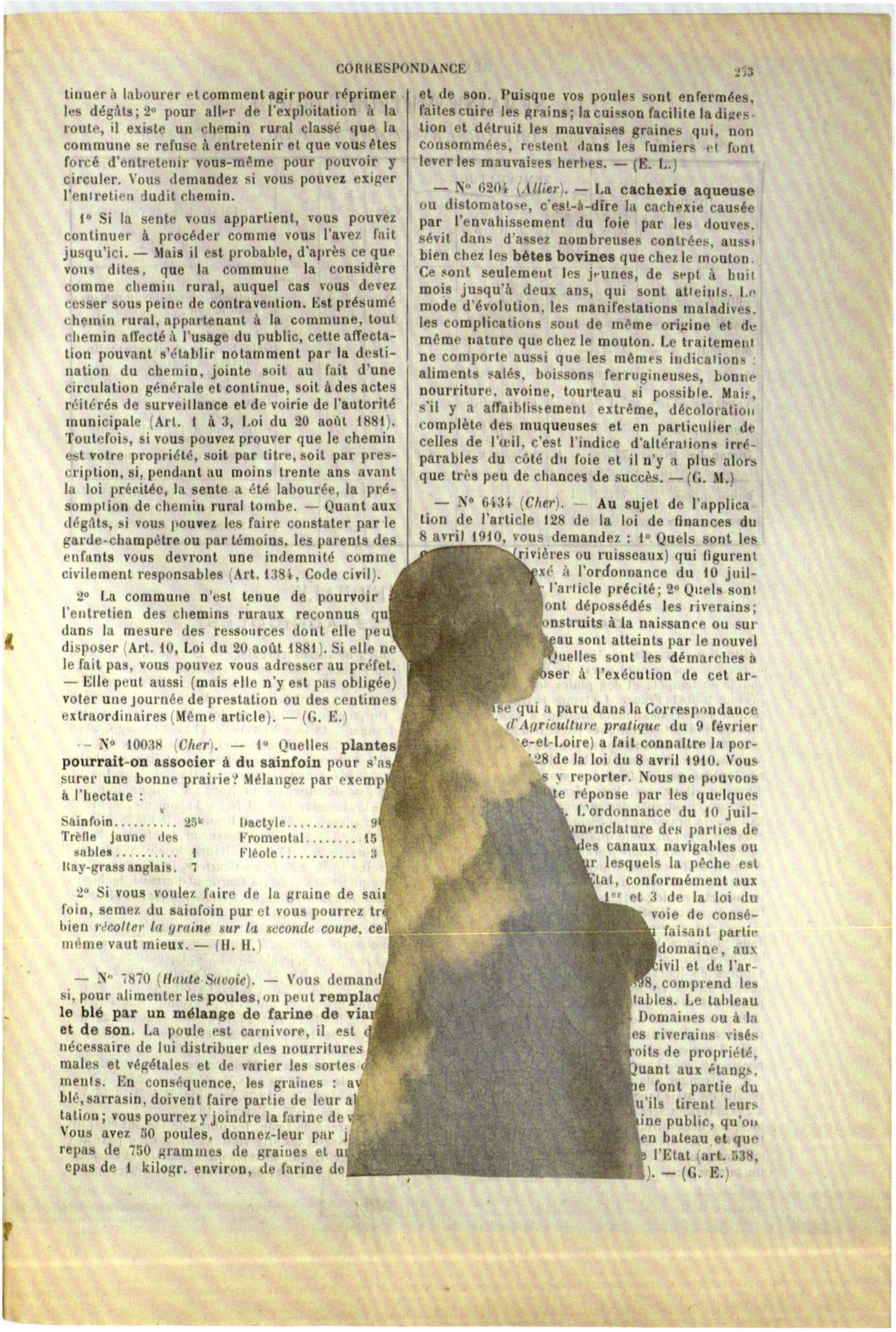

CORRESPONDANCE 253

tinuer à labourer et comment agir pour réprimer les dégâts; 2° pour aller de l'exploitation à la route, il existe un chemin rural classé que la commune se refuse à entretenir et que vous êtes forcé d'entretenir vous-même pour pouvoir y circuler. Vous demandez si vous pouvez exiger l'entretien dudit chemin.

1° Si la sente vous appartient, vous pouvez continuer à procéder comme vous l'avez fait jusqu'ici. — Mais il est probable, d'après ce que vous dites, que la commune la considère comme chemin rural, auquel cas vous devez cesser sous peine de contravention. Est présumé chemin rural, appartenant à la commune, tout chemin affecté à l'usage du public, cette affectation pouvant s'établir notamment par la destination du chemin, jointe soit au fait d'une circulation générale et continue, soit à des actes réitérés de surveillance et de voirie de l'autorité municipale (Art. 1 à 3, Loi du 20 août 1881). Toutefois, si vous pouvez prouver que le chemin est votre propriété, soit par titre, soit par prescription, si, pendant au moins trente ans avant la loi précitée, la sente a été labourée, la présomption de chemin rural tombe. — Quant aux dégâts, si vous pouvez les faire constater par le garde-champêtre ou par témoins, les parents des enfants vous devront une indemnité comme civilement responsables (Art. 1384, Code civil).

2° La commune n'est tenue de pourvoir à l'entretien des chemins ruraux reconnus qu dans la mesure des ressources dont elle peu disposer (Art. 10, Loi du 20 août 1881). Si elle ne le fait pas, vous pouvez vous adresser au préfet. — Elle peut aussi (mais elle n'y est pas obligée) voter une journée de prestation ou des centimes extraordinaires (Même article). — (G. E.)

— N° 10038 (*Cher*). — 1° Quelles **plantes pourrait-on associer à du sainfoin** pour s'as surer une bonne prairie? Mélangez par exemp à l'hectare :

Sainfoin	25k	Dactyle	9
Trèfle jaune des sables	1	Fromental	15
Ray-grass anglais	7	Fléole	3

2° Si vous voulez faire de la graine de sai foin, semez du sainfoin pur et vous pourrez tr bien *récolter la graine sur la seconde coupe*, ce même vaut mieux. — (H. H.)

— N° 7870 (*Haute-Savoie*). — Vous demand si, pour alimenter les **poules**, on peut **remplac le blé par un mélange de farine de via et de son**. La poule est carnivore, il est d nécessaire de lui distribuer des nourritures males et végétales et de varier les sortes ments. En conséquence, les graines : av blé, sarrasin, doivent faire partie de leur al tation; vous pourrez y joindre la farine de v Vous avez 50 poules, donnez-leur par j repas de 750 grammes de graines et u epas de 1 kilogr. environ, de farine de et de son. Puisque vos poules sont enfermées, faites cuire les grains; la cuisson facilite la digestion et détruit les mauvaises graines qui, non consommées, restent dans les fumiers et font lever les mauvaises herbes. — (E. L.)

— N° 6204 (*Allier*). — La **cachexie aqueuse** ou distomatose, c'est-à-dire la cachexie causée par l'envahissement du foie par les douves, sévit dans d'assez nombreuses contrées, aussi bien chez les **bêtes bovines** que chez le mouton. Ce sont seulement les jeunes, de sept à huit mois jusqu'à deux ans, qui sont atteints. Le mode d'évolution, les manifestations maladives, les complications sont de même origine et de même nature que chez le mouton. Le traitement ne comporte aussi que les mêmes indications : aliments salés, boissons ferrugineuses, bonne nourriture, avoine, tourteau si possible. Mais, s'il y a affaiblissement extrême, décoloration complète des muqueuses et en particulier de celles de l'œil, c'est l'indice d'altérations irréparables du côté du foie et il n'y a plus alors que très peu de chances de succès. — (G. M.)

— N° 6434 (*Cher*). — **Au sujet de l'application de l'article 128 de la loi de finances du 8 avril 1910**, vous demandez : 1° Quels sont les rivières ou ruisseaux) qui figurent xé à l'ordonnance du 10 juil- l'article précité; 2° Quels sont ont dépossédés les riverains; onstruits à la naissance ou sur eau sont atteints par le nouvel Quelles sont les démarches à oser à l'exécution de cet ar-

se qui a paru dans la Correspondance *d'Agriculture pratique* du 9 février e-et-Loire) a fait connaître la por- 28 de la loi du 8 avril 1910. Vous s y reporter. Nous ne pouvons te réponse par les quelques L'ordonnance du 10 juil- menclature des parties de des canaux navigables ou r lesquels la pêche est Etat, conformément aux 1er et 3 de la loi du voie de consé- faisant partie domaine, aux civil et de l'ar- 98, comprend les tables. Le tableau Domaines ou à la es riverains visés roits de propriété, Quant aux étangs, ne font partie du u'ils tirent leurs ine public, qu'on en bateau et que l'Etat (art. 538,). — (G. E.)

FIG. 1.15 Joseph Cornell, *Untitled Book Object (Journal d'Agriculture Pratique et Journal de L'Agriculture)*, p. 253, with incised silhouette.

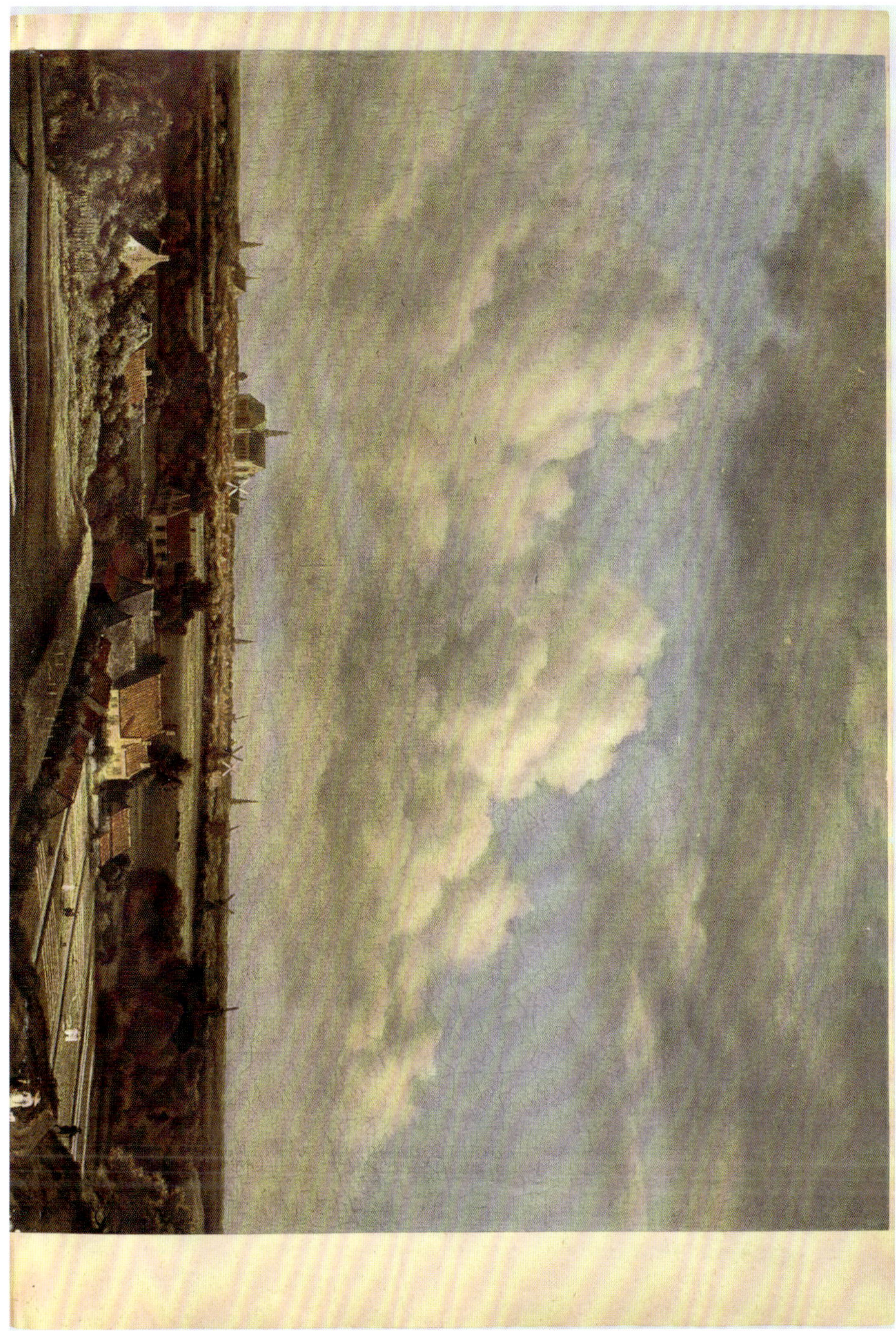

FIG. 1.16 Joseph Cornell, *Untitled Book Object (Journal d'Agriculture Pratique et Journal de L'Agriculture)*, with inset reproduction of Jacob van Ruysdale's *The Bleaching Grounds near Haarlem.*

and shadow become the contours of her face and hair, and the tranquil sky transforms into fabric. By suggesting the inseparability of body and sky, common and cosmos, the silhouette augments art historian Analisa Leppanen-Guerra's trenchant observation that the *Journal d'Agriculture Pratique* attempted to link the celestial and the terrestrial.[63] Like the edges of Stieglitz's photograph, Cornell's cut gives shape to the ineffable. His sky silhouette refuses binary oppositions—far and near, land and sky, vast and bounded—and instead pictures their paradoxical coexistence within a single figure. The correspondences created among these realms figure their inseparability, the fundamental connection of all things in the world.

TRANSCENDENTAL MONTAGE

The purpose of this section is to explore Cornell's description of his collages as "montages."[64] As early as 1932, the artist insisted that his two-dimensional images be described with this term, even when designing for commercial publications such as *Vogue* and *Harper's Bazaar*.[65] Many of Cornell's early works also take the form of protocinematic devices, such as stereographs, daguerreotypes, and zoetropes. As Cornell wrote in a 1960 diary entry, his work of the 1930s could be described as "a kind of 'forgotten game,' a philosophical toy of the Victorian era, with poetic or magical 'moving parts.'"[66] This description of his "philosophical toys" as both poetic and magical speaks to the effect he hoped to achieve through montage.

Cornell was a passionate cinephile. During the 1920s, he inhaled films by Ernst Lubitsch, Dimitri Kirsanoff, and Carl Theodor Dreyer at New York's movie palaces and began amassing a collection of rare film prints, which he lent out for extra income and used as the basis for his subsequent cinematic experiments.[67] Dreyer's *La passion de Jeanne d'Arc* (1928, fig. 1.17), the director's last silent film and a touchstone for Cornell, suggests the lessons he drew from cinema. Dreyer's famed use of montaged close-ups dramatizes the dialogue between the saint and her inquisitors. The intentional contrasts between the inquisitors' harsh, sneering faces and Jeanne's beatific visage are more than just a narrative technique, but materialize contrasts between doctrinal and visionary belief. As Dreyer wrote in his 1929 essay "Realized Mysticism," "I wanted to interpret a hymn to the

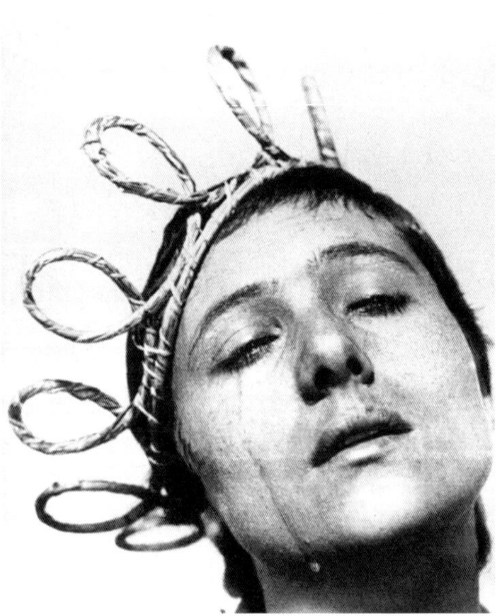

FIG. 1.17 Film still from *La passion de Jeanne d'Arc* (Carl Theodor Dreyer, 1928). Digital print, Almay Archives.

triumph of the soul over life. What streams out to the possibly moved spectator in strange close-ups is not accidentally chosen."[68]

So it was with one of Cornell's earliest cinematic experiments, the unrealized film scenario *Monsieur Phot (Seen through a Stereoscope)* from 1933 (fig. 1.18).[69] This written scenario is composed of five loosely connected vignettes set in 1870 New York. *Monsieur Phot* opens with the titular photographer assembling a group of children for a picture in a snowy park. The moment before his shutter clicks, a magnificent pheasant erupts from a basket at their feet, and suddenly the film becomes saturated with color. Subsequent scenes feature the photographer examining his images, and the children gazing into a shop window's "forest of exquisite glass and ceramics." The repeated musical refrain, "Si mes vers avaient des ailes" (If my verses had wings), ties these disparate scenes together. Taken from a poem by Victor Hugo, which was set to music in 1888 by the child composer Reynaldo Hahn, this melodic leitmotif punctuates and connects the film scenario much like the winged pheasant, which reappears across several scenes, at one point accompanied by the strains of Stravinsky's *The Firebird*. The scenario's epilogue, performed "entirely in color and the action carried out as in a ballet" ends with the photographer picking up a gun and taking aim at the pheasant, now trapped under a glass dome.

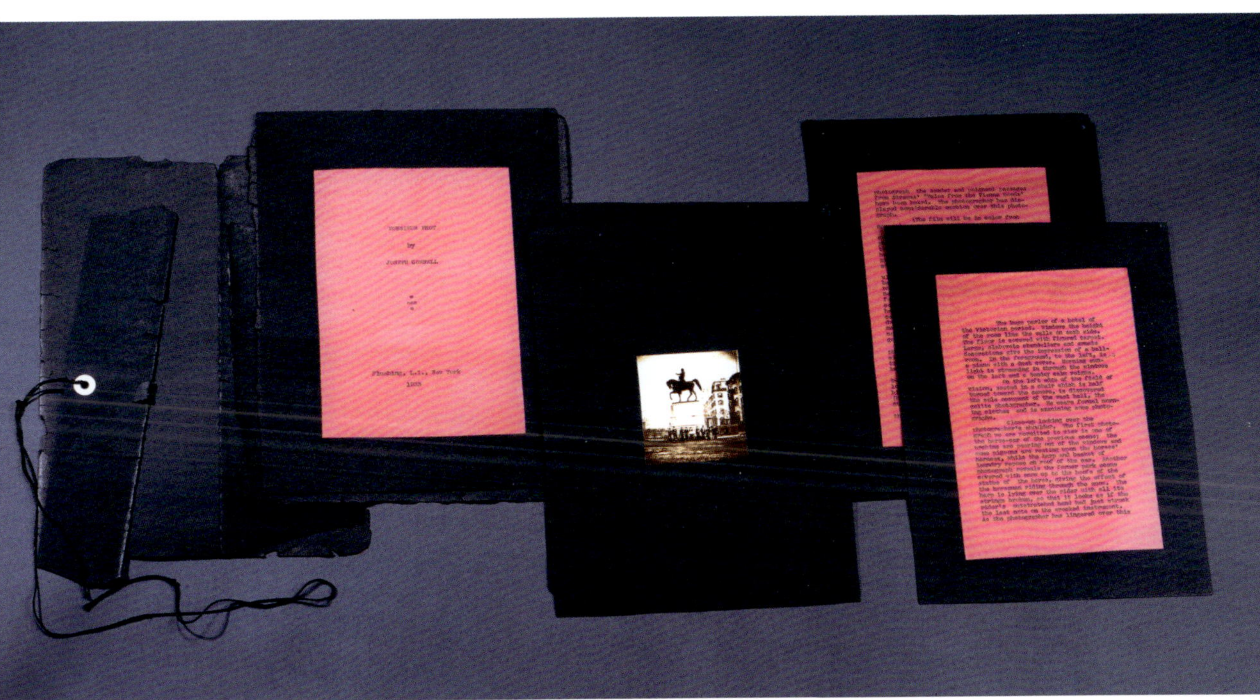

FIG. 1.18 Joseph Cornell, *Monsieur Phot (Copy no. 5)*, 1933. Paper folio with typed film scenario illustrated with stereopticon photographs, 1/4 × 11 3/8 × 8 7/8 inches, when closed. Smithsonian American Art Museum, Washington DC, gift of the Joseph and Robert Cornell Memorial Foundation.

An earlier moment in the scenario clarifies the true target of Monsieur Phot's gun. As he considers a photograph of the pheasant, he is interrupted by a maid wielding a feather duster "identical in size and color to the pheasant." This striking moment of montage relies on the formal similarity of distinct forms (photograph of pheasant and feather duster), as well as the disjuncture between image and object, nuancing Sergei Eisenstein's famed description of montage as a "collision" between two unlike images.[70] Cornell's scenario thus intensifies film theorist Pavle Levi's observation that "there is something inherently equivocal about the cinematic cut. It brings two shots together while setting them apart."[71] The formal congruence *and* the material distance between photograph and feather duster crystalizes montage's equivocal affordances. Moreover, both feather duster and photograph are material remnants of the pheasant, inanimate substitutes for the living creature. What is the difference between a photograph and the world around it? At this moment, Monsieur Phot does not know. He is shaken; he grows pale; tears fall from his eyes. This moment of profound disturbance sets the stage for him to take up the gun (a historic corollary to the camera).[72] Neither the presumed illusionistic quality of the photograph nor the pheasant is his true target. Rather, he takes aim at the barrier that separates the two, a Victorian bell jar, a form that often contained taxidermy specimens. His shot shatters the glass enclosure, destroying the transparent plane between bird and world. Did Monsieur Phot free the bird from its confines, or kill it? The scenario plunges into darkness and silence. The last scene returns us to the park, where snow falls softly on the basket that once held the pheasant, now empty.

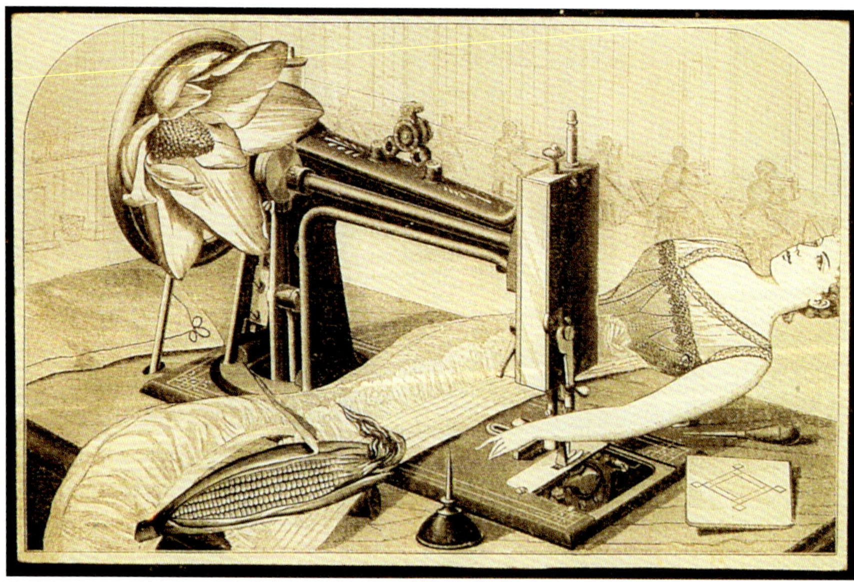

FIG. 1.19 Joseph Cornell, *Untitled (Woman and Sewing Machine)*, ca. 1932. Collage, 5 1/4 × 8 1/16 inches. Osaka City Museum of Modern Art.

Cornell's investigation of montage's capacity to close the distance between work and world extends to works such as *Untitled* (ca. 1932, fig. 1.19). Pieced together from nineteenth-century steel engravings, the montage features a sewing machine stitching a fin-de-siècle woman, whose stiff pose and blank expression suggests that she is not a flesh-and-blood body but a paper doll. The delicate thread that runs across the top of the sewing machine; the gossamer spiderweb nestled within the center of the rose of Cornell's earliest collage: these are meditations on montage as a mode of unification, on creation as an attempt to give life to the inanimate. As with the schooner, the work's physical congruence is achieved through Cornell's precise matching of the sizes of the blossom and the sewing machine's balance wheel. While these formal choices imbue the composition with a sense of organic continuity, its subject remains strikingly lifeless. Like *Monsieur Phot*, this work uses montage to figure the connection between art and the world around it but stops short of proposing that art may take on the quality of life. Perhaps, even at this early stage in his career, Cornell was coming up against the limitations of enchantment.

As Rachael Z. DeLue has shown, Arthur Dove's *Hand Sewing Machine* (1927) likewise uses needle and thread to emblematize connections among its disparate components (fig. 1.20). For DeLue, Dove's assemblages "spell out and make literal Dove's belief that art's ideal state consists in its entanglement in the world and, also, that art's entanglement with the world can

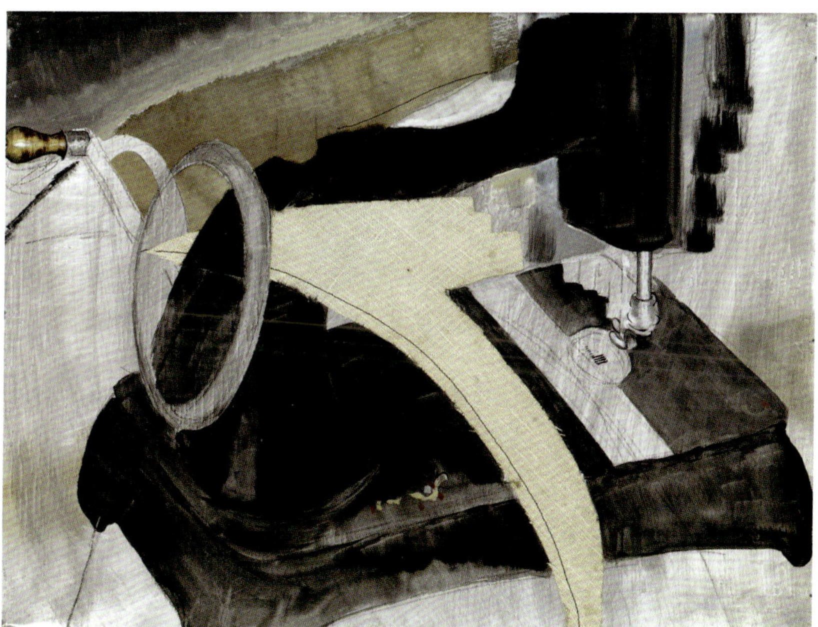

FIG. 1.20 Arthur Dove, *Hand Sewing Machine*, 1927. Oil, cut and pasted linen, resin, and graphite on sheet metal, with artist-made frame, $14\frac{7}{8} \times 19\frac{3}{4}$ inches. Alfred Stieglitz Collection, Metropolitan Museum of Art, New York.

serve as a model for forging material connections among diverse physical and phenomenal entities."[73] Her description applies equally to Cornell's 1932 montage. Although DeLue traces Dove's interest in connection to theories of language and contemporaneous scientific discourses rather than religious belief, her argument suggests that relations among "diverse physical and phenomenal entities" was a consequential question in early-twentieth-century American culture.

This impulse can also be discerned in the efflorescence of interest in Transcendentalism during the 1920s.[74] As Kristina Wilson has argued, Stieglitz and the artists in his orbit were influenced by the Transcendentalist belief that "any given object symbolized both material and spiritual existence, which meant that the material world could always be read as an indication of the existence of a spiritual realm."[75] Early twentieth-century artists and writers saw an implicit critique of capitalist modernity in Transcendentalism's insistence on a realm beyond material value. In his 1919 book, *Our America*, for example, the writer Waldo Frank rejects the idea of Whitman as a mere emblem of Americanness and warns that to describe him as such would be to "dangerously reduce him." Rather, Frank sees Whitman as a symbol of a departed era. In the years since Whitman roamed New York's streets, Frank asserts that the country has "withdraw[n] into the encompassing darkness." The cause of this darkness is the rise of "Capitalist Industrialism," manifested in American journalism, education, industrialization, and popular culture.[76] By contrast, modern-day Transcendentalists such as Alfred Stieglitz seek alternative ways of living life. As Frank wrote of Stieglitz's famed gallery, " '291' is a religious fact: like all such, a miracle. It is an altar where talk was often loud, heads never bared, but where no lie and compromise could live. A little altar at which life was worshipped above the noise of a dead city. Here was refuge, certain and solitary, from the tearing grip of industrial disorder."[77] The description of 291 as an "altar" gains sacredness by contrast to the "dead" city around it. Yet to worship at this altar is not to succumb to individualism. In the face of industrial capitalism's "encompassing darkness," Transcendentalism offers a means of building a "multitude who have a reverence for life, a margin of energy for living, understanding of the sacrament of life's interpretation," to "step out from the American theaters into the streets of American life."[78] In Frank's telling, to assume Whitman's "poetic view of life" is not to turn away from the world but to refuse modernity's individualism and alienation.[79]

Paul Strand and Charles Sheeler's film *Manhatta* (1921) likewise offers Transcendentalism as an alternative to modern alienation. Taking intertitles from Walt Whitman's similarly titled poem, *Manhatta* features shots of New York's towering buildings, bustling crowds, and busy harbor from the vantage of its roofs and streets (fig. 1.21). From here, the city's inhabitants became as anonymous as a swarm of ants. The film concludes with two shots of the sun shining through clouds, whose serenity contrasts with the frenetic activity of the preceding footage (figs. 1.22, 1.23). A final intertitle offers an entreaty from Whitman: "Gorgeous clouds of sunset! drench with your splendor me or the men and women generations after me." Nature's splendor links the singular speaker ("me") with subsequent generations of city dwellers. Sheeler and Strand remind the viewer that the faceless crowds, the anonymous men and women who exist beneath the city's imposing edifices, exist beneath the same clouds, the same sky, as Whitman once did.

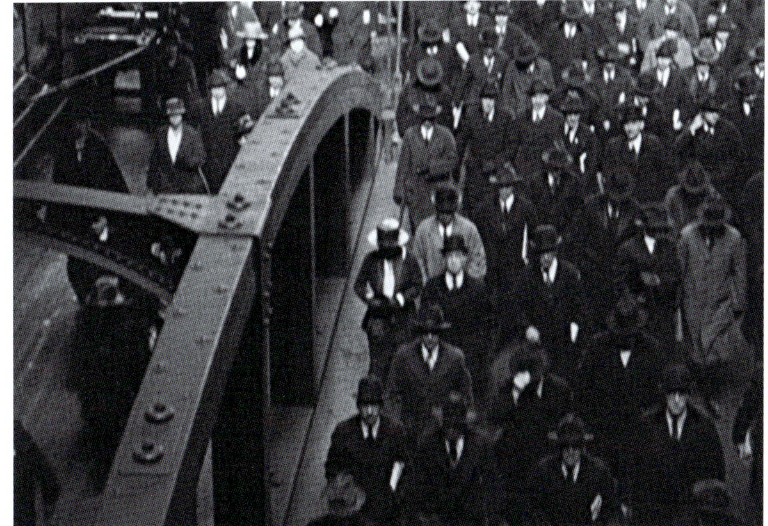

FIG. 1.21 Film still from *Manhatta* (Charles Sheeler and Paul Strand, 1921). 35-mm film transferred to video. Museum of Modern Art, New York.

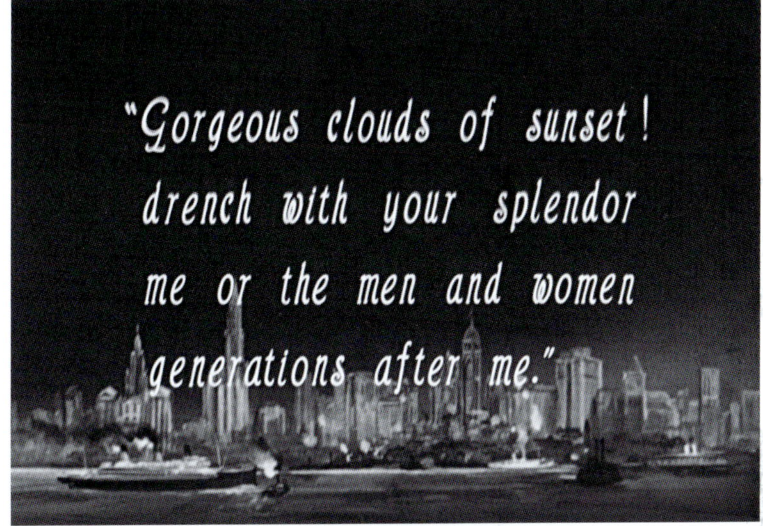

FIG. 1.22 Film still from *Manhatta*, showing Walt Whitman intertitle.

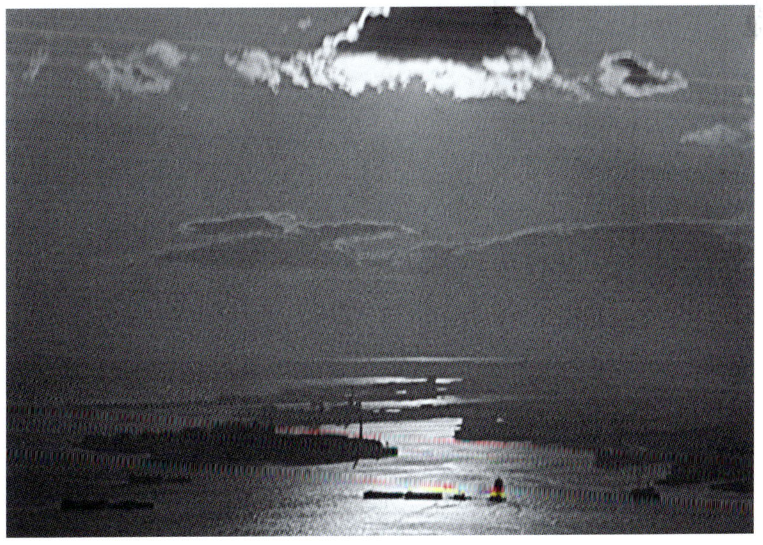

FIG. 1.23 Film still from *Manhatta*, showing sun over the harbor.

In "Science and Vocation," Weber described the emergence of the individual subject as among disenchantment's most consequential effects. The sociologist's most famous book-length work, *The Protestant Ethic and the "Spirit" of Capitalism*, is the classic text on this issue. He describes capitalism's ethic of work and individualism as a substitution for that which has been lost in a disenchanted world: metaphysical religious calling.[80] Like the critics and artists described in this chapter, Cornell sought an alternative to this state of affairs. In Transcendentalism, Romanticism, and Symbolism, in browsing Book Row and attending the cinema, Cornell found a way of experiencing the world in which objects are repositories of experience rather than commodities, in which the past is living rather than dead. He found ways to extract images and materials from their given contexts, reconfiguring and connecting them. He found a different way of experiencing a world that would seek to reduce him to one of *Manhatta*'s anonymous, black-coated city dwellers.

SURRÉALISME

Despite his enchantment, Cornell could not eschew the pressures of daily life. His public emergence as an artist coincided almost exactly with the second exhibition of Surrealism in the United States. This was no coincidence. One need only consider the timeline of the events that preceded his visit to Levy to arrive at a possible motivation for his emergence as a Surrealist artist in 1931. May 1929: The Cornell family purchases a home on Utopia Parkway in Flushing, Queens, the first they owned since the death of Cornell Sr. September 1929:

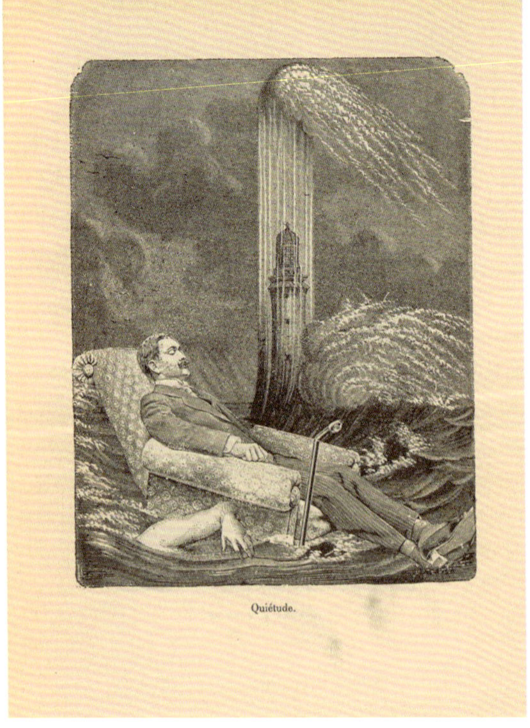

FIG. 1.24 Max Ernst, page from *The Hundred Headless Woman* (*La femme 100 têtes*), 1929. Illustrated book with 147 reproductions after collages, $9\frac{7}{8} \times 7\frac{9}{16}$ inches. Museum of Modern Art, New York.

The stock market crash ushers in the Great Depression. October 1929: Cornell is fired from William Whitman after nine years of employment. The period between Cornell's termination and his visit to Levy were beset by hardship. While the family never resorted to the breadlines, they depended on the charity of wealthy relatives.[81] By 1931, Cornell had been out of work for nearly two years and was desperate to support his family. Levy's support helped alleviate these monetary pressures, and Cornell remained grateful to him. Writing to Levy in 1960, he ruminated, "What wd I be doing now without that 'generosity' of yours in the depression days . . ."[82]

Surrealism offered Cornell a way to present himself as an artist at the outset of his career. The movement's importance to the legibility of his work suggests one reason for the artist's almost too-literal adoption of its principles in the early 1930s. *Untitled* (1932) is after all close to an illustration of Comte de Lautréamont's famous description of the marvelous as "the chance meeting on a dissecting table of a sewing machine and an umbrella."[83] Cornell likely got the idea of turning nineteenth-century prints into montages from Max Ernst's Surrealist collage novel *La femme 100 têtes* (fig. 1.24).[84] Ernst was also interested in esoteric phenomena such as alchemy, which spoke to the broader Surrealist engagement with magic and occultism. As Gavin Parkinson has recently argued, André Breton saw the movement in dialogue with literary and artistic Symbolism, seeing itself an inheritor to that movement's ambition to "bring forth the invisible and not represent the visible."[85]

Le voyageur dans les glaces: Jouet surréaliste (fig. 1.25) invokes the marvelous in an altogether less literal way than Cornell's earliest Surrealist experiments. Collaged images of stars and athletes adorn the disks of a thaumatrope. It takes but a push of a thumb to set them in motion. They spin with such speed that their sides combine into a single blur. A fencer and a picture of a shooting star become a man dueling the heavens. Body and stars, near and far, immaterial and material become one. The work places a miniature universe in the palm of our hand, a twinkling orb that disappears the moment the disk stills.

One could describe the thaumatrope's momentary illusion as a form of the Surrealist marvelous. Hal Foster writes:

> As a medieval term the marvelous signaled a rupture in the natural order, one, unlike the miraculous, not necessarily divine in origin. This challenge to rational causality is essential to the medievalist aspect of surrealism, its fascination with magic and alchemy, with mad love and analogical thought. It is also fundamental to its spiritualist aspect, its attraction to mediumistic practices and gothic tales (e.g., Matthew Gregory Lewis, Ann Radcliffe, Edward Young) where the marvelous is again in play. These enthusiasms suggest the project to which the surrealist marvelous is implicitly pledged: the reenchantment of a disenchanted world, of a capitalist society made ruthlessly rational.[86]

Foster describes the Surrealist marvelous through the lens of psychoanalysis, specifically repression and trauma. For him, the Surrealist search for the marvelous is

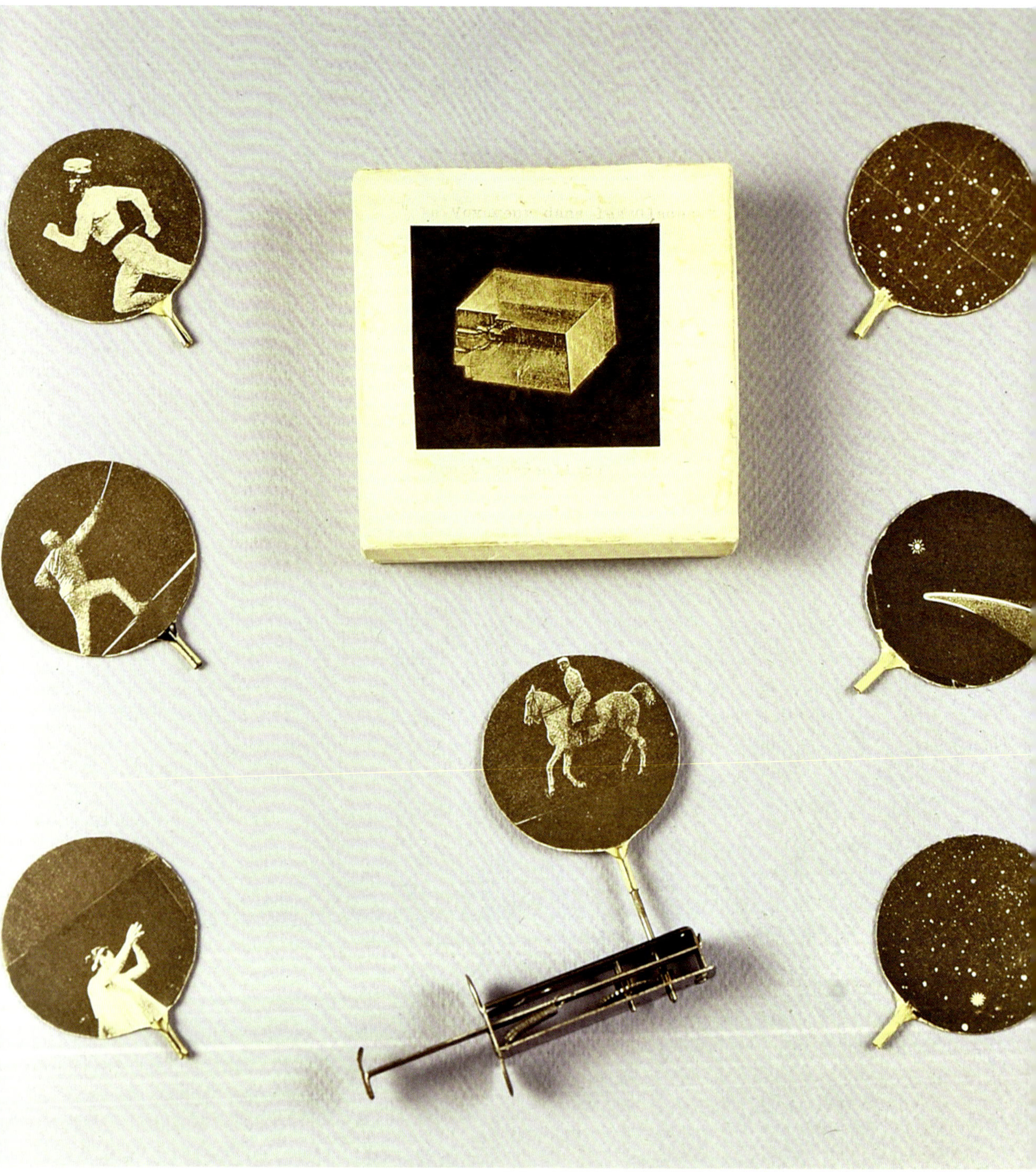

FIG. 1.25 Joseph Cornell, *Le voyageur dans les glaces: Jouet surréaliste*, ca. 1935. Altered thaumatrope, 3¾ × 3¾ × 1¹⁄₁₆ inches. Collection of Mark Kelman, New York.

repetitive desire for loss, and thus an enactment of the psychoanalytic death drive.[87] Cornell's enchantment was grounded instead in his religious beliefs, which of course would have been anathema to orthodox Surrealists. Although one might dismiss Cornell's focus on this aspect of Surrealism as a simplistic misreading of the movement's aims, his thaumatrope suggests a more complex story. As cinema theorist Tom Gunning has observed of this "philosophical toy," as the thaumatrope was often called, "its ontology wobbles and amazes us precisely because it plays with our vision, exposing its limits and possibilities."[88] In this, the thaumatrope is particularly well-suited to probe the possibility of the marvelous in an ostensibly disenchanted world. Cornell's floating, flickering man in the stars creates a moment of magic that is at once intangible and real. Like all moments of enchantment, this one cannot last. It was there; we saw it; but we could not hold it. This ephemeral sphere vanishes into air like smoke, consolidated back into the material form of the paper disk, into the dualism of a disenchanted world.

For Julien Levy, Surrealism was not a rarified avant-garde movement, but a worldview. Writing in the 1935 book *Surrealism*, Levy opines, "Surrealism should not be difficult to understand. It is not a specialized monopoly of a few mysterious initiates. . . . Its fundamental doctrine is that poetry originates in, and appeals to, the subconscious. Everyone shares the subconscious. Everyone can enjoy poetry and everyone can make it."[89] In Cornell, he found the perfect exemplar of this thesis.

Levy's approach to Surrealism was shaped by his studies in the Fine Arts Department at Harvard. For Harvard's art history students, which included future art world luminaries such as Lincoln Kirstein and Alfred Barr, the department provided one of the few alternatives to Harvard's emphasis on conventional success in business, law, or medicine.[90] Within Harvard's potent environment, these young men began to nurture ambitions of elevating Modernist art and literature to a central place in American culture.[91] At Harvard, Levy found himself drawn to the art history courses of Chandler Post, a Renaissance specialist who often held classes at the cinema, where he would "talk about the chiaroscuro of a Gloria Swanson film, or the composition of Chaplin's beginnings and endings."[92] According to cultural historian Steven Watson, this approach encapsulated the group's "catholic embrace of media and the desire to topple existing hierarchies."[93]

Post's class sparked Levy's interest in film and photography, which he pursued in an independent study that concerned the "physics of optics and the psychology of vision," a specialization that surely lent him a special sensitivity to Surrealism.[94] After dropping out of Harvard and a brief sojourn in Paris, Levy decided to open his own gallery. *Surréalisme*, only the third show in the gallery's history, debuted on December 12, 1931.[95] The exhibition was an adapted version of an exhibition curated by Levy's classmate and collaborator A. Everett "Chick" Austin at Wadsworth Atheneum in Hartford, and together they constituted the movement's first official presentations in the United States.[96]

In its previous iteration in Connecticut, Austin had chosen to promote Surrealism as the newest "fashion" in the art world, packing the show with luscious examples of Surrealist painting, including works by Salvador Dalí and Pablo Picasso.[97] Levy consciously expanded the canon of Surrealist art beyond European painting. To Austin's original checklist Levy added work by Jean Cocteau; Bauhaus designer Herbert Bayer; and photographs by Jacques-André Boiffard, Eugène Atget, George Platt Lynes, and even anonymous nineteenth-century photographers. He also held film screenings of Fernand Léger and Dudley Murphy's *Ballet mécanique,* Jay Leyda's *A Bronx Morning,* and Man Ray's *L'étoile de mer*.[98] With this capacious range of objects, Levy hoped to present Surrealism as not just a "fashionable" avant-garde movement but as the overarching condition of American life.

To this point, among Levy's most daring additions to *Surréalisme* was a series of collaged covers from the tabloid *Evening Graphic* (fig. 1.26). These covers illustrate the notorious "Peaches" and "Daddy Browning" divorce trial, which pitted the sixteen-year-old ingénue against her fifty-two-year-old-husband.[99] In the absence of courtroom photographs, the daily tabloids created collages worthy of Max Ernst to adorn their front pages. Levy distanced these images from their newsprint origins by creating photostats of the original *Evening*

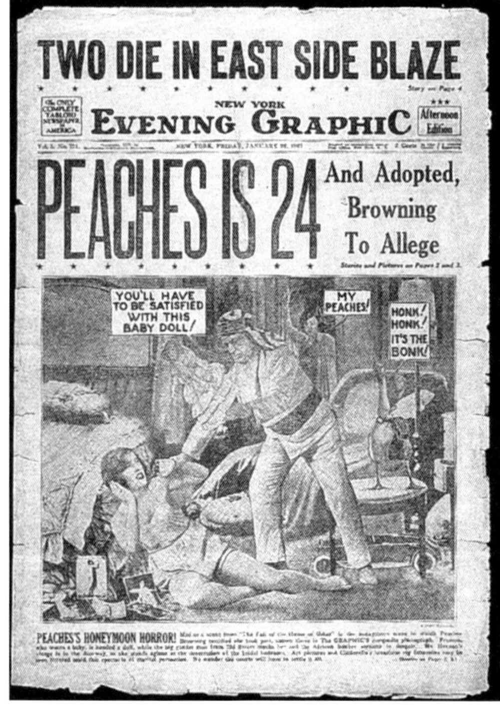
TWO DIE IN EAST SIDE BLAZE
NEW YORK EVENING GRAPHIC
Afternoon Edition
PEACHES IS 24 And Adopted, Browning To Allege

PEACHES'S HONEYMOON HORROR!

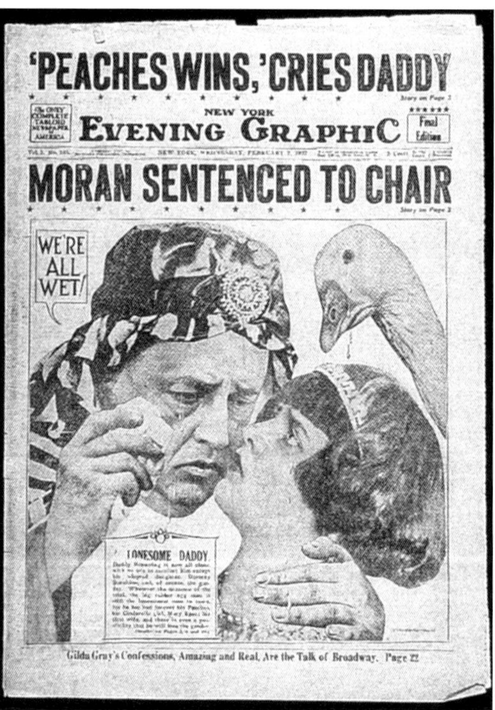
'PEACHES WINS,' CRIES DADDY
NEW YORK EVENING GRAPHIC
Final Edition
MORAN SENTENCED TO CHAIR

LONESOME DADDY
Gilda Gray's Confessions, Amazing and Real, Are the Talk of Broadway. Page 22

FIG. 1.26 Covers from the *New York Evening Graphic* reporting the "Peaches" and "Daddy" Browning scandal, 1927. Illustrated in Lisa Jacobs and Ingrid Schaffner, eds., *Julien Levy: Portrait of an Art Gallery* (Cambridge, MA: MIT Press, 1998).

Graphic covers, reversing the images and rendering their seams imperceptible.[100] As critic Matthew Josephson wrote in his assessment of the exhibition: "The lesson of *The Evening Graphic* is that we have long been producing super realist art in the raw state."[101] Surrealism could, in Levy's presentation, puncture the rarified air of fine art and demonstrate the relevance of recent artistic ideas to a broad public. The long-lamented Surrealist migration into mass culture was in fact embedded within its earliest presentations in the United States.[102]

Levy's ambitions for Surrealism suggests a reason for his immediate interest in Cornell. While the formal proximity of Cornell's montages and Ernst's collages initially drew his attention, Cornell's status as an amateur artist was a crucial piece of evidence for his thesis. In Levy's telling, Cornell was an untrained American artist who had instinctively intuited the principles of Surrealism from the basement of his mother's home; what better proof of the movement's universality? With this narrative, Levy intensified a latent implication of Surrealist automatism. In his 1924 manifesto, Breton defined Surrealism as "[p]sychic automatism in its pure state," and even included instructions for automatic writing.[103] This process of free association was intended to ease the rational mind's grip on the unconscious, allowing anyone to produce art.[104] Automatism thus implicitly critiqued the idea of fine art as the exclusive province of trained professionals, and by extension suggested that art may be produced by anyone. Levy's strategy proved wildly successful. The exhibition not only launched his gallery to prominence but also set the terms for the American public's subsequent understanding of the movement. People lined up to see the exhibition, and *New York Times* critic Edward Alden Jewell praised it as "[o]ne of the most entertaining exhibitions of the season (possibly the most profound)."[105] And most important for Levy, the exhibition garnered the first substantial sales in the gallery's brief history.

Cornell's work made its public debut in *Surréalisme*.[106] Levy also gave Cornell, one of only two Americans in the show, the plum assignment of designing the catalogue. Cornell's cover montage features a boy blowing a fantastical floral instrument made from a pastry bag, which pipes out florid letters that, unlike the sans serif font of the exhibition checklist, take on the aspect of musical notes floating in a serpentine curve across the page (fig. 1.27). While Cornell's montage literally spells out his allegiance to Surrealism, his transmutation of letters into musical notes and his keen attention to language's visual dimensions shares more with Symbolist poetry than its twentieth-century descendant.[107] Despite Cornell's liminal position with respect to Surrealism, Levy's choice designated Cornell as the movement's public face, cementing the gallerist's simplistic account of how he came to make art.

Yet at this early moment in his career, Cornell did not shy away from creating work that fit the Surrealist mold. An early glass bell jar, likely exhibited in *Surréalisme*, features a disembodied hand overlaid with a black-and-white rose and surrounded by miniature kitchen implements and shoes (fig. 1.28). Cornell combines textbook Surrealist compositional principles and motifs with a method of display popular in late-nineteenth-century homes, integrating avant-garde artistic principles with American vernacular practices. Like his paper doll montage, the work signals Cornell's alliance with the movement in altogether literal terms, suggesting Surrealism's importance to his newfound legibility (and employment) as an artist. His success at casting himself as a Surrealist was such that an altered version of the bell jar was illustrated in the Winter 1937 issue of the Surrealist journal *Minotaure* (fig. 1.29).[108] Cornell had become an artist.

And yet, doubts remained. Doubt that participation in a single movement could encapsulate the breadth of his artistic concerns. Doubt, too, in his ability to fully convey that which he wished to capture. A boy grasping a paper parasol glimmering with pink sequin floats within

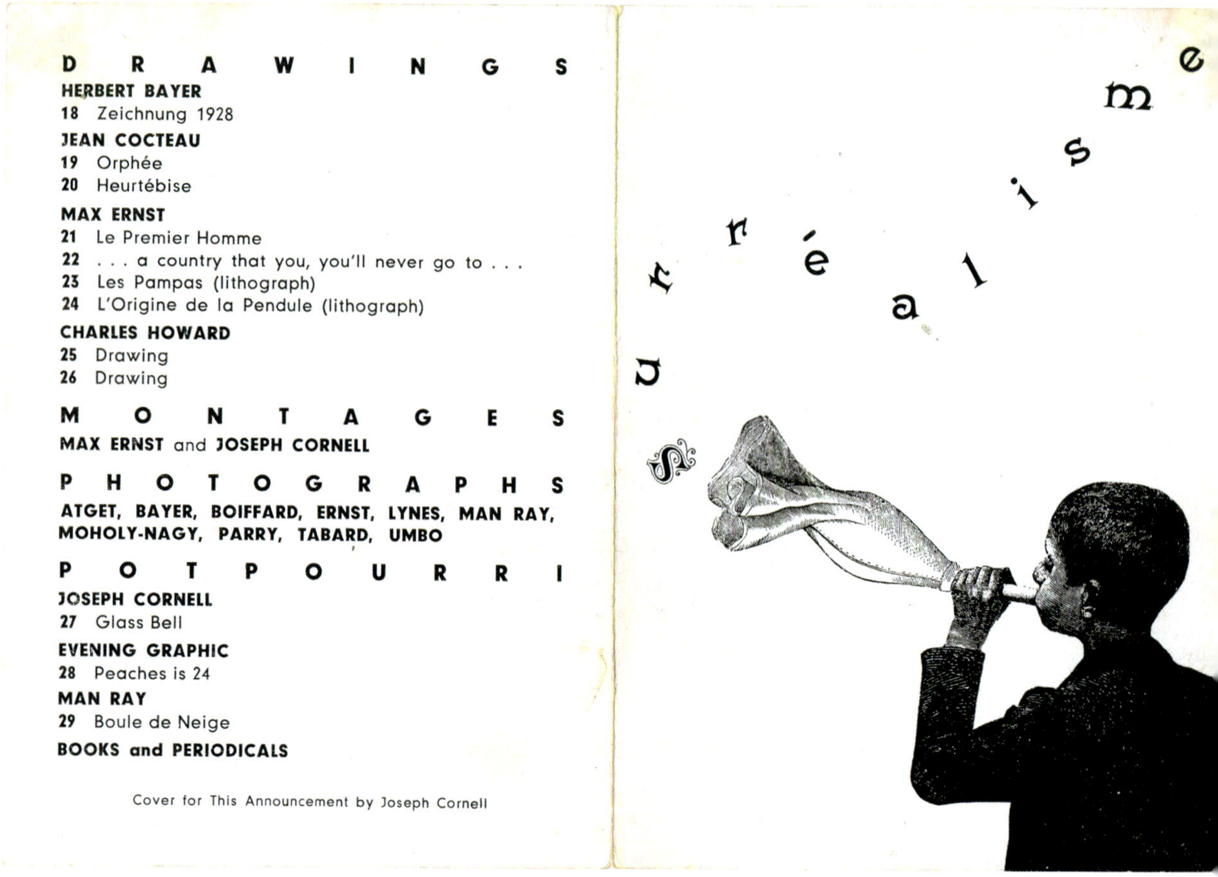

D R A W I N G S
HERBERT BAYER
18 Zeichnung 1928
JEAN COCTEAU
19 Orphée
20 Heurtébise
MAX ERNST
21 Le Premier Homme
22 . . . a country that you, you'll never go to . . .
23 Les Pampas (lithograph)
24 L'Origine de la Pendule (lithograph)
CHARLES HOWARD
25 Drawing
26 Drawing
M O N T A G E S
MAX ERNST and JOSEPH CORNELL
P H O T O G R A P H S
ATGET, BAYER, BOIFFARD, ERNST, LYNES, MAN RAY, MOHOLY-NAGY, PARRY, TABARD, UMBO
P O T P O U R R I
JOSEPH CORNELL
27 Glass Bell
EVENING GRAPHIC
28 Peaches is 24
MAN RAY
29 Boule de Neige
BOOKS and PERIODICALS

Cover for This Announcement by Joseph Cornell

Surréalisme

FIG. 1.27 Joseph Cornell, printed exhibition announcement for *Surréalisme* at Julien Levy Gallery, New York, 1931. 5 1/2 × 4 1/8 inches. Joseph Cornell Study Center, Smithsonian American Art Museum, Washington, DC, gift of Mr. and Mrs. John A. Benton.

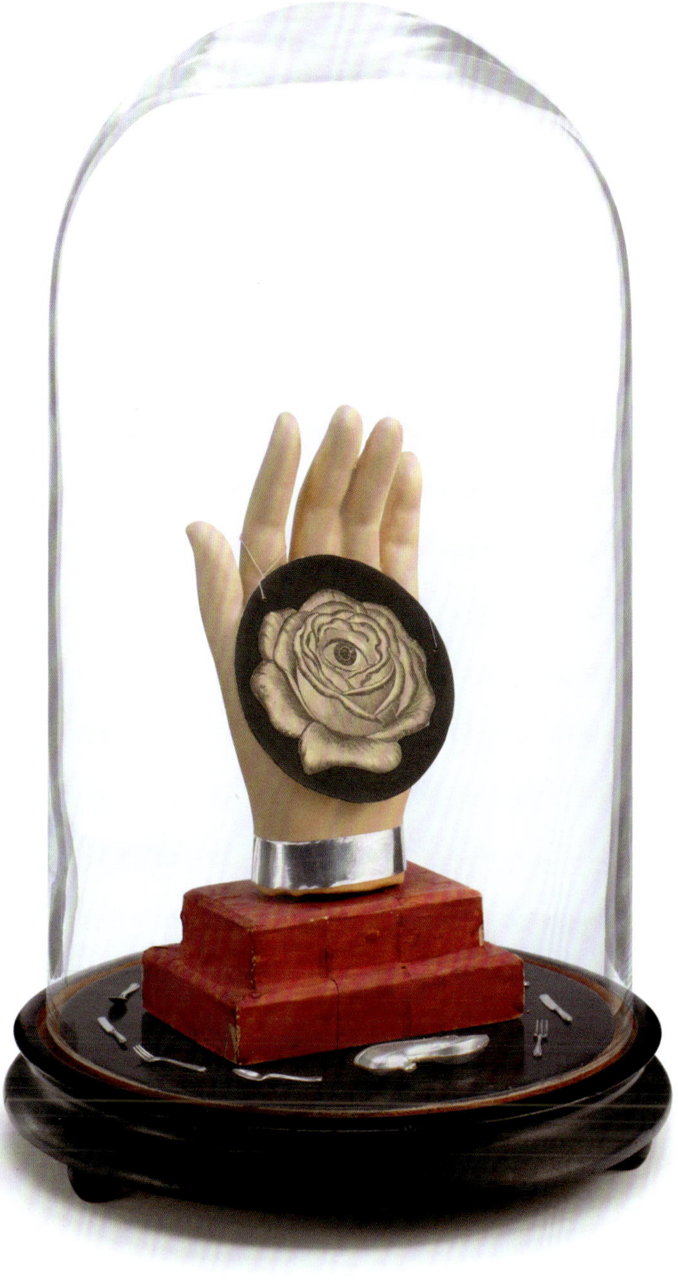

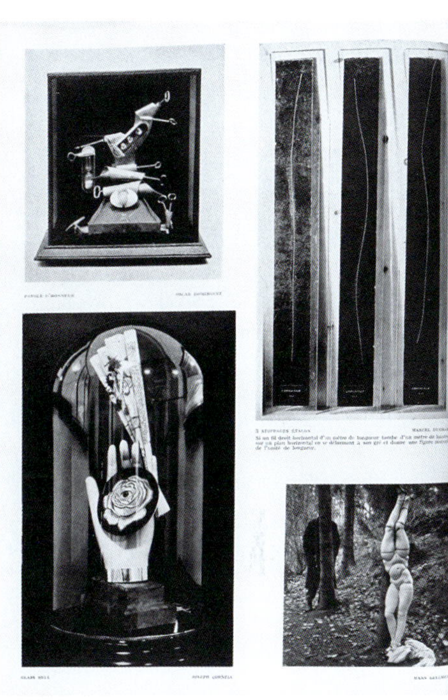

FIG. 1.29 Joseph Cornell, *Untitled (Glass Bell)*, ca. 1932. Illustrated (*lower left*) in *Minotaure* (Winter 1937): 36.

FIG. 1.28 Joseph Cornell, *Untitled (Glass Bell)*, ca. 1932. Assemblage, 16 × 9 inches. Private collection.

another early bell jar (fig. 1.30). His arched back and billowing shirt create a sense of upward movement, as if to lift him from his former life into the heavens. The vitreous enclosure entices us to look closer, and as we do, our gaze falls upon a tiny chain around his ankle (fig. 1.31). Suddenly, the trinket under glass becomes a gripping narrative of escape. As we become aware of the boy's earthly restraints, we also engender his escape: the glass dissolves under our vision, much as Monsieur Phot shattered the pheasant's enclosure. The boy floats unobstructed through the air, free. Or so it seems. For although he appears to float, he remains trapped under glass. And if he escapes in our imagination, he does so only for a moment. Cornell sought to break the material bonds of human life and signal the existence of an

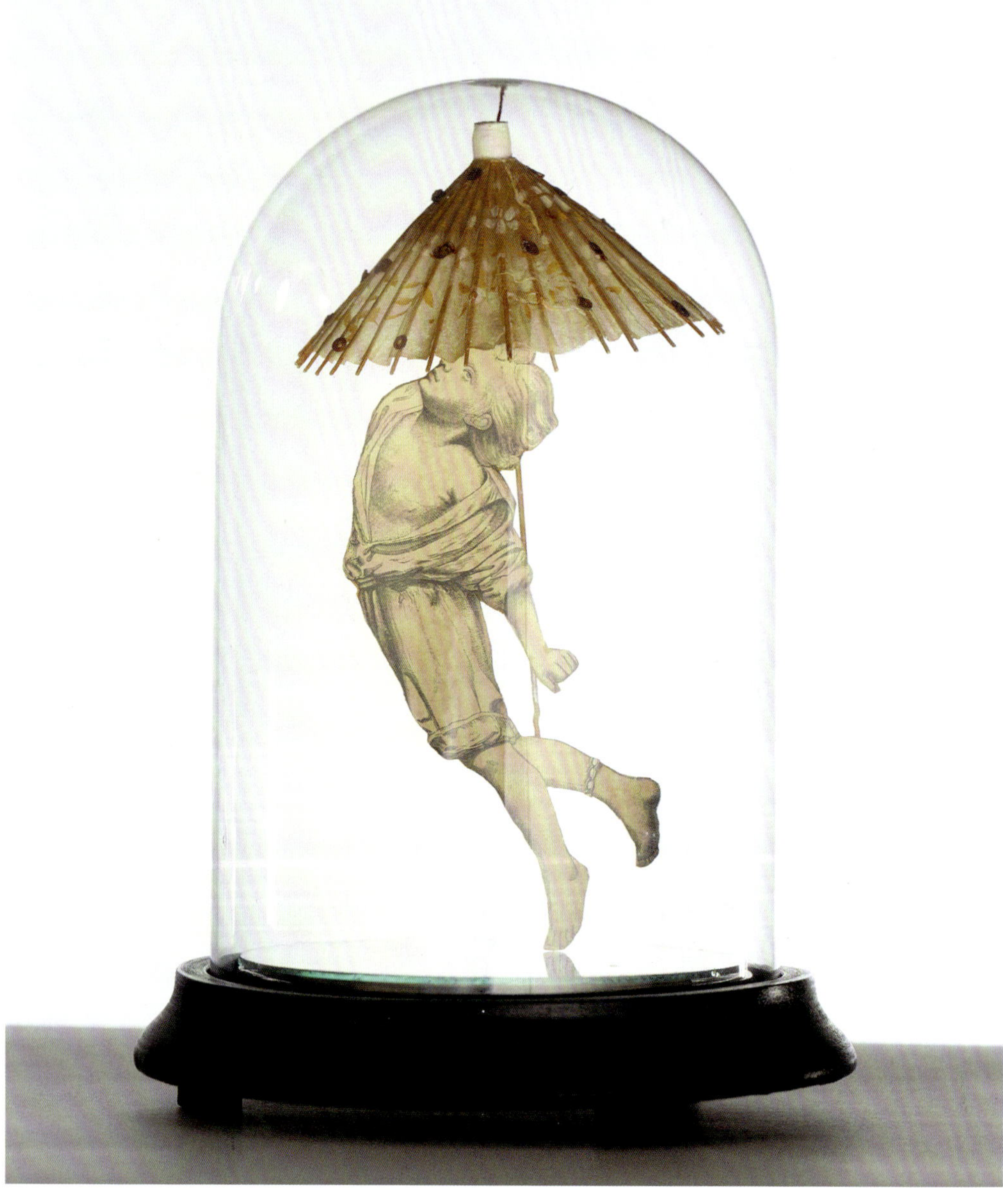

enchanted realm of experience, yet his decision to place the boy under a protective glass shell reveals the tenuousness of such an ambition. His complex artistic and personal motivations were subsumed under the mantle of a legible and emergent artistic movement. Levy's exhibition framed Cornell as a textbook Surrealist, an association that clings to the artist to this day, despite his renunciation of its aims just five years later.

Axel's Castle, Edmund Wilson's famed 1931 study of Symbolism, has been described as "a work of the twenties catching up page by page to the thirties."[109] The book takes its name from Auguste Villiers de L'Isle-Adam's *Axel*, published in 1890. The young count Axel lives alone in a castle filled with treasure. Upon finally finding true love, he decides that this real experience pales in comparison with his rich imaginary world. The melancholic young man enters into a suicide pact with his lover, choosing death over the perceived impoverishment of daily life. For Wilson, Axel represented the ultimate endpoint of Symbolism, one of the movement's heroes who "would rather drop out of the common life than to have to struggle to make themselves a place in it."[110] Wilson's comments encapsulate the frequent criticism of enchantment as elitist and escapist, and illustrates the purchase of this question in the late 1920s. As he writes, "The question begins to press us again as to whether it is possible to make a practical success of human society, and whether, if we continue to fail, a few masterpieces, however profound or noble, will be able to make life worth living even for the few people in a position to enjoy them."[111] What, in other words, were the uses of enchantment not simply for one, but for all? As we will see in the next chapter, this question would shape Cornell's work—and the course of American Modernism in the 1930s.

FIG. 1.30 (Facing page) Joseph Cornell, *Untitled (Bell Jar Object)*, ca. 1939. Engraving on paperboard, paper, sequins, foil, and mirror on wood in glass bell jar, 9 1/4 × 6 1/4 inches. Smithsonian American Art Museum, Washington, DC, gift of Katharine Sergava Sznycer in honor and loving memory of Bernard W. Sznycer and Eugene Berman.

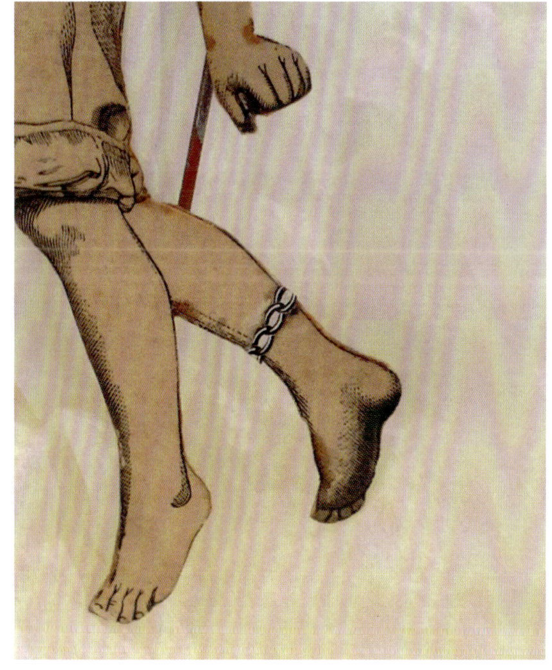

FIG. 1.31 Detail of Joseph Cornell, *Untitled (Bell Jar Object)*, ca. 1939.

CHAPTER 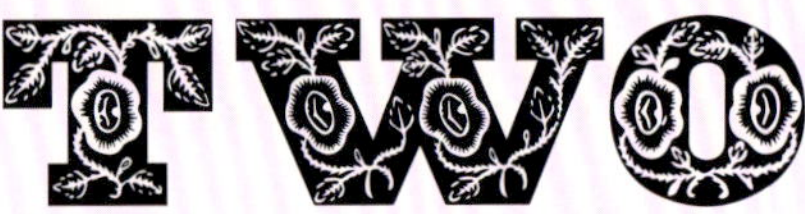

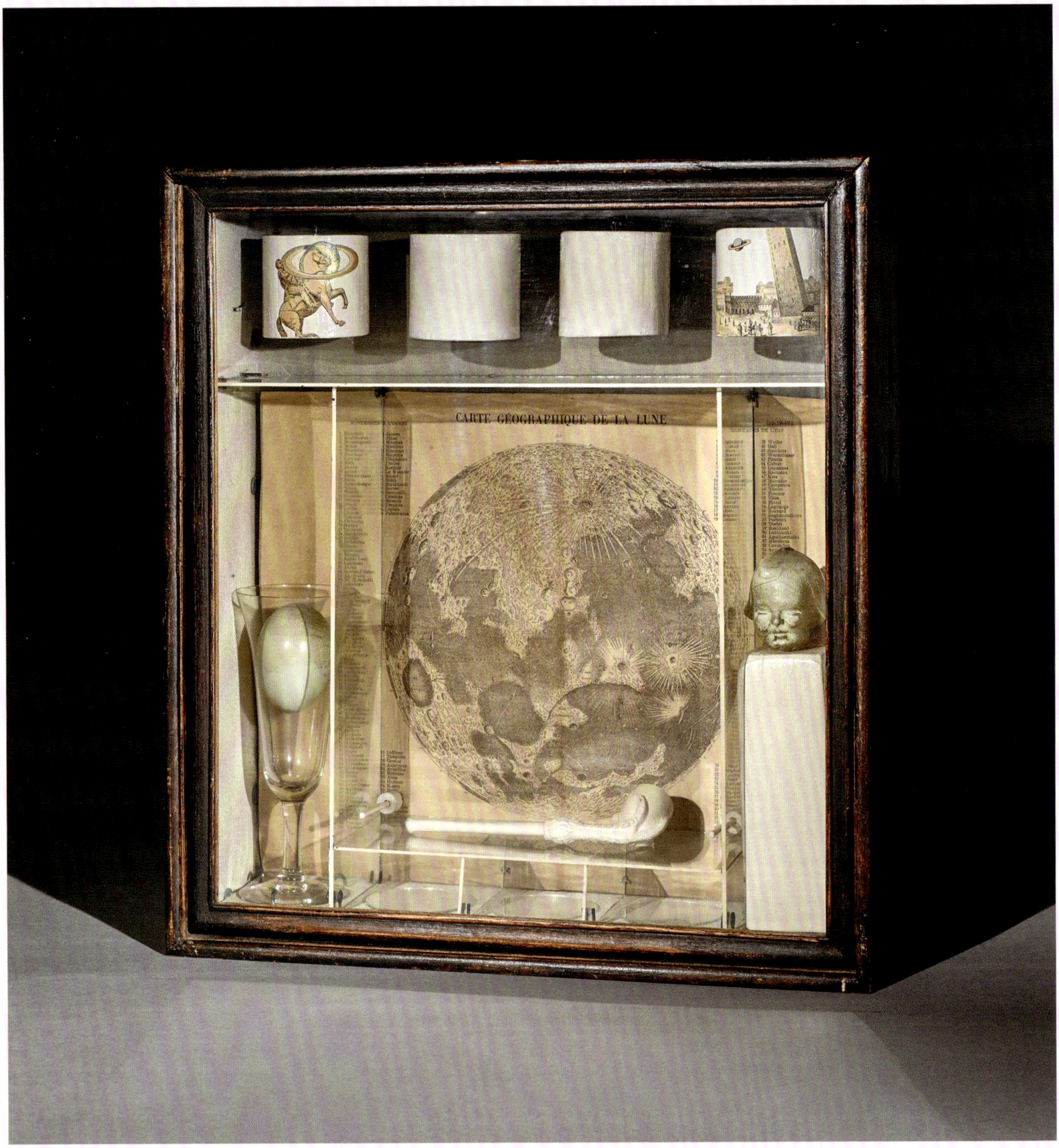

FIG. 2.1 Joseph Cornell, *Soap Bubble Set*, 1936. Mixed media, $14\frac{3}{16} \times 15\frac{1}{2} \times 5\frac{7}{16}$ inches. Wadsworth Atheneum, Hartford, CT, purchased through the gift of Henry and Walter Keney.

Universe to Cosmos

Capit quod non capit.

Guilielmus Hesius, *Emblemata sacra de fide, spe, charitate*

☾

"It was a real 'first-born' of the type of case that was to become my accepted milieu."[1] Thus Joseph Cornell described *Soap Bubble Set* (1936, fig.2.1), a wooden box lined with blue silk, now faded, and divided by glass shelves.[2] An exquisite engraving of the moon's craters, rendered in radiating starbursts and penumbral impressions of ink, lines the back of the lower panel.[3] A white pedestal crowned with a doll's head, and a single egg suspended in a cordial glass flank the moon. Painted the same shade of robin's egg blue, these orbs create a visual link to the celestial bodies adorning the white cylinders in the box's upper compartment. Like the artist's earlier work, *Soap Bubble Set* relies on scalar shifts to create a sense of otherworldliness. The large moon and small terrestrial objects evoke the sky and the earth, while the round mirrors at bottom figure the ocean's glassy surface. For Cornell, bubbles are "fragile, shimmering globules" that "become the shimmering but more enduring planets—a connotation of moon and tides," spheres that drift from the earth to the sky, liquid circles that expand to form the infinite surface of the sea.[4] Sky, earth, and sea are brought into intimate proximity within the box. Their connection is literalized by the bubble of the work's title, which would presumably emanate from the lip of the Dutch clay pipe suspended on a glass shelf above the mirrors.[5] *Soap Bubble Set* is a cosmos.

Soap Bubble Set was also Cornell's first box construction, the format for which he remains best known. With their precise display of quotidian objects, arranged within a wooden frame and sealed behind a pane of glass, Cornell's boxes transpose his early montages into three-dimensional space. The box format's emergence in 1936 marked a turning point in the artist's practice, signaling the growing complexity and ambition of his work and initiating new lines of inquiry he would explore for the remainder of his career. *Soap Bubble Set* also comprises a rich commentary on the continuity between the natural and human worlds, a subject that was among the artist's most enduring preoccupations. Why did the box form appear at this moment, and what to make of the meticulously ordered world within?

This chapter explores these questions by considering Cornell's engagement with natural philosophy, the early modern form of inquiry combining scientific and theological investigation. Upon completing *Soap Bubble Set,* Cornell placed it in a glass vitrine alongside ten objects encased in glass bells (now lost), and another work, *Cabinet of Natural History (Object)*, which he began in 1934 and completed in 1940 (fig. 2.2). He called the full installation *Elements of Natural Philosophy* (fig. 2.3). By invoking natural philosophy, Cornell signaled his ambition to create a space in which scientific inquiry, theology, and art were connected rather than distinct: a cosmos rather than a universe.

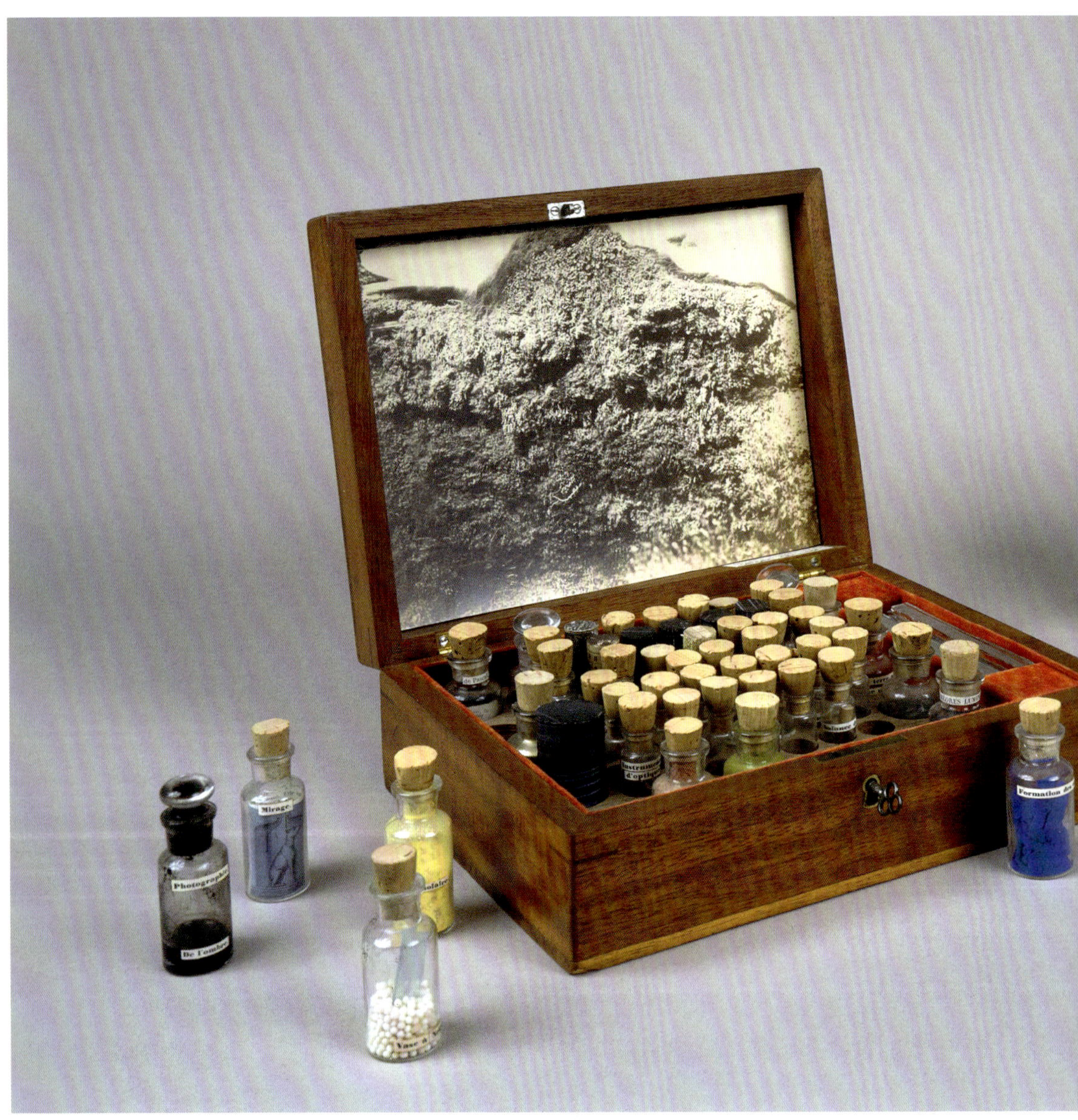

As Charles Taylor has discussed, a cosmos is a model of the world governed by "the sense of the ordered whole." Within a cosmos, science, religion, and being itself emerge from a single set of divine laws. Natural philosophy was the study of these cosmic laws. A universe is instead a world explained by "exceptionless natural laws."[6] For Max Weber, the separation of scientific, philosophical, religious, and artistic inquiry into distinct disciplines—the transition from cosmos to universe—was a key consequence of disenchantment. If Leonardo saw science as "the path to true art," and early modern natural philosophers understood science as a means of apprehending the workings of the divine, disenchantment's rationalist convictions render

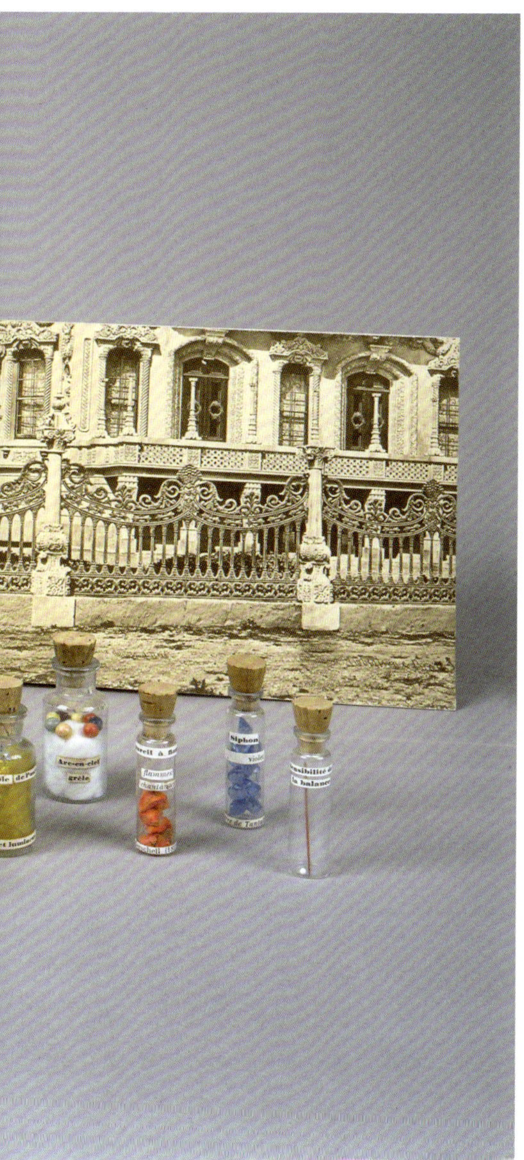

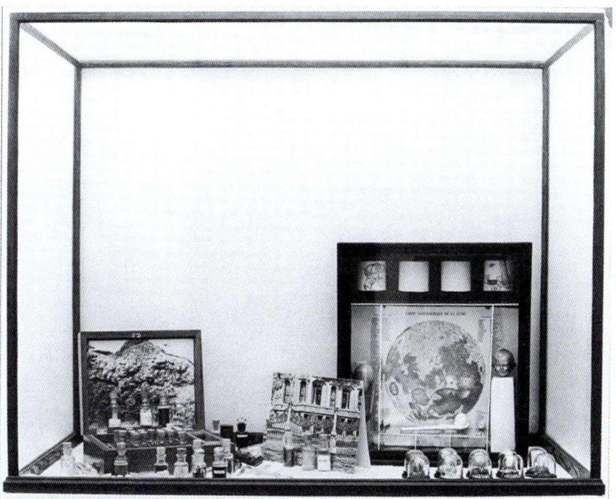

FIG. 2.2 Joseph Cornell, *Cabinet of Natural History (Object)*, 1934, 1936–40. Box construction, $3\frac{1}{4} \times 9\frac{3}{4} \times 7\frac{3}{8}$ inches, when closed. Private collection.

FIG. 2.3 Installation view of the exhibition *Fantastic Art, Dada, Surrealism*, December 7, 1936–January 17, 1937. Shown is Joseph Cornell's *Elements of Natural Philosophy; (left to right) Cabinet of Natural History (Object)*, 1934, 1936–40; *Soap Bubble Set*, 1936; and ten unidentified bell jar objects. Photographic Archive, Museum of Modern Art, New York.

such connections patently absurd.[7] Many of Cornell's most cherished subjects—optical devices, astronomy, early cinema—likely appealed to him precisely because of their liminal position between science and art. In turning to natural philosophy, Cornell sought to create a cosmos from the material leavings of the universe; to show, in other words, how enchantment lingers within an ostensibly disenchanted world.

Although *Elements of Natural Philosophy* took early modern inquiry as its basis, it also responded to contemporary concerns. Cornell created *Soap Bubble Set* specifically for the Museum of Modern Art's famed 1936 exhibition *Fantastic Art, Dada, Surrealism*, curated by Alfred Barr.[8] This exhibition, and Cornell's position therein, were shaped by pressing questions about Modernism's public relevance and ethical obligations. The artist's famed box constructions emerged from this fraught context. With the box format, he found a means of carving out an ordered cosmos from the chaotic world around it, creating a brief moment of stillness and connection in the midst of relentless and inexorable social change.

BUBBLES

At first glance, *Soap Bubble Set* raises a deceptively simple question: Where are the bubbles? These delicate spheres should emerge from the white pipe beneath the moon. Yet no bubbles appear in the box. In their place, Cornell offers an array of suspended spheres. The doll's head perched on a pedestal; the egg floating in a clear cordial glass; the shining white cylinders hanging from hooks; and of course the moon itself: all stand for the box's absent bubbles. As art historian Kirsten Hoving has observed, Cornell created the collaged vignettes adorning the cylinders at top from scientific diagrams illustrating the principles of gravity (fig. 2.4).[9] *Soap Bubble Set* seems to evoke these rules in order to break them. The mounted rider encircled with rings on the cylinder at the left takes its place in the sky on the cylinder at right, transformed into a ringed planet below a diagonal building recalling the Leaning Tower of Pisa, a structure that at once defies gravity and succumbs to its pull. To the moon's left, the cordial glass "proffers rather than contains" its egg, in the apt words of poetry scholar Bonnie Costello.[10] Aloft in a glass container, the egg floats alongside the moon just as a bubble defies gravity. At once absent and figured by the quotidian spheres that populate the box, *Soap Bubble Set*'s

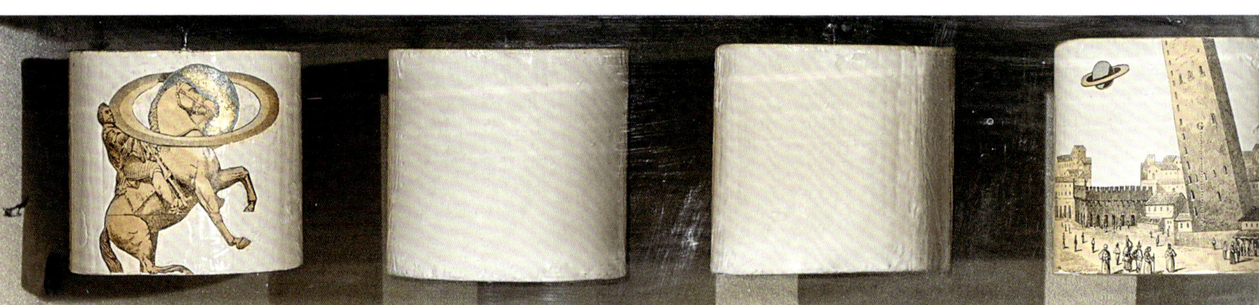

FIG. 2.4 Detail of *Soap Bubble Set*, 1936, showing the four cylinders in the top section.

bubbles present a paradox: how can a work of art, a material form, capture something as ephemeral and magical as a bubble?

To explore this paradox, Cornell turned to natural philosophy. The history of natural philosophy is long and complex, beginning with ancient Greek philosophy and extending through the early modern period.[11] Cornell gleaned natural philosophy's basic tenets from a scattershot assortment of antiquarian books on physics, optics, and astronomy, as well as texts by natural philosophers such as Sir Francis Bacon.[12] Although the artist's understanding of natural philosophy was necessarily incomplete and lacked historical specificity, he grasped its core tenet of theology and scientific inquiry's connection. Paralleling this idea, Mary Baker Eddy described Copernicus's discovery that the earth orbits around the sun as a more precise description of divine perfection than had come before.[13]

The cosmos described by natural philosophy is bound together by similitudes, or deep kinships among ostensibly unlike elements. As Michel Foucault argued, analogy is a type of similitude that "makes possible the marvelous confrontation of resemblances across space; but it also speaks, like [convenience or juxtaposition, another kind of similitude] of adjacencies, of bonds and joints. Its power is immense, for the similitudes of which it treats are not the visible, substantial ones between things themselves; they need only be the more subtle resemblances of relations."[14] In analogy, resemblance is not simply physical resemblance, as in representation, but an ontological affinity that connects materially distinct phenomena. Like a joint, a point of articulation that is at once a break and a bond, analogy signals sympathy without obliterating distinction. Giovanni di Paolo's painting *The Creation of the World and the Expulsion from Paradise* (1445, fig. 2.5) visualizes the analogies that bind a cosmos. The picture is divided into two parts, befitting its title. At right, Adam and Eve are ushered out of paradise by a nude angel. Adam looks over his shoulder to see what he has lost: a blessed world, embodied by a marvelous multicolored wheel. At the cosmos's center is a

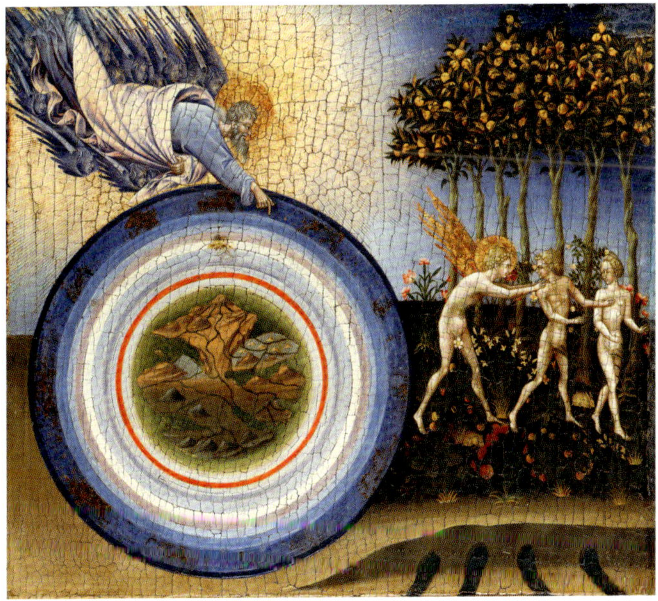

FIG. 2.5 Giovanni di Paolo, *The Creation of the World and the Expulsion from Paradise*, 1445. Tempera and gold on wood, 18¼ × 20½ inches. Robert Lehman Collection, Metropolitan Museum of Art, New York.

Emblems and analogies signal ontological connection among distinct phenomena; they are paradoxes. They are thus well suited to the paradox of trying to capture the divine in material form. Vermeer's sphere embodies Hesius's paradoxical idea of "it captures what it cannot hold." Unlike Jan van Eyck's famed mirror, it does not reflect the contents of the painting but rather shows all that it excluds from it. Gleaming white squares suggest the windows that line the room, while amorphous dark forms indicate the presence of a table or fireplace. The space of the room bends across the sphere, transforming the geometric perspective of Vermeer's meticulously rendered interior into a convex plane of exquisite delicacy. The world is captured with a few indelible strokes of light and color, compressing the infinite into something graspable, conceivable.

As Smith notes, the painting, and the orb in particular, give the lie to the Protestant denigration of representation as deceit rather than transformation.[21] While Vermeer's glass orb is not a bubble, it might as well be, delicate to the point of immateriality, more reflection than object. Vermeer's painting also presages the central visual incident in *Soap Bubble Set*'s most proximate art historical antecedent, Jean Siméon Chardin's beloved eighteenth-century painting *Soap Bubbles* (ca. 1733–34, fig. 2.8). As with Vermeer's sphere, it is no exaggeration to describe Chardin's bubble as a miracle of painting, viscous oil giving way to an object that hovers on the edge of materiality. With a few flicks of the wrist, Chardin lays down a warm sienna outline burnished with daubs of white and limned with blue, suggesting the iridescence of its luminous skin, and forming a chromatic link with the cluster of honeysuckles emerging from the glass of liquid soap at the boy's elbow. Flower and bubble are made from the same substance, materializing a world in paint, much as bubbles give form to breath.

Like Vermeer's sphere, Chardin's bubble is at once reflective and transparent, at once of and not of the world. And like Vermeer, Chardin painted at a moment of intense religious debate over the meaning of representation. As Thomas Crow has argued, Chardin, a practicing Jansenist, followed that Catholic sect's condemnation of material excess and idolatry.[22] Rather, Chardin turned his attention to the humble, everyday manifestations of divine grace in accordance with Jansenism's figurist tendencies, which located divine truth in common occurrence.[23] While acknowledging the different geographic and historical contexts in which Vermeer, Chardin, and Cornell worked, one might note that the artists faced parallel structural problems: how to maintain their conviction in the religious potency of art amidst moments of intense doubt. These artists turned to the transparent sphere, whether made of glass or soap, to figure this problem. Vermeer and Chardin's orbs are at once material and evanescent, representative and limited, embodying the paradoxical truth of *capit quod non capit* by indexing precisely that which it is impossible to fully grasp. The extended caption accompanying the Dutch painter's source image makes explicit this point: "The vast universe can be shown in something small / A small globe encompasses endless skies / And captures what it cannot hold. Our mind is large enough / Though people think it small. / If only I believe in God, nothing can be larger than that mind; / Nothing broader than that mind; never can he who believes / Appreciate the greatness of this mind. / The mind is larger than the largest sphere because it is human."[24] Hesius's passage is threaded with attempts to close the distance between large and small, near and far, much as Cornell's box relies on the convergence of multiple scalar relationships to condense cosmic distance into a few centimeters. To return to the artist's own description of soap bubbles, "these fragile, shimmering globules . . . become the shimmering but more enduring planets." For Cornell, Vermeer, and Chardin, the bubble was a device for collapsing the distance between the earthly and the divine.

It was no coincidence that Cornell's first box construction featured bubbles. Like a Cornell box, a bubble is a humble form that evokes more than its material origins would suggest. It is an emblem of the transience and vulnerability of faith. Cornell places all of this behind a pane of glass, a shimmering surface that itself resembles the skin of a bubble. These glass fronts embody the compatibility and disjuncture of the world inside the box, and the world that lies beyond its frame. Their reflective surfaces transfigure common incident into light and color, evanescent flashes that negotiate the distance between impossible and perfect representation.

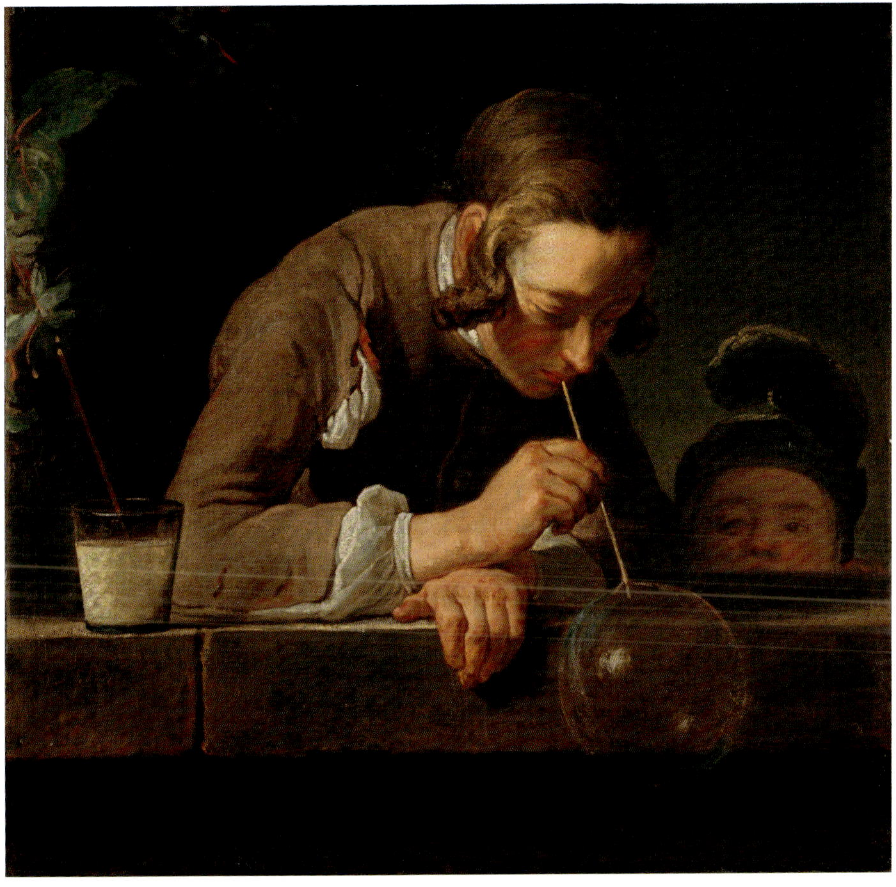

FIG. 2.8 Jean-Baptiste-Siméon Chardin, *Soap Bubbles*, ca. 1733–34. Oil on canvas, 24 × 24⅞ inches. Metropolitan Museum of Art, New York.

(fig. 2.9).[44] While these cases are convincingly argued, one might note that the museum's display of common objects also connotes the obverse. Rather than desacralizing art, MoMA's displays might be thought of as *sacralizing* all manner of cultural production, elevating cinema, design, and industrial goods to the exalted level of fine art. To this point, in the same interview with Macdonald, Barr allowed that showing fine and popular art together would "dignify [them] through exhibition under the same roof with some of the best paintings, sculptures, etc. of the present and recent past."[45]

That common objects might be thus elevated had profound social implications during the 1930s. Ralph Ellison's 1980 essay "Going to the Territory" details the author's childhood in the '30s, a period when he wore blue jeans, listened to the radio, and learned European folk dances. As Ellison recalls, such lessons helped him learn "a bit more about how to live within the

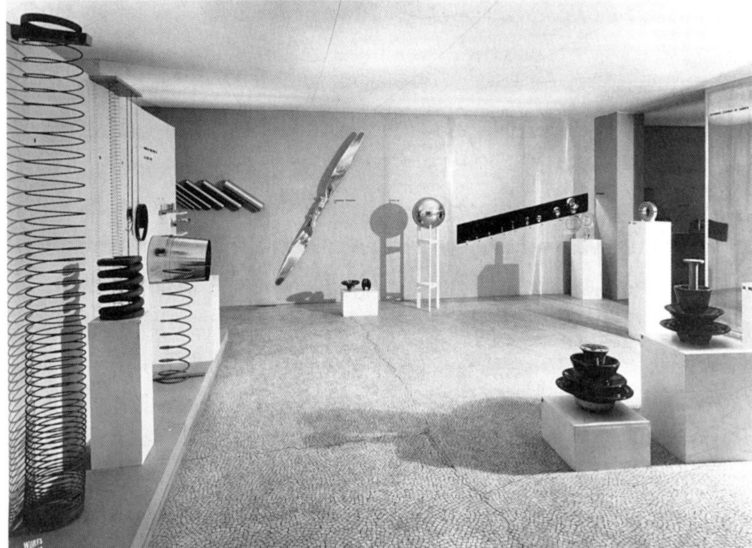

FIG. 2.9 Installation view of the exhibition *Machine Art*, March 5–April 19, 1934. Photographic Archive, Museum of Modern Art, New York.

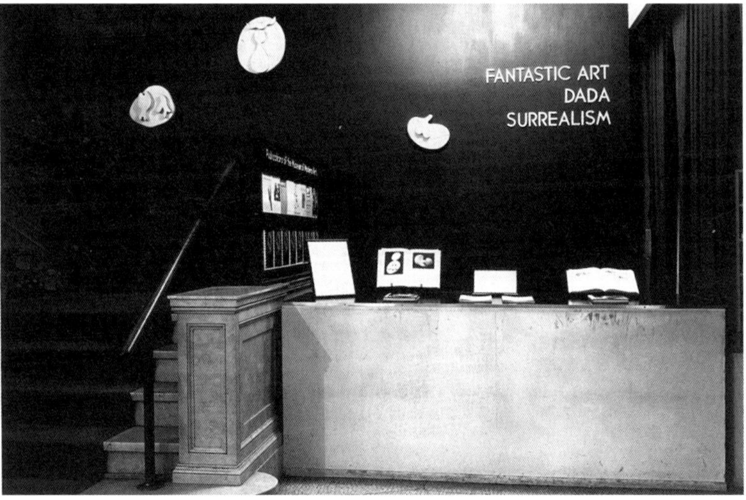

FIG. 2.10 Installation view of the exhibition *Fantastic Art, Dada, Surrealism*, December 7, 1936–January 17, 1937. Photographic Archive, Museum of Modern Art, New York.

sphere because it is human."[24] Hesius's passage is threaded with attempts to close the distance between large and small, near and far, much as Cornell's box relies on the convergence of multiple scalar relationships to condense cosmic distance into a few centimeters. To return to the artist's own description of soap bubbles, "these fragile, shimmering globules . . . become the shimmering but more enduring planets." For Cornell, Vermeer, and Chardin, the bubble was a device for collapsing the distance between the earthly and the divine.

It was no coincidence that Cornell's first box construction featured bubbles. Like a Cornell box, a bubble is a humble form that evokes more than its material origins would suggest. It is an emblem of the transience and vulnerability of faith. Cornell places all of this behind a pane of glass, a shimmering surface that itself resembles the skin of a bubble. These glass fronts embody the compatibility and disjuncture of the world inside the box, and the world that lies beyond its frame. Their reflective surfaces transfigure common incident into light and color, evanescent flashes that negotiate the distance between impossible and perfect representation.

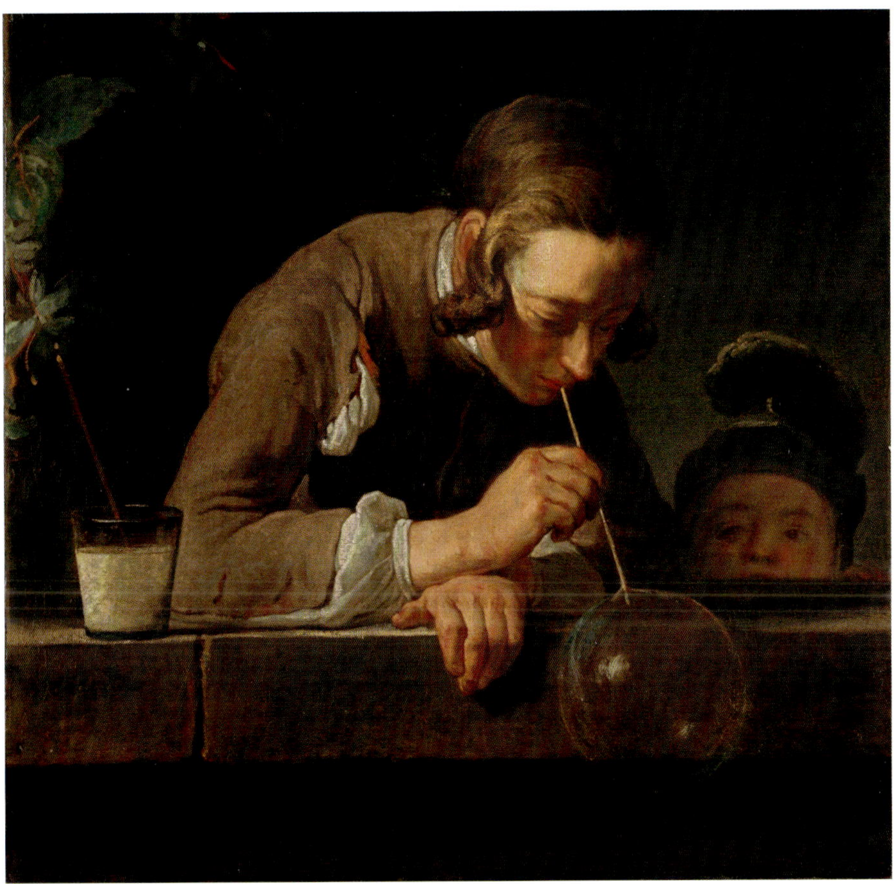

FIG. 2.8 Jean-Baptiste-Siméon Chardin, *Soap Bubbles*, ca. 1733–34. Oil on canvas, 24 × 24 7/8 inches. Metropolitan Museum of Art, New York.

Paint, bubble, glass: these corollary devices of creation recombine the quotidian stuff of the world into an interconnected realm not by elevating them but by embodying all that exceeds their material limitations.

THE MODERN ON THE EDGE OF THE 1930S

How did Cornell's complex artistic experiment relate to the strident politics of 1930s America? To answer this question requires a brief detour away from the artist to explore the competing imperatives that shaped the Museum of Modern Art's early history.

In an oft-cited irony, MoMA officially opened its doors just days after the Great Crash of 1929. The museum's first three years of operation coincided with the nadir of the Great Depression, the pre–New Deal era famously described as the "years of the locust."[25] As Franklin Roosevelt noted during his first inaugural address in 1933, "We now realize as we have never realized before our interdependence on each other; that we cannot merely take but we must give as well; that if we are to go forward, we must move as a trained and loyal army willing to sacrifice for the good of a common discipline."[26] Roosevelt offers implicit critique of Gilded Age individualism and proposes collectivity as the solution to the crisis. The emergent collectivist imperative of the 1930s was marshaled by both ends of the political spectrum. On the right, jingoistic demagogues such as Father Coughlin capitalized on social instability to push an anti-Semitic and pro-Fascist platform, while on the left, the Great Depression was understood as a spur to political action and a portent of the coming revolution. As Edmund Wilson wrote in his 1932 essay, "The Literary Consequences of the Crash," "To the writers and artists of my generation who had grown up in the Big Business era and had always resented its barbarism, its crowding-out of everything they cared about, these years were not depressing but stimulating."[27]

To Wilson's point, the early 1930s saw many artists undertake a searching reconsideration of their perceived elitism.[28] Poet Wallace Stevens described this impulse as the "pressure of reality," or an obligation to respond directly to the exigencies of the political moment.[29] This "pressure of reality" can be discerned in the fervent leftism of the period, encapsulated in what Michael Denning has described as the Cultural Front.[30] The sheer heterogeneity of artistic production from this period, which included printmaking, photography, painting, and muralism in idioms ranging from realism to abstraction, suggests the difficulty of settling on a single definition of what was optimistically known in period parlance as "art for the people."[31]

Philosopher John Dewey offered a potential answer in his 1927 book *The Public and Its Problems*.[32] This influential text diagnosed elitism and expertise as the primary obstacle in creating a truly public culture, which Dewey defined as one that could provide answers to urgent social issues. With a tinge of pragmatic wisdom, he remarks, "The man who wears the shoe knows best that it pinches and where it pinches, even if the expert shoemaker is the best judge of how the trouble is to be remedied."[33] What Dewey describes as the expertise of "scientific investigators and artists" is not enough: "What is required is that they have the ability to judge of the bearing of the knowledge supplied by others upon common concerns."[34]

Dewey proposes that it is only through practical, everyday experience—rather than the "elite" knowledge offered by artists and scientists—that one might create a culture that would be of *use* to a public. Yet for British literary critic William Empson, the solution was not so simple. In a 1935 essay on proletarian literature, a genre also concerned with questions of accessibility and "common experience," Empson succinctly diagnoses the paradox endemic in Dewey's approach to expertise—and by extension, the period call for an "art for the people." The heart of the matter is a question of prepositions: is an "art for the people," *for* them, *about* them, or *by* them?[35] For Empson, art *by*, *for*, and *about* the proletariat presented distinct, and often contradictory aims, which no single work could hope to fulfill.[36]

The paradox described by Empson shaped MoMA's early history. As Suzanne Hudson has observed, the question of the public was in fact embedded into MoMA's institutional mission from its founding. The museum's original charter stated its primary mission as the education of a broad public, "encouraging and developing the study of modern arts and the application of such arts to manufacture and practical life, and furnishing popular instruction."[37] Despite its efforts, the museum's three wealthy founders, and especially Abby Aldrich Rockefeller, led many to see MoMA as a symbol of the elitist culture that gave rise to the Great Depression.[38] As New Dealer Edward Bruce sneered in 1933, MoMA was considered by many to be "the little snob which was recently dedicated by the Rockefellers and who have put their dead hand on it as on everything they touch."[39] By virtue of its unchangeable identity as a museum and its association with the Rockefellers, MoMA found itself at odds with the emergent demotic tenor of the 1930s. The "pressure of reality" described by Stevens was an ingrained part of MoMA's institutional identity: its charge was to show the relevance of modern art to a broad public.

These ambitions suggest one motivation for MoMA's remarkably eclectic early exhibition program. Long condemned as a bastion of teleological formalism, recent scholarship has demonstrated the catholic nature of the museum's interests.[40] During the early 1930s, Barr organized exhibitions of Mexican and American murals, Persian frescoes, theater, and graphic and industrial design, and established curatorial departments devoted to film and architecture. Barr understood this broad scope crucial to Modernism, as well as a means of achieving broad legibility. "We hope," he later explained to critic Dwight Macdonald, "that showing the best in these arts of popular entertainment and of commercial and industrial design will mitigate some of the arcane and difficult atmosphere of painting and sculpture."[41]

Barr's point explicates the social implications of the porous boundaries between fine art and vernacular culture during the 1930s.[42] In the vernacular, cultural elites such as Barr and Julien Levy found a potential avenue for expanding the audience of fine art. This narrative has found purchase among art historians such as Joan Saab, who describes MoMA's goal of mitigating the abstruseness of Modernism as an attempt to "desacralize" art in order to "democratize" the museum.[43] In a related line of inquiry, Jennifer Jane Marshall positions the museum's 1934 exhibition *Machine Art* as extending from the period's "positivism," displaying common objcets such as ball bearings as "empirical proof" of abstraction's universalism (fig. 2.9).[44] While these cases are convincingly argued, one might note that the museum's display of common objects also connotes the obverse. Rather than desacralizing art, MoMA's displays might be thought of as *sacralizing* all manner of cultural production, elevating cinema, design, and industrial goods to the exalted level of fine art. To this point, in the same interview with Macdonald, Barr allowed that showing fine and popular art together would "dignify [them] through exhibition under the same roof with some of the best paintings, sculptures, etc. of the present and recent past."[45]

That common objects might be thus elevated had profound social implications during the 1930s. Ralph Ellison's 1980 essay "Going to the Territory" details the author's childhood in the '30s, a period when he wore blue jeans, listened to the radio, and learned European folk dances. As Ellison recalls, such lessons helped him learn "a bit more about how to live within the

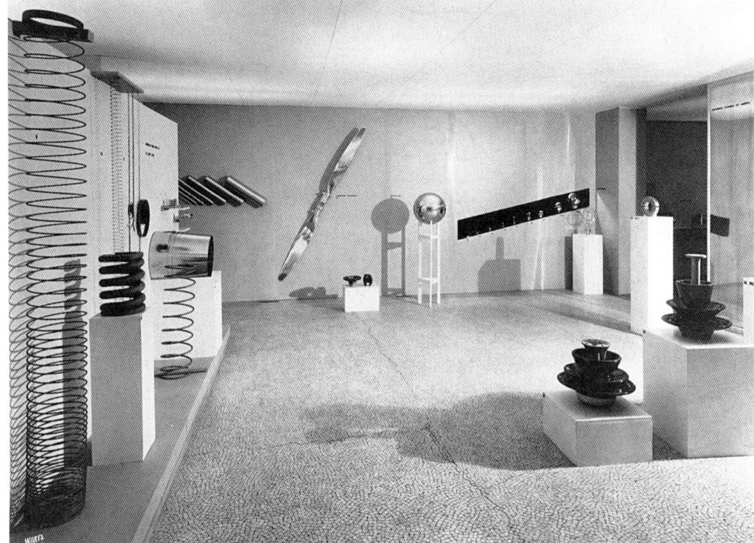

FIG. 2.9 Installation view of the exhibition *Machine Art*, March 5–April 19, 1934. Photographic Archive, Museum of Modern Art, New York.

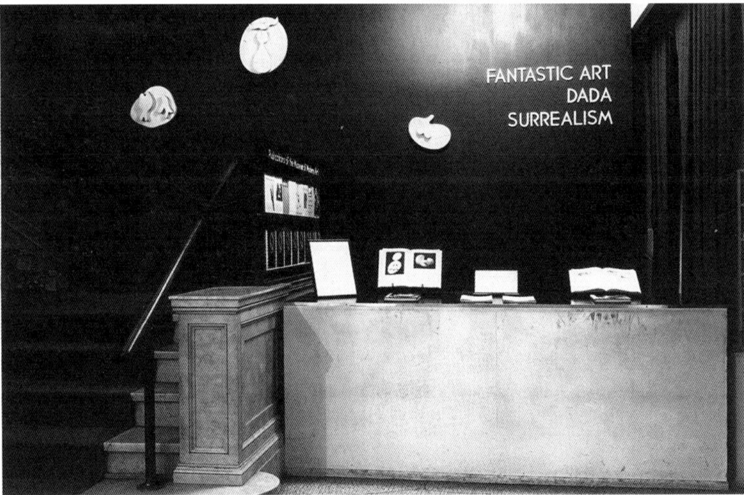

FIG. 2.10 Installation view of the exhibition *Fantastic Art, Dada, Surrealism*, December 7, 1936–January 17, 1937. Photographic Archive, Museum of Modern Art, New York.

mystery which haunts American experience, and that is the mystery of how we are many and yet one." He continues:

> It seems to me that our most characteristic American style *is* that of the vernacular. But by "vernacular" I mean far more than popular or indigenous language. I see the vernacular as a dynamic process in which the most refined styles from the past are continually merged with the play-it-by-eye-and-by-ear improvisations which we invent in our efforts to control our environment and entertain ourselves. . . . In it the styles and techniques of the past are adjusted to the needs of the present, and in its integrative action the high styles of the past are democratized. From this perspective the vernacular is, no less than the styles associated with aristocracy, a gesture toward perfection.[46]

Ellison's description of the vernacular as a "process" returns the phrase to its linguistic roots. He defines the vernacular in terms of its everyday use, rather than its means of production. The vernacular's capacity for "perfection" resides in its leveling of cultural hierarchies, which he understands as a requirement for a truly equitable society. In Ellison's idealistic telling, diverse cultural artifacts such as Hollywood film, graphic design, folk dance, and photography need not be characterized by their means of production, as in "mass culture," but might instead be understood as a potential site for the creation of a common cultural language.

Writing in 1929, Erich Auerbach similarly described Dante's decision to write in Italian rather than Latin as motivated by his desire to serve the general Italian public. In the *Comedy*, Dante constructs what Auerbach describes as the *volgare illustre*, the "illustrious vernacular," a language that "maintains a constant give and take with the language of everyday usage and so makes the living element in thought and tradition, the part that is really worth knowing, available to all who are eager to receive it."[47] In Auerbach and Ellison's writing, the vernacular emerges as a site of social mediation, where elite aesthetic traditions may be merged with everyday language. Within this historical context, MoMA's investment in a broad swath of culture and Cornell's elevation of everyday objects seemed, at least in 1936, one way of answering Empson's paradox.

FANTASTIC ART, DADA, SURREALISM

With *Fantastic Art, Dada, Surrealism*, Barr attempted to merge MoMA's wide-ranging interests and an established European avant-garde movement into a single exhibition. The show was the second of five enormous survey exhibitions that sought to "present in an objective and historical manner the principal movements of modern art.[48] *Fantastic Art, Dada, Surrealism* was truly dizzying in scope, featuring over seven hundred objects, including painting and sculpture from the fifteenth- to twentieth-centuries installed alongside Disney animation cels, folk art, and the work of children and "the insane"[49] (fig. 2.10). Barr's catalogue describes Cornell as "American constructivist. Born in New York, 1904. Self-taught. Author of two Surrealist scenarios."[50] In addition to misstating Cornell's birth year, Barr's entry calls him an "American constructivist." The lowercase "c" of constructivist (in contrast to the capitalization of "Surrealist") suggests that this designation was meant to describe the artist's working methods rather than affiliation with the Russian movement. More telling is Barr's decision to characterize Cornell as "self-taught," which situated the artist within the history of the museum's promotion of so-called folk art.[51]

The man responsible for introducing folk art to the museum was Holger Cahill, who took over as MoMA's director while Barr was on sabbatical in 1932.[52] Best known for his subsequent directorship of the Federal Arts Project (FAP) of the Works Progress Administration (WPA), Cahill viewed folk art as a means to reconcile what he descried as Modernism's "revolution in form" with his ardent leftist politics.[53] Cahill's choice of a subtitle for his exhibition *American Folk Art: The Art of the Common Man* is telling in this respect (fig. 2.11).[54] The exhibition, which opened at MoMA in 1932, focused exclusively on "the work of craftsmen and amateurs of the eighteenth and nineteenth centuries," and included examples of itinerant portraiture, weathervanes, and carved figureheads. Cahill defined the "expression of the common people" through labor and education: for him, "common people" were "amateurs and craftsmen" who acquired skill through daily labor rather than formal artistic training.[55] The curator described industrialization as a threat to these vernacular practices, noting that this type of skill "has declined rapidly with the progress of the machine age." Cahill's idealization of America's preindustrial history is echoed in Malcolm Cowley's retrospective account of the period: "Many of them were also unconsciously seeking a religious solution, a faith that would supply certain elements heretofore lacking in their private and professional lives as middle-class Americans. I suspect that the element most acutely missed was a sense of comradeship, or cooperation or, to use the religious word, communion."[56] Cowley diagnoses the atavism inherent in period calls for "comradeship" or "cooperation." If Cahill turned to American history as a source of preindustrial collectivity, Cowley discerned a desire for an earlier, more communal model of religious practice as motivating this retrospective gaze.

Yet even within this idealistic framing, Cahill positioned folk art as secondary to the work of professionally trained artists. His catalogue essay concludes with the following qualification: "Folk art cannot be valued as highly as the work of our greatest painters and sculptors, but it is certainly entitled to a place in the history of American art."[57] His privileging of fine art elucidates the paradox inherent to locating Modernism's most cherished principles in the work of amateurs, outsiders, and children.[58] Exhibiting folk art placed MoMA in a precarious situation: while it needed the form to answer the period's demotic imperative, the very definition of folk art threatened to destabilize the logic of the museum itself, which since the Gilded Age had been charged with displaying "unique aesthetic and spiritual properties that rendered it inviolate, exclusive, and eternal," to quote Lawrence Levine's foundational study of cultural hierarchies in the United States.[59]

Surrealism appeared to offer a resolution to this paradox. As discussed in chapter 1, Surrealist theories of automatism carried an implicit challenge to the category of fine art, suggesting that art could be made by anyone. Levy and Austin's popular early exhibitions of Surrealism illustrated the viability of this idea. In *Fantastic Art, Dada, Surrealism,* Barr combined the museum's promotion of folk art as the "art of the common man," with Surrealism's emphasis on untrained artistic expression.[60] Following Levy's original presentation of the movement in *Surréalisme*, Barr's arrangement of *Fantastic Art, Dada, Surrealism* sought to unveil a vibrant modern tendency toward the "bizarre, dreamlike, absurd, uncanny, enigmatic; objects of 'concrete irrationality,' " a host of characteristics that he dubbed "the fantastic."[61] Barr continued that he considered Surrealism "a serious affair and that for many it is more than an art movement; it is a philosophy, a way of life a cause to which some of the most brilliant painters and poets of our age are giving themselves with consuming devotion."[62] This description of Surrealism and the fantastic as sensibilities rather than discrete artistic movements encapsulates Barr's attempts to reconcile two ostensibly incommensurate value systems: vernacular legibility and vanguard artistic practice. Like all primitivizing formulations, his framing of Surrealism was an argument for universality: by including work by those ostensibly unencumbered by the lessons of modern society—children, folk artists, "the insane"—Barr's construed the fantastic as an essential element of human nature.

The popular appeal of this narrative can be seen in the fashion magazine *Harper's Bazaar*, which devoted an article to *Fantastic Art, Dada, Surrealism*. The article describes Surrealism as a popular trend and declares, "This is Their Year all over America."[63] About Cornell, the magazine writes, "Finally, there is Joseph Cornell, who is, according to Mr. Levy, one of the few Americans who fully and creatively understand the surrealist viewpoint. Cornell does not paint, he 'objectifies.' If he dreams of a wooden ball with a long needle sticking through it, that is what he puts together when he wakes up. Cornell's little surrealist gadgets might be called imagination-toys for adults. (That's what Mr. Levy calls them, and nobody in America knows more about surrealism than he does)."[64]

This passage encapsulates Cornell's early reception. While Levy's description of the artist as an American Surrealist helped him attain public recognition, the gallerist also contributed to this condescending view of the artist's work. To promote Cornell's first solo exhibition in December 1932, Levy, no doubt thinking of André Breton's mention of adult fairy tales in the first Surrealist manifesto, described the

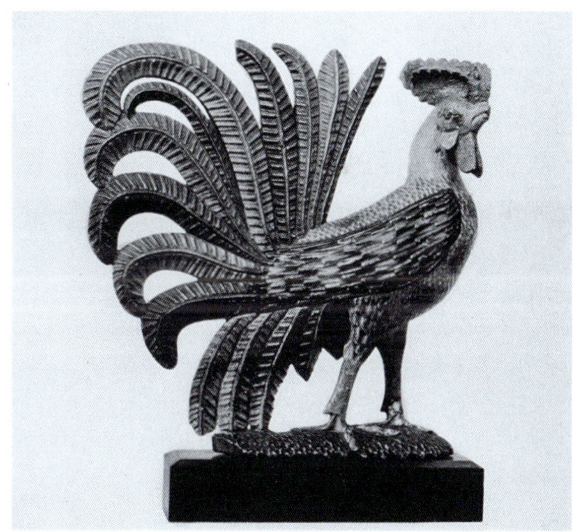

FIG. 2.11 *Rooster*, n.d. Wood sculpture, polychromed. Reproduced in the catalogue for the exhibition *American Folk Art: The Art of the Common Man in America, 1750–1900* (1932). Library of the Museum of Modern Art, New York.

artist's work as "toys for adults" and noted that they would make excellent Christmas presents.[65] Infantilization was the price of Cornell's growing public profile.

Cornell vehemently objected to this characterization. While corresponding with Barr about his participation in *Fantastic Art, Dada, Surrealism,* he asked the curator to correct the magazine's description of his work as "the objectification of dreams" and complained that it had stated, "if I dream of sticking a needle into a wooden ball, when I awake that is what I do." Cornell continued firmly, "I do not share in the sub-conscious and dream theories of the Surrealists. While fervently admiring much of their work, I have never been an official Surrealist, and I believe that Surrealism has healthier possibilities than have been developed."[66] This 1936 letter, Cornell's earliest recorded statement about Surrealism, vividly articulates his rejection of his art as unconscious expression, which the artist would later describe as "black magic" in contrast to his own "white magic."[67] *Harper's Bazaar*'s description of his process as a literal translation of his dreams obscured the painstaking care Cornell took researching, gathering, and arranging his work. Perhaps this also motivated his decision to include the doll's head in *Soap Bubble Set*. The same object, pierced with threaded needles and placed under a glass dome, appeared in Surrealist Lee Miller's 1933 photograph of a Cornell work (fig. 2.12). With its pricked central form and enigmatic atmosphere, Miller's photograph calls to mind the phrase "sticking a needle into a wooden ball" that so pained Cornell.

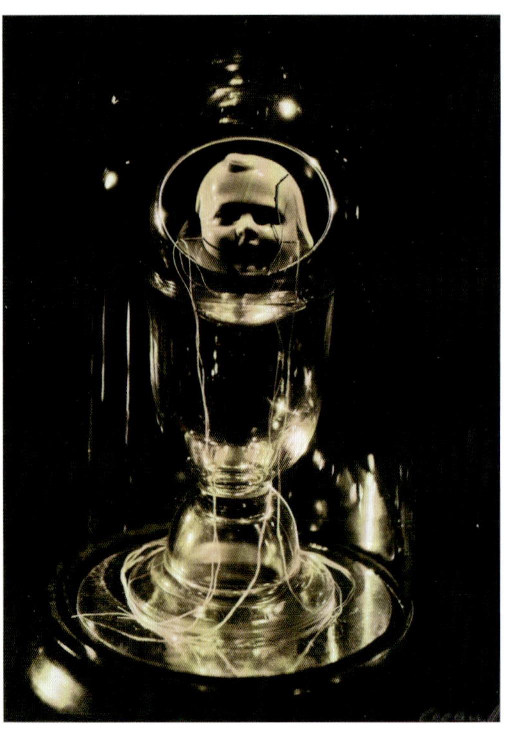

FIG. 2.12 Lee Miller, *Object by Joseph Cornell (Glass Dome)*, 1933. Gelatin silver print, 8½ × 6 inches. Private collection.

Cornell's fears were not without basis. Despite his objections, the artist became a crucial figure in Barr's attempts to navigate the competing imperatives of accessibility and vanguard experimentation in *Fantastic Art, Dada, Surrealism*. Barr installed Cornell's vitrine alongside works such as *Object* by Joan Miró, which features a stuffed parrot perched above a dangling mannequin leg, and a drawing by eleven-year-old Grand Rapids native Jean Hoisington (figs. 2.13–2.15), works he grouped in the exhibition catalogue under the heading "confrontation of incongruities."[68] The display positioned Cornell as a mediator between European avant-garde traditions and the fantastic impulse undergirding the work of amateur practitioners such as Hoisington.

If Barr's attempt to negotiate this paradox was a means of institutional

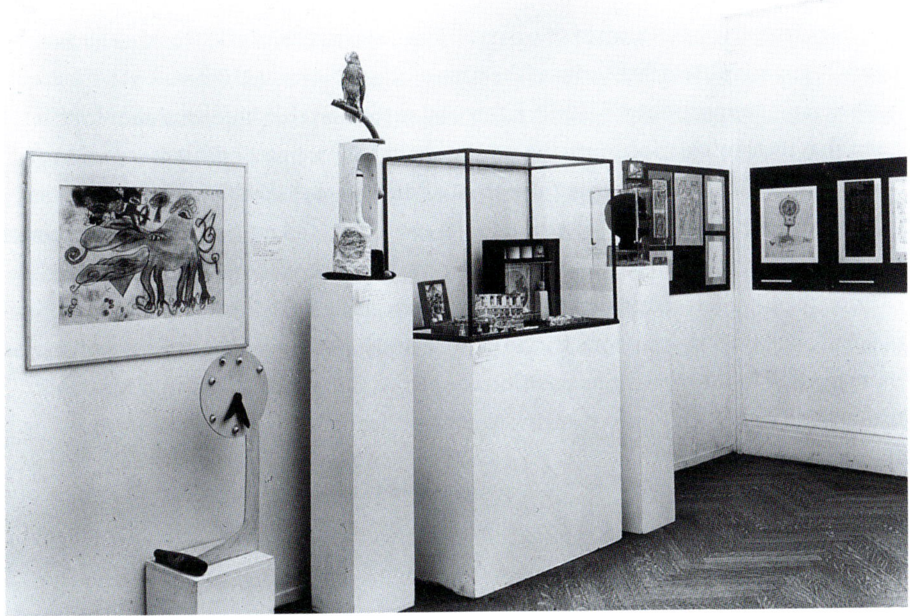

FIG. 2.13 Installation view of the exhibition *Fantastic Art, Dada, Surrealism*, December 7, 1936–January 17, 1937. Shown are *(from left)* works by Jean Hoisington, Wolfgang Paalen, Joan Miró, Joseph Cornell, and Marcel Jean. Photographic Archive, Museum of Modern Art, New York.

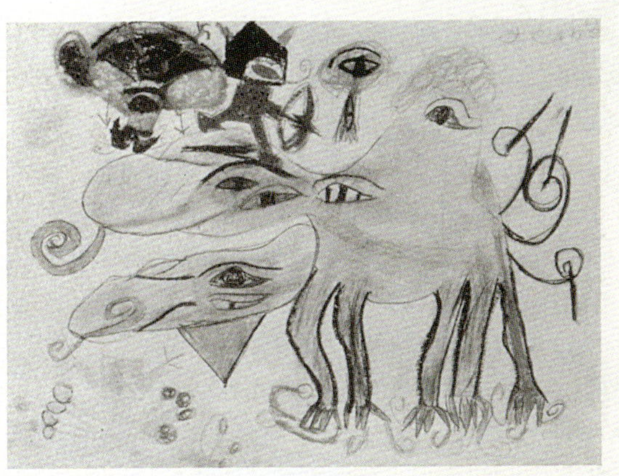

FIG. 2.14 Jean Hoisington, *A God of War Shooting Arrows to Protect the People*, ca. 1936. Reproduced in the catalogue for the exhibition *Fantastic Art, Dada, Surrealism* (1936), ed. Alfred H. Barr Jr. Library of the Museum of Modern Art, New York.

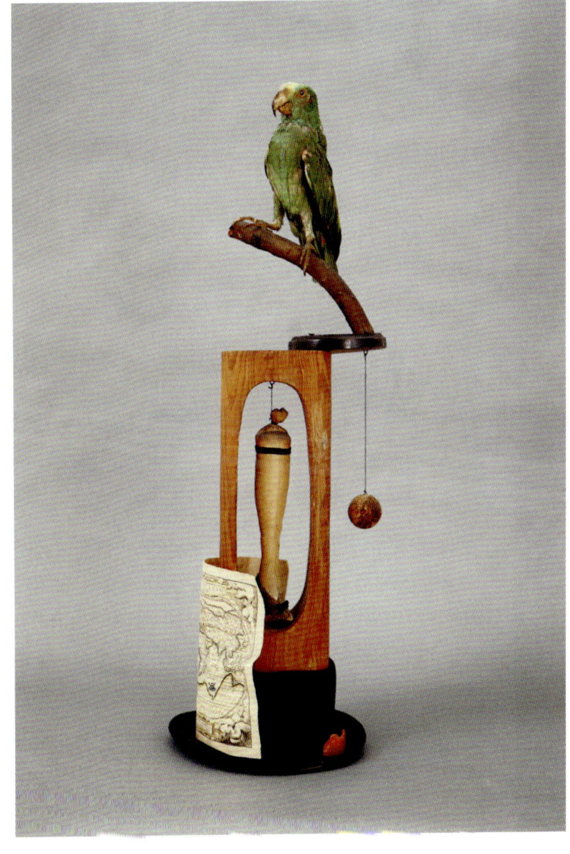

FIG. 2.15 Joan Miró, *Object*, 1936. Stuffed parrot on wood perch, stuffed silk stocking with velvet garter and doll's paper shoe suspended in hollow wood frame, derby hat, hanging cork ball, celluloid fish, and engraved map, 31 7/8 × 11 7/8 × 10 1/4 inches. Museum of Modern Art, New York.

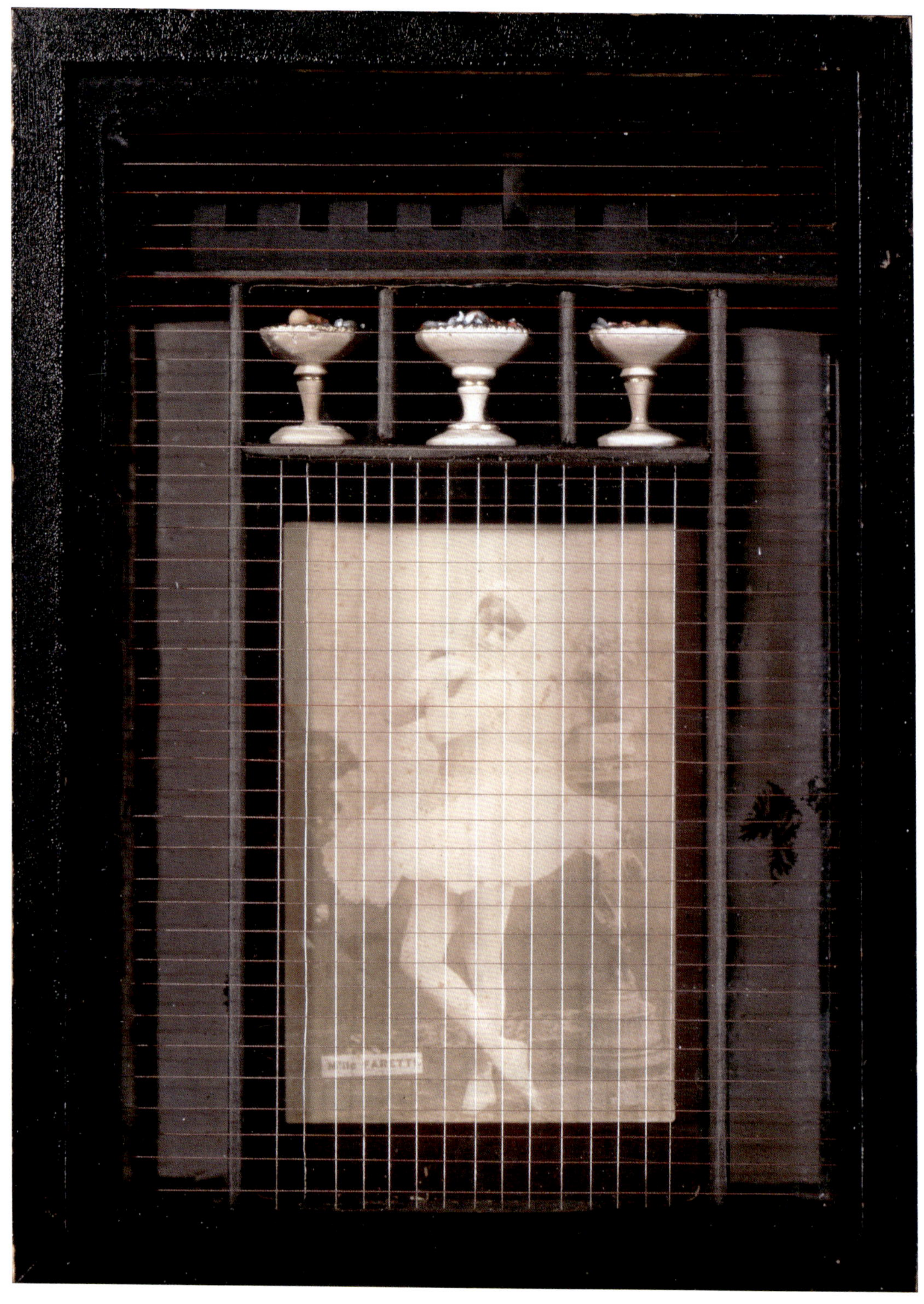

FIG. 2.18 Joseph Cornell, *Untitled (Mlle Faretti)*, 1933. Box construction, 11 × 8 × 2 inches. Private collection.

a play of two and three dimensions. While *Untitled (Mlle Faretti)*'s rectilinear frame and internal formal relationships cast it as a clear predecessor to *Soap Bubble Set*, the boxes differed in one crucial respect: at roughly one-third the depth of *Soap Bubble Set*, *Untitled (Mlle Faretti)* inhabits a frame more than a box. *Soap Bubble Set*'s additional physical depth gave Cornell a third axis with which to work, to dramatic effect.

Soap Bubble Set expands *Untitled (Mlle Faretti)*'s grid into three dimensions. Rather than veiling the object, the grid penetrates and organizes the box's space. As Rosalind Krauss has argued, the grid's prominence in Modern art can be traced to its ability to mediate distinct epistemological structures. Although the grid's orderly geometry and ostensible resistance to narrative would seem the apogee of Modernist self-sufficiency, the form also implies infinite expanse and Albertian perspectival depth. As Krauss writes, "I do not think it is an exaggeration to say that behind every twentieth-century grid painting there lies—like a trauma that must be repressed—a symbolist window parading in the guise of a treatise on optics."[73] Krauss articulates the grid's capacity to "allow *both* views to be held in some kind of para-logical suspension," holding in suspension, in other words, Modernism's pretension to rationalism and its lingering investment in illusionism.[74]

Krauss's brilliant essay helps to explain the effect of *Soap Bubble Set*'s internal grid, and indeed, she illustrates (although does not discuss) a box by Cornell in her essay.[75] If *Soap Bubble Set* is guided by natural philosophy's sympathetic relationships, in the box these similitudes arise from the grid structure. The grid allows us to see the moon, egg, head, and cylinders as related yet distinct. Their juxtaposition transforms the physical millimeters that separate moon and egg into the miles between heaven and earth, a depth that emerges from the physical relation of its objects rather than illusionistic perspective. Materialism and idealism are shown as subtending, rather than opposing one another.

WONDERS

In his aforementioned letter to Barr, Cornell asked that his work be displayed in a separate vitrine, to be called *Elements of Natural Philosophy*.[76] Certainly, this request was partially motivated by the physical vulnerability of his delicate objects. Yet the glass case also formed a barrier between his boxes and the surrounding works. These transparent planes allowed Cornell to parcel out a space at once connected to the exhibition and distinct from the uncanny juxtapositions that governed works such as Joan Miró's *Object*. The vitrine's pellucid walls thus served a similar function to *Soap Bubble Set*'s wooden frame.

Cabinet of Natural History (Object) served as the pendant to *Soap Bubble Set* in the *Elements of Natural Philosophy* vitrine. Natural history, the study of living organisms in their environment, was a key element of Sir Francis Bacon's attempts to reform natural philosophy. As Lorraine Daston and Katherine Park have observed, Bacon hoped natural history's emphasis on physical phenomena would offer an empirical corrective to the universalist generalizations that had come to characterize natural philosophy. Bacon's natural history encompassed both "nature in course" and "nature erring."[77] "Nature erring," or "wonders" were physical specimens so extraordinary that they seemed crafted by a divine hand.[78] These unique and dazzling specimens embody the natural world's creativity and were seen as akin to works of art. For example, in Johann Georg Hinz's painting of an imaginary *wunderkammer* (1664, fig. 2.19), whorled nautilus shells and spiky coral sit alongside boxes of beads, strings of pearls, and intricately carved ivory objects, suggesting that both natural and manmade objects are ultimately the creations of a divine being.

Cabinet of Natural History is structured by a similar logic. Seventeen cork-stoppered bottles and thirty-five glass vials sit in an antique wooden apothecary cabinet. Each holds bits of ephemera such as beads, sequins, strands of cotton, or grains of sand, labeled with notable figures in art, science, and literature, as well as natural phenomena.[79] A vial of bright yellow powder boasts the title "sol solaire," while a picture of a dog on blue paper is labeled "Mirage" (figs. 2.20, 2.21). "Arc-en-ciel grèle" (rainbow after a thunderstorm) holds a tuft of white cotton and a few multicolored balls, evoking the texture of clouds and the colors of a rainbow (fig. 2.22). Rather than the magnificent spiky shells or precious gems on display in Hinz's *wunderkammer*, this bottle captures the wonder of daily occurrence.[80] A rainbow after a thunderstorm is no rare event, but available to anyone who would think to look up. As with all his work, the modest size of Cornell's vitrine belies its ambition. The installation instantiates connections among a range of materials, from the rocks of the moon to the dirt of the earth. Together they form a cosmos, not a world re-enchanted, but a world in which the forces of disenchantment have never fully triumphed.

Consider the colored powders that fill a number of the work's vials, which look like the pulverized mineral pigments used by early modern painters. Cornell equated the cabinet's contents with the substance of art in a bottle filled with opaque black ink and labeled "shadow of a photograph." Arrayed in neat rows, black, gold, cerulean, and canary powder look like the materials of artistic practice, and ready to be combined with oil. Painting's special alchemy is its ability to conjure a world from the primordial ooze of its raw materials, obliterating the difference among discrete objects. As poet Mark Doty observes in his marvelous consideration of Dutch still life painting, "When both are made of paint, is a cabbage any less precious than a golden cup?"[81] Painting is an act of metamorphosis, transforming elemental material into a world of infinite variety. Within Cornell's enchanted vitrine, cotton becomes cloud, yellow pigment sunlight, and vermillion

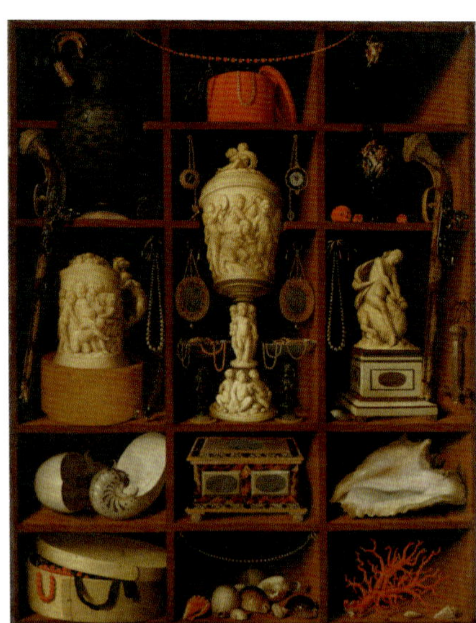

FIG. 2.19 Johann Georg Hinz, *A Collector's Cabinet*, 1664. Oil on canvas, 50 1/4 × 40 1/8 inches. Royal Collection Trust, London.

dust spiky coral. And hiding in plain sight, perhaps the most miraculous transformation of all: the everyday alchemy that allows the goopy liquid interior of *Soap Bubble Set*'s egg to become the living, feathered flesh of the scaly claw gripping the bowl of the clay pipe.

MASS ENCHANTMENTS

While Cornell sought to create a space that temporarily suspended modernity's epistemological divisions, Barr had no such option. Soon after its debut, *Fantastic Art, Dada, Surrealism* was summarily dismissed by both cultural conservatives and defenders of the avant-garde for its willingness to elevate the work of "madmen" to art. In a characteristically vituperative remark, critic Thomas Craven declared it "one of the foulest doses of art ever compounded by the international apothecaries. . . . The freaks of art belong in the tent show along with the two-headed calf and the tattooed idiot."[82] It was precisely this reaction that Société Anonyme doyenne Katherine Dreier feared when she wrote to Barr, "It seemed as if you had deliberately hung the pictures to give the emphases to the abnormal!"[83] Barr did little to dispel Dreier's fears, replying, "Genius consists in the ability to retain in security the imaginative faculties of childhood."[84] Unconvinced by his response, Dreier withdrew her loans from the exhibition's subsequent venues. Although diametrically opposed in their understanding of art, Drier and Craven understood that Barr's attitude posed an inherent threat to the sanctity of fine art. If folk art and Surrealism proposed that Modernism could encompass work created without artistic intention or training, by what criteria could art distinguish itself from the rest of the world?

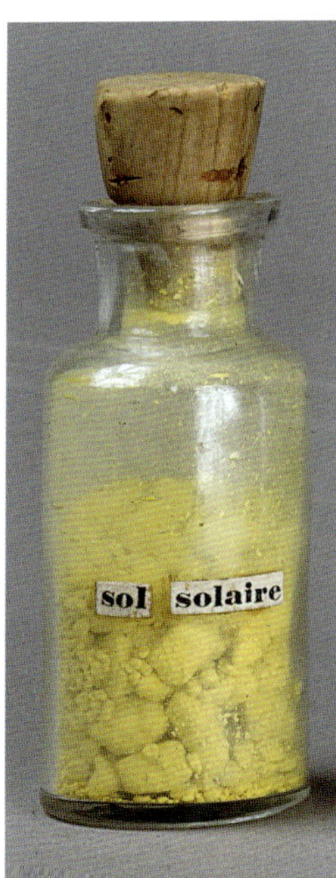

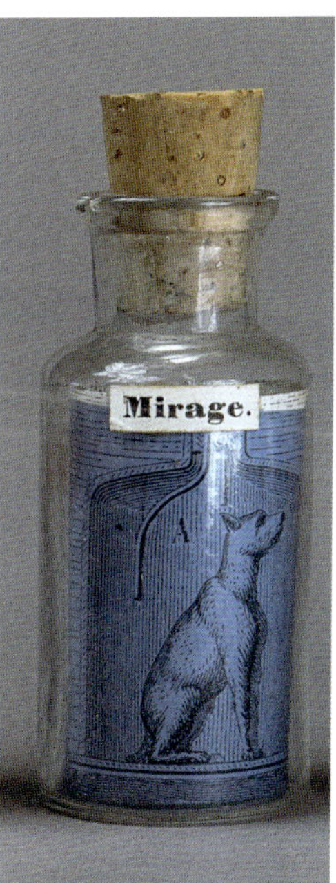

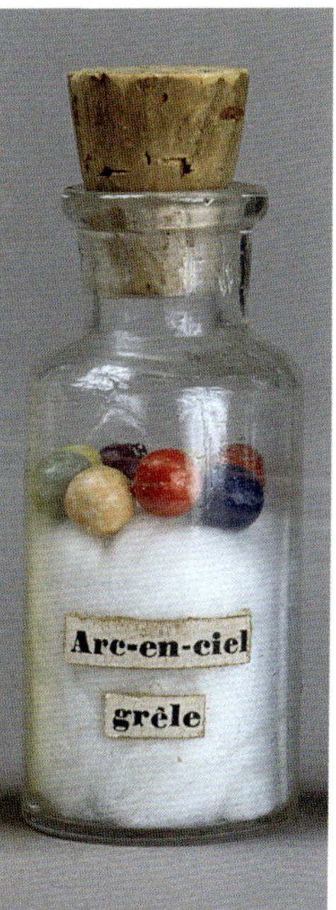

FIG. 2.20 Detail of Joseph Cornell, *Cabinet of Natural History (Object)*, 1934, showing "sol solaire" bottle.

FIG. 2.21 Detail of Joseph Cornell, *Cabinet of Natural History (Object)*, 1934, showing "Mirage" bottle.

FIG. 2.22 Detail of Joseph Cornell, *Cabinet of Natural History (Object)*, 1934, showing "Arc-en-ciel grèle" bottle.

Art critic Emily Genauer's notorious article, "The Fur-Lined Museum," published in *Harper's Magazine* in 1944, posed similar questions. Genauer's furious screed against the Museum of Modern Art pinpoints *Fantastic Art, Dada, Surrealism* as the origin of its decline, as evidenced by her titular evocation of Meret Oppenheim's disturbingly tactile teacup, which had by this time become synonymous with the exhibition. For Genauer, *Fantastic Art, Dada, Surrealism* paved the way for "stunts like the display of a tinsel-bedecked shoeshine chair, of the doodlings of inmates of insane asylums, and of the pathetic efforts of frustrated amateurs," referencing the museum's 1943 controversial exhibition of the Italian immigrant Joe Milone's decorated shoeshine stand, whose display became a flashpoint of contention (fig. 2.23).[85] Trained by the Federal Arts Project to see artistic practice as labor worthy of remuneration, critics such as Genauer argued that MoMA's focus on amateur artists siphoned away support from "real" artists: "While serious professional artists fight for the recognition that means life to them, the Modern fiddles away its resources, building a precious cult around amateurism."[86]

Genauer's invocation of "chi-chi pandering" encapsulates the period suspicion that MoMA's advocacy of Surrealism was motivated by money.[87] As numerous scholars have discussed, Surrealism's animation of objects became powerful visual tools for advertising and fashion.[88] Desperate to support his family, Cornell took full advantage of this period vogue for Surrealism, contributing graphic design work to fashion publications that sought to capitalize on the trend. His design for *Harper's Bazaar*'s February 1937 issue (fig. 2.24) sandwiches the article's text between a pair of 1932 montages featuring women and sewing machines. The sinuous curves and variable fonts of the article's title recall Cornell's aforementioned 1932 design for Julien Levy's *Surréalisme* catalogue, which Levy also used

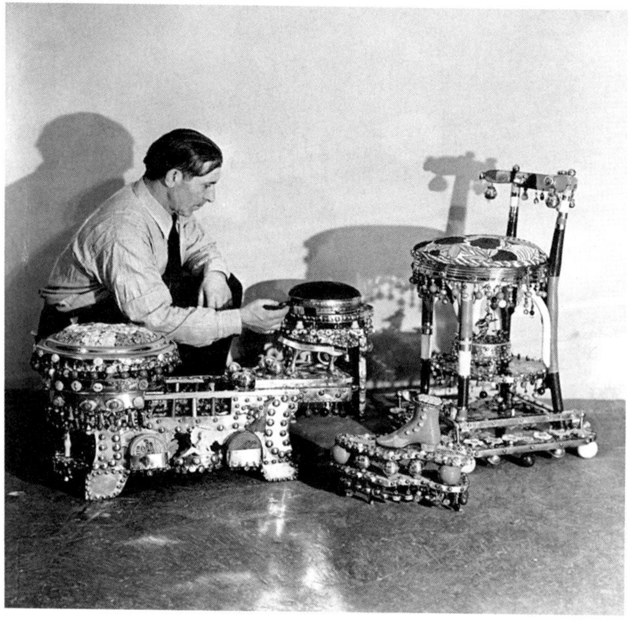

FIG. 2.23 Joe Milone and his shoeshine equipment in the exhibition *Joe Milone's Shoe Shine Stand*, December 22, 1942–January 10, 1943. Photographic Archive, Museum of Modern Art, New York.

for the cover of his 1936 book on the movement (fig. 2.25). The near-identical formats of Cornell's 1932 exhibition catalogue, the 1936 cover, and his 1937 layout allegorize the ease with which Surrealist forms migrated between the worlds of fine and commercial art. Cornell took full advantage of the midcentury affinity between fine art and fashion, working as a graphic designer throughout the 1940s and '50s for *Vogue, Harper's Bazaar*, and *Good Housekeeping*.

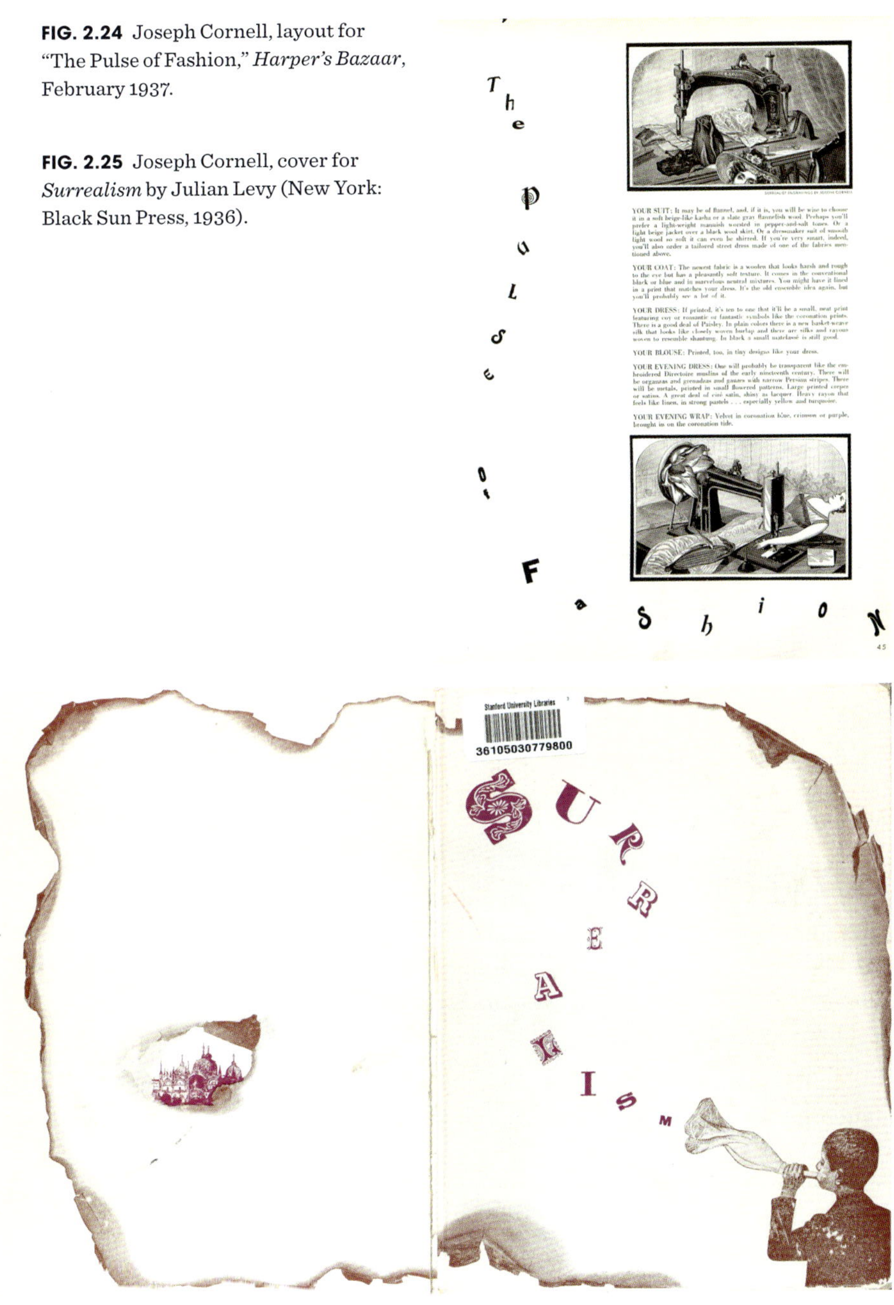

The Pulse of Fashion

SURREALIST ENGRAVINGS BY JOSEPH CORNELL

YOUR SUIT: It may be of flannel, and, if it is, you will be wise to choose it in a soft beige-like kasha or a slate gray flannelish wool. Perhaps you'll prefer a light-weight mannish worsted in pepper-and-salt tones. Or a light beige jacket over a black wool skirt. Or a dressmaker suit of smooth light wool so soft it can even be shirred. If you're very smart, indeed, you'll also order a tailored street dress made of one of the fabrics mentioned above.

YOUR COAT: The newest fabric is a woolen that looks harsh and rough to the eye but has a pleasantly soft texture. It comes in the conventional black or blue and in marvelous neutral mixtures. You might have it lined in a print that matches your dress. It's the old ensemble idea again, but you'll probably see a lot of it.

YOUR DRESS: If printed, it's ten to one that it'll be a small, neat print featuring coy or romantic or fantastic symbols like the coronation prints. There is a good deal of Paisley. In plain colors there is a new basket-weave silk that looks like closely woven burlap and there are silks and rayons woven to resemble shantung. In black a small matelassé is still good.

YOUR BLOUSE: Printed, too, in tiny designs like your dress.

YOUR EVENING DRESS: One will probably be transparent like the embroidered Directoire muslins of the early nineteenth century. There will be organzas and grenadzas and gauzes with narrow Persian stripes. There will be metals, printed in small flowered patterns. Large printed crepes or satins. A great deal of ciré satin, shiny as lacquer. Heavy rayon that feels like linen, in strong pastels . . . especially yellow and turquoise.

YOUR EVENING WRAP: Velvet in coronation blue, crimson or purple, brought in on the coronation tide.

45

FIG. 2.24 Joseph Cornell, layout for "The Pulse of Fashion," *Harper's Bazaar*, February 1937.

FIG. 2.25 Joseph Cornell, cover for *Surrealism* by Julian Levy (New York: Black Sun Press, 1936).

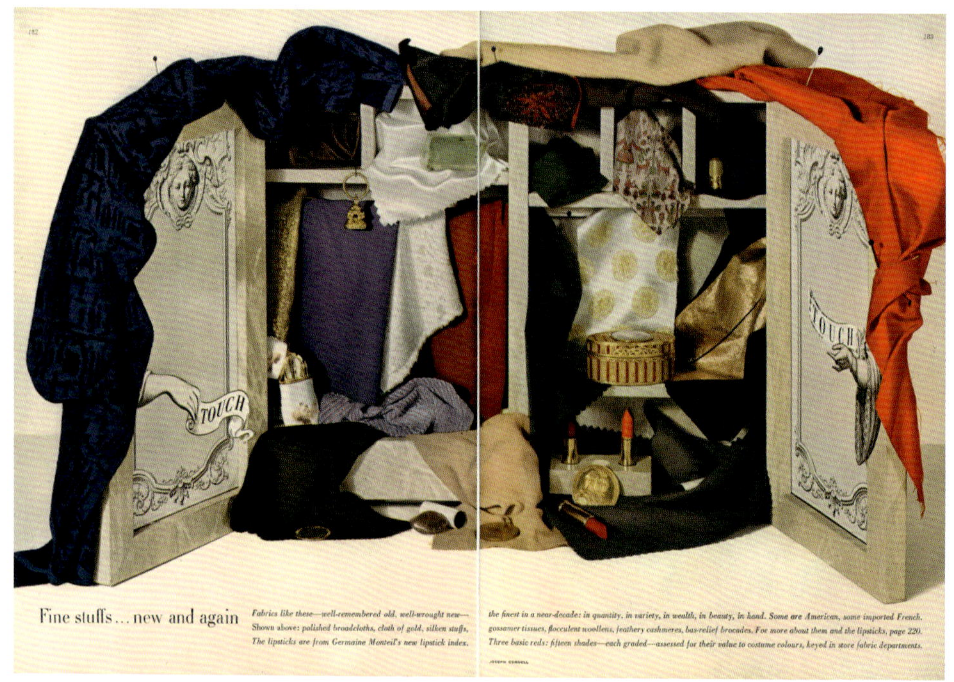
Fine stuffs ... new and again

Fabrics like these—well-remembered old, well-wrought new— Shown above: polished broadcloths, cloth of gold, silken stuffs, The lipsticks are from Germaine Monteil's new lipstick index.

the finest in a near-decade: in quantity, in variety, in wealth, in beauty, in hand. Some are American, some imported French, gossamer tissues, flocculent woollens, feathery cashmeres, bas-relief brocades. For more about them and the lipsticks, page 220. Three basic reds: fifteen shades—each graded—assessed for their value to costume colours, keyed in store fabric departments.

FIG. 2.26 Joseph Cornell, layout for "Vogue Designs for Dressmaking: Dressmaker Dresses," *Vogue* 110, no. 6 (September 15, 1947): 182–83.

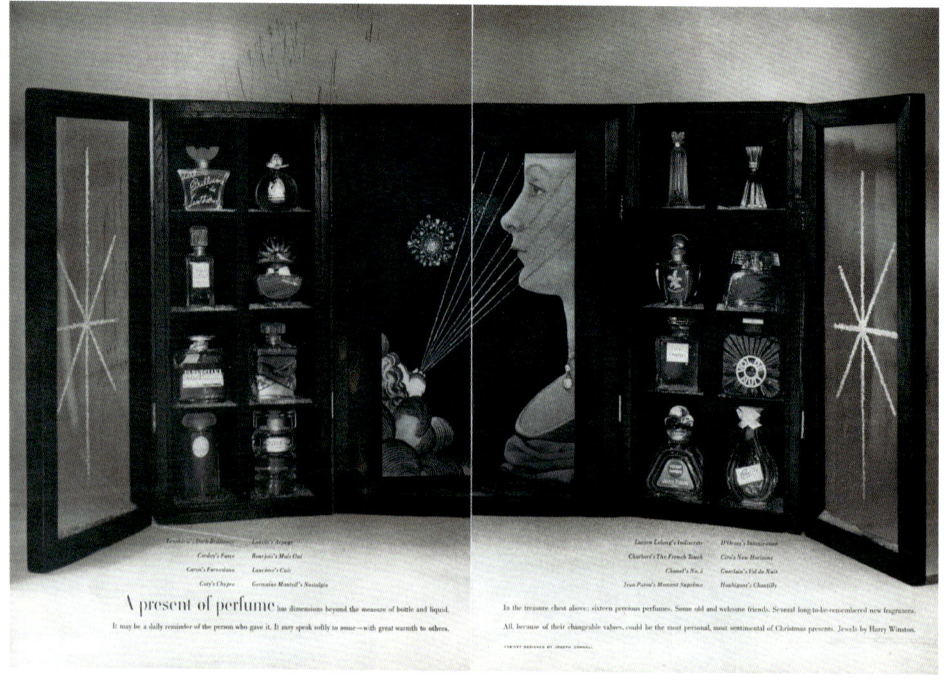

A present of perfume has dimensions beyond the measure of bottle and liquid. It may be a daily reminder of the person who gave it. It may speak softly to some—with great warmth to others.

In the treasure chest above: sixteen precious perfumes. Some old and welcome friends. Several long-to-be-remembered new fragrances. All, because of their changeable values, could be the most personal, most sentimental of Christmas presents. Jewels by Harry Winston.

FIG. 2.27 Joseph Cornell, layout for "A Present of Perfume," *Vogue* 110, no. 11 (December 1947): 154–55.

His layout for the 1947 issue of *Vogue* shows a trompe l'oeil cabinet overflowing with luxurious swaths of fabric and tubes of crimson lipstick (fig. 2.26). Victorian graphics invite the viewer to "Touch," transposing the implicit address of Oppenheim's teacup into the realm of fashion. Cornell used the same compositional principle in December of the same year, repurposing the cabinet format as a display case for perfume bottles (fig. 2.27). A Renaissance woman in profile inhales delicate wisps of scent blown into her nose by a putto, rendering visible perfume's olfactory promise and transposing Cornell's talent for visualizing the invisible to the commercial realm.

Cornell's example suggests that Surrealism's oft-commented upon appropriation by commercial interests cannot be blamed on Salvador Dalí's gleeful self-promotion alone.[89] Rather, the artist whose name André Breton famously sneered could be anagrammed into the phrase "Avida Dollars" simply intensified a latent implication in the movement's adaptation to its American context, beginning with Levy's exhibition and extending through *Fantastic Art, Dada, Surrealism*. From the expanded perspective provided by Cornell's work, the well-documented backlash against Dalí might be understood as more than a protest against the artist's crass commercialism, but as a shift in priorities away from the vernacular and toward a more hermetic mode of expression.[90]

Clement Greenberg's canonical essay "Avant-Garde and Kitsch" emerged from this heated context.[91] From the perspective of the history delineated in this chapter, Greenberg's essay is most masterful in its ability to unite the various threads of 1930s art and politics into a powerful statement of compelling moral clarity—a quality sorely lacking during this decade of drastic political reversals. For Greenberg, kitsch is an "ersatz art" whose power lies in its ability to manipulate. Like totalitarianism, it is not beholden to a single ideology (he notes that both Stalin and the Nazis make use of it) and can be used to indoctrinate the masses or trick them into consumption. "Kitsch" allowed Greenberg to place propaganda and commercial culture on the same plane and attribute their dangers to formal representation, now recast as deceptive illusion.[92] For Greenberg, representation combined disingenuous folk simplicity with enchanting qualities of Surrealism. Kitsch literalized Marx's commodity fetish, allowing commercial objects to take on powers of control or manipulation.[93]

Yet it was the issue of audience rather than representation that first prompted Greenberg to write "Avant-Garde and Kitsch." The essay had its genesis in Greenberg's letter to critic Dwight Macdonald regarding a series of articles on Soviet cinema he published in *Partisan Review*. In the last article, Macdonald wonders what to make of the disparity in attendance between the Modernist Moscow Museum of Western Art and the Tretyakov Gallery, whose recent exhibition of the Russian Academic painter Ilya Repin drew large audiences. "The scales," Greenberg explained to Macdonald, "are weighted in favor of kitsch to start with, by the very ignorance of the peasant." The figure of the ignorant peasant appears again at the end of the letter, in a far more ignominious form, as Greenberg drives home the political stakes of his argument: "And I'm pretty pessimistic now, for it seems to me that in England, France, and this country, as well as in the dictatorships, avant-garde culture is beginning to retreat all along the line under the pressure of the demoralization of the left and in the face of the increasing boldness with which hill billies everywhere are coming into the light to attack all culture. Where Hitler came with Wotan, in this country they come with the Bible."[94]

Greenberg's disdain for what was previously called the "common man" (never a woman) signals the growing discontent with populism as a viable artistic and political goal, as well as with the deployment of enchantment (here figured as both religion and Wagner's *gesamtkunstwerk*) to achieve it. And although Greenberg was a leftist, his concerns were echoed from the other side of the ideological spectrum by the former Communist Eugene Lyons, who wrote in an alarmist 1941 tome, "During the Red Decade we are confronted, in the main, with a horde of part-time pseudo-rebels who have neither courage *nor* convictions, but only a muddy emotionalism and a mental fog which made them an easy prey for the arbiters of a political racket."[95] Easy prey, in other words, for the enchantments of totalitarianism.

Greenberg's assessment was not without merit; one only has to look at the demagogues of the 1930s—and the use to which Johann Gottfried von Herder's discussion of *volksgeist*, or national spirit, was put by National Socialism—to discern the dangers of a populist political ideology.[96] If Cahill had described folk art as "the sense and sentiment of a community" just six years earlier, Greenberg's letter represents the eclipse of Cahill's formulation at the decade's end.

Like Genauer and Lyons, Greenberg called for a reassertion of rationality over the period's flirtation with fantasy. The end result, Greenberg's well-known and endlessly discussed return to Kantian aesthetics in the guise of "medium specificity" and "autonomy," finds a historical parallel in the Enlightenment transformation of natural philosophy into distinct scientific disciplines. As Daston and Park explain, during the late seventeenth-century, wonder became "a disreputable passion in workday science, redolent of the popular, the amateurish, and the childish."[97] This discrediting of wonder as a flight from reason, and thus the sign of a "weak" mind, emerged as a means of social control and distinction, instantiating the Enlightened individual at the top of the social hierarchy. Exercising will, control, and above all reason, this (Western, male) figure stood in contrast to "women, the very young, the very old, primitive peoples, and the uneducated masses, a motley group collectively designated as 'the vulgar.'"[98]

One can also situate Greenberg's denigration of kitsch within centuries-old religious debates over idolatry. Taylor describes the Reformation's prohibition on vernacular forms of piety as a means of consolidating authority in the elite strata of life, that is to say, the aristocracy, the church, and the state.[99] The condemnation of carnivals and relics—lay customs that located religious power in a range of practices and objects—and the related efforts to suppress or limit their popularity are "uniformizing: they aim to apply a single model or schema to everything and everybody; they attempt to eliminate anomalies, exceptions, marginal populations, and all kinds of non-conformists."[100] Taylor elucidates the social implications of Greenberg's aesthetic theory. To condemn the potential enchantment of objects—to recast the vernacular as kitsch—has historically been deployed as a means of social control and distinction.

Macdonald responded enthusiastically to Greenberg, encouraging him to turn the letter into what would eventually become "Avant-Garde and Kitsch." In its final form, the essay would focus on the definition and historical character of kitsch, spending comparatively little time on the issue of audience. Yet as evidenced by Greenberg's letter, kitsch requires the figure of the ignorant peasant, whose lack of sophistication and knowledge would render her wholly susceptible to its empty promises. To claim for kitsch the power Greenberg ascribed to it required a corresponding lack of agency on the part of public, now recast as mindless consumers. If kitsch takes advantage of the ignorant, then it stands to reason that Greenberg and his enlightened brethren can see through its empty promises; thus Greenberg's "hill billies" also implicitly inoculate him against kitsch's enchantments, hardening the divide between the intellectual elite and the denigrated masses.

Despite his condemnation of kitsch, Greenberg thought highly of Cornell. In 1942, he wrote of Cornell's work, "The stuffed birds, thimbles, bells, cardboard cut-outs, and so forth . . . mean or represent nothing but themselves."[101] What led Greenberg to approve of Cornell's work and to see his boxes not as kitsch, but as "nothing but themselves"? As this chapter has argued, Cornell's boxes emerged from the artist's need to set himself apart from Surrealism's connotations of irrationality and madness. In doing so, they present an interconnected, enchanted world that would seem antithetical to the Kantian formalism Greenberg championed. Yet numerous commentators have noted that despite Greenberg's pretentions to rationality, his concept of autonomy maintained a Romantic-theological investment in aesthetic experience as a realm apart from daily life.[102] Cornell's boxes did not seek to maintain this separation but rather to render it mute. His boxes are both of and not of this world. The true fantasy of Cornell's *Elements of Natural Philosophy* vitrine is not its presumably whimsical subject matter but its attempt to suspend this division. As Greenberg himself put it, contra to his own literalist take on the artist, "Cornell could construct landscapes ten feet square inside his boxes."[103] Cornell's boxes are worlds in which the impossible contradictions defining modern life in 1936 America are suspended, if only for a moment.

CODA: CONSTELLATIONS

On December 8, 1948, Cornell sat beneath Grand Central Station's magnificent vaulted ceiling (fig. 2.28). Although he had been commuting through this terminal for over two decades, on this day he felt a striking "elation" upon "looking up at the celestial blue heavens and golden constellations on the ceiling." The sight sparked "thought of the Milky Way star dust and scattering of bread crumbs in the morning for the birds at home."[104] At this moment the distance between grand and humble, between the stars above and the dusting of bread crumbs on the ground, vanished.

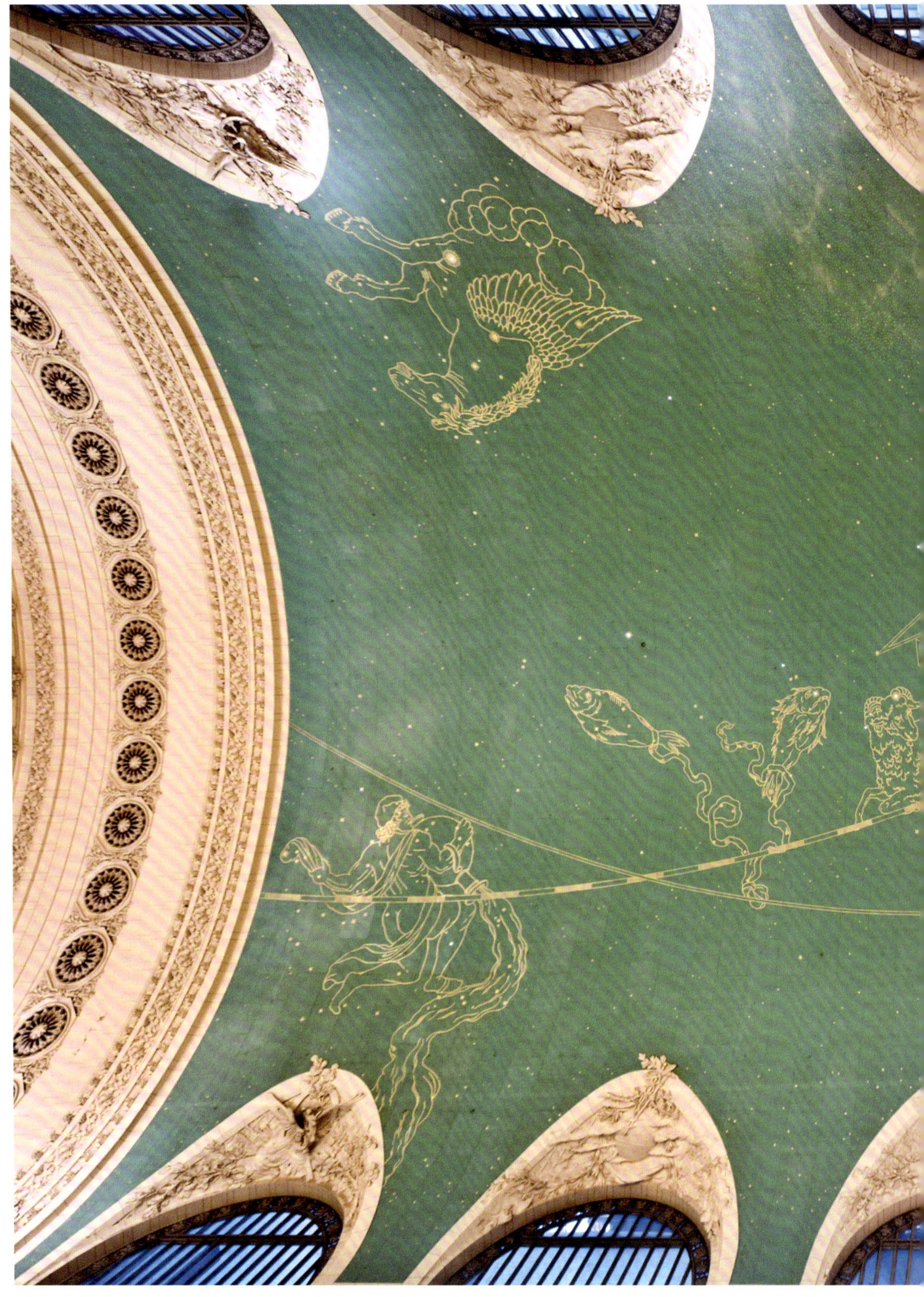

FIG. 2.28 Ceiling of Grand Central Station, 2011. Digital print. Almay Archives.

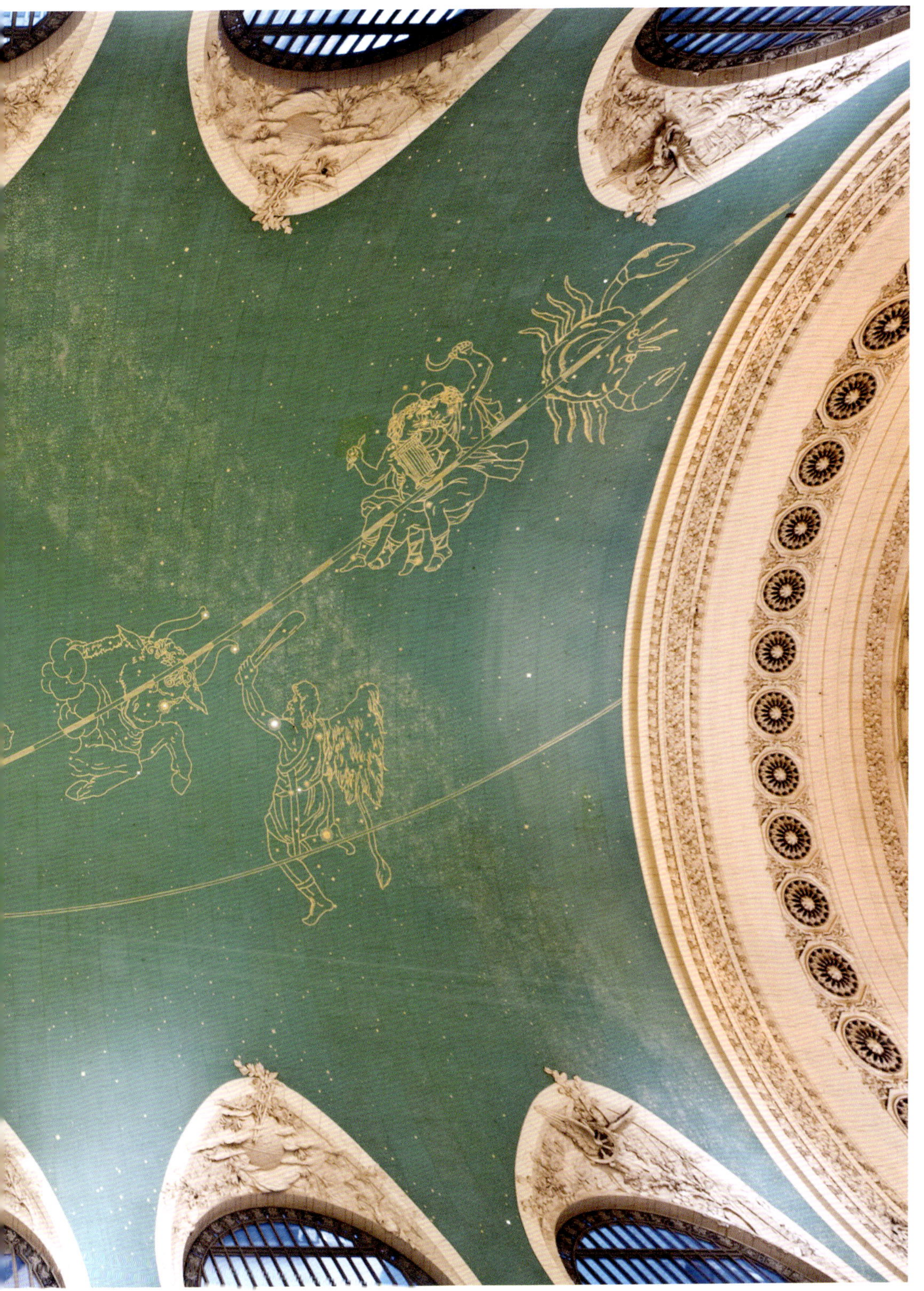

Grand Central Station opened to the public in 1913, eight years before Cornell moved to New York City. The starry sky crowning its Main Concourse was designed by French painter Paul César Helleu, who studied with Jean-Léon Gérôme at the École des Beaux-Arts and was close friends with John Singer Sargent and James McNeill Whistler. Helleu's aqua ceiling is adorned with personified constellations that curve across its blue expanse like a golden necklace. These shining ornaments glow in the light streaming in from the Main Concourse's arched skylights and enormous windows, as well as the four thousand incandescent lightbulbs arrayed around the hall. The morning the ceiling was completed, Helleu remarked to an acquaintance, "I have been nearly bowled over with worries, but now all is well—for the stars shine in the firmament."[105]

To ensure the accurate placement of the constellations, Helleu consulted Dr. Harold Jacoby, a professor of astronomy at Columbia University. Jacoby in turn based his plan on Johann Bayer's famed 1603 *Uranometria,* an atlas of the constellations of the Northern Hemisphere. The *Uranometria* also served as the basis for several Cornell montages, created just three years before *Soap Bubble Set*. That Cornell associated these works with *Uranometria* is evidenced by their subtitle: "Atlas de Bayer."[106] *Le Grand Chien (Atlas de Bayer, 1603)* (ca. 1934, fig. 2.29), shows Canis Major as a magnificent dog with a juicy steak under its paw and a waffle at its rear. Sirius, the brightest star in the constellation, forms his nose. The base of this work is Alexander Mair's marvelous copperplate engraving for *Uranometria* (fig. 2.30). Mair's delicate shading and intricate rendering of the beast's fur contrast with its graphic outline and the lines of longitude and latitude that divide the composition. As art historian Matthew Hunter has written of Mair's fantastical engravings, such figures "visualiz[e] these distinctions between the verified and the imagined . . . plott[ing] cutting-edge, certified coordinates into ancient, useful fictions."[107] Cornell's addition of the steak and waffle augments Hunter's salient observation. Placed at a slight angle, the waffle imparts the illusion of depth onto the otherwise flat image, much as Mair's stipples provide Canis Major flesh and fur. The steak perched under is paw is not merely playful, but weaves through lines of longitude and latitude, entwining the constellation within these "cutting-edge, certified coordinates."[108]

Literary theorist Joshua Landy has described the constellation as the guiding structure of re-enchantment. Constellations map meaning onto disparate points in the sky. Like poetry, whose self-contained structure creates order from the infinite expanse of human language, constellations "replace religious faith." For in both poetry and constellations, "[w]hat before was chaos now comes forth as order; where contingency reigned, now there is a certain internal necessity, as each point of light has to be just where it is for the posited shape to hold."[109] Landy's insight demonstrates how poetic structure might create connection and meaning among words on a page, or dots of light in the sky. Weaving the *Uranometria*'s lines of measurement and its fantastical images into a single space, Cornell's montage dissolves the boundaries between faith, fantasy, and scientific fact.

FIG. 2.29 Joseph Cornell, *Le Grand Chien (Atlas de Bayer, 1603)*, ca. 1934. Collage with watercolor on paper, 5 5/8 × 5 1/16 inches (image). Collection Mickey Cartin.

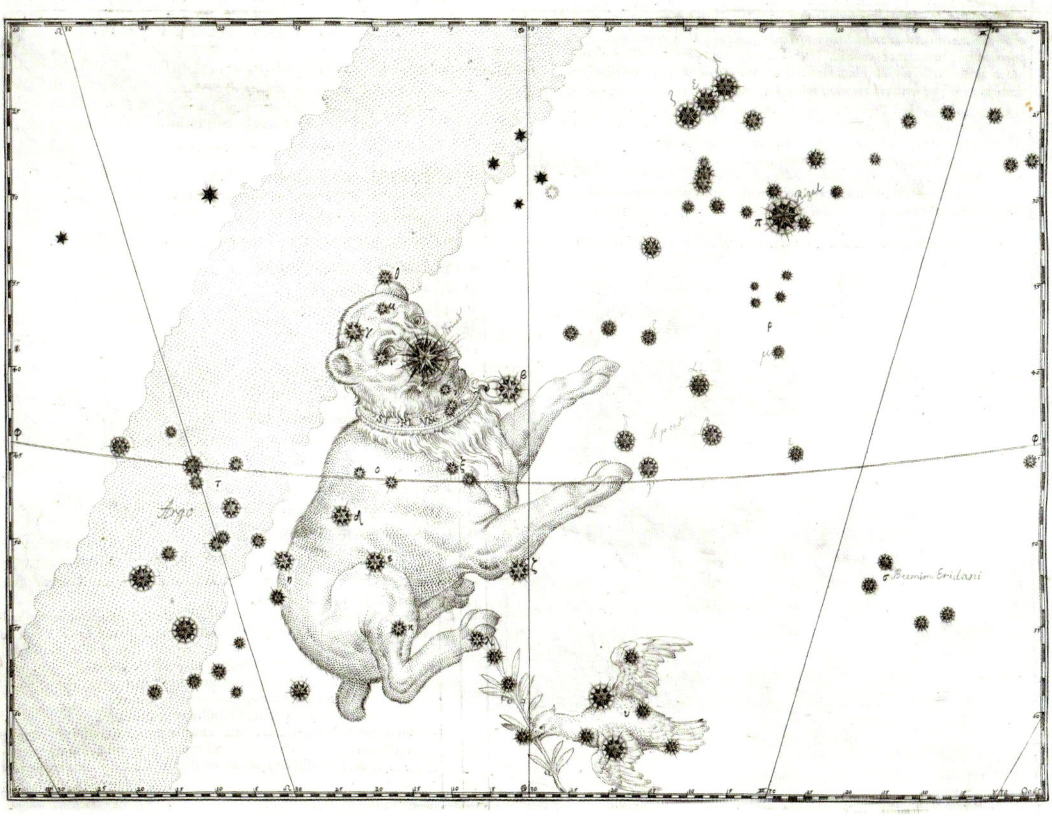

FIG. 2.30 Alexander Mair, *Canis Major Star Map*, 1603. Verso page 00 in Johann Bayer, *Uranometria*. Linda Hall Library, Kansas City, MO.

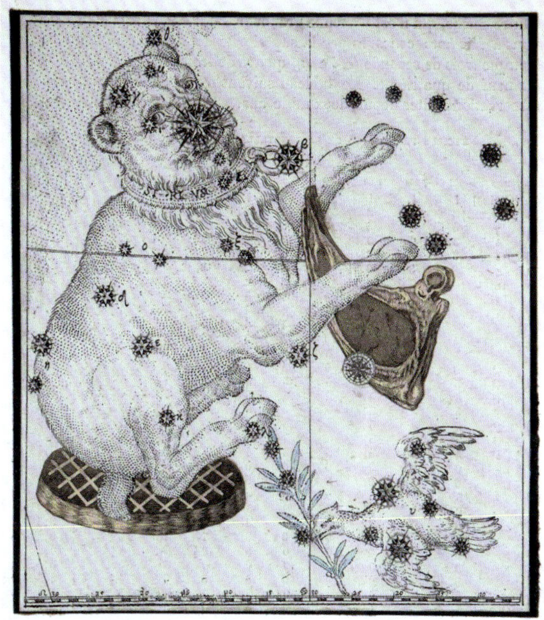

Consider another early work, dedicated to the Danish astronomer Tycho Brahe, whose observations formed the basis of Bayer's *Uranometria* (fig. 2.31). In this unaltered engraving, which Cornell likely intended to include in a larger series, the astronomer gazes upward at a bright star. The picture commemorates the moment on November 11, 1572, when Tycho discovered a new star in the constellation Cassiopeia.[110] Head tilted back and arms reaching outward, Tycho is pictured at the moment he catches sight of this view. The crowd mimics his ecstatic pose, gazing at the sky with outstretched arms. To the right of the astronomer, a woman falls to her knees and another clasps her hands, as if in prayer. Their enraptured reactions suggest that this is a moment of both scientific and religious reverence, and indeed, the structure behind Tycho is Herrevad Abbey, the site of his first discovery and his first laboratory. The golden lines of a constellation, the montaged elements in Cornell's box constructions, are moments of enchantment—moments in which the connections that bind a cosmos flicker briefly into view.

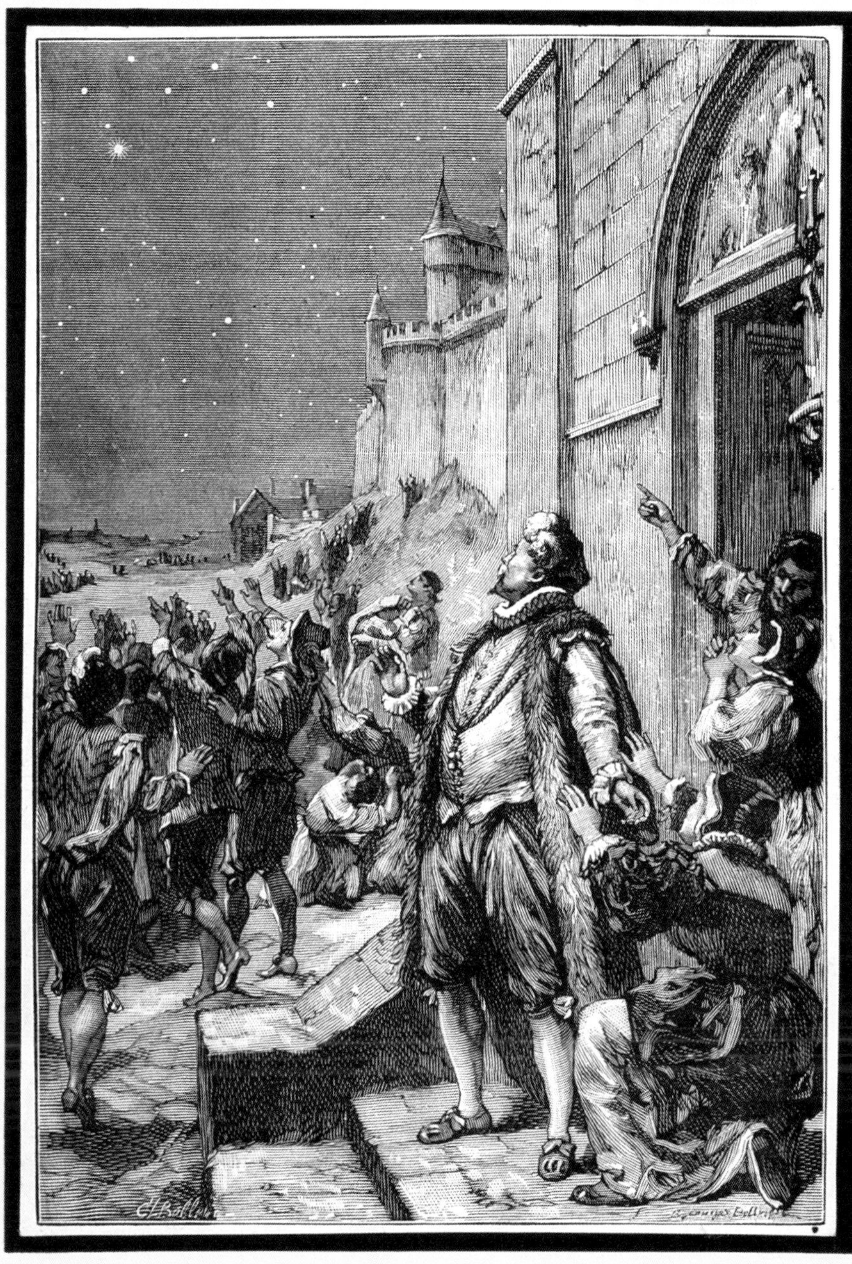

FIG. 2.31 Joseph Cornell, *Tycho's Star*, date unknown. Paperboard, 10 × 7 3/8 inches. Smithsonian American Art Museum, Washington, DC, gift of the Robert and Joseph Cornell Foundation.

CHAPTER THREE

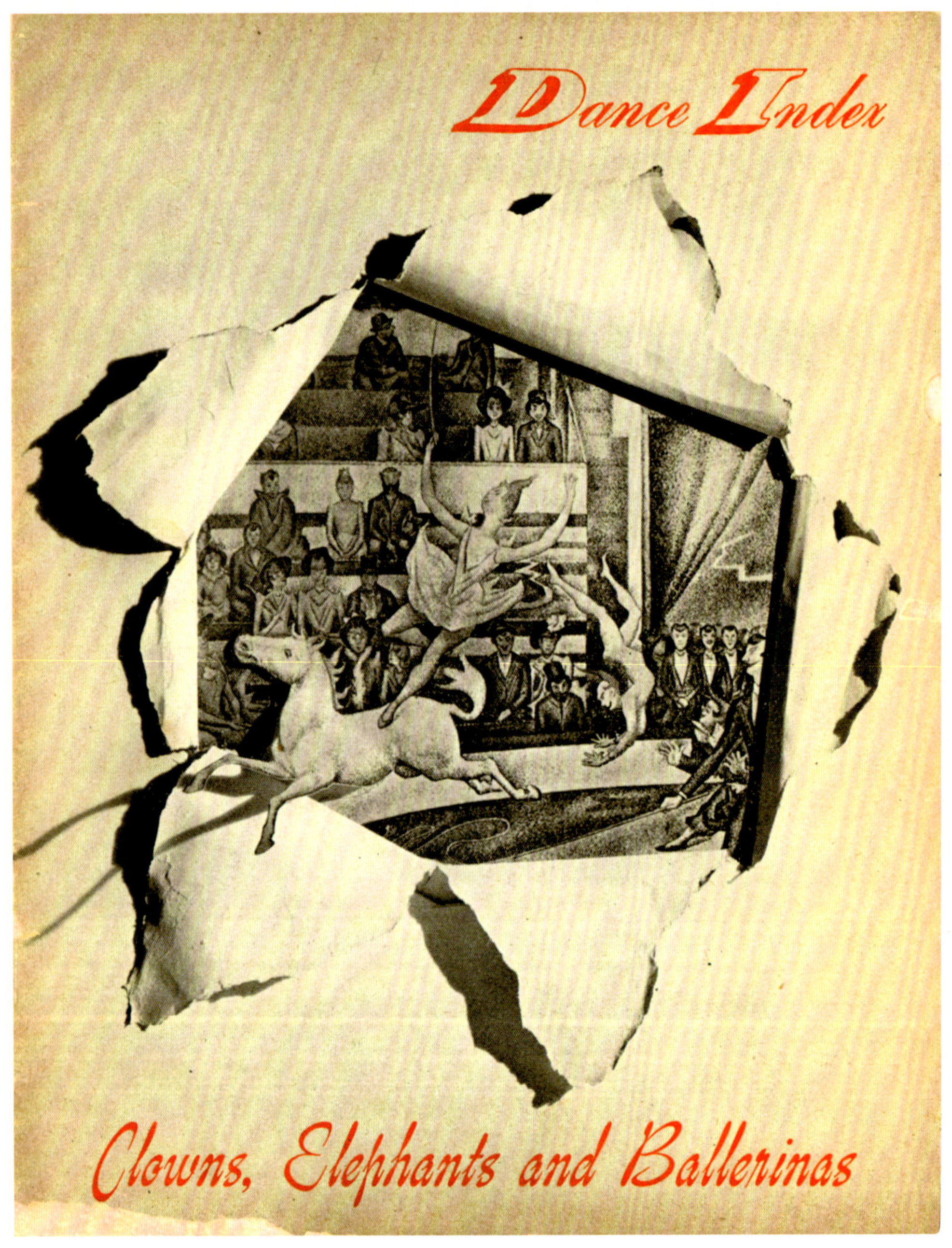

FIG. 3.1 Joseph Cornell, ed., cover design for "Clowns, Elephants and Ballerinas," special issue, *Dance Index* 5, no. 6 (June 1946). Joseph Cornell Study Center, Smithsonian American Art Museum, Washington, DC.

Folk into Myth

. . . It is as when,
In the dead of freezing winter the mistletoe,
Engrafted from another tree, brings forth
New leaves, strange leaves, yellow flowers and yellow berries;
This is what, upon the shadowy ilex,
The golden leafage on the bough looked like,
And this is how the gold-foil leaves were gently
Rustling in the breeze.

Virgil, *The Aeneid*

In 1946, Cornell guest-edited a special issue of the periodical *Dance Index* titled "Clowns, Elephants and Ballerinas."[1] Cornell's cover design shows the white steed of Georges Seurat's 1890–91 painting *Le cirque* galloping *through* a paper screen (figs. 3.1, 3.2).[2] To achieve this cheeky trompe l'oeil effect, Cornell placed a reproduction of Seurat's painting behind a sheet of torn paper and commissioned photographer Larry Colwell to take a picture of the arrangement.[3] The result is a homage to both Seurat and to Charlie Chaplin, whose 1928 silent film *The Circus* opens with an acrobat bursting through a black title card. In the next shot, a blur of white streaks across the screen as a horse canters past the rip in the barrier (figs. 3.3–3.5). Cornell's cover compresses and freezes Chaplin's opening scene into a single image, just as Seurat's painting suspends its acrobats in the air. Exaggerated shadows cast by the screen's torn edges and the horse's forelegs augment the cover's trompe l'oeil effect. Suspended mid-stride, the horse leaps the barrier between the illusionistic space of Seurat's painting and the outside world.

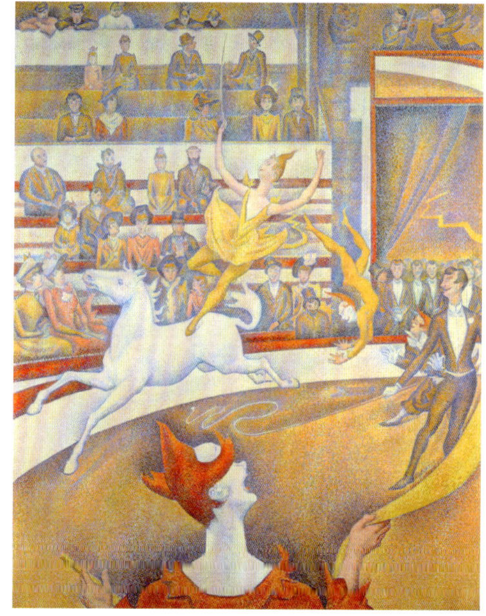

FIG. 3.2 Georges Seurat, *Le cirque (The Circus)*, 1890–91. Oil on canvas, 73 1/8 × 59 7/8 inches. Musée d'Orsay, Paris.

With this cover, Cornell proposes that the rarified realm of ballet and the popular entertainment of the cinema and circus are not as far apart as they may appear. As the artist writes in the issue, "Clowns do not always dance, but essentially they were trained as dancers; their hands, feet, their whole bodies express themselves as precisely, as dancers."[4] To convey this idea, Cornell populated "Clowns, Elephants and Ballerinas" with an eclectic array of sources suggesting the balletic grace of clowns and beasts, including photographs of Chaplin and Harpo Marx performing pantomime, a drawing by Picasso showing acrobats balanced on the back of a horse, and a description of the Théâtre des Funambules from the Jules Janin

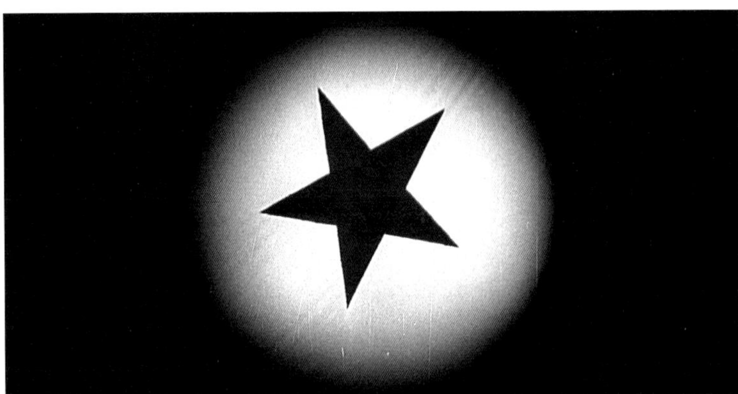

FIG. 3.3 Film still from *The Circus* (Charlie Chaplin, 1928), showing the intact barrier.

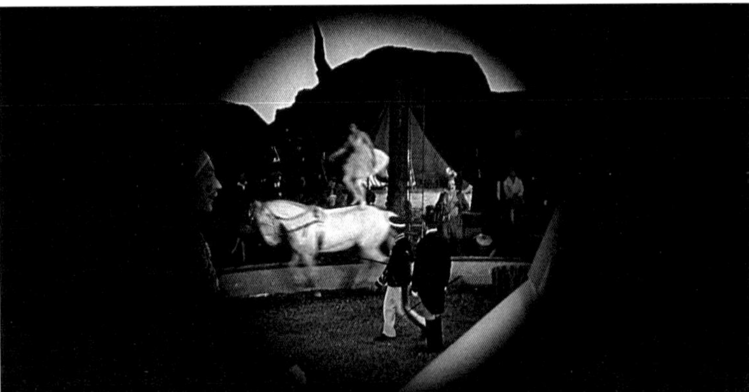

FIG. 3.4 Film still from *The Circus*, showing a white horse cantering past a rip in the barrier.

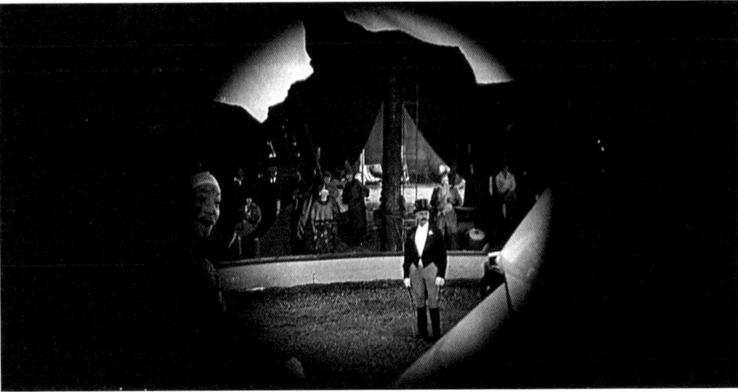

FIG. 3.5 Film still from *The Circus*, showing the clown and ringleader looking through the ripped screen after the horse has left the scene.

feuilleton. (figs. 3.6, 3.7).[5] Enchantment, Cornell suggests in this issue, is not the province of a single sphere of culture but cuts across the fine and the vernacular, the elevated and the lowly.

This chapter examines Cornell's remarkable body of graphic design projects for the periodicals *Dance Index* (1942–48) and *View* (1940–47). Although Cornell worked as a graphic designer throughout the 1940s, his projects for these specialist publications were created in partnership with like-minded collaborators, including Lincoln Kirstein, Charles Henri Ford, and Parker Tyler, and thus constitute a category of production apart from his commercial

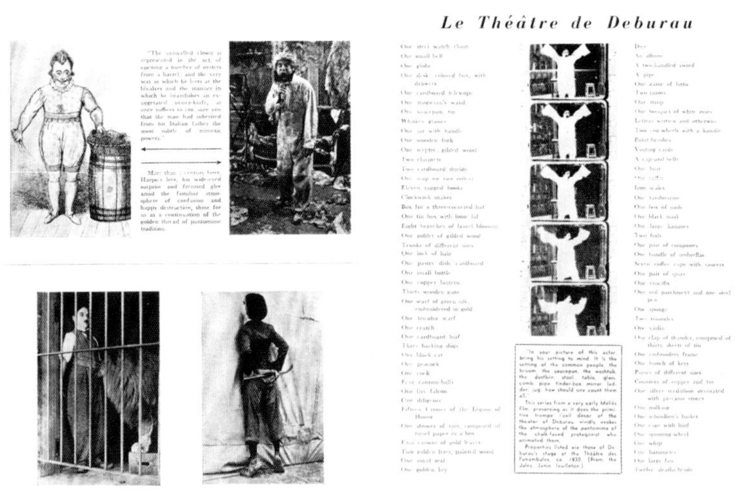

"The unrivalled clown is represented in the act of opening a number of oysters from a barrel; and the very way in which he leers at the bivalves and the manner in which he brandishes an exaggerated oyster-knife, at once suffices to convince you that the man had inherited from his Italian father the most subtle of mimetic powers."

More than a century later, Harpo's leer, his wide-eyed surprise and frenzied glee amid the familiar atmosphere of confusion and happy destruction, shine for us as a continuation of the golden thread of pantomime tradition.

Le Théâtre de Deburau

"In your picture of this actor, bring his setting to mind. It is the setting of the common people, the broom, the saucepan, the washtub, the dustbin; stool, table, glass, comb, pipe, tinder-box, mirror, ladder, jug: how should one count them all."

This series from a very early Méliès film, preserving as it does the primitive trompe l'oeil décor of the theater of Deburau, vividly evokes the atmosphere of the pantomime of the chalk-faced protagonist who animated them.

Properties listed are those of Deburau's stage at the Théâtre des Funambules, ca. 1830. (From the Jules Janin feuilleton.)

FIG. 3.6 "Clowns, Elephants and Ballerinas," 140–41.

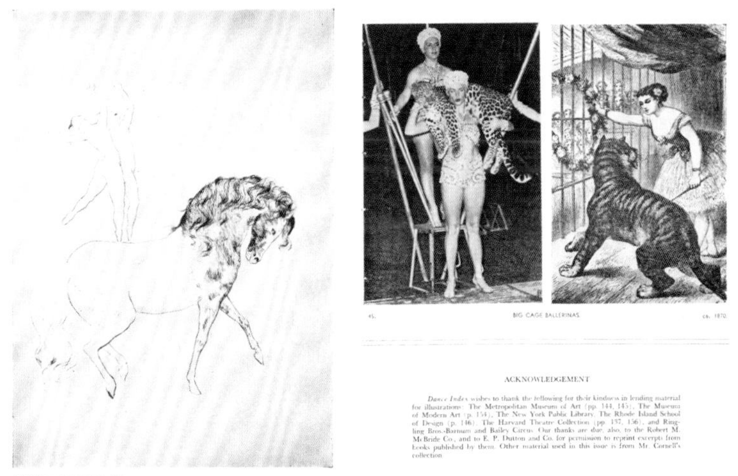

45. BIG CAGE BALLERINAS ca. 1870.

ACKNOWLEDGEMENT

Dance Index wishes to thank the following for their kindness in lending material for illustrations: The Metropolitan Museum of Art (pp. 144, 145), The Museum of Modern Art (p. 154), The New York Public Library, The Rhode Island School of Design (p. 146), The Harvard Theatre Collection (pp. 137, 156), and Ringling Bros.-Barnum and Bailey Circus. Our thanks are due, also, to the Robert M. McBride Co., and to E. P. Dutton and Co. for permission to reprint excerpts from books published by them. Other material used in this issue is from Mr. Cornell's collection.

FIG. 3.7 "Clowns, Elephants and Ballerinas," 154–55.

work. If the late 1930s and the 1940s saw a growing hostility to the enchantments of vernacular culture, now recast as kitsch, Cornell and the coterie of largely queer artists, dancers, and poets associated with these publications instead found resources in the folkloric, the cinematic, the mythic, and the fantastic.[6]

Cornell's enchantment at once augmented the core mission of these publications and allowed him to extend his artistic ambitions to audiences outside of museum walls. The public, collaborative nature of these projects also sheds light on a moment of close alignment between the artist and a circle of sympathetic interlocutors. To elucidate the relevance of Cornell's enchanted worldview to midcentury dance and poetry, this chapter necessarily expands beyond the artist to consider the overlapping groups of creators that orbited around these publications.[7] While neither *Dance Index* nor *View* shared Cornell's precise definition of enchantment, they understood and respected it and, crucially, found concordances with their own artistic projects. To track the varied approaches to enchantment in these circles, this chapter explores two entwined artistic impulses during the 1930s and '40s: the folkloric and the mythic.

FOLK BALLET

In the 1930s, ballet emerged as a vital sphere of cultural production in the United States. Like the first decade of the Museum of Modern Art's exhibition program, ballet's early history in America was shaped by questions of audience and accessibility. Its growing prominence during this decade can be attributed to a number of factors, including the Ballets Russes's decision to tour the United States after the death of legendary impresario Sergei Diaghilev in 1929, and the work of English-language scholars and critics such as Edwin Denby and Cyril Beaumont, whose writing and translation of Romantic-era critics including Théophile Gautier raised ballet's intellectual profile in America.[8] Most significant, in 1933 former Ballets Russes choreographer George Balanchine and the self-styled impresario Lincoln Kirstein partnered to found the School of American Ballet and subsequently collaborated on several dance companies, including what would eventually become the New York City Ballet.[9]

Like Julien Levy, Kirstein studied art history at Harvard, where he cofounded the Modernist little magazine *Hound & Horn* with Varian Fry and started the Harvard Society of Contemporary Art with John Walker II and Edward M. M. Warburg. If Levy and Chick Austin (who would become an important Kirstein collaborator) hoped to position Surrealism within mainstream American life, Kirstein held similar ambitions for the ballet. Kirstein's efforts to promote ballet in the United States included authoring popular publications and cofounding the touring dance company Ballet Caravan. Established in 1936, Ballet Caravan staged fifty-two performances at forty-one venues across the United States including Las Cruces, New Mexico, Austin, Texas, and Fayetteville, Arkansas, where the audience included the local football team.[10] Although some contemporaneous critics decried the "nationalist prejudice" or "blind chauvinism" of the endeavor, Kirstein did more than try to codify an essential American art.[11] Rather, he believed that infusing ballet with American vernacular sources would help to modernize it, reflecting in his 1937 pamphlet *Blast at the Ballet*, ". . . I still think that given half a chance, ballet even by Americans, would please an opera-house audience if the atmosphere were a trace less snobbish."[12]

To achieve this, Kirstein cannily positioned ballet as a form of "American folklore," a phrase that invoked both the period understanding of folk as "the art of the common man," as well as Russian and Romantic ballet's engagement with folktales.[13] During the 1930s, Kirstein produced and funded numerous ballets whose titles read as a repository of American folkways: *Folk Dance, Pocahontas, Yankee Clipper, Filling Station* (based on the adventures of Mac, a gas station attendant), *Billy Budd,* and *Billy the Kid* (figs. 3.8, 3.9). This last performance featured choreography by Eugene Loring, whom Kirstein described as "the son of a Wisconsin saloon keeper"; costumes by artist Jared French; and a score by Aaron Copland that famously incorporated cowboy tunes and other folk melodies.[14]

Numerous dance scholars, including Lynn Garafola and James Steichen, have discussed Kirstein's efforts in relation to the leftist politics of the 1930s.[15] A remarkable portrait of Balanchine by George Platt Lynes explicitly makes this point (fig. 3.10). Balanchine faces the

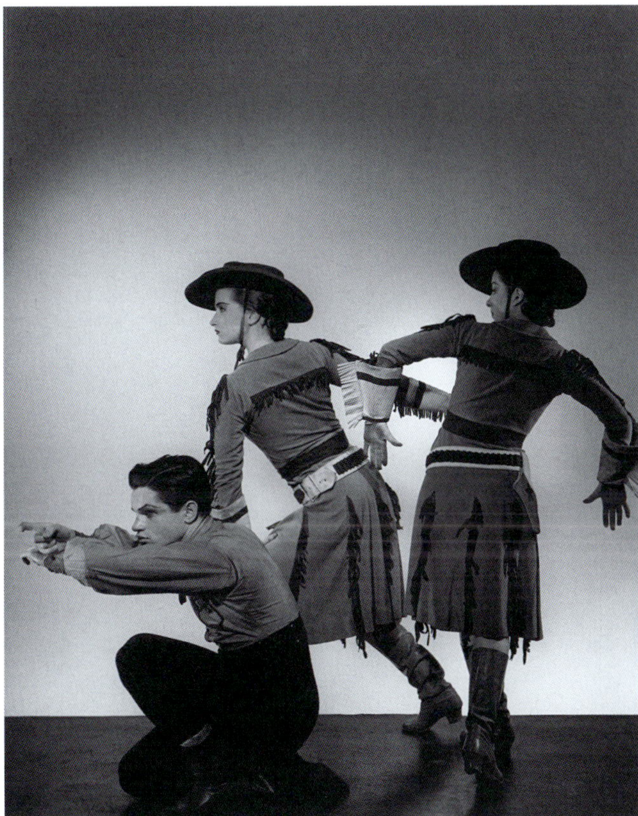

FIG. 3.8 George Platt Lynes, *Michael Kidd, Beatrice Tompkins, and Ruth Asquith in "Billy the Kid,"* 1938, printed ca. 1953. Gelatin silver print, 13 1/4 × 10 7/16 inches. Metropolitan Museum of Art, New York.

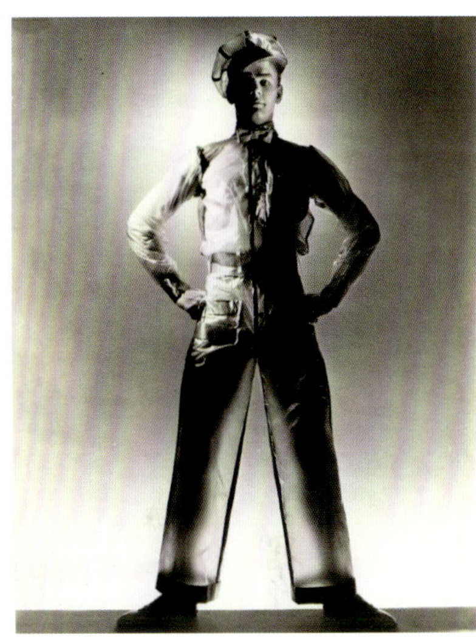

FIG. 3.9 George Platt Lynes, *Filling Station,* 1938. Christensen-Caccianza Papers, Museum of Performance + Design, San Francisco, CA.

camera grasping a priapic drill in one hand and a hammer in the other, no doubt intentionally referencing the Communist hammer and sickle, and hence the choreographer's Russian heritage. His carefully styled costume—tweed jacket draped over his shoulders, tie pushed back—casts him as a sophisticate playing the role of a laborer, while the wooden arm that replaces his right hand recalls the simplified forms of folk sculpture. Rather than contradicting these markers of labor, Balanchine's debonair bearing and pristine coif thematize the connection between choreographer and folk sculptor, choreography and labor, underscoring the compatibility of vernacular tradition and formal sophistication described by Ralph Ellison in the previous chapter.

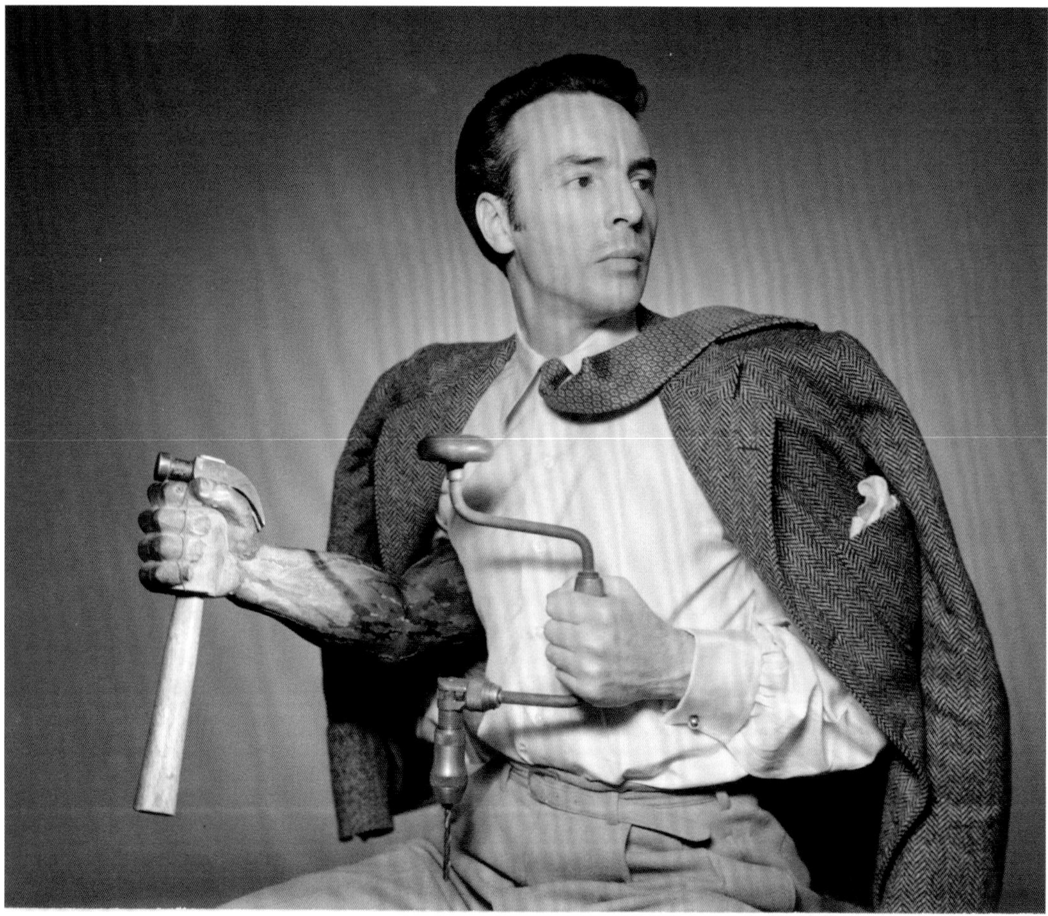

FIG. 3.10 George Platt Lynes, *George Balanchine*, 1941. Gelatin silver print, 7 1/2 × 9 inches. National Portrait Gallery, Smithsonian Institution, Washington, DC.

DANCE INDEX

Dance Index was the cornerstone of Kirstein's attempt to cement dance's place in American culture. First published in 1942, *Dance Index* commissioned articles from scholars and critics such as John Martin and George Chaffe on a broad range of dance-related topics. The publication's low price point ($2 for its debut issue) and broad scope accorded with Kirstein's attempts to make ballet "a trace less snobbish."[16] In Cornell, Kirstein found a designer uniquely positioned to visualize *Dance Index*'s ethos of scholarly accessibility.[17] At the time of the publication's founding, the artist was already an amateur scholar of ballet, attending performances regularly during the 1920s and '30s, and amassing a vast trove of ballet-related ephemera.[18] Over the course of the publication's six-year run, Cornell designed fourteen covers and guest-edited four special issues, drawing on both his personal collection and MoMA's newly established Dance Archives.[19] The artist's centrality to the publication's visual identity was such that he was the only graphic designer the magazine credited by name.[20] Cornell approached each issue as he would a work of art, explaining to Kirstein that a single special issue "consumed nine months to a year," requiring "endless research, chasing around, and exaltations of going to press." In the same letter, he noted that these exertions were so great that they caused his own artistic output to dramatically decrease.[21]

In ballet, the artist found a subject particularly well-suited to his attempts to convey enchantment. From its origins in the Neoplatonic philosophy of the sixteenth-century, ballet attempted to mediate the divide between the metaphysical and material. Ballet's rigid repertoire of steps and poses were developed to convey a higher spiritual order through the bodies of its dancers.[22] Romantic ballet, the nineteenth-century form Cornell cherished most, pushed this dematerialization of the body to its logical conclusion by establishing the conventions we associate with classical ballet today: delicate dancing *en pointe*, tulle tutus, gravity-defying leaps—innovations intended to create the illusion of the human body unencumbered by earthly forces such as gravity or mass. Through *Dance Index*, Cornell found a circle that shared his intense devotion to ballet and, moreover, respected his approach to it. In Kirstein's foreword to "Clowns, Elephants and Ballerinas," he astutely observed, "For [Cornell], the inconsequential past is neither frivolous nor dead." Kirstein continued:

> The horse spectacles of Astley's Ampitheater, the Funambuels of Deburau's boulevards are as alive, human and significant to him as Coney Island or the Ballets Russe, maybe even more so. Many amateurs love the vaguely preposterous past, but few pursue it with the affectionate surgery and relentless skill of Joseph Cornell. He is brother to the scientist who recreated a whole pre-historic age from the glimpse of a dinosaur's tooth. From a fragment of a program, a set of lithographs, a couple of footnotes and a reference in a letter, Mr. Cornell evokes splendid evenings completely lost. Only now we find they are merely sleeping, waiting for him to surprise them back to life.[23]

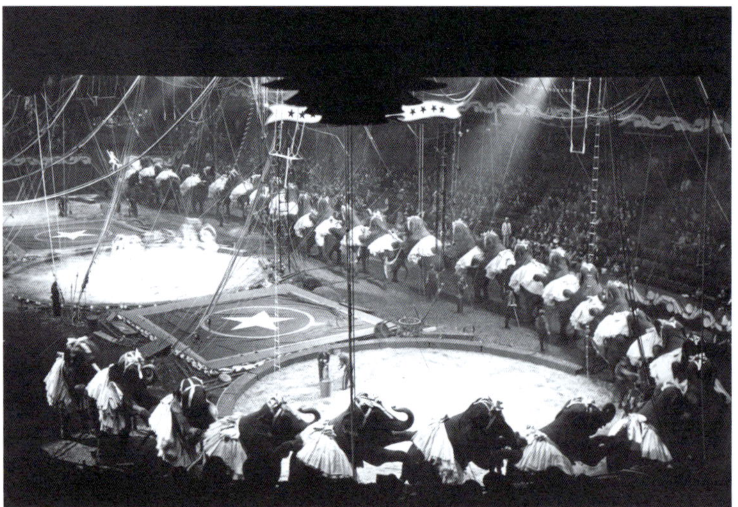

FIG. 3.11 Scene from George Balanchine's *Elephant Ballet*, 1942. Black-and-white photo print, 7 5/8 × 9 1/2 inches. Tibbals Circus Collection, John and Mable Ringling Museum of Art, Sarasota, FL.

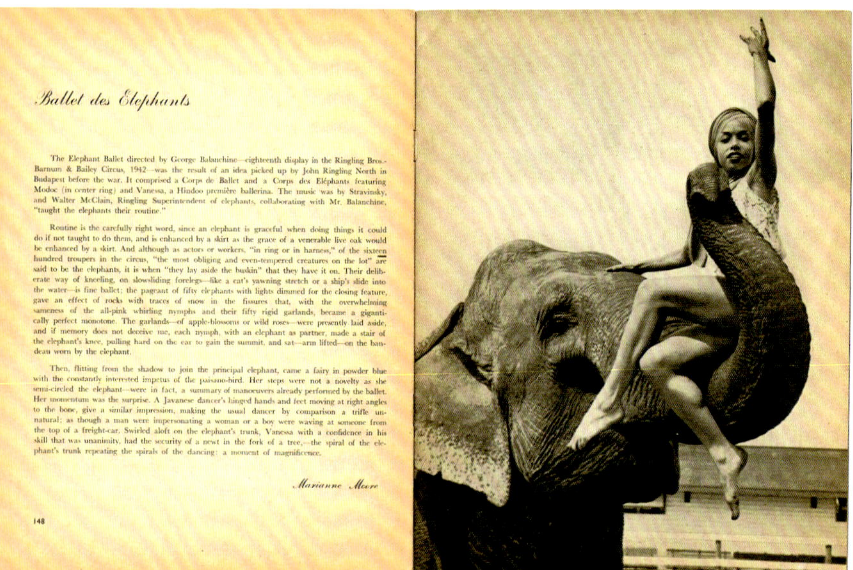

Ballet des Elephants

The Elephant Ballet directed by George Balanchine—eighteenth display in the Ringling Bros.-Barnum & Bailey Circus, 1942—was the result of an idea picked up by John Ringling North in Budapest before the war. It comprised a Corps de Ballet and a Corps des Eléphants featuring Modoc (in center ring) and Vanessa, a Hindoo première ballerina. The music was by Stravinsky, and Walter McClain, Ringling Superintendent of elephants, collaborating with Mr. Balanchine, "taught the elephants their routine."

Routine is the carefully right word, since an elephant is graceful when doing things it could do if not taught to do them, and is enhanced by a skirt as the grace of a venerable live oak would be enhanced by a skirt. And although as actors or workers, "in ring or in harness," of the sixteen hundred troupers in the circus, "the most obliging and even-tempered creatures on the lot" are said to be the elephants, it is when "they lay aside the buskin" that they have it on. Their deliberate way of kneeling, on slowsliding forelegs—like a cat's yawning stretch or a ship's slide into the water—is fine ballet; the pageant of fifty elephants with lights dimmed for the closing feature, gave an effect of rocks with traces of snow in the fissures that, with the overwhelming sameness of the all-pink whirling nymphs and their fifty rigid garlands, became a gigantically perfect monotone. The garlands—of apple-blossoms or wild roses—were presently laid aside, and if memory does not deceive me, each nymph, with an elephant as partner, made a stair of the elephant's knee, pulling hard on the ear to gain the summit, and sat—arm lifted—on the bandeau worn by the elephant.

Then, flitting from the shadow to join the principal elephant, came a fairy in powder blue with the constantly interested impetus of the paisano-bird. Her steps were not a novelty as she semi-circled the elephant—were in fact, a summary of manoeuvers already performed by the ballet. Her momentum was the surprise. A Javanese dancer's hinged hands and feet moving at right angles to the bone, give a similar impression, making the usual dancer by comparison a trifle unnatural; as though a man were impersonating a woman or a boy were waving at someone from the top of a freight-car. Swirled aloft on the elephant's trunk, Vanessa with a confidence in his skill that was unanimity, had the security of a newt in the fork of a tree,—the spiral of the elephant's trunk repeating the spirals of the dancing: a moment of magnificence.

Marianne Moore

148

FIG. 3.12 Marianne Moore, "Ballet des Elephants," in "Clowns, Elephants and Ballerinas," 148–49.

Theatre-Royal, Liverpool.

The Public is respectfully informed, that the Theatre WILL OPEN FOR THE SEASON, This present MONDAY, June 14, and that an engagement has been made with

Messrs. Mathews & Yates,

Of the Theatre Royal, Adelphi, for **TWELVE NIGHTS'** performance of the

STUPENDOUS ELEPHANT,

THE TALENTED AND COLOSSAL

MADEMOISELLE D'JECK,

WHO WILL APPEAR IN A

GORGEOUS and SPLENDID NEW DRAMA,

Which has been honoured during the whole of the season in London, with the most distinguished patronage. An engagement has also been made with the Three extraordinary

SIAMESE DANCERS,

Whose performance at the Adelphi Theatre, during the whole of last season, was nightly honoured with the loudest plaudits.

This present MONDAY, June 14, 1830,

Will be performed an entirely new gorgeous **INDIAN DRAMATIC SPECTACLE,** with new and splendid Pageants, Music, Scenery, Dresses, Banners, and Decorations, called the

Elephant of Siam,

And the FIRE FIEND!

The **MUSIC** composed by *G. H. RODWELL*.—**SCENERY** by *Mr. BEVERLY, Mr. MORELLI and Assistants*.—**MACHINERY** by *Messrs. WILMORE, EVANS, and Assistants*.—**DRESSES** by *Messrs. GODBEE, SMITHERS, MARSHALL, &c.*—**TROPHIES, BANNERS,** *&c. by Messrs. GODBEE, PEARCE, HARRISON, &c.*

ENGLISH resident at SIAM.

Theophilus Giraffe ...... travelling for the Zoological Society) ...... Mr. BAKER,

(From the Theatres Royal, York, Norwich, &c. his first appearance here.)

Titchi ....(Valet de Chambre to the Royal Elephant)...... ...... Mr. BENWELL

Mrs. Giraffe, alias Zillah ......(the attendant on the Princess) ...... Mrs. CLARKE

SIAMESE.

Prince Almanza ...... Mr. HAINES | Malee ......(High Priest of Siam)...... Mr. WEBSTER

Chittagong, (Grand High Chamberlain to the Elephant) Mr. SMITH | Principal Officer, Mr. LEAVES

Iudamora ...... (Princess of Siam) ...... Miss SEYMOUR,

(From the Theatre-Royal, Bristol, her first appearance here.)

Ludicia .... Miss SCRUTON | Irma .... Miss M. CLARKSON

Principal Dancing Slaves... Mrs. CLARKSON, and Miss CLARKSON

Ladies of the Serai ... . Messds. GARDINER, MORELLI, WEBSTER, &c. &c.

Priests, Dervises, Soldiers, &c. &c.

BURMESE.

Korassan the Usurper...... Mr. CLARKSON | Saib ......(his first officer) ...... Mr. HUNT

Kaherbad, the Traitor Priest ...... Mr. GARDINER

SUPERNATURALS.

Hafed......(the Fire Fiend) ...... Mr. SIMPSON

Slaves of Fire... Messrs. BENNETT, BARRETT, MORELLI, &c. &c.

Incidental to the Piece, the following Scenery, &c.

Mystic Cave of the Fiend, & Descent on his Throne of Fire.

SPLENDID KIOSK AND GARDENS OF THE PRINCESS.

Visit by the Royal Elephant,

TEMPLE OF THE HEATHEN DEITY, SOMONA KODAM.

Funeral Dance of the Jugglers of the King of Siam.

BY THE SIAMESE DANCERS OF THE ADELPHI THEATRE.

DEFEAT OF THE CONSPIRATORS BY THE ROYAL ELEPHANT.

Exterior of the Elephant's Pavilion.—Grand Banquet Chamber.

The ROYAL ELEPHANT at DINNER.

Dance by the Royal Elephant, and the Ladies of her Court.

Grand Square in Siam.—DECISION of the ROYAL ELEPHANT, who snatches the Crown from the Head of the Usurper, places it on the rightful Prince, & Triumphantly Carries him off over the heads of his Enemies.

Asiatic Pavilion.—The Bivouac of the Royal Elephant.

Extraordinary Sagacity evinced by her contrivance for the Escape of the Prince.

FIRE FIEND'S CAVE.—SPLENDID LAST SCENE.

TRIUMPH OF THE ELEPHANT—GRAND PROCESSION AND PAGEANT.

FIG. 3.13 Advertisement for Theatre-Royal, Liverpool, in "Clowns, Elephants and Ballerinas," 147.

With this passage, Kirstein demonstrates his deep respect for Cornell's enchantment, while also recognizing that the "relentless skill" Cornell applied to his practice set him apart from the fervent passion of other amateur balletomanes.[24] In citing Cornell's combination of amateur intensity and discipline, Kirstein was likely drawing a parallel between the artist and his own theory of American ballet. As he wrote in 1938, "The most important thing about American dancers is the retention of their amateur status and their nearness to the audience.... Our dancing artists have selected and amplified all that is most useful in amateur spirit to make of it a conscious and brilliant frame for their individual theatrical projection."[25] Cornell was gratified by this recognition, writing to *Dance Index* editor Donald Windham that working on the publication "makes me feel less 'escapist' in my work."[26]

Kirstein's statement also suggests Cornell's relevance to *Dance Index*'s attempts to broaden dance's audience. Cornell's enchantment allowed him to find value in a range of culture, from the Ballets Russes to Philip Astley's nineteenth-century spectacles; from *ballet blanc* to the elegant pantomimes of Jean-Gaspard Deburau. His broad yet exacting taste accorded with the publication's editorial program, which included issues on Romantic ballet as well as Shaker dance, dance films, and even the specialized topic of European dance teachers in the United States. For both Kirstein and Balanchine, vernacular forms were crucial to leavening what they described as the Ballets Russes's outmoded "European decadence." To this point, Balanchine incorporated elements of what critic Irving Howe described as "jazz, social dancing, Busby Berkeley–style razzmatazz, and vernacular movements like walking" into his choreography.[27] Balanchine also relied on ballet's public appeal to support himself in his adopted country: to make money in the early 1930s, he choreographed popular vaudeville productions and was later recruited by MGM to invent dance numbers for the studio's 1938 Technicolor extravaganza *The Goldwyn Follies*, among other productions.[28]

Most spectacularly, in 1942 Balanchine choreographed the Ringling Brothers Barnum & Bailey Circus's *Elephant Ballet*, which featured fifty tutued pachyderms adorned with garlands of roses and apple blossoms dancing alongside a corps de ballet, to music by Igor Stravinsky (fig.3.11).[29] The *Elephant Ballet* was the subject of the only original content in "Clowns, Elephants and Ballerinas," an essay by poet Marianne Moore (fig. 3.12) that Kirstein described as "a defense of the Elephant as Dancer."[30] Moore praised Balanchine's choreography for highlighting the elephant's innate grace, observing, "Their deliberate way of kneeling, on slowsliding forelegs—like a cat's yawning stretch or a ship's slide into the water—is fine ballet." The essay concludes with a description of Vanessa, a "Hindoo première ballerina" nesting in the elephant's trunk, "the spiral of the elephant's trunk repeating the spirals of the dancing: a moment of magnificence."[31] Balanchine's choice to cast Vanessa as the production's star evokes the pantomime *Elephant of Siam*, an orientalist spectacle performed in 1830 at the Theatre-Royal in Liverpool.[32] Cementing this link, Cornell reproduced the program for the June 14, 1830, performance on the page before Moore's article (fig. 3.13). This montage of motifs across time is typical of Cornell's attempts to convey enchantment's romantic temporality. His layout places *Elephant of Siam*, Balanchine's ballet, and Moore's text into physical proximity, as if to show the nineteenth-century performance "surprised back to life" in the present moment. And in another contemporary resonance, the sheer delight of seeing supposedly earthbound beasts transfigured by ballet had been intuited two years earlier by none other than Walt Disney, whose 1940 *Fantasia* featured ostriches, alligators, elephants, and hippos pirouetting to Ponchielli's *Dance of the Hours*.[33]

Moore's discussion of "the Elephant as Dancer" also offered Cornell a potent opening to connect his enchantment with the aims of *Dance Index*. As he wrote in the issue, "The elephant has become a kind of dialectical symbol for theatrical dancing; its huge grey bulk the opposite of the flashing ballerina's mercurial evanescence."[34] Cornell continues, "Later, he performed under Louis XIV, and a hundred years ago was loudly applauded for his patient balance, his solemn trunk and his rhythmical adagio foot-work."[35] Although an elephant's "huge grey bulk" might appear the polar opposite of a ballet dancer's impossible lightness, Cornell admires the animal's balance, solemnity, and rhythm, much as Moore marvels at the moment in which dancer and elephant seem to spiral into one another. There is enchantment to be found even in the heaviest of creatures, provided we are willing to see beyond mere appearances.

MARBLE AND PAPER

From its debut issue, published in January 1942, *Dance Index* was indelibly marked by the Second World War. In their opening comment, coeditors Baird Hastings, Paul Magriel, and Kirstein explained that they had planned the issue before Pearl Harbor and printed it soon thereafter. They were preparing to halt production on the issue when they were contacted by "a number of men in service who expressed a lively interest [in the magazine], and this, if nothing else, convinced us to persevere." Reflecting on the publication's future, they write, "A year from now it may be undesirable or impossible even to think of manufacturing anything as apparently useless as a sober review concerned with one rather specific branch of theater, and that lyric and unrealistic."[36]

The only note of solace is their mention of dance's persistence in Western culture. "Like other arts," they write, "dancing has survived every disaster the Western world has known. It seems to exist instinctively in response to some blind necessity, which in an almost preposterous sense, ignores all the frightening facts of human survival."[37] Cornell's cover design offers an apt visual corollary to this discussion of cultural survival (fig. 3.14). Its star is the dancer Isadora Duncan, revered for her deployment of classical sources as well as her innovative choreographic grammar. To visualize Duncan's classical inheritance, Cornell arranged photographs, reviews, and dance programs into a montage that spills beyond the graphic outline of an amphora.[38] Duncan looks out from the montage's center, clad in a draped garment trimmed with a Greek meander pattern and wearing her hair in a Hellenistic coiffure. She sits atop columnar forms built from a newspaper clipping with the headline "La Danse grecque antique" and a photograph of women arrayed before a classical frieze. Cornell flanks her with images from Renaissance painting, including the Three Graces of Sandro Botticelli's *La primavera* at right, and a striding figure trailed by a loop of drapery at left. This figure in motion is none other than Aby Warburg's time-traveling "Nympha," her presence

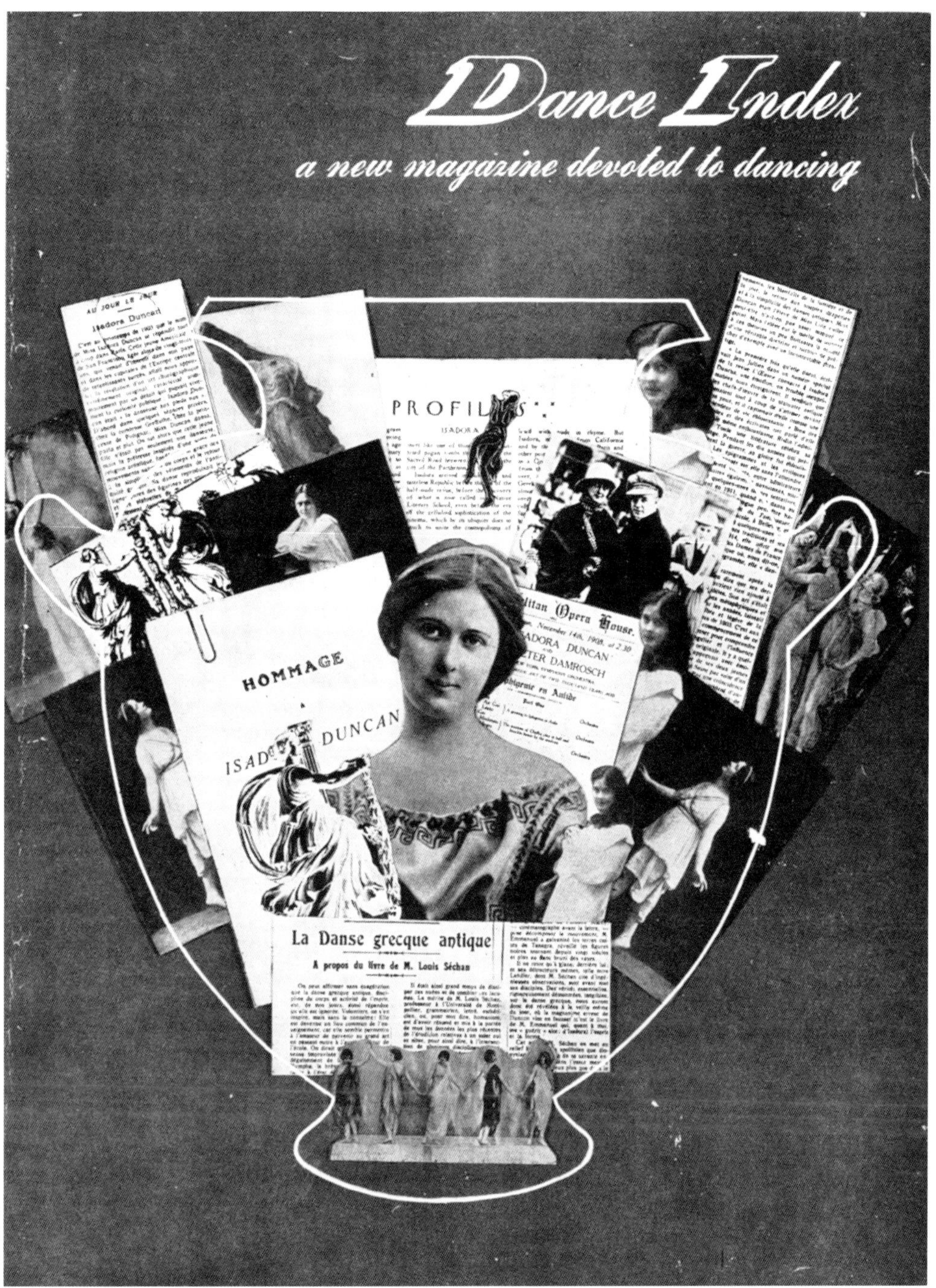

FIG. 3.14 Joseph Cornell, "Hommage à Isadora," cover design for *Dance Index* 1, no. 1 (January 1942).

reverberating through antiquity, the Renaissance, and the present.[39] Although there is no evidence Cornell knew of Warburg's work, Nympha's presence in this collage is no coincidence: the German art historian famously attended performances by Duncan while developing his theory of *pathosformel*.[40]

Classicism's relevance to the present moment can also be seen in Paul Cadmus's *Arabesque* (1941, fig. 3.15), reproduced directly across from the issue's opening comment. The picture shows three figures, one man and two women, posing in a dance studio. Their sharp outlines, elegantly defined muscles, and hieratic poses evoke Greek sculpture, while the chalky tones of egg tempera on board recall the earthy tones of fresco. Queer desire permeates the painting, particularly in the tight fit of the male figure's pants, which cling to his sculpted buttocks like a second skin. As Richard Meyer and others have shown, Cadmus was one of many artists during the period to associate classicism with queer desire.[41] In *Arabesque*'s "threesome," to use Meyer's phrase, the entwined graces of *La primavera* are distributed across a crisply rendered perspectival room, reconfiguring sexual desire to show the "range of intimate possibilities" in which Cadmus and Kirstein participated.[42]

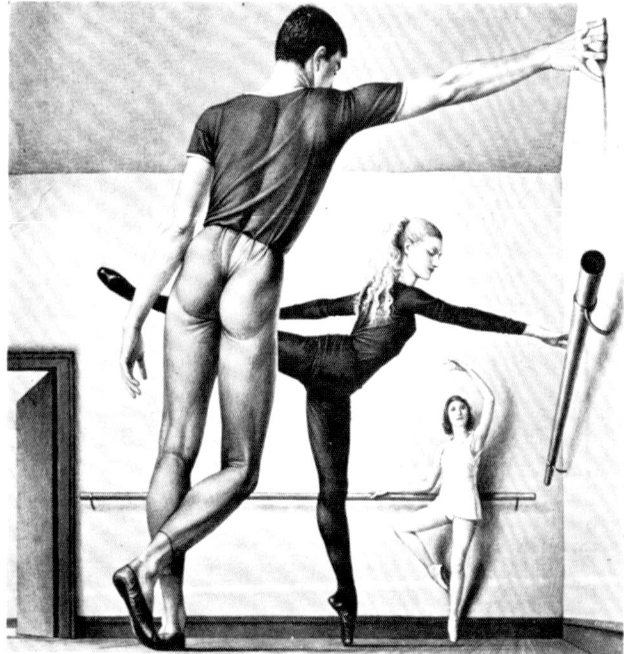

ARABESQUE : PAUL CADMUS : 1941
(Courtesy: Midtown Galleries)

FIG. 3.15 Paul Cadmus, *Arabesque*, 1941, frontispiece for *Dance Index* 1, no. 1 (January 1942).

The idealized inviolability of Cadmus's male dancer takes on additional resonance in relation to the pendant article. The servicemen who clamored for *Dance Index*'s publication had already begun to leave for war, and editors Kirstein, Magriel, and Hastings would soon join them. Ballet Caravan was forced to close after many of its dancers left to fight. *Dance Index*'s introductory section tracked this circulation of bodies, diligently noting the magazine's personnel changes as the war pulled ever more men into its brutal orbit.[43]

The experience of the war had a decisive impact on Kirstein, attuning him to the vulnerability of the human body. Kirstein spent part of the war as a member of the famed Monuments Men division, rescuing Europe's cultural patrimony from destruction. The war's toll registered most profoundly for Kirstein when he came across the dancer Lew Christensen burying bodies as a member of the Graves Registration Agency, his honed dancer's muscles repurposed for physical labor.[44] As Garafola has noted, Christensen was revered by Balanchine and Kirstein, who saw him as "an Orpheus and Apollo for America. . . . An American hero with the technique of an Olympian (fig. 3.16)."[45] The war brought the god back to earth. As Kirstein later wrote, "Nothing is more frail or transient than a ballet. Every action is evanescent, and after its enactment it is gone for good, or until a next time, when the same conditions obtain. Human bodies are frail."[46]

After the war, Kirstein channeled this concern with the fragility of the human body into championing the Polish Jewish sculptor Elie Nadelman, who committed suicide in 1946. Nadelman lost numerous family members to the concentration camps, and his suicide was the horrific culmination of a decade of struggles including financial ruin and a worsening heart condition. During the 1940s, the artist abandoned the sensuous wood and marble sculptures he had produced in the 1920s in favor of small, handmade figurines sculpted from plasticine clay, whose voluminous forms were inspired by kewpie dolls, Mae West, and Greek terra-cotta votives (fig. 3.17). These intimate sculptures bear the traces of Nadelman's fingers as he pinched and smoothed their delicate bodies. Rather than preserving them under an electrolyte coating, Nadelman left them to dry in the air, vulnerable to the ravages of light and time.[47]

Within a week of Nadleman's suicide, Kirstein began work on a lifelong project to preserve the sculptor's legacy. In the catalogue for Nadelman's 1948 MoMA retrospective, he writes of visiting the

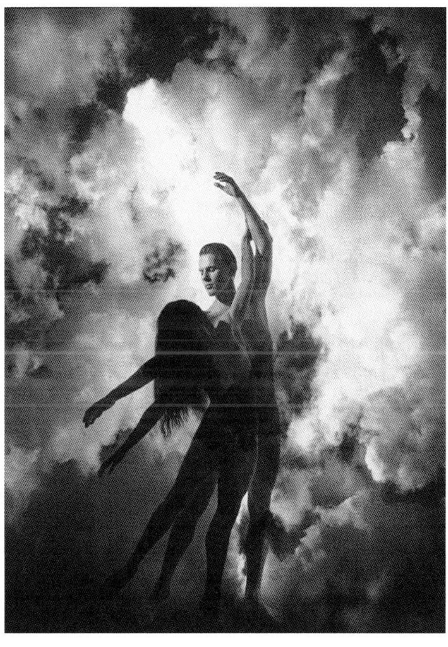

FIG. 3.16 George Platt Lynes, *Cover for the American Ballet's South American Tour*, showing Lew Christensen and Marie-Jeanne, May 1941. Metropolitan Museum of Art, New York.

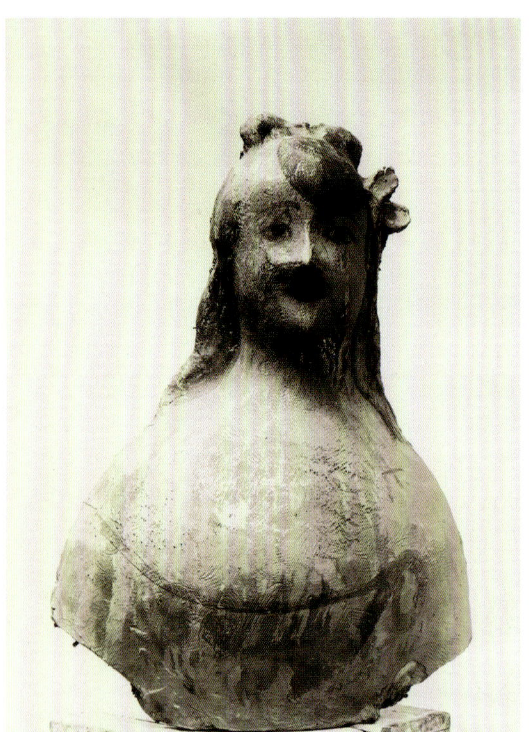

FIG. 3.17 Elie Nadelman, *Girl's Half-Length Torso*, 1925–27. Painted Galvano-plastique, 30 in. Lincoln Kirstein Papers, Jerome Robbins Dance Division, New York Public Library for the Performing Arts, box 4, Nadelman 1, no. 7.

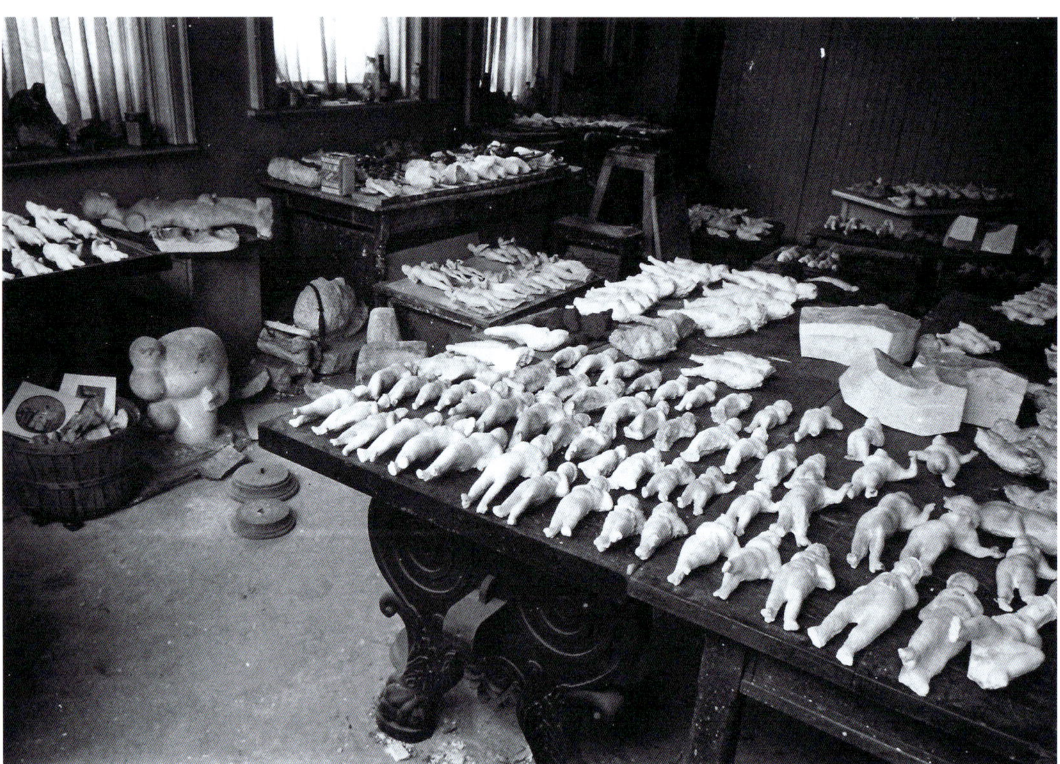

FIG. 3.18 Konrad Cramer, *Elie Nadelman's Studio with Multiple Plasters*, ca. 1948. Estate of Elie Nadelman.

artist's studio in winter 1947, after his death, and seeing "dozens of these small white corpses . . . laid out was as if one had stumbled upon archeological treasures, relics of hecatomb or mass sacrifice" (fig. 3.18).[48] Kirstein's description of Nadelman's sculptures as corpses suggests the intense emotional charge of his posthumous championing of the artist. He attempted to preserve these vulnerable lumps of clay by recasting them into durable materials such as bronze or marble, as if to save Nadelman's legacy from further decay.

Kirstein's most ambitious intervention involved overseeing the casting of two of the artist's papier-mâché figures of circus women in pristine Carrara marble. He installed these colossal nineteen-foot sculptures at either end of the newly built New York State Theater at Lincoln Center (figs. 3.19, 3.20).[49] With their swollen limbs and polished surfaces, these gargantuan figures exhibit none of the fragile intimacy of their predecessors. This was precisely the point. By remaking them in the most vaunted of classical materials, Kirstein rendered Nadelman's sculptures impervious to time and destruction. These figures embody Kirstein's wish to make culture—and the bodies that created them—whole and enduring, fixing time's flow into static eternity.

Cornell responded to the war in his own ways. *Habitat Group for a Shooting Gallery* (1943, fig. 3.21) made its public debut at Julien Levy's exhibition *Through the Big End of the Opera Glass*, alongside a group of small objects by Yves Tanguy and Marcel Duchamp.[50] Reviewing the show, *New York Times* art critic Edward Alden Jewell criticized Cornell for his perceived escapism: "Cornell's art I shall have to leave altogether, I'm afraid, in the reader's hands (but handle with care, for it is fragile). Somehow, while looking with curiosity at his neat little bottles filled with this and that, his pretty shells and devious gadgets and the doll

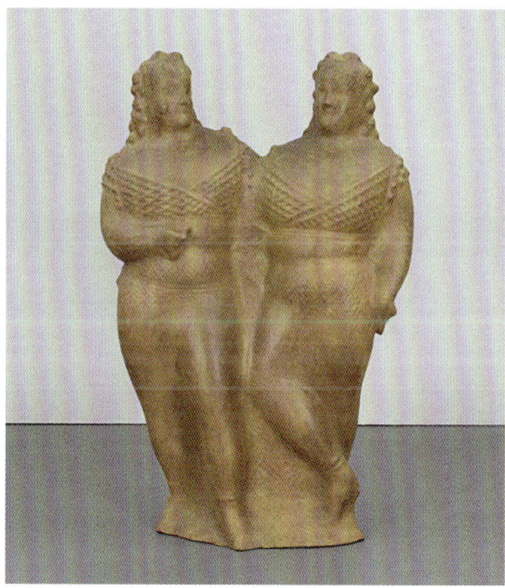

FIG. 3.19 Elie Nadelman, *Two Circus Women*, ca. 1928–29. Plaster covered with paper, overall 62 × 40⅞ × 17½ inches. Whitney Museum of American Art, New York; purchase, with funds from The Lauder Foundation, Evelyn and Leonard Lauder Fund. Inv.: 99.90.4.

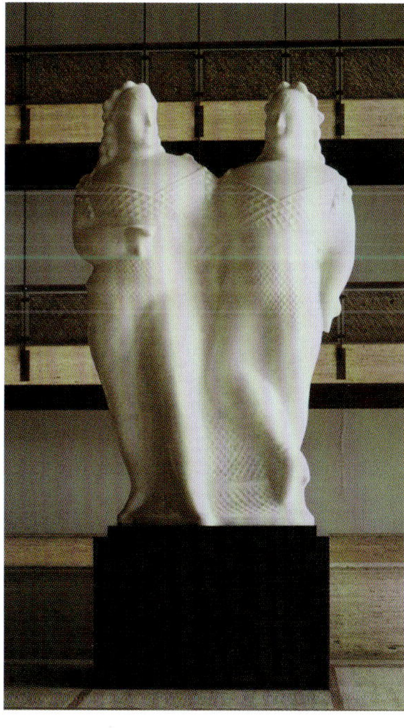

FIG. 3.20 Elie Nadelman, *Two Circus Women*, 1964. Monumental sculpture for New York State Theater (original papier-mâché version created ca. 1928–29). Carrara marble, 19 feet tall. Lincoln Center, New York.

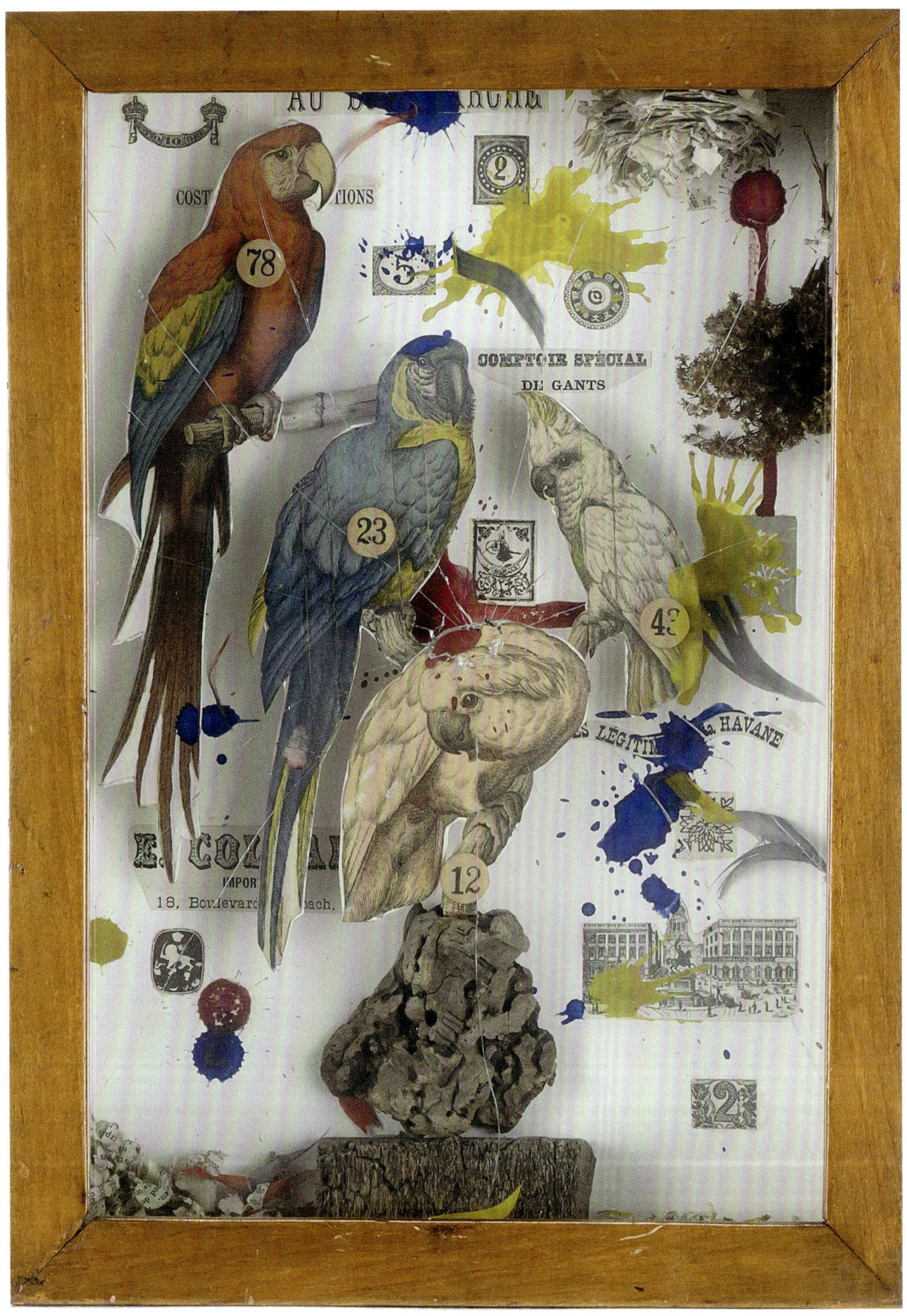

FIG. 3.21 Joseph Cornell, *Habitat Group for a Shooting Gallery*, 1943. Mixed media, 15½ × 11⅛ × 4¼ inches. Collection of the Des Moines Art Center, 1975.27; purchased with funds from the Coffin Fine Arts Trust; Nathan Emory Coffin.

enmeshed in silvered twigs, I remembered that there is a war, and after that, try as I might, I couldn't find my way back into Mr. Cornell's dreamworld."[51]

Jewell's commentary is emblematic of the questions asked of art during times of turmoil and tragedy: what is it for, and what good does it do in the world? *Habitat Group for a Shooting Gallery* suggests that Cornell asked himself these very questions. The work is among the most literal in Cornell's oeuvre. A single hole pierces its glass front, as if a bullet has ripped through the box to splatter the primary-colored blood of Cornell's beloved birds across its interior. The work of art is an abattoir. A vulgar bloom of red paint crowns the cranium of the central cockatoo (fig. 3.22).[52] Clippings redolent of Europe line the box: a picture of a mounted equestrian statue in a city square at bottom right, and French phrases such as "Comptoir spécial de gants," and "Au Bon Marché." The phrases' connotations of shopping correspond with the box's reduction of the birds to mere commodities, labeling them with numbers as if for easy purchase. As if we needed another reminder of the box's precise time and place, the number "43"—the year of the its assembly—adorns the tail of the cockatoo at right. Feathers, bullet holes, blood; all attempt to depict the violence of the war. But the cost of this literal engagement with the historical moment was the reduction of Cornell's avian characters to corporal bodies.

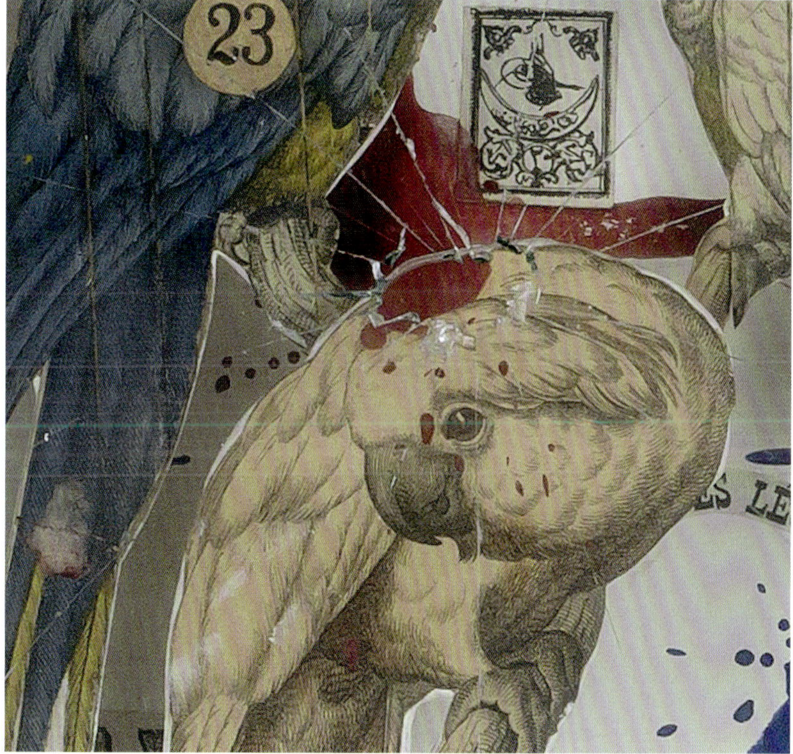

FIG. 3.22 Detail from Joseph Cornell, *Habitat Group for a Shooting Gallery*.

Two years later, Cornell took an altogether different approach to bringing current events into his work. In September 1945, *Dance Index* published the artist's special issue devoted to Danish author Hans Christian Andersen (fig. 3.23). In the issue's foreword, Cornell connected Andersen to the war's conclusion: "The Constant Tin Soldier has been through more fiery trials, and the Little Match Girl more long cruel winters. Rejoicing with them in the liberation of the land that gave them birth we can better appreciate the imponderables of the Tales—to survive the terror and tragedy that have been their lot the past half decade. Perennial and universal as has been their appeal renewed acquaintance with them now becomes even more rewarding."[53] Despite its celebratory tone, Cornell's choice of tales is telling: at their end, the Tin Soldier is melted down into a metal heart, and the Little Match Girl freezes to death.

Just five months earlier, Denmark had been liberated from the Nazis. The issue is illustrated by paper silhouettes created by Andersen, which Cornell borrowed from Copenhagen's Hans Christian Andersen Museum.[54] The frontispiece features a ballet dancer balancing delicately on pointed toes (fig. 3.24). To create her perfectly symmetrical figure, Andersen folded a piece of paper and snipped along its central crease, layering this ornate black web on a sheet of white paper.[55] The resulting figure oscillates between negative and positive, flesh and fabric, her body created by these elemental contrasts. She is the tin soldier's beloved, the paper ballerina who falls into the flames and is incinerated into ash.

Cornell wrote that he admired Andersen's fairy tales for "their release, their escape, their flight, their defiance of the limitations of a physical world; their amiability; the subtler sense of light and air."[56] Their enchantment survives conflagration, and this is what Cornell means when he describes "the imponderables of the Tales." Yet if enchantment endures, it reverses neither the tales' tragic endings, nor the war's violence. In contrast to the literalism of *Habitat Group for a Shooting Gallery* as well as Kirstein's classicism, which attempted to fix and preserve in the

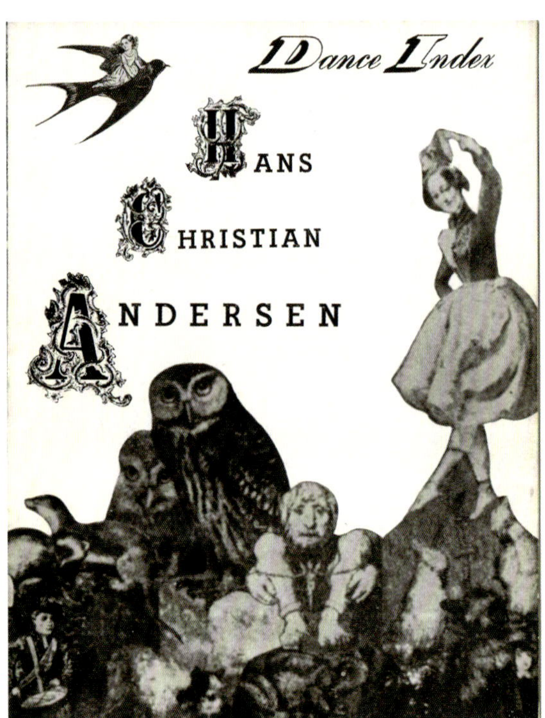

FIG. 3.23 Joseph Cornell, cover design for "Hans Christian Andersen," special issue, *Dance Index* 4, no. 9 (September 1945). Joseph Cornell Study Center, Smithsonian American Art Museum, Washington, DC.

face of incomprehensible violence, here Cornell neither depicts nor attempts to forestall tragedy. Rather, tragedy makes the survival of Andersen's tales all the more miraculous. Andersen's stories, Cornell's enchantment do not—cannot—repair violence and death. Their continued existence, even in the face of the world's brutality, is the miracle. This is the source of their limited strength.

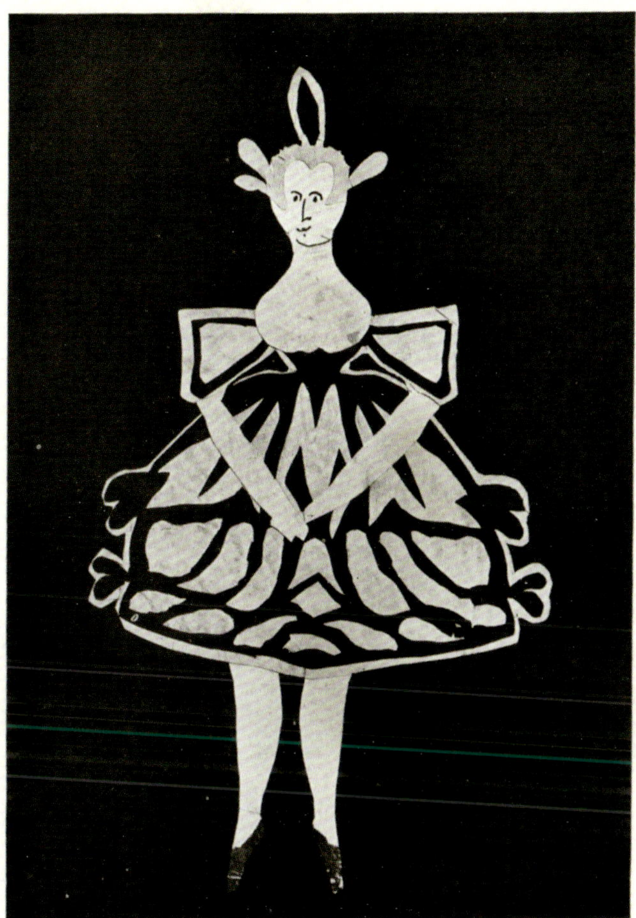

Silhouette cut in paper by H. C. Andersen, from the Hans Andersen Museum.

FIG. 3.24 Frontispiece for "Hans Christian Andersen."

In 1940, Charles Henri Ford and Parker Tyler cofounded the publication *View*. Hoping to capitalize on the recently arrived wave of European exiles, Ford and Tyler promoted *View* as an American vehicle for Surrealist thought.[57] Like *Dance Index*, *View* addressed a wide range of culture, including literature, film, photography, the work of children, and poetry. The predominantly queer circle around *View* also overlapped significantly with that of *Dance Index*: Ford's partner, the Russian émigré painter Pavel Tchelitchew, was a noted balletomane who collaborated with Kirstein and Balanchine on costumes and set designs.

From its founding, Cornell was a key participant in the *View* milieu, even lending Ford and Tyler boxes to decorate the publication's office.[58] The affectionate, decades-long correspondence among the artist and *View*'s editors attests to the respect and admiration among the men. While Cornell's letters to Kirstein maintained a distant, professional tone, his correspondence with Ford and Tyler reads instead as an intimate conversation among artists. The men often traded suggestions for locating source material, as when Ford tipped Cornell off to a Carl Van Vechten photograph for sale at the Gotham Book Mart.[59] Even more telling is the litany of insecurities and frustrations Cornell detailed in his letters to the men, who responded by encouraging him to write about his artistic practice. As he replied to Tyler after one of these entreaties, "I think I'd always shrink away from publishing anything about my own work. I'd want to feel a little surer of myself, at least have more solid things to my credit than have evolved so far from my dilettante manner of working."[60] Cornell's candor speaks to his genuine trust in the poets. Their admiration in turn is evidenced by the dedications written in books of poetry they gave to him in the early 1940s, which describe him as "the Benvenuto Cellini of Flotsam and Jetsam," and the one "who woke to find the winter landscape in his own jewel box" (fig. 3.25).[61]

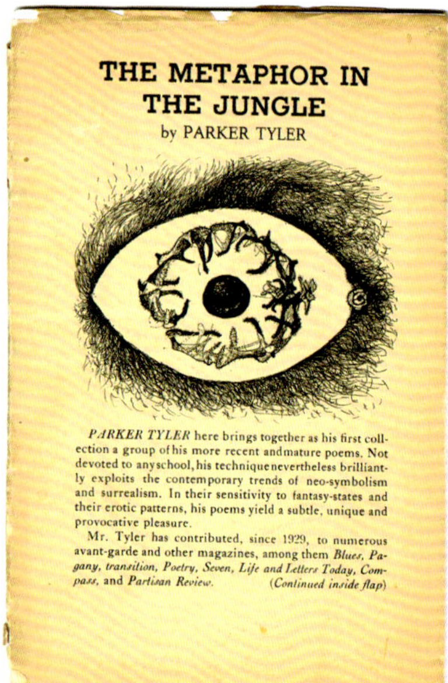

FIG. 3.25 Parker Tyler, *The Metaphor in the Jungle: And Other Poems*, inscribed to Joseph Cornell, January 18, 1941. Joseph Cornell Study Center, Smithsonian American Art Museum, Washington, DC.

Although Cornell was not queer, the artist's deep engagement with poetry and cinema, and his agonistic relationship with Surrealism positioned him as an important predecessor and collaborator for the *View* milieu. In Cornell, Ford and Tyler found an artist with the imprimatur of an established Surrealist who had also spent the past decade negotiating his relationship to the movement. Despite the artist's attempts to distance himself from Surrealism, in 1938 André Breton and Paul Éluard picked Cornell for inclusion in their famed *Exposition Internationale du Surréalisme* at the Galerie Beaux-Arts in Paris, cementing his Surrealist credentials.[62] The association was significant for Ford and Tyler, who remained acutely aware of the outsider status imputed to them by their queerness. Unlike other prominent gay figures of the period, they could rely on neither social status nor money to shield them. In an undated letter to Ford during their first collaborative editorial effort *Blues*, Tyler recounted a party where he was asked "before 7 or 8 people why blues wasn't called orchid and I fairly screamed out: we were thinking of calling it the international fairy review but reconsidered that it wouldn't be good policy."[63] Ford and Tyler also encountered hostility from Breton, the self-declared leader of Surrealism and supposed champion of unleashed desire, who had recently arrived in the United States. Breton's transparent homophobia is evidenced by a private letter between Ford and Tyler skewing his pompous hypocrisy: "He is revolted by obvious Lesbians as well as 'fairies' like we used to be.... Which doesn't OBVIATE his looking like a woman in the first place without wearing his hair long in the 2nd.... Velvet knee pants and silk stockings would make him the REINCARNATION of O. Wilde, for whom, as is, he's much more of a DEAD-RINGER than Robert Morley.... In fact Miss Morley has to be made up to the high g-ds in order to HOLD A CANDLE to Miss Breton."[64] In another telling anecdote, *View*'s managing editor, John Bernard Myers, recalled seeing Ford scrawl "What a terribly designed page!" on the title page of Breton's novel *Nadja*.[65]

Breton matched this private irreverence with public viciousness, referring to *View* as "pederasty international" and founding his own publication, *VVV*, to compete with it.[66] And for all their camping, Ford and Tyler were acutely aware of the real toll of Breton's hostility, privately blaming him for the suicide of gay poet René Crevel, Tchelitchew's former lover.[67] As art historian Tirza Latimer has argued, with *View*, Ford and Tyler sought to counter Surrealism's homophobia to create a queer "collective history—as recorded in various aesthetic forms ... a tissue of fictionalized or strategically falsified memoirs."[68] From this vantage, *View*'s eclectic range of subjects can be understood as their attempt to circumvent the increasingly strident dictums of the Surrealist intelligentsia.[69]

Ford and Tyler turned to mythopoeia, or myth-making, as a means of weaving *View*'s eclectic sources into a queer "collective history." Jean-Pierre Vernant's discussion of myth helps elucidate enchantment's relevance to their project. Vernant observes that in the West, "myth is defined in terms of what is not myth, being opposed first to reality (myth is fiction) and, second, in what is rational (myth is absurd)."[70] He locates the root of myth's opposition to reality and rationality to the historical divide between *muthos*, or constructed speech, and *logos*, or rational written discourse intended to establish truth. As a follower of Claude Lévi-Strauss, Vernant is well-aware of the poststructuralist understanding of myth as means of entrenching ideology. Yet he also admits another function of myth, which is to "bring into play

compendium of myths, *The Golden Bough*.[81] Although Tyler also cited Frazier's work for his *Magic and the Myth of the Movies*, he warned that such stories were not to be taken literally, instead describing myth as "a free, unharnessed fiction, a basic, prototypic pattern capable of many variations and distortions, many betrayals and disguises, even though it remains *imaginative* truth."[82] Tyler draws on myth's noncontradictory affordances to join "imaginative" and "truth," creating a conceptual structure in which "*desires* may have the same power over the mind and behavior, indeed, a much greater power, than *facts*."[83] In myth's field of noncontradiction, the supposedly irrational force of desire can be elevated to the status of Truth.

Tyler elaborated on his understanding of myth in a 1956 talk at the Creative Film Foundation: "Now, to invent a myth—what does that mean? I think it means simply to conceive all human action in terms of symbolism. . . . It suggests the element of ritual, the element of the dance figure, of the formalized pantomime, that reduces action to its dramatic and poetic fundamentals; that represents birth and death, and everything between and everything beyond; that represents physically the discovery of love and its sacred realization. And if everything in life is sacred, death cannot escape. Death, too, is sacred."[84] The quotation suggests the resonances Ford and Tyler likely found in Cornell's enchantment. The artist shared their conviction that there are forces beyond the purview of rational facts and sought to capture this in his work. His figuration transforms the ephemera of daily life into embodiments of these forces, paralleling Ford and Tyler's attempts to construct myths from the folklore of queer life.

Tyler's esteem for Cornell's enchantment is evident in a 1939 catalogue essay, which describes the artist's ability to elevate commonplace objects as central to his artistic achievement: "The poor people and children collect strings, useless articles, fetishes beyond price. Joseph Cornell transforms this practice and raises it into art. We would transform our world into a more livable one, a kinder and more solidly glamorous one. Joseph Cornell, master of the world as a biblioquet, transformed the tired brooding on messy things into the crystal perfection of forms and colors; he cathedralizes thought too silly to mention and returns lost articles of the imagination."[85] Like Kirstein, Tyler deliberately sets Cornell apart from the "poor people and children" who collect things out of passion. To transform these "messy things" into art, Cornell refines them into "crystal perfection of forms and colors," a process akin to reducing human action to "its dramatic and poetic fundamentals." Cornell thus "cathedralizes" what is silly and useless, what is merely material, into the eternal elements of myth.

Consider, for example, Cornell's *Medici Slot Machine* (1942, fig. 3.28). The serious young boy within is Massimiliano Stampa, the nine-year-old marquess of the Italian city Soncino.[86] Painted in 1557 with characteristic tenderness by artist Sofonisba Anguissola, the boy's gaze is at once mature and youthful. Cream pillars clipped from maps of Rome bracket his body. A vertical line painted on the box's glass front draws our gaze down, to a lower compartment filled with marbles, jacks, dice, and the interior mechanism of a nineteenth-century compass. Backed by a mirror and framed by a thick black border, this lower chamber bears a striking resemblance to a film strip. The cinematic analogy is confirmed by the sequential repetition of

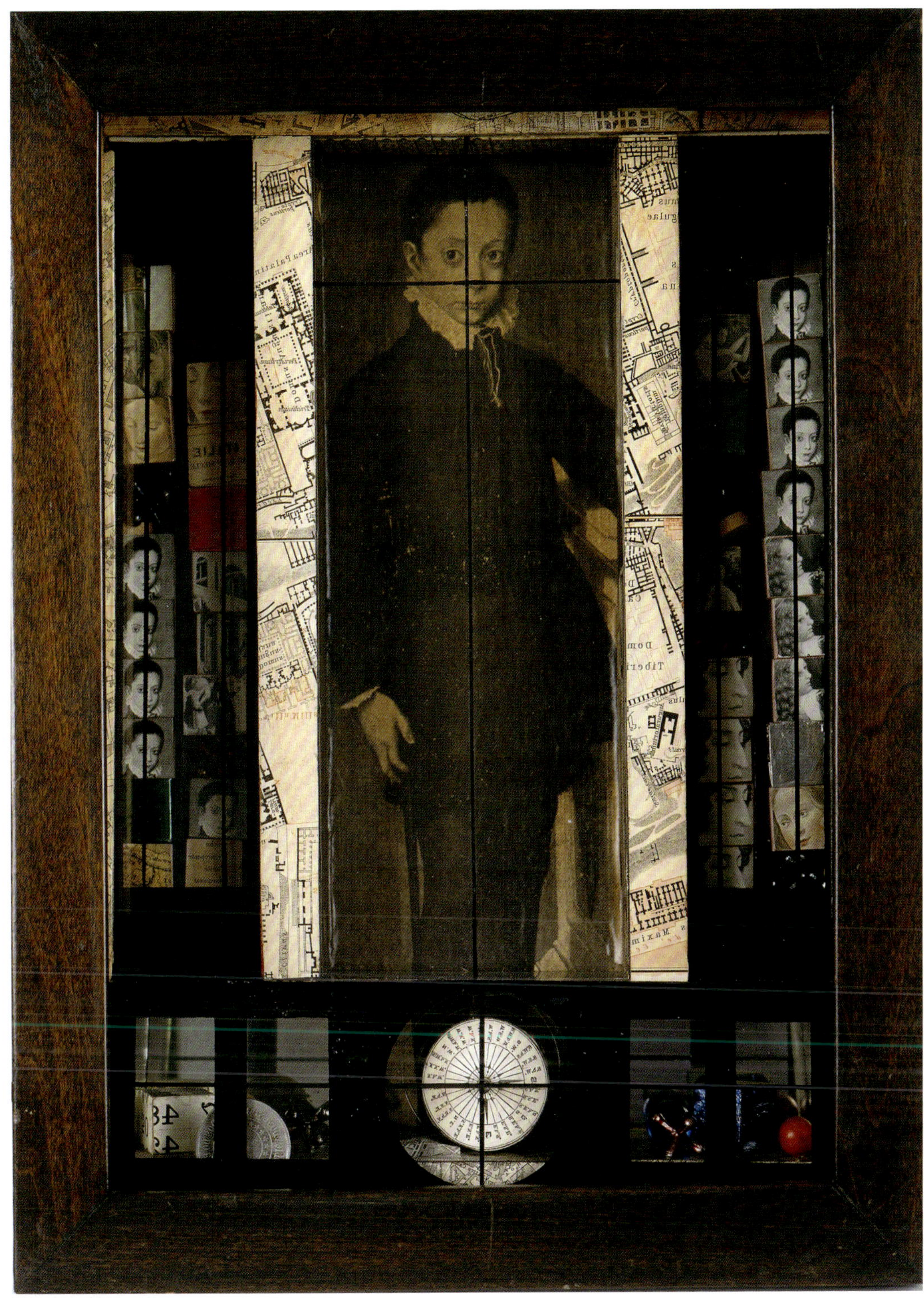

FIG. 3.28 Joseph Cornell, *Medici Slot Machine: Object*, 1942. Box construction with painted glass, 15 1/2 × 12 1/4 × 4 3/8 inches. Private collection.

faces stacked in the compartments flanking the portrait, film strips that have ceased their incessant forward movement to become as still as the boy in Anguissola's portrait. The box is what film theorist Pavle Levi describes as "cinema by other means," evoking the formal and phantasmagoric structure of film without resorting to celluloid.[87] Horizontal and vertical; movement and stillness; maturity and youth; high culture and childish games; the nearness of the boy's body and the distance of Rome: the structure of Cornell's box extracts these elemental contrasts from its eclectic array of materials. Placed behind a pane of glass, Anguissola's portrait embodies the most elemental contrast of all. The liveliness of childhood becomes an image preserved in amber, as if to remind us of the breath that will never cloud the box's front. Life and death are at stake here. Cornell's precise calibration of images and objects distills or "cathedralizes" them into evocations of these foundational themes—life, death, desire—creating a material corollary to Ford and Tyler's mythopoeia.

During the 1940s, Cornell looked to painting as a model for how to condense his enchantment into the "crystal perfection" described by Tyler. Upon seeing a reproduction of Jan van Eyck's *Ghent Altarpiece* in a 1949 issue of *Life* (fig. 3.29), he noted that the painting "glows as beautifully realized, metamorphosed, sublimation ... [w]ith the feeling of the grasses, fields, the flowers, the rarified quality of a dream." This, he continued, constituted a "concrete presentation of a vision."[88] Cornell appreciated painting's ability to achieve such moments crystalline intensity. Painting's materialization of experience does not sacrifice the "rarified quality of a dream" but rather intensifies it by condensing it into a single image.

Cornell shared this understanding of painting with others in the 1940s. In 1943, the exhibition *Americans 1943: Realists and Magic-Realists* opened at the Museum of Modern Art. Curated by Dorothy Miller with advice from Kirstein, the show was the fourth in the series of

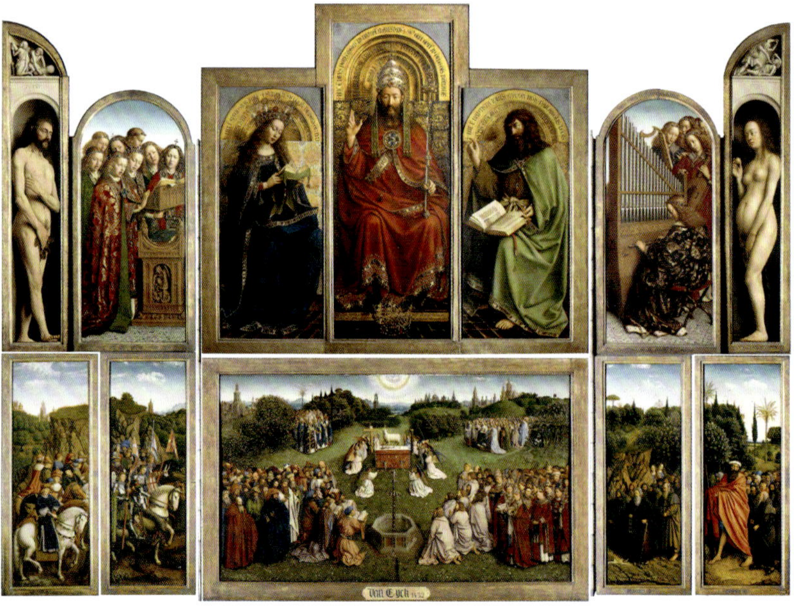

FIG. 3.29 Jan van Eyck, *Ghent Altarpiece* (showing twelve interior panels), completed 1432. Oil on oak panel, 11 × 15 feet. Saint Bavo's Cathedral, Ghent, Belgium.

broad survey exhibitions that also included *Fantastic Art, Dada, Surrealism*. Like that earlier show, *Americans 1943: Realists and Magic-Realists* covered a broad chronological scope, including early American paintings by Edward Hicks and Raphaelle Peale; leftist artists such as Peter Blume, Ben Shahn, and O. Louis Guglielmi; and "magic realists" such as Tchelitchew and Paul Cadmus, whose *Arabesque* was included in the exhibition. Although distinct in aim and period, these artists shared a commitment to realist painting techniques. "By a combination of crisp hard edges, tightly indicated forms, and the counterfeiting of material surfaces such as paper, grain of wood, flesh, or leaf," Kirstein writes, "our eyes are deceived into believing the reality of what is rendered, whether factual or imaginary."[89] Painting's illusionism *can* deceive, as Greenberg had suggested in 1939. Yet unlike Greenberg, Kirstein did not see this effect as entirely pernicious, observing admiringly that magic realists "try to convince us that extraordinary things are possible simply by painting them as if they existed."[90]

Take Guglielmi's 1941 painting *Terror in Brooklyn* (fig. 3.30), which was included in the MoMA exhibition. The picture shows three nuns trapped in a Cornell-esque bell jar, cowering before a bloody arrangement of pelvic bones. The scene's eeriness is heightened by the exaggerated perspective of the empty street and unsettling details such as the lamppost that terminates in a point rather than a glowing bulb. Guglielmi described this painting as trying to convey a feeling rather than a specific event, a "mood because of irrational events in the object world—murder in the streets, war, subjective reality."[91] Guglielmi's use of Dalí's crisply illusionistic painting style across the composition allows the picture's disparate vignettes—pelvic bones, Brooklyn street, cowering nuns—to cohere together into a single composition, as airless as the bell jar that encases the nuns. Like Cornell's deliberately constructed contrasts in *Medici Slot Machine*, Guglielmi's uniformly realist style imparts the scene with a mythic structure, transforming an array of fantastical images into a seamless whole. The painting crystalizes the horror and dread of the early 1940s into a myth that is at once "factual and imaginary." However irrational the spectacular violence of this historical moment might seem, it was all too real. To paraphrase Kirstein, extraordinary things exist.

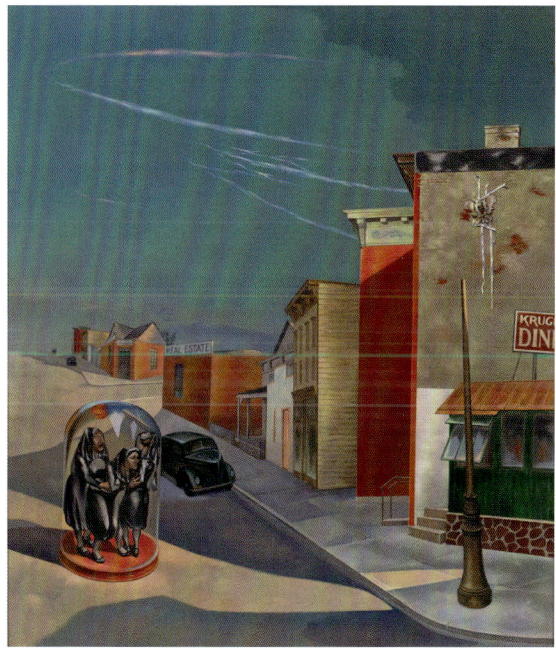

FIG. 3.30 Louis Guglielmi, *Terror in Brooklyn*, 1941. Oil on canvas, 34 1/8 × 30 3/16 inches. Whitney Museum of American Art, New York.

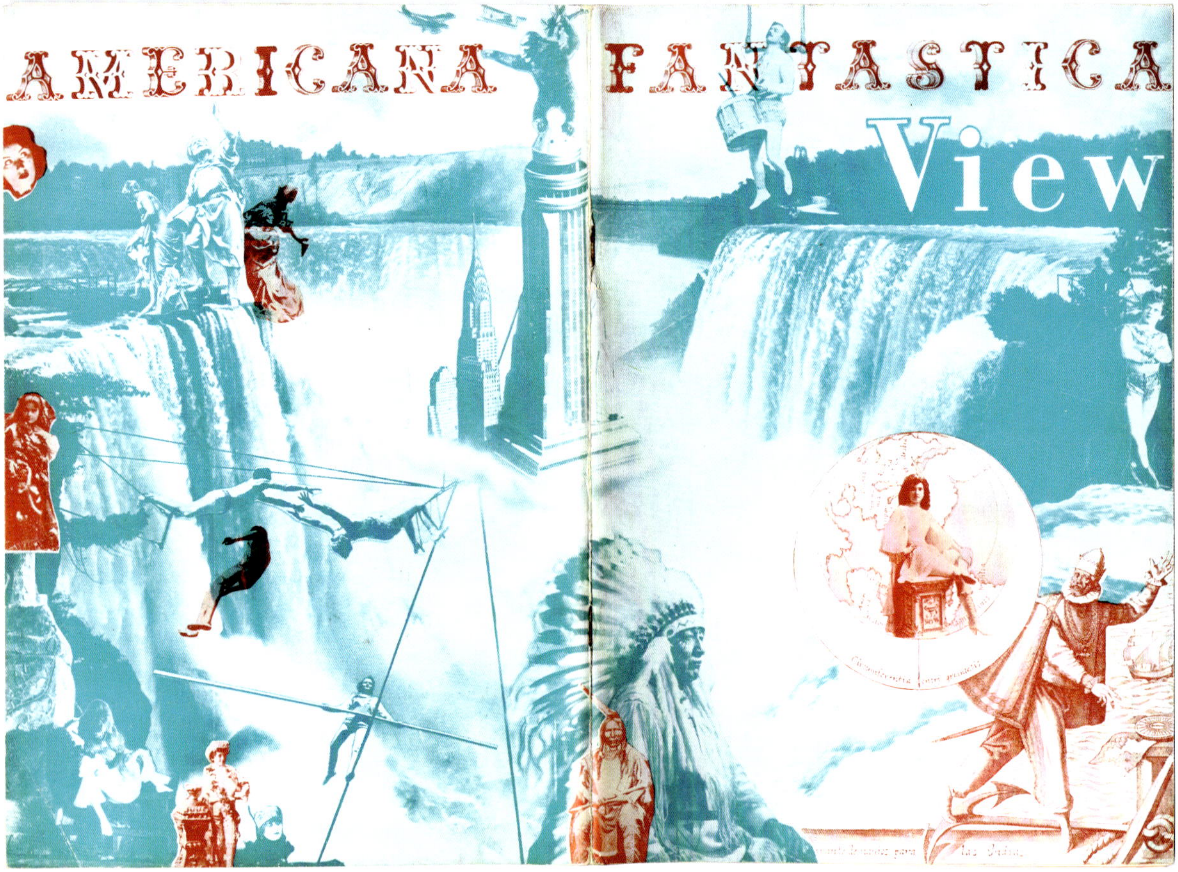

FIG. 3.31 Joseph Cornell, cover design for "Americana Fantastica," special issue, *View* 2, no. 4 (January 1943). Joseph Cornell Study Center, Smithsonian American Art Museum, Washington, DC.

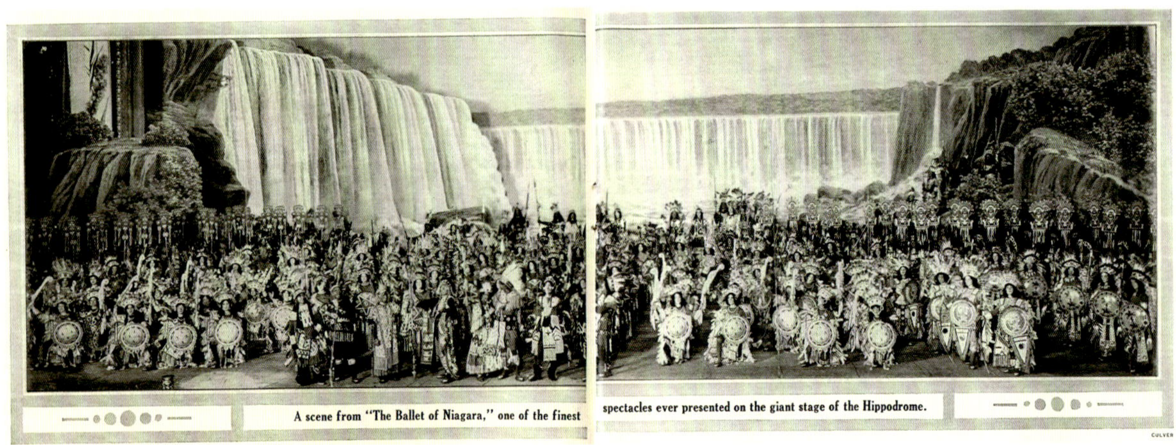

FIG. 3.32 Scene from *The Ballet of Niagara* at the Hippodrome Theater, *Stage*, no. 1911 (August 1936): 58–59. Joseph Cornell Study Center, Smithsonian American Art Museum, Washington, DC.

RISE AND FALL

Cornell's work for *View* makes explicit the sympathies between his project and that of Ford and Tyler. His cover design for *View*'s 1943 issue titled "Americana Fantastica" (fig. 3.31) features popular historical icons of American culture layered across a compressed view of Niagara Falls. The sublime curtains of falling water become a theatrical setting for an array of American culture, akin to the backdrop of the Hippodrome Theater's 1910 *Ballet of Niagara*, whose playbill was in Cornell's collection (fig. 3.32).[92] As Kirsten Hoving has argued, the figure at bottom right might stand for Christopher Columbus, who looks over his shoulder at a globe overlaid with a picture of the vaudeville actress Fanny Ward.[93] The Empire State Building rises from the ethereal mists of the falls, with none other than King Kong perched at its apex. A circus strongman, a group of women, and a boy playing a drum hover at the falls' precipice, while at bottom left the French daredevil Charles Blondin repeats his 1862 feat of crossing Niagara on a tightrope.[94] Many of the figures on Cornell's cover appear moments away from plunging into Niagara's watery depths. An acrobat, tinted blood red, appears to have missed his catch. And of course, King Kong will eventually fall from his summit, succumbing to the same inexorable force that hurtles water over Niagara's formidable ledge. Even Columbus is not immune: the spine of the folded cover creates a physical precipice recalling the fictional one that threatened to swallow the Italian colonist as he sailed to the edge of the world (fig. 3.33).

Cornell's cover image relies on the contrast of rise and fall to weave together distinct fragments of American culture into a single mythic scene, offering a visual corollary to Tyler's discussion of the "fantastic" on *View*'s editorial page in the same issue (fig. 3.34). Tyler describes the fantastic as the sui generis emergence of some force outside of rational comprehension. Departing from Barr's earlier formulation of the fantastic as a universal

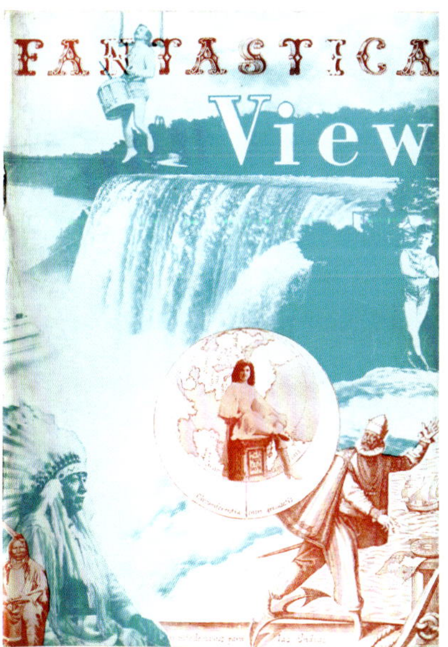

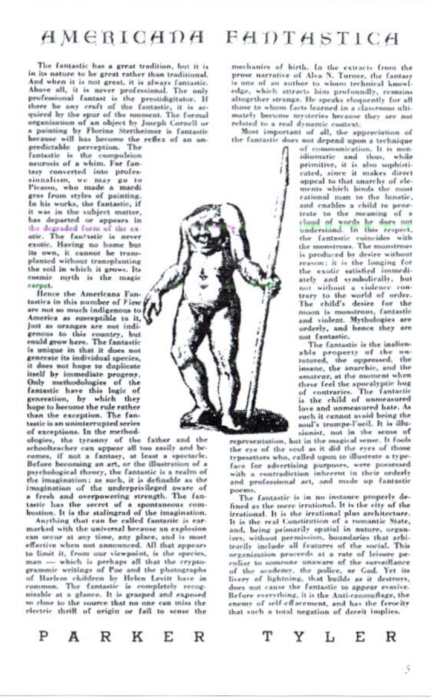

AMERICANA FANTASTICA

The fantastic has a great tradition, but it is in its nature to be great rather than traditional. And when it is not great, it is always fantastic. Above all, it is never professional. The only professional fantast is the prestidigitator. If there be any craft of the fantastic, it is acquired by the spur of the moment. The formal organization of an object by Joseph Cornell or a painting by Florine Stettheimer is fantastic because will has become the reflex of an unpredictable perception. The fantastic is the compulsion neurosis of a whim. For fantasy converted into professionalism, we may go to Picasso, who made a mardi gras from styles of painting. In his works, the fantastic, if it was in the subject matter, has departed or appears in the degraded form of the exotic. The fantastic is never exotic. Having no home but its own, it cannot be transplanted without transplanting the soil in which it grows. Its cosmic myth is the magic carpet.

Hence the Americana Fantastica in this number of *View* are not so much indigenous to America as susceptible to it, just as oranges are not indigenous to this country, but could grow here. The fantastic is unique in that it does not generate its individual species, it does not hope to duplicate itself by immediate progeny. Only methodologies of the fantastic have this logic of generation, by which they hope to become the rule rather than the exception. The fantastic is an uninterrupted series of exceptions. In the methodologies, the tyranny of the father and the schoolteacher can appear all too easily and becomes, if not a fantasy, at least a spectacle. Before becoming an art, or the illustration of a psychological theory, the fantastic is a realm of the imagination; as such, it is definable as the imagination of the underprivileged aware of a fresh and overpowering strength. The fantastic has the secret of a spontaneous combustion. It is the stalingrad of the imagination.

Anything that can be called fantastic is earmarked with the universal because an explosion can occur at any time, any place, and is most effective when not announced. All that appears to limit it, from our viewpoint, is the species, man — which is perhaps all that the cryptogrammic writings of Poe and the photographs of Harlem children by Helen Levitt have in common. The fantastic is completely recognizable at a glance. It is grasped and exposed so close to the source that no one can miss the electric thrill of origin or fail to sense the mechanics of birth. In the extracts from the prose narrative of Alva N. Turner, the fantasy is one of an author to whom technical knowledge, which attracts him profoundly, remains altogether strange. He speaks eloquently for all those to whom facts learned in a classroom ultimately become mysteries because they are not related to a real dynamic context.

Most important of all, the appreciation of the fantastic does not depend upon a technique of communication. It is non-idiomatic and thus, while primitive, it is also sophisticated, since it makes direct appeal to that anarchy of elements which binds the most rational man to the lunatic, and enables a child to penetrate to the meaning of a cloud of words he does not understand. In this respect, the fantastic coincides with the monstrous. The monstrous is produced by desire without reason; it is the longing for the exotic satisfied immediately and symbolically, but not without a violence contrary to the world of order. The child's desire for the moon is monstrous, fantastic and violent. Mythologies are orderly, and hence they are not fantastic.

The fantastic is the inalienable property of the untutored, the oppressed, the insane, the anarchic, and the amateur, at the moment when these feel the apocalyptic hug of contraries. The fantastic is the child of unmeasured love and unmeasured hate. As such it cannot avoid being the soul's trompe-l'oeil. It is illusionist, not in the sense of representation, but in the magical sense. It fools the eye of the soul as it did the eyes of those typesetters who, called upon to illustrate a typeface for advertising purposes, were possessed with a contradiction inherent in their orderly and professional act, and made up fantastic poems.

The fantastic is in no instance properly defined as the mere irrational. It is the city of the irrational. It is the irrational plus architecture. It is the real Constitution of a romantic State, and, being primarily spatial in nature, organizes, without permission, boundaries that arbitrarily include all features of the social. This organization proceeds at a rate of leisure peculiar to someone unaware of the surveillance of the academy, the police, or God. Yet its livery of lightning, that builds as it destroys, does not cause the fantastic to appear evasive. Before everything, it is the Anti-camouflage, the enemy of self-effacement, and has the ferocity that such a total negation of deceit implies.

PARKER TYLER

5

FIG. 3.33 Joseph Cornell, cover design for "Americana Fantastica" (folded).

FIG. 3.34 Parker Tyler, editorial page, "Americana Fantastica," 5.

human impulse, Tyler instead calls it "the inalienable property of the untutored, the oppressed, the insane, the anarchic, and the amateur, at the moment when these feel the apocalyptic hug of contraries." The fantastic also requires the structure of myth: "The fantastic is in no instance properly defined as the mere irrational. It is the city of the irrational. It is the irrational plus architecture. It is the real Constitution of a romantic State, and, being primarily spatial in nature, organizes, without permission, boundaries that arbitrarily include all features of the social."[95] There is no better description of Cornell's cover, which uses the backdrop of the falls and the space of the page to unite its eclectic denizens into a single mythic tale.

A map by Flemish engraver Theodor de Bry was Cornell's source for the figure at bottom right of "Americana Fantastica." *America Sive Novus Orbis Respectu Europaeorum Inferior Globi Terrestris Pars* (1596) places four colonists in the four corners of its map: Columbus, Vespucci, Magellan, and Pizarro (fig. 3.35). Cornell used the image of Pizarro to stand for Columbus, the figure's off-kilter pose and delicate maneuvering over an anchor better according with his cover's depiction of precarious movement than the comparatively stable figure of de Bry's rendering. This comparison expands Hoving's description of this work as a map of the constellations.[96] While Cornell was certainly concerned with the connection of stars and earth, he also transforms de Bry's image into a map of the Americas, now populated with allegorical figures drawn from its presumed margins: cinema, vaudeville, the circus, and Indigenous culture. At once a map of the stars, a map of the Americas, and a *mappa mundi*, Cornell's cover compresses rise and fall, life and death, far and near, into a single scene.

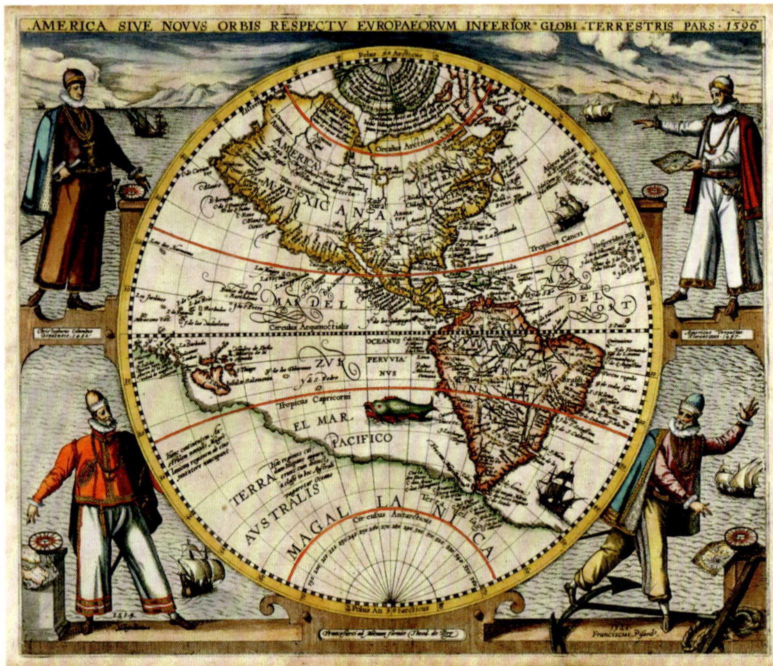

FIG. 3.35 Theodor de Bry, *America Sive Novus Orbis Respectu Europaeorum Inferior Globi Terrestris Pars*, printed in Frankfurt, 1596. Hand-colored print, 16 × 13 inches. David Rumsey Map Center, Stanford, CA.

Cornell's combination of fragments into a unified view recalls the compositional logic of Pavel Tchelitchew's remarkable painting *Phenomena* (1936–38, fig. 3.36). Tchelitchew was close with Cornell, who peppered his letters to Ford with questions for the painter.[97] *Phenomena,* the first painting in a cycle of works devoted to Dante's *Divine Comedy,* depicts hell, a prologue to the purgatory of the painter's better-known *Cache-Cache* (*Hide Seek*). Here the marginal figures of Cornell's "Americana Fantastica" are distorted into grotesquerie. Tchelitchew populates the picture with a dense panoply of characters, including conjoined twins, an elderly woman hunched with scoliosis, and a reclining nude bearing six breasts. As Angela Miller has recently argued, Tchelitchew sought to create a visual system that "situated the flux of nature, organic growth, and sexuality inside an integrated universe mapped by ordered cosmological systems," thereby creating "an integrated vision that transcended the dualisms of reason/magic, matter/spirit, body/nature."[98] In his paintings, nothing is contained,

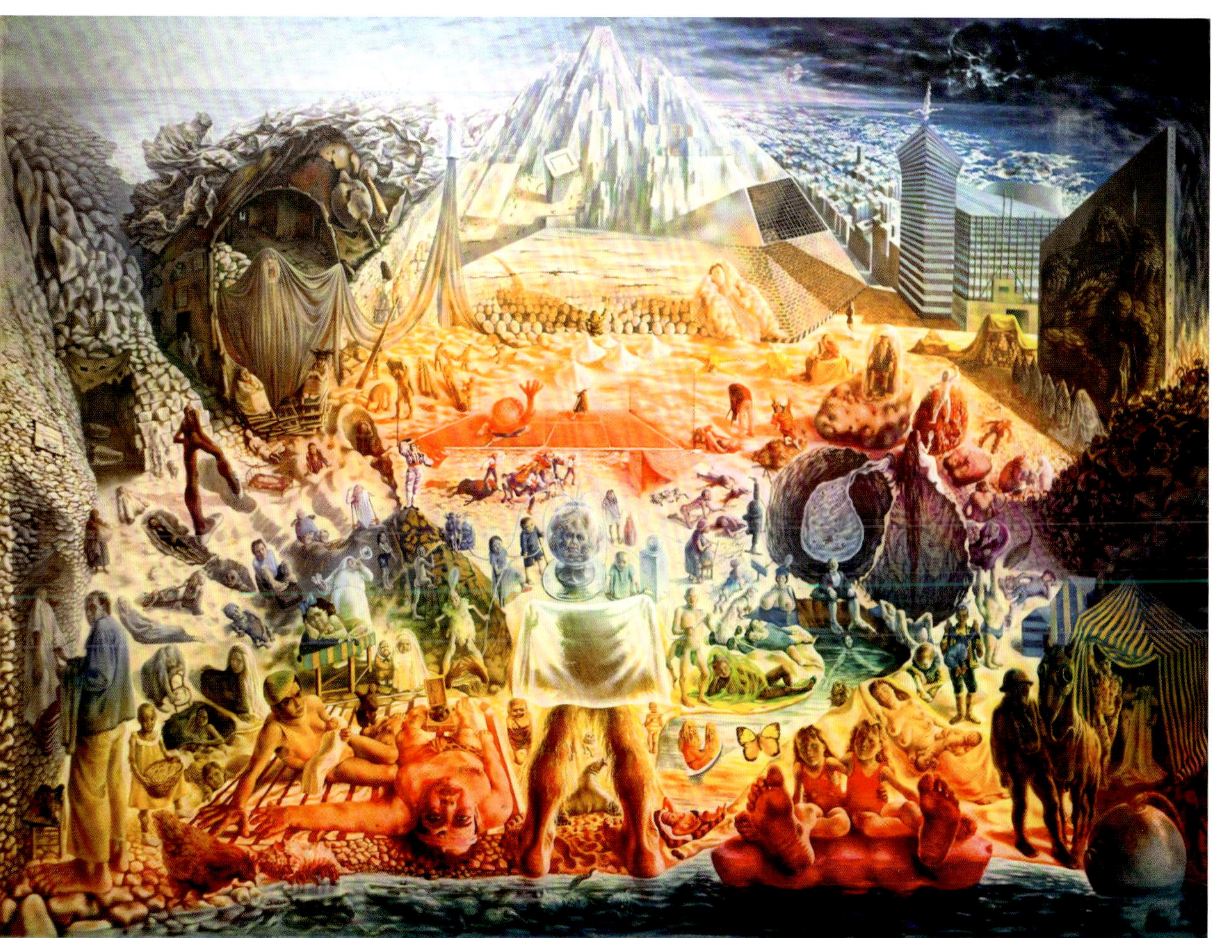

FIG. 3.36 Pavel Tchelitchew, *Phenomena,* 1936–38. Oil on canvas, 79 × 106½ inches. Tretyakov Gallery, Moscow.

and all is malleable: bodies stretch, transform, and flow into trees and flowers to create intricate, organic structures that dissolve divisions among flesh, plant, and paint. In *Phenomena*, Tchelitchew's interest in metamorphosis as a means of breaking normative categorization is evident in his selective application of perspectival illusion (drawn from the painter's intensive study of Paolo Uccello), which swells the figures' bottom limbs and shrinks their upper halves. Despite their distortion, their faces are not caricatures but portraits of Tchelitchew's closest friends, an inclusion he described as an act of affection rather than mockery. As he wrote to Julien Levy, "My dear friends are freaks. And freaks are beautiful people."[99]

Like Michelangelo's *Last Judgment* (fig. 3.37), the picture is divided into two halves by the imprint of the artist's right palm print at left and his footprint at right, reversing the earlier painting's latinate associations of *dexter* and *sinister*. Heaven and hell, saved and damned; *Phenomena* at once traffics in and scrambles their connotations. The rainbow hues overlaying the picture, which Tchelitchew pushed to their highest chromatic key to render them "poison," unite the scene of freaks into a coherent whole. Similarly, his use of perspectival illusionism at once distorts their bodies and places them within a single landscape. Here is "the irrational plus architecture." The world of *Phenomena* is neither heaven nor hell but a world in which the hard distinctions between these realms break down. Here, the denizens of the cultural margins congregate and populate, live and die. Their "freakishness" is no longer distinctive in a world where everything is subject to distortion. This idea is also at the heart of *View*'s

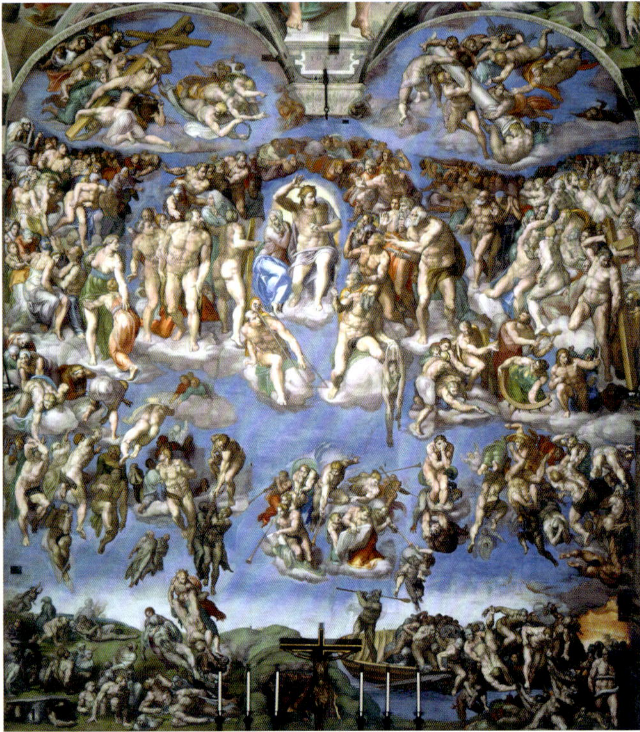

FIG. 3.37 Michelangelo, *The Last Judgment*, 1536–41. Fresco, 45 × 40 feet. Sistine Chapel, Vatican City.

queer mythopoeia: the invention of a world in which erotic desire is central rather than marginal, where fantastic elements of myth need not be opposed to the real but offer a different, exquisite view of it. As Tchelitchew's painting suggests, this mythic realm is no utopia, for there is no respite from the gas mask–clad man and horse at bottom right, signaling the looming Fascist threat. Rather, this is the world where we all live, but that only some have the special sight to perceive.

Yet at this historical moment, the efflorescence of myth was accompanied by a mounting awareness of its dangers. The overt colonialism of de Bry's source image seeps into Cornell's design, which includes two photographs of the Hunkpapa Lakota holy man Sitting Bull at the falls' base. Excised from his historical context and made to stand in for the generalized Indigenous figures that dot nineteenth-century paintings of Niagara Falls, his presence embodies the violence of universalism, of the Western colonial desire to abstract specific bodies and histories into mythology. Similarly, Tyler's choice to illustrate his article with a reproduction of a woodcut *blemmyes*, or headless man, uses a racialized figure to stand for all those relegated to the margins of society. As classics scholar Walter D. Ward has noted, the *blemmyes* was first associated in Greco-Roman texts with either Ethiopia or Egypt. Although their precise geographical origin was contested, "[w]hat is not ambiguous," Ward writes, "is the image of these groups as barbarians and the consistency of denunciations against them."[100] By the medieval period, *blemmyes* were symbols of faraway places. De Bry used the figure to represent the Americas in his map of Guiana, printed in his 1595 *The Discoverie of the Large, Rich and Beautiful Empire of Guiana, with a Relation of the Great and Golden Citie of Manoa (Which the Spaniards call El Dorado), and the Provinces of Emeria, Arromaia, Amapaia, and other Countries, with Their Rivers Adjoyning*, whose lengthy title outlines the general narrative of the book (fig. 3.38).[101] The marginalization of white queer men in early-twentieth-century New York was all too real, but in no way equivalent to the violence enacted by

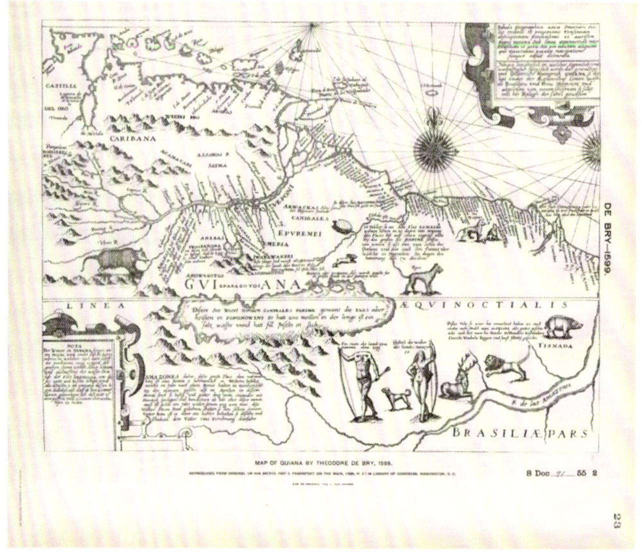

FIG. 3.38 Theodor de Bry, *Maps of the Orinoco-Essequibo Region, South America. Compiled for the Commission Appointed by the United States "To Investigate and Report upon the True Divisional Line between the Republic of Venezuela and British Guiana,"* 1599 (1897 facsimile). Lithograph, 13¾ × 16⅛ inches. David Rumsey Map Center, Stanford, CA.

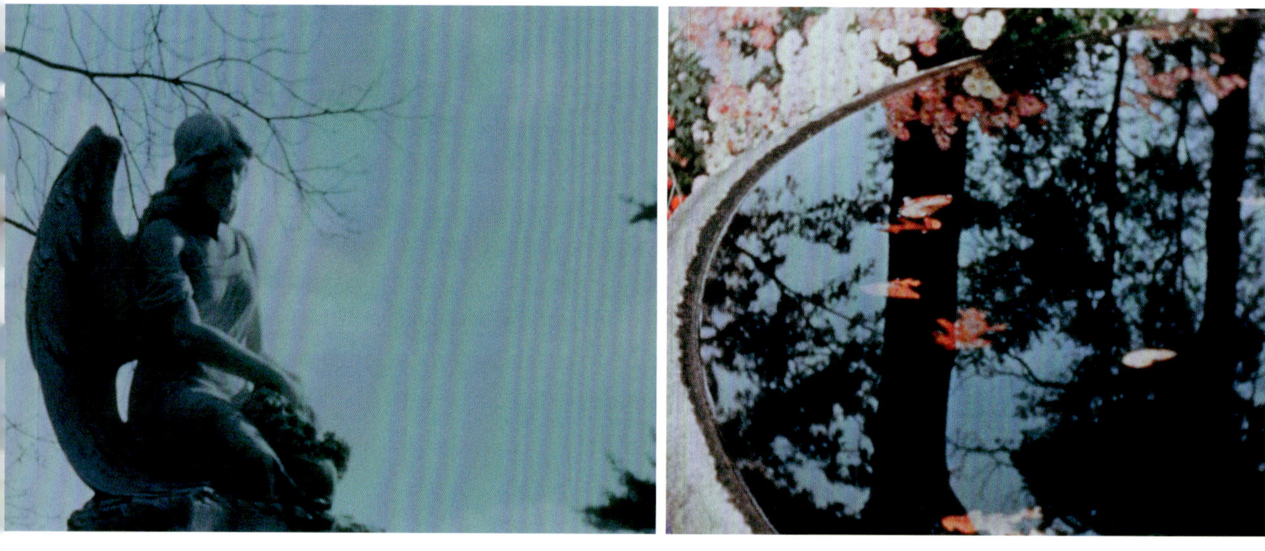

FIG. 3.39 Film still from *Angel* (Joseph Cornell, 1957). Austrian Film Museum.

FIG. 3.40 Film still from *Angel*, showing water from the fountain with flowers reflected.

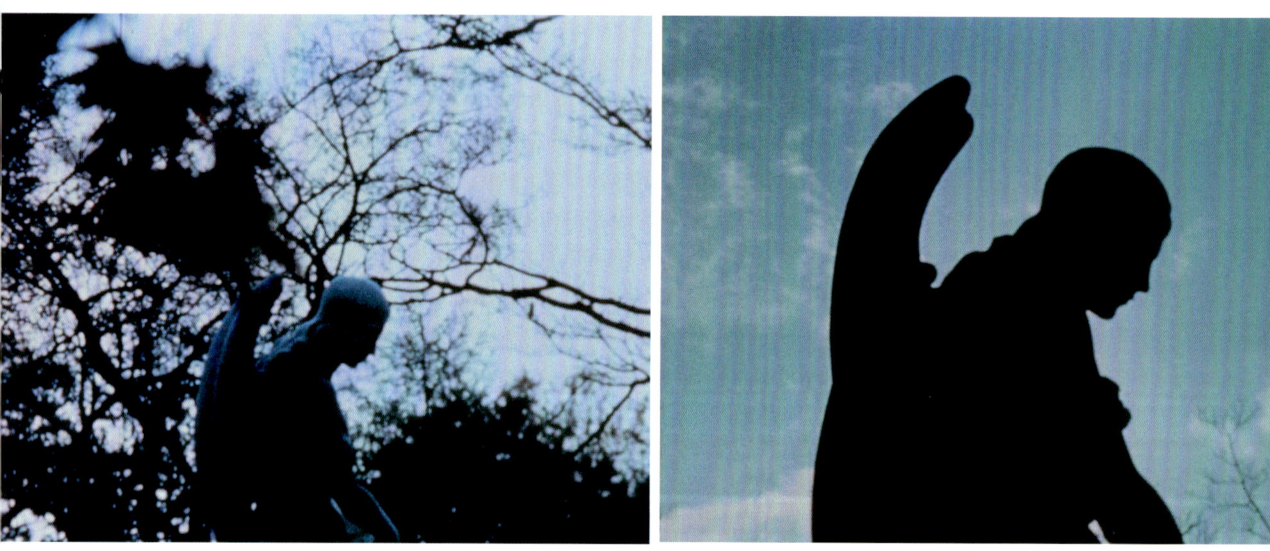

FIG. 3.41 Film still from *Angel*, showing side view of the statue.

FIG. 3.42 Film still from *Angel*, showing silhouetted statue.

best when they're statuary. They commemorate death but they suggest a world without dying. They are made of the heaviest things on earth, stone and iron, they weigh tons but they're winged, they are engines and instruments of flight."[116]

Death was on Cornell's mind as he composed his own angel. When Tchelitchew passed away in 1957, Cornell sent Ford a tender condolence letter. "Believe me," hc wrote in apology for the tardiness of the note, "hardly a week has gone by but I've been searching for the right words to adequately express my sympathies to you."[117] He continued, "Just recently I asked someone to take an especially moving color movie of an angel and fountain nearby and in spirit at least it is dedicated to Pavlik [Tchelitchew]."[118] Here, film expressed what words could not.

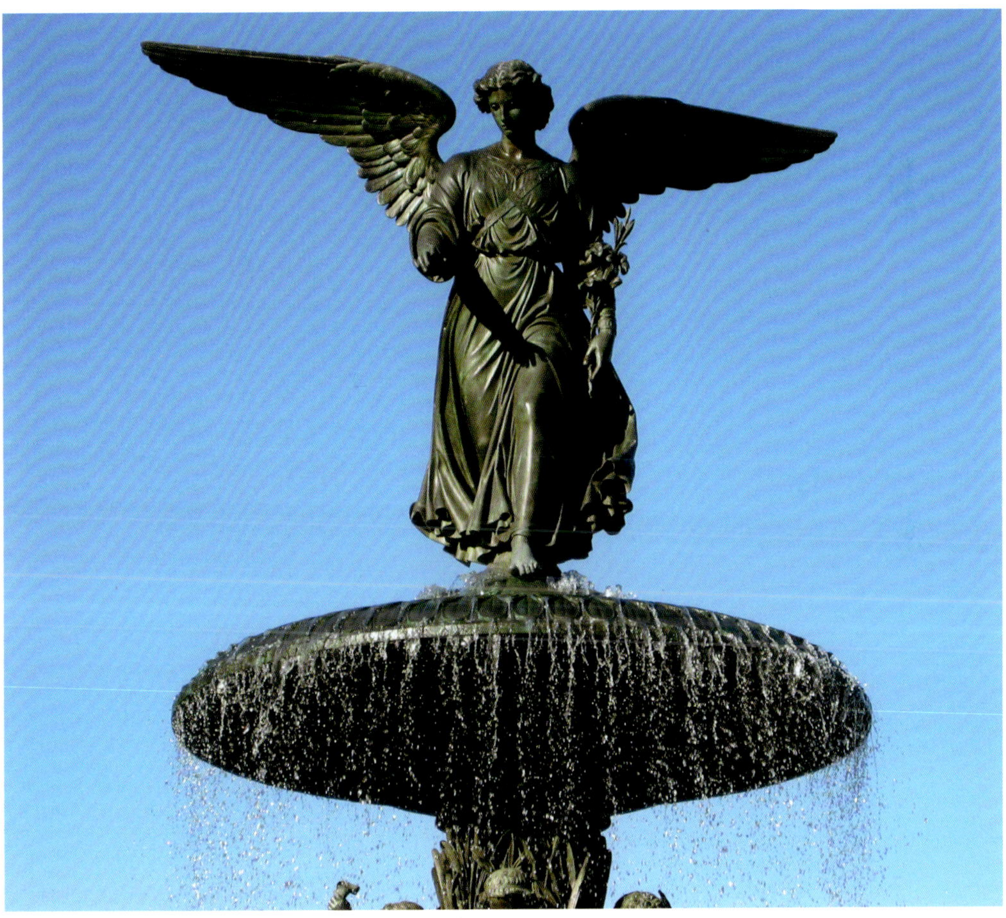

FIG. 3.43 Emma Stebbins, *Angel of the Waters (Bethesda Fountain)*, 1859–64. Bronze, 25 × 15 feet. Central Park, New York City.

CHAPTER FOUR

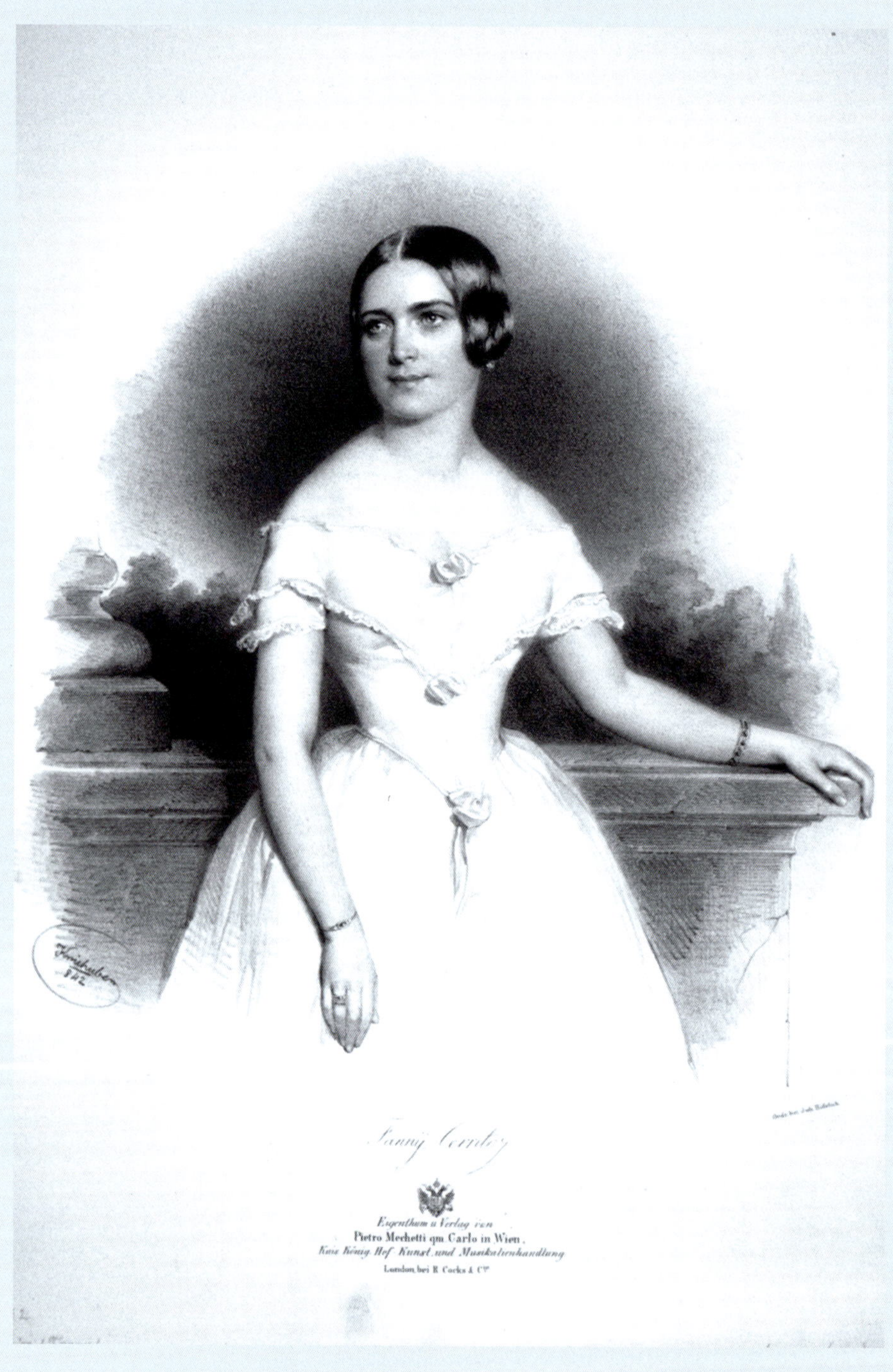

FIG. 4.1 Josef Kriehuber, *Fanny Cerrito*, 1842. Lithograph.

Enchantresses

Cordelia
(Aside) What shall Cordelia speak?
Love, and be silent.

William Shakespeare, *King Lear*

It was one of those late summer afternoons New Yorkers know well. The air was hot and thick, dense with an invisible moisture that clings to the skin. On this "sultry and monotonous" afternoon in 1940, Joseph Cornell once again took to the Fourth Avenue bookstalls in search of source material.[1] Yellow paper crumbled beneath his fingertips as he browsed the prints crammed into boxes. Suddenly, he stopped.

Perhaps he was arrested by her eyes (fig.4.1). Looking out from beneath a straight brow and a crown of center-parted hair, her gaze is at once distant and direct. These eyes belong to Fanny Cerrito, the famed Romantic ballet dancer who graced the stages of Milan, Paris, and London during the 1840s.[2] Unlike contemporaneous prints of Cerrito (fig. 4.2), this 1848 image by Austrian printmaker Josef Kriehuber pictures her as a woman rather than a performer.[3] Clad in a simple white dress trimmed with delicate satin rosettes, she stands with one arm casually draped over the wall behind her. Washes of gray and black capture the delicacy of her features, the satiny shine of her hair, the supple grace of her arms. The verisimilitude of these details contrasts with the dark trees in the distance, an impressionistic mass that seems to exhale a dark vapor, forming a shadowy halo behind her head. In a 1944 letter to poet Marianne Moore, Cornell described his initial encounter with Kriehuber's print as akin

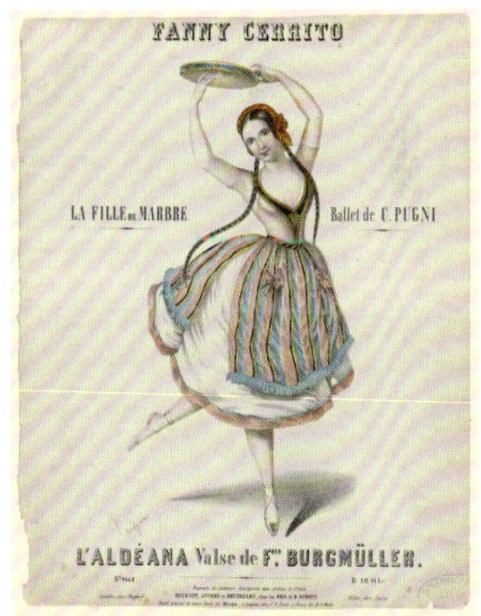

FIG. 4.2 *Fanny Cerrito, La fille de marbre. Ballet de C. Pugni*, ca. 1840–50. Colored lithograph, 10 1/8 × 5 1/16 inches. Jerome Robbins Dance Collection, New York Public Library.

to meeting Cerrito in the flesh: "A ballerina of the eighteen forties came to life for me about four years ago with such a complete vividness and unspeaking grace that I have since been collecting romantic material."[4]

Cornell shared his admiration for Cerrito with nineteenth-century critic Théophile Gautier. As Gautier wrote of the dancer, "There are moments when she recalls Canova's statue of Psyche leaning over Cupid; her white muslin skirt gives the illusion of white marble, and certainly no sculptor ever fashioned out of Paris or Carrara marble arms more supple, more caressing or more beautifully moulded."[5] Seeing Cerrito dance, Gautier felt the distinctions between marble, fabric, and flesh dissolve before his eyes. At this moment, sculpture came to life; dancer became animate sculpture. Cornell described his encounter with Cerrito in similar terms: "[The] portrait brought me face to face with the radiant and starry-eyed ballerina bringing the fair Italian disturbingly to life."[6] Both descriptions grant Cerrito the power to bring art "to life." The grace of her dancing and intensity of her dancing blur the boundaries among sculpture, print, and body.

Cornell was devoted to enchantresses. Among his most frequent subjects are women bestowed with creative power: ballet dancers, movie stars, opera singers, artists. Cornell's enchantresses *transgress boundaries*. They slip the earthly tethers of the bodies, flutter across stages and pages, and traverse oceans of time and space. The artist was not alone in granting women this power. As art historian Mary D. Sheriff has discussed, in eighteenth-century France, enchantresses were imbued with the power to cross both physical and moral borders. "In what was considered the 'natural' course of events," she writes, "a woman was defeated and a man victorious when he overcame her modesty, and here her resistance to sexual adventure. The enchantress, however, reversed this dynamic, for she captivated and captured a hero who fell prey to her physical charms and the magical arts."[7] By bewitching the male hero, the enchantress reverses the normative power structure of heterosexual conquest. Yet as Sheriff shows, this power was a double-edged sword: the enchantress at once challenged gender norms and upheld conventional sexual mores, casting desire as an occult power and women who wielded it as unnatural. The figure of the enchantress, like enchantment itself, can be put to a variety of uses.

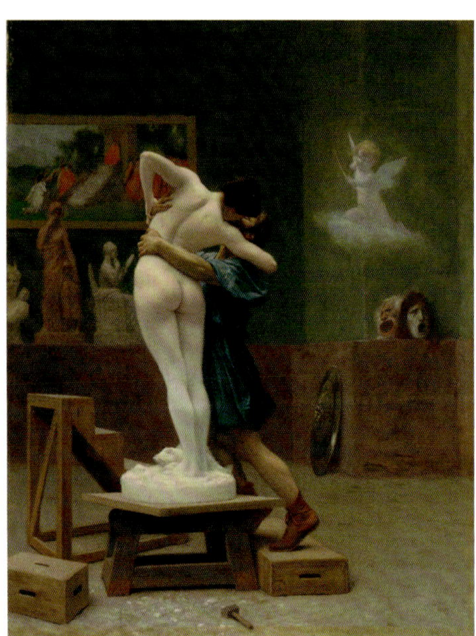

FIG. 4.3 Jean-Léon Gérôme, *Pygmalion and Galatea*, ca. 1890. Oil on canvas, 35 × 27 inches. Metropolitan Museum of Art, New York, gift of Louis C. Raegner.

Gender and desire are at the heart of Cornell's work. Sophisticated studies by Jodi Hauptman and Michael Moon have discussed this in terms of the complex workings of desire, alternately describing his practice as withholding or evoking the female body.[8] Their scholarship usefully pushes back against the idea of Cornell as "objectifying" women by "trapping" them in boxes or collages.[9] This chapter builds on their studies to consider the complex interchanges of power among Cornell and the enchantresses who were his most cherished subjects. As David Morgan has discussed, heterosexual desire is often equated with enchantment, the erotic aura of a woman seeming to exert a spell over the minds and bodies of supposedly rational men.[10] The ur-myth of enchantment and desire is the story of Pygmalion and Galatea, the sculptor who falls so deeply in love with his own creation that Venus grants her life (fig. 4.3).[11] The gendered dynamics of this story are clear: Galatea is at once created and animated by Pygmalion's desire; she remains an object even as she is brought to life. By contrast, Cornell's enchantresses do not rely on him for their power. For him, they are akin instead to the goddess who animated Galatea, residing on Mount Olympus and only occasionally deigning to bestow her grace on the mortals below.

The figure of the enchantress offered Cornell a means of mediating the tension between ideal and real that characterizes his work. With her earthly form and supernatural power, the enchantress is at once of and not of this world. As she changes form, her body is both the source of enchantment and that which must be transcended to achieve it. Yet idealization is also a form of objectification. Idealization's violence is its transformation of women into abstracted renderings of the artist's vision, no matter how vaunted. To this point, Cornell's veneration of enchantresses contrasted with his experiences of real women, many of whom understandably bristled at being turned into an image, no matter how powerful. Cornell's enchantresses render stark the tension between his idealized worldview and the vicissitudes of the real world. In them, enchantment's entanglement of beauty, frustration, and violence comes sharply into view.

FIXING BALLET

Portrait of Ondine (1940–72, fig. 4.4), is Cornell's attempt to transform his discovery of Kriehuber's print into a single work of art. Named after the dancer's most famous role, the water sprite Ondine of the 1843 ballet *Ondine, ou la Naïde,* the unfinished portfolio holds Kriehuber's Cerrito print as well as reproductions of paintings, prints, photographs, and excerpts from nineteenth-century sources. Cornell selected each component for its connection to Cerrito's biography.[12] Photographs of London and Naples show the cities where Cerrito debuted as Ondine, and the dancer's birthplace while a work by Italian painter Giorgio de Chirico, labeled "Toys of a Prince," and a nineteenth-century engraving of Bologna refer to the dancer's Italian heritage (figs. 4.5, 4.6).[13] Like all of Cornell's work, *Portrait of Ondine* relies on the artist's deep historical research for its associative, imaginative connections. Below the image of Bologna, for example, the artist's caption imagines the engraving's creation as contemporaneous with Cerrito's birth (fig. 4.7).[14] Cornell envisioned the completed work as a widely disseminated publication, writing of the project in the aforementioned letter to Marianne Moore, "I have already given it more thought than anything I have ever worked on."[15]

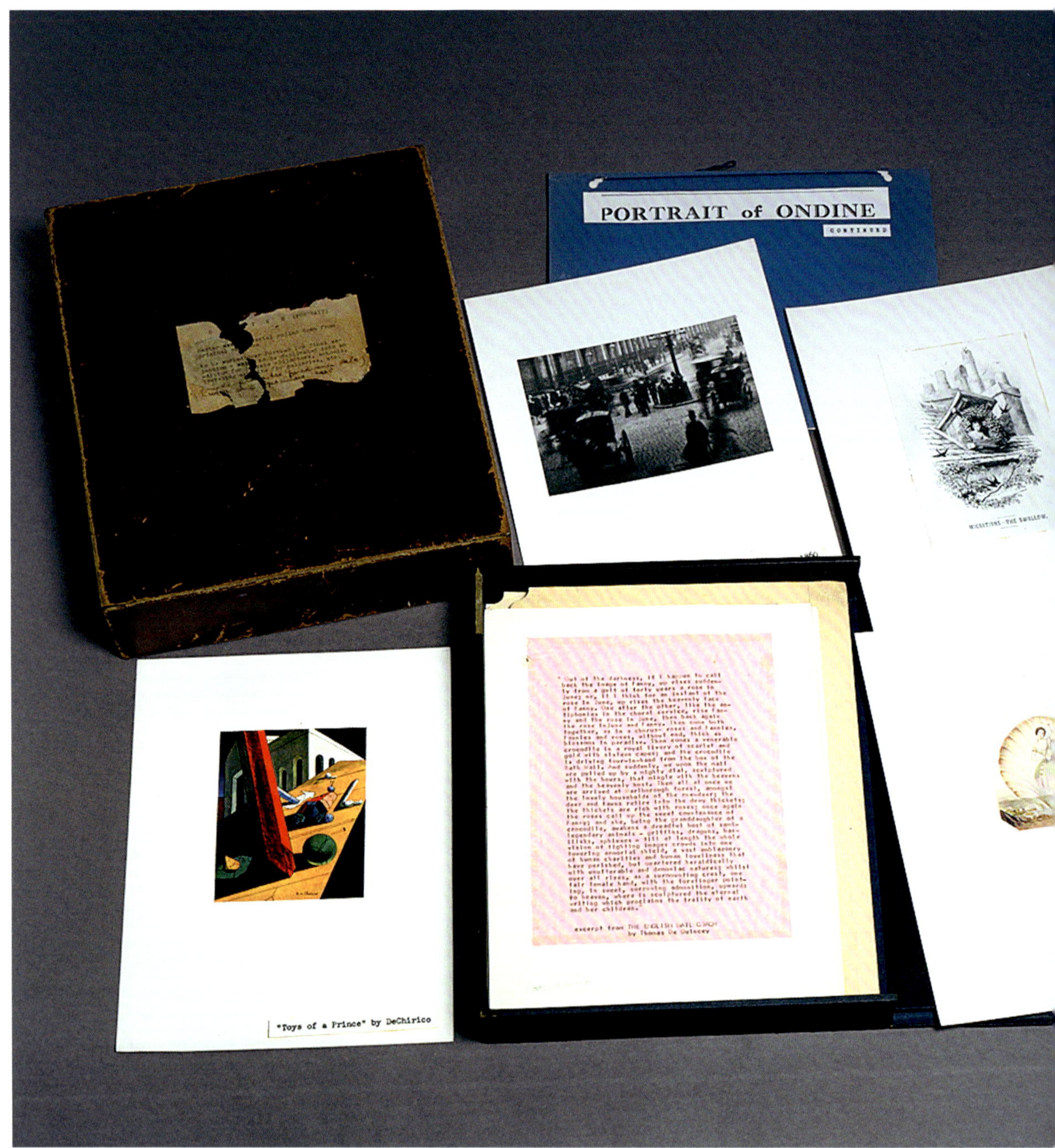

FIG. 4.4 Joseph Cornell, *Portrait of Ondine*, 1940. Mixed media: paperboard, cardboard, paint, prints, maps, 2 1/2 × 10 3/4 × 12 3/4 inches. Smithsonian American Art Museum, Washington, DC, gift of the Robert and Joseph Cornell Foundation.

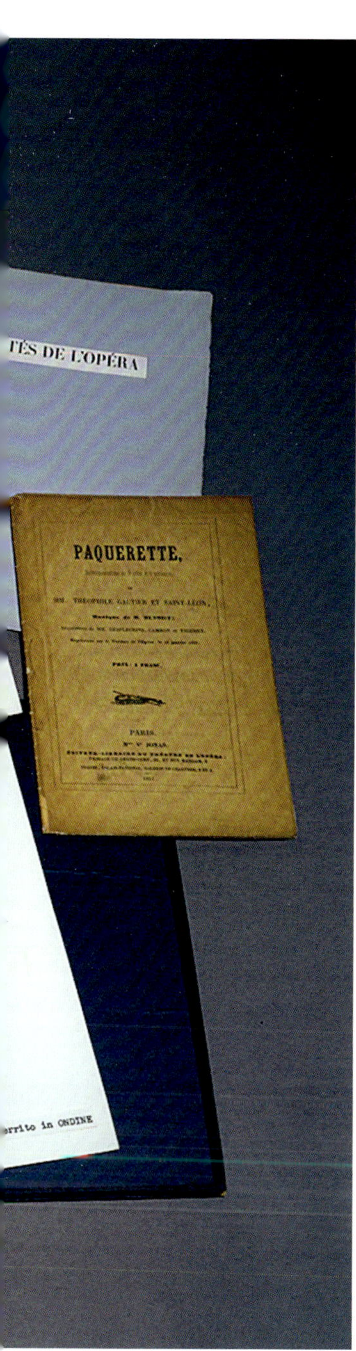

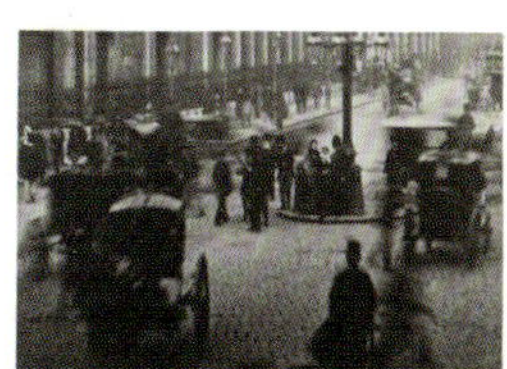

FIG. 4.5 Detail of Joseph Cornell, *Portrait of Ondine*, showing a photograph of London, ca. 1860.

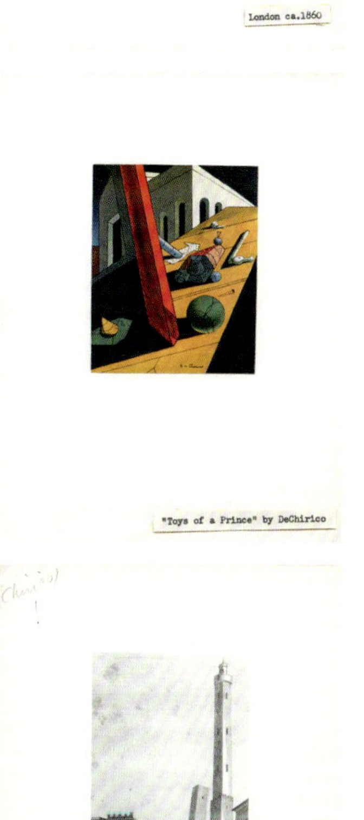

FIG. 4.6 Detail of Joseph Cornell, *Portrait of Ondine*, showing a reproduction of a painting by Giorgio de Chirico, 1914, labeled "Toys of a Prince."

FIG. 4.7 Detail of Joseph Cornell, *Portrait of Ondine*, showing a line engraving with caption: "Bologna—line engraving done approx. the time of Cerrito's birth."

Given the artist's investment in *Portrait of Ondine*, why did it remain unfinished? To answer this question requires a deeper understanding of Cornell's ambition for the work and the role of the enchantress within.

Portrait of Ondine was the first of several portfolio works Cornell began during the 1940s. Over the course of his life, Cornell assembled over 150 dossiers of clippings, which were not works of art but rather an organizational system for his vast collections.[16] With portfolio works such as *Portrait of Ondine*, Cornell attempted to transform these dossiers into discrete art objects. He hoped these portfolios would afford the viewer an experience akin to his own in assembling the research dossiers.[17] *GC44*, for example, was intended to encapsulate Cornell's experiences during the summer of 1944, when he worked at the Garden Center nursery in Queens (fig. 4.8). As he explained in a note about the portfolio, he hoped the format would "exercise a method [that] may be worked out for the recording of other past experiences seemingly insignificant." He continued, "GC 44 realized successfully can become a 'method' for crystalizing

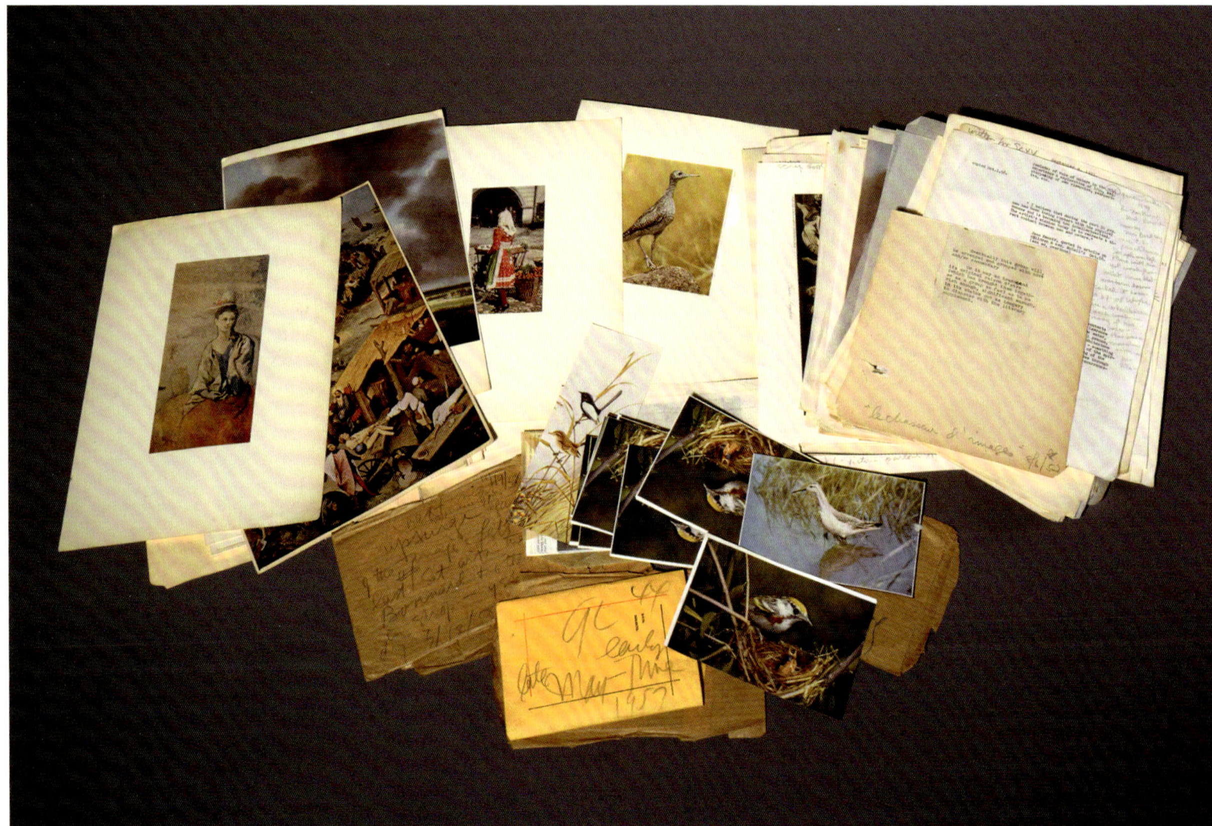

FIG. 4.8 Joseph Cornell, *GC44*, 1944–72. Paper folder, paper bags, and envelopes with mounted and loose photomechanical reproductions, photographs, postcards, and notes, 3½ × 9½ × 11 inches, when closed. Joseph Cornell Study Center, Smithsonian American Art Museum, Washington, DC.

experiences of the above sort never before considered."[18] By consolidating ephemeral and previously unconsidered experiences into a single archive, Cornell hoped to preserve and communicate the enchantment of these "seemingly insignificant" moments to others.

The success of these works therefore hinged on the experience of the viewer. In a letter to curator Jermaine MacAgy, Cornell described *Portrait of Ondine* as "depend[ing] upon an imaginative collaboration with the other and in its present form."[19] One might describe Cornell's portfolios as attempts to create epiphanic moments for their viewers. As literary scholar Sharon Kim has discussed, the term "epiphany" derives from the Greek *epiphaneia*, meaning "a coming into light" or "view." Its Greek root *phaneia* is also the root of *phantasia*, or "fantasy." Such fantasies are not simply escapist reveries but revelations of a deeper truth, a specifically Christian experience of what Kim describes as "full presence . . . a charged fullness of being, a saturation of being."[20] Epiphanies are moments of enchantment whose significance resides in their revelation of divine presence. With *Portrait of Ondine*, Cornell attempted to create the conditions for an epiphany modeled on his experience of Kriehuber's print. Just as Cerrito came "disturbingly to life" at the moment Cornell beheld her image, *Portrait of Ondine* was created to "exhale a 'romantic vapor' . . . ," evoking a sense of the dancer's presence.[21]

Cornell drew on several sources when selecting the portfolio as the vehicle for this epiphanic moment. The first was the logic of Romantic ballet itself, and specifically *Ondine, ou la Naïde*.[22] This performance allegorizes Romantic ballet's transformation of female bodies through the figure of the enchantress Ondine. Over the course of the ballet, Ondine attempts to win the love of mortal fisherman Matteo by assuming a range of forms: Venus floating on a shell, a vision in a dream, and even Matteo's own fiancée (fig. 4.9). Ondine's power is her ability to change form, to move among water, earth, and dreams. For Cornell, the surprise of finding the Kriehuber print seemed to fit with *Ondine, ou la Naïde*'s story of transformation; it was as if the dancer had slipped her time-bound form to travel, in the guise of print, to twentieth-century New York. The artist connected the ballet and his discovery of the print in a diary entry: "Like the capricious Ondine of her favorite ballet she [Cerrito] seemed once more to have assumed mortal guise," evoking the enchantress's power to change form.[23]

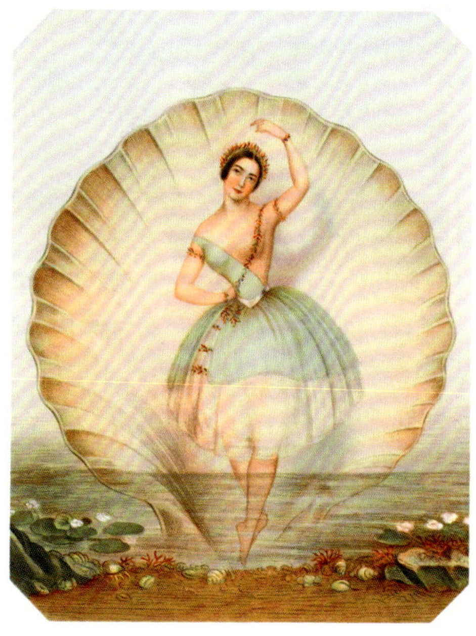

FIG. 4.9 Fanny Cerrito as *Ondine*. Print included in *Portrait of Ondine*.

In Ondine—Cerrito—Cornell found an enchantress endowed with the power to cross borders not just among media but between fact and fiction. The artist deliberately blurred these lines by merging Cerrito and

Boîtes or *Boîte* variants, a task that required him to "assemble the precut cardboard structure of the *Boîte* edition's container with linen tape, ordering the wood sticks that formed the "M" on the lid of the box, and pasting labels and reproductions onto paper folders."[35] A drawing made by Duchamp for Cornell shows a rough sketch of the *Boîte*'s expandable interior frame, labeled with numbers to indicate the placement of each reproduction (fig. 4.13). *Boîte-en-valise*'s reproducibility and portability likely guided Cornell's attempts to transform *Portrait of Ondine* into a single printed booklet. As his close friend Donald Windham recalled, Cornell hoped to produce the work "as cheaply as possible" so it could be sold at "five-and-ten-cent stores."[36] Rather than the luxurious and expensive *pochoir* and collotype printing that ensured the precise chromatic fidelity of Duchamp's reproductions, Cornell planned instead to render *Portrait of Ondine* in what the artist described as the "humble garb" of black-and-white print, allowing him to price the work for far less than Duchamp's $200 *Boîte*.[37] In this, Cornell went further in challenging the conventions of fine art than even the Dadaist, whose *Boîte-en-valise* was first displayed and sold at Peggy Guggenheim's chic Art of This Century gallery.

Cornell's work on *Boîte-en-valise* coincided with his struggles to finish *Portrait of Ondine*, as well as his employment at Allied Control Company in Long Island City.[38] Just a year before Pearl Harbor, Cornell quit his despised and underpaid job at Traphagen Textile Studio, assuming that his burgeoning graphic design career would be sufficient to support his family. The tightened wartime economy pushed Cornell to return to work, and in 1943 he began a ten-month stint assembling radio controls at Allied Control, hoping, as his sister recalled, to "contribute to the war effort."[39] The year Cornell arrived at Allied Control, the company employed 270 workers who manufactured electric switches, power relays, and circuit breakers.[40] Period advertisements offer a clue to the types of objects Cornell assembled at the factory. In one (fig. 4.14), a relay designed for aircraft use is pictured in a transparent case, revealing the intricate coils and wires within, calling to mind the erotic mechanical figures of Duchamp's *Large Glass* (fig. 4.15). While both the factory work and *Boîte-en-valise* required manual dexterity and intricate assembly, Cornell experienced a

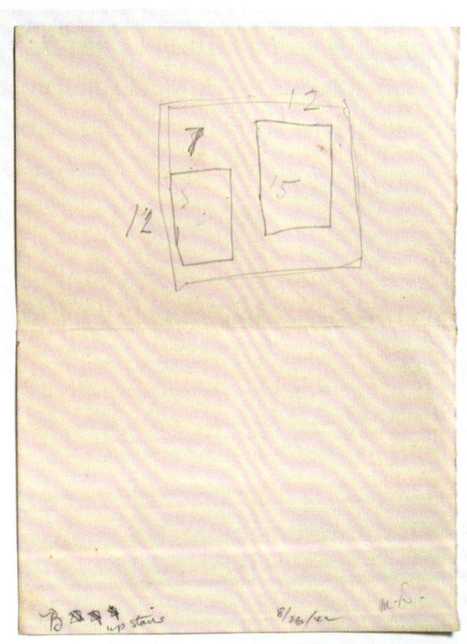

FIG. 4.13 Drawing by Marcel Duchamp, included in Joseph Cornell, *Untitled*, ca. 1942–53. Ephemera and objects contained in the Duchamp Dossier, 14¼ × 12⅝ × 3⅛ inches. Philadelphia Museum of Art, gift of the Robert and Joseph Cornell Foundation, 1990-33-1(72).

sharp distinction between Allied Control and the rarified world represented by Duchamp and Art of This Century, and his time at Allied Control. Cornell admired Duchamp, and the feeling was apparently mutual. Not only did Duchamp own several works by Cornell, at the outset of their collaboration he gave Cornell a box of LePage's glue, Cornell's favored adhesive, altered to read "gimme strength," as if to acknowledge the painstaking manual labor required by the project (fig. 4.16).[41] By contrast, the artist despised his job at Allied Control, describing in his notes the factory's "inferno like nature of the soldering table."[42]

Cornell's female coworkers provided his only solace during his hours at the factory. In another diary entry, he describes the "beautiful feeling of seeing [women] enjoy themselves talking looking bright + fresh after day's work," as a "compensation" for the "aggressive thoughts of being dissatisfied with work + place."[43] Cornell made several attempts to

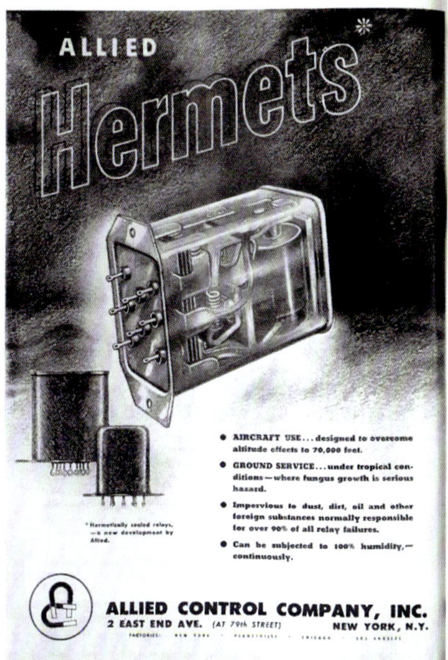

FIG. 4.14 Allied Control Company, advertisement for "Hermets" relays, *Electronics* magazine, September 1944.

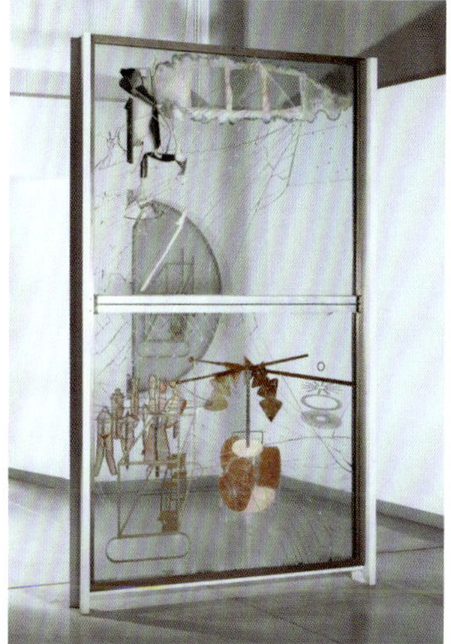

FIG. 4.15 Marcel Duchamp, *The Bride Stripped Bare by Her Bachelors, Even (The Large Glass)*, 1915–23. Oil, varnish, lead foil, lead wire, and dust on two glass panels. 9 ft., 1¼ inches. × 70 inches. × 3⅜ inches. Philadelphia Museum of Art: Bequest of Katherine S. Dreier, 1952-98-1.

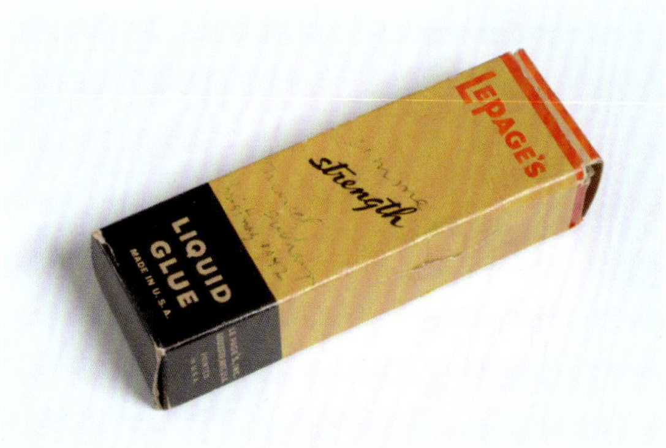

FIG. 4.16 Glue box inscribed "gimme [strength], Marcel Duchamp Christmas 1942," from Joseph Cornell, *Untitled*, ca. 1942–53. Ephemera and objects contained in the Duchamp Dossier, 14¼ × 12⅝ × 3⅛ inches. Philadelphia Museum of Art, gift of the Robert and Joseph Cornell Foundation.

communicate with these women, at one point even contemplating "mak[ing] a velvet box to carry around–floral arrangements" to bring to the factory.[44] Such efforts seem to have failed. In a note written on Allied Control ephemera, the artist agonized that the "signif. of my method notes + docs of summary lost in the past to others etc."[45] If the artist hoped to communicate his experiences of enchantment to his fellow workers, here he laments his failure to do so. To this point, Windham recalled that during this period Cornell "would telephone and tell me, with pauses, how depressed he was because he could not capture and preserve some experience that had been, he felt, full of rare sensations, 'thick enough,' he would say, 'to cut with a knife.' "[46] No matter how vividly real enchantment was for the artist, it remained "lost in the past" for others. Cornell's time at Allied Control thus highlighted the gap between his enchantment and the harsh realities of work in an wartime factory. Even the women he venerated, whose presence seemed to represent his most cherished ideals, did not understand him. Pressed into work by the necessities of the war, these women had more urgent matters to attend to.

Cornell exhibited *Portrait of Ondine* on three separate occasions: in a special Dance Archives–related exhibition at MoMA in 1945, in his *Romantic Museum* exhibition at Hugo Gallery in 1946, and at the Wittenborn Bookstore in 1956.[47] Each time, he hoped the exhibition would serve as a prelude to a finished version, even drawing up a list of possible recipients for the unrealized publication of *Portrait of Ondine*.[48] Each time, he could not bring himself to complete the work. His unsuccessful 1945 application for a Guggenheim grant to work on the portfolios suggests one possible reason. As he wrote, "My ultimate purpose as a scholar and artist is in the exploration of the possibilities of my work in general, and in particular in making available to as many as possible the beauty and knowledge of the monograph albums."[49] Yet as his experiences at Allied Control suggest, the artist's enchantment—the deeply felt "beauty and knowledge" of his subjects—was ultimately a personal experience. It was not so easily communicated to others. In his decades of ministrations over *Portrait of Ondine*, one glimpses the unruly and expansive nature of experience, its unwillingness to be condensed into a single narrative. As Cornell later wrote, "At first the material was gathered in the same spirit as one hoards souvenirs of every description of an especially precious journey—eventually to realize the subjective nature of the experience & consequent bric-a-brac of such englamoured objects."[50]

SOUND AND SILENCE

Although Cornell never completed *Portrait of Ondine*, he continued to engage with enchantresses in subsequent works. *"Enchanted Wanderer": Excerpt from a Journey Album for Hedy Lamarr* appeared in the December 1941–January 1942 issue of *View* (fig. 4.17). The single-page layout features an image of Lamarr, which the artist described as a "Quattrocento Montage portrait."[51] The actress's face glows against the inky darkness of the composition, atop the body of an unidentified old master painter whose self-portrait forms the montage's base. Just as this montage bridges the distance between painting and photograph, old master artist and contemporary film star, Cornell's accompanying text describes Lamarr as

View Page 3

"ENCHANTED WANDERER"

★ Excerpt from a Journey Album for Hedy Lamarr ★

By

JOSEPH CORNELL

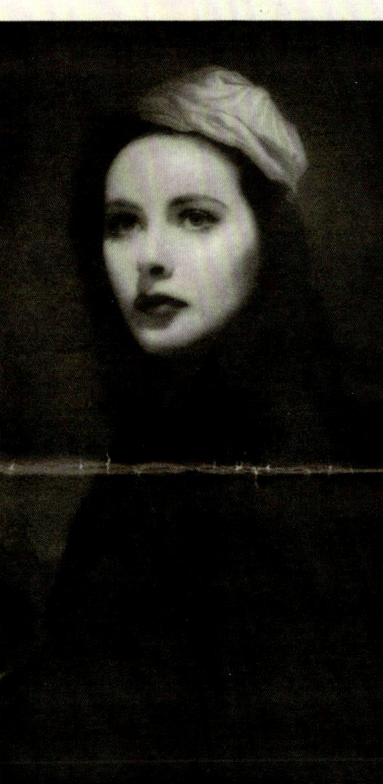

Among the barren wastes of the talking films there occasionally occur passages to remind one again of the profound and suggestive power of the silent film to evoke an ideal world of beauty, to release unsuspected floods of music from the gaze of a human countenance in its prison of silver light. But aside from evanescent fragments unexpectedly encountered, how often is there created a superb and magnificent imagery such as brought to life the portraits of Falconetti in "Joan of Arc," Lillian Gish in "Broken Blossoms," Sibirskaya in "Menilmontant," and Carola Nehrer in "Dreigroschenoper?"

And so we are grateful to Hedy Lamarr, the enchanted wanderer, who again speaks the poetic and evocative language of the silent film, if only in whispers at times, beside the empty roar of the sound track. Amongst screw-ball comedy and the most superficial brand of clap-trap drama she yet manages to retain a depth and dignity that enables her to enter this world of expressive silence.

Who has not observed in her magnified visage qualities of a gracious humility and spirituality that with circumstance of costume, scene, or plot conspire to identify her with realms of wonder, more absorbing than the artificial ones, and where we have already been invited by the gaze that she knew as a child.

Her least successful roles will reveal something unique and intriguing — a disarming candor, a naivete, an innocence, a desire to please, touching in its sincerity. In implicit trust she would follow in whatsoever direction the least humble of her audience would desire.

*"She will walk only when not bid to, arising from her bed of nothing, her hair of time falling to the shoulder of space. If she speak, and she will only speak if not spoken to, she will have learned her words yesterday and she will forget them to-morrow, if to-morrow come, for it may not."**

(Or the contrasted and virile mood of "Comrade X" where she moves through the scenes like the wind with a storm-swept beauty fearful to behold).

* * * * * * * * *

At the end of "Come Live With Me" the picture suddenly becomes luminously beautiful and imaginative with its nocturnal atmosphere and incandescence of fireflies, flashlights, and an aura of tone as rich as the silver screen can yield. Her arms and shoulders always covered, our gaze is held to her features, where her eyes glow dark against the pale skin and her earrings gleam white against the black hair. Her tenderness finds a counterpart in the summer night. In a world of shadow and subdued light she moves, clothed in a white silk robe trimmed with dark fur, against dim white walls. Through the window fireflies are seen in the distance twinkling in woods and pasture. There is a long shot (as from the ceiling) of her enfolded in white covers, her eyes glisten in the semi-darkness like the fireflies. The reclining form of Snow White was not protected more lovingly by her crystal case than the gentle fabric of light that surrounds her. A closer shot shows her against the whiteness of the pillows, while a still closer one shows an expression of ineffable tenderness as, for purposes of plot, she presses and intermittently lights a flashlight against her cheek, as though her features were revealed by slow-motion lightning.

In these scenes it is as though the camera had been presided over by so many apprentices of Caravaggio and Georges de la Tour to create for her this benevolent chiaroscuro . . . the studio props fade out and there remains a drama of light of the *tenebroso* painters . . . the thick night of Caravaggio dissolves into a tenderer, more star-lit night of the Nativity . . . she will become enveloped in the warmer shadows of Rembrandt . . . a youth of Giorgione will move through a drama evolved from the musical images of "Also Sprach Zarathustra" of Strauss, from the opening sunburst of sound through the subterranean passages into the lyrical soaring of the theme (apotheosis of compassion) and into the mystical night . . . the thunderous procession of the festival clouds of Debussy passes . . . the crusader of "Comrade X" becomes the "Man in Armor" of Carpaccio . . . in the half lights of a prison dungeon she lies broken in spirit upon her improvised bed of straw, a hand guarding her tear-stained features . . . the bitter heartbreak gives place to a radiance of expression that lights up her gloomy surroundings . . . she has carried a masculine name in one picture, worn masculine garb in another, and with her hair worn shoulder length and gentle features like those portraits of Renaissance youths she has slipped effortlessly into the role of a painter herself . . . le chasseur d'images . . . out of the fullness of the heart the eyes speak . . . are alert as the eye of the camera to ensnare the subtleties and legendary loveliness of her world. . . .

[The title of this piece is borrowed from a biography of Carl Maria von Weber who wrote in the horn quartet of the overture to "Der Freischutz" a musical signature of the Enchanted Wanderer.]

* Parker Tyler

FIG. 4.17 *"Enchanted Wanderer": Excerpt from a Journey Album for Hedy Lamarr*, 1941. Photomontage with text by Joseph Cornell, *View* 1, nos. 9–10 (December 1941–January 1942): 3. Joseph Cornell Study Center, Smithsonian American Art Museum, Washington, DC.

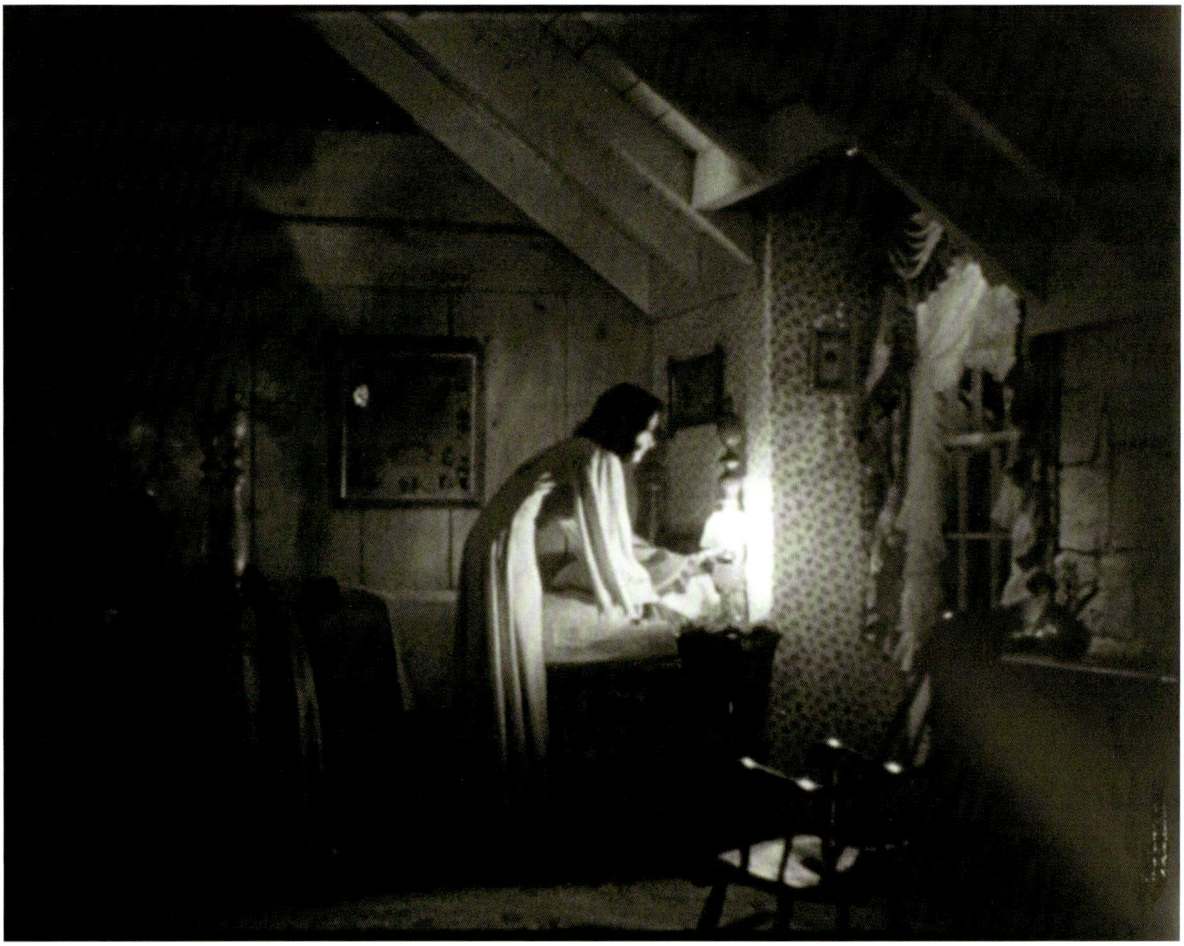

FIG. 4.21 Film still from *Come Live with Me* (Clarence Brown, 1941), showing Hedy Lamarr turning off the lamp. Austrian Film Museum.

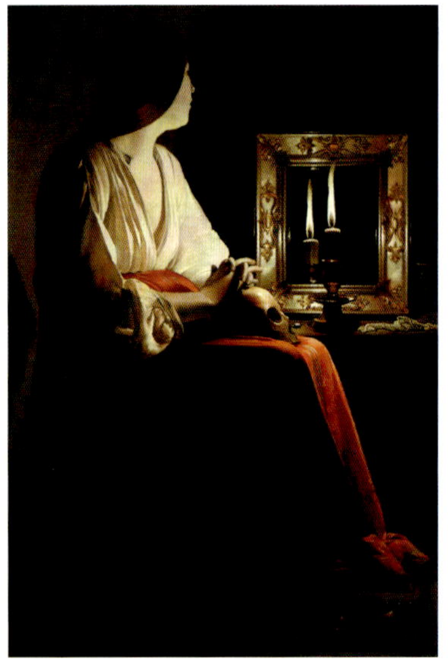

FIG. 4.22 Georges de La Tour, *The Penitent Magdalen*, ca. 1640. Oil on canvas, 52 ½ × 40 ¼ inches. Metropolitan Museum of Art, New York.

her bedside table. With this, the scene plunges into a dramatic composition of light and shadow (fig. 4.21). "It is as though the camera had been presided over by so many apprentices of Caravaggio and Georges de la Tour to create for her this benevolent chiaroscuro," Cornell writes.[59] Bathed in illumination from the open window and captured in profile, Lamarr becomes the central figure in La Tour's *Penitent Magdalene* (1625–50, fig. 4.22), which Cornell studied at the Met.

For the artist, the true drama of *Come Live with Me* was not its plot but the drama of light itself, embodied by the gentle coronas cast by fireflies outside Lamarr's bedroom window, and the blinking flashlight she uses to signal to Stewart that she has chosen him at the film's end (fig. 4.23). As T. J. Clark has observed, "Painting's muteness gives it a peculiar advantage over the spoken or written word."[60] This insight applies equally to silent film. Color, light, and shadows are *not* language, although they are often taken as such. Although language is often imposed on their muteness, they resist being frozen into a single narrative. Lamarr's gestures communicate in the hieroglyphic language of silent film, defying the cacophony that surrounds her. She would not be controlled. Her presence dissolves boundaries between sound and silence, painting and film, showing the constructed nature of these categories and embodying all that escapes narrative.

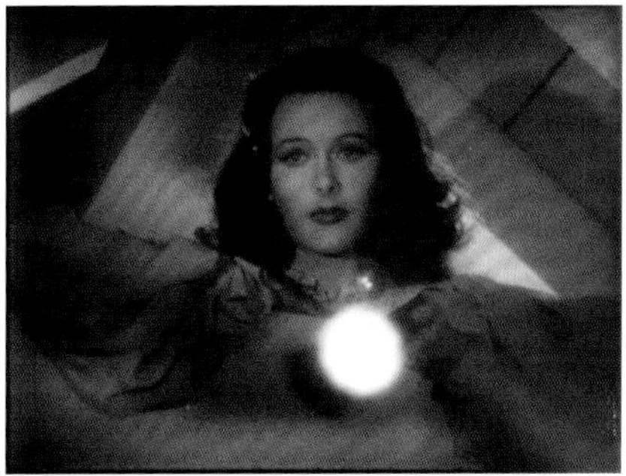

FIG. 4.23 Film still from *Come Live with Me*, showing Hedy Lamarr with a flashlight.

Like Hobart and Cerrito, Cornell's Lamarr also blurs fact and fiction. In *Come Live with Me*, Johnny Jones is an Austrian exile, nodding to Lamarr's own peregrinations through Austria and Germany before arriving in the United States in 1938. In a rhyme with this canny filmic touch, Cornell borrowed the title "Enchanted Wanderer" from a biography of the Austrian-German composer Carl Maria von Weber. Published in 1940, *The Enchanted Wanderer: The Life of Carl Maria von Weber* details the composer's peripatetic movements across Europe in search of opportunities, education, and patronage.[61] In tying the actress's life to that of a male composer, Cornell not only alludes to her masculine name in *Come Live with Me*, but also to her role in *Comrade X*,

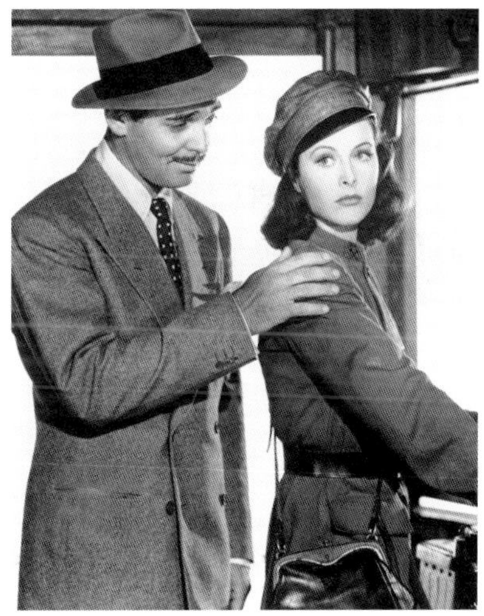

FIG. 4.24 Publicity still from *Comrade X* (King Vidor, 1940), showing Hedy Lamarr in a trolley conductor's uniform with Clark Gable. Everett Collection, New York.

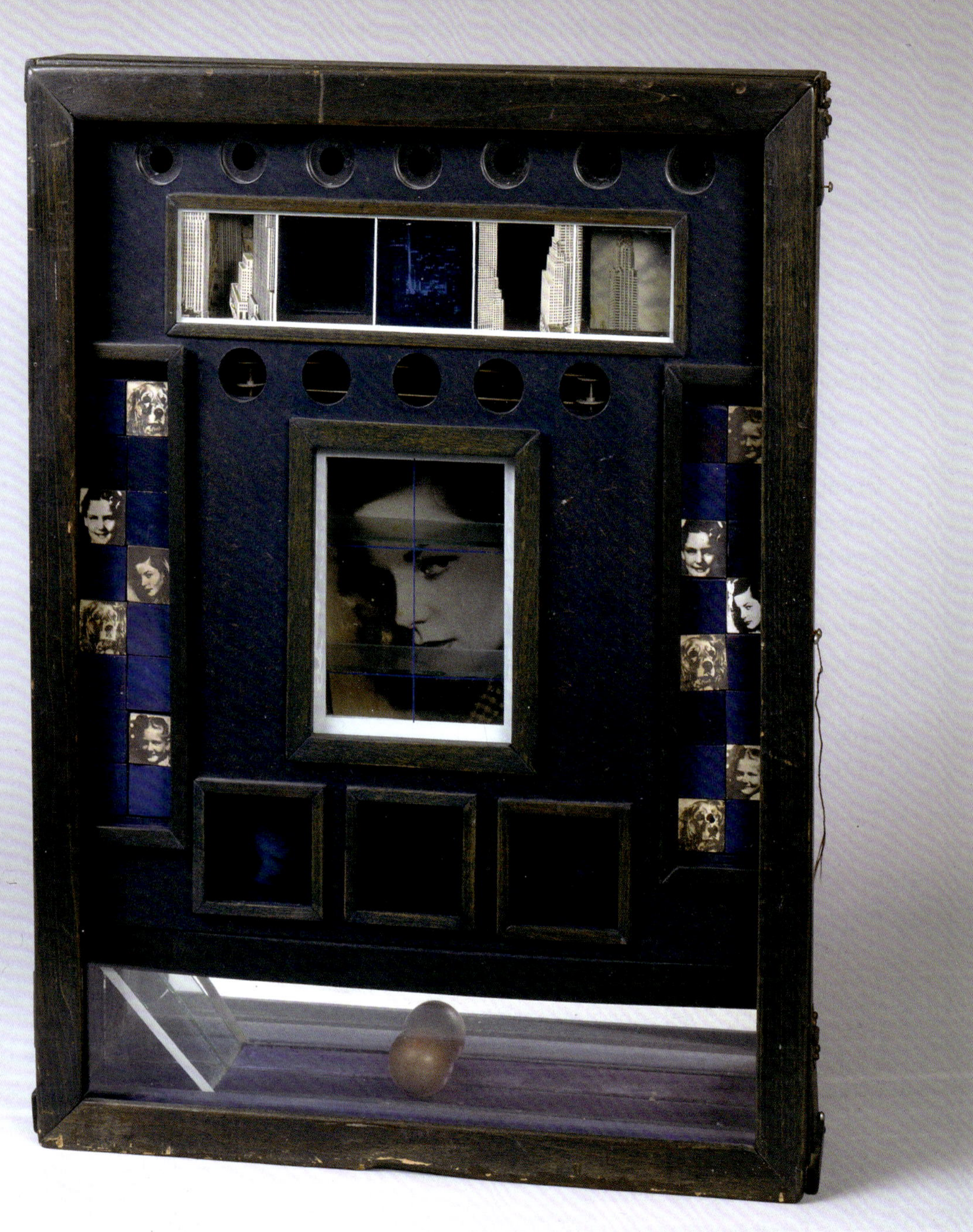

FIG. 4.28 Joseph Cornell, *Untitled (Penny Arcade Portrait of Lauren Bacall)*, ca. 1945–46. Wood box construction—wood, glass, paint, tinted glass, mirror, foil paper, string, thread and printed paper collage, 20½ × 17 × 3½ inches. Private collection.

Cornell's description elucidates the gamelike structure of *Penny Arcade Portrait of Lauren Bacall*. To play, one deposits a ball in the hatch at the top of the box frame, where it whizzes down a series of metal ramps before being deposited in the mirrored chamber below. As the ball travels downward, it rolls past the city skyline and is briefly visible in the cut-outs above Bacall's central portrait. Ricocheting between images showing Bacall's childhood and rolling past her achingly mature present form, the ball's gentle clicks evoke the sound of a film projector. Bacall's portrait is at once a moment of stillness in the midst of action, and that which seems to initiate it. Looking out from behind a turned shoulder and under an artfully arched eyebrow, her gaze forms a direct line to the hatch at top right, where the game begins.

As Hauptman has noted, Cornell tied this work to Delacroix's *Une sibylle qui montre le rameau d'or (The Sybil with the Golden Bough)* (1845, fig. 4.29). The painting, he wrote, shows "the ideal type of the Renaissance, with her gaze lost in the infinite, with her slow and cadenced movement and her relaxed attitude . . . lovely and meditative like the ancient statues."[68] Delacroix's sibyl is indeed as still as a classical sculpture, offering a moment of respite amidst the painter's quivering brushstrokes. She gestures upward at a golden bough above her head, which like her, seems to emit a radiant glow. This bough identifies her as Deiphobe, who assists Aeneas in his quest to find a path to the underworld, and whose story structures James Frazier's aforementioned compendium of myths, *The Golden Bough*. Like Deiphobe's finger,

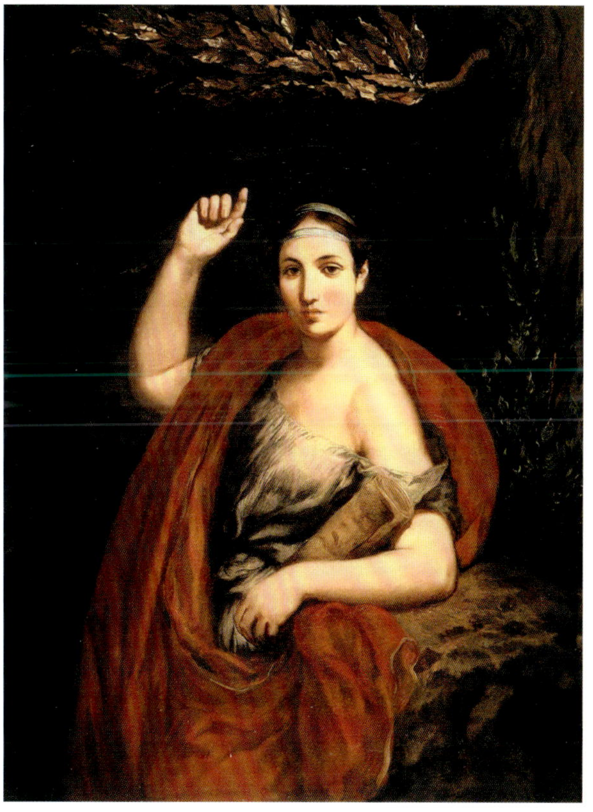

FIG. 4.29 Eugène Delacroix, *Une sibylle qui montre le rameau d'or*, 1845. Private collection.

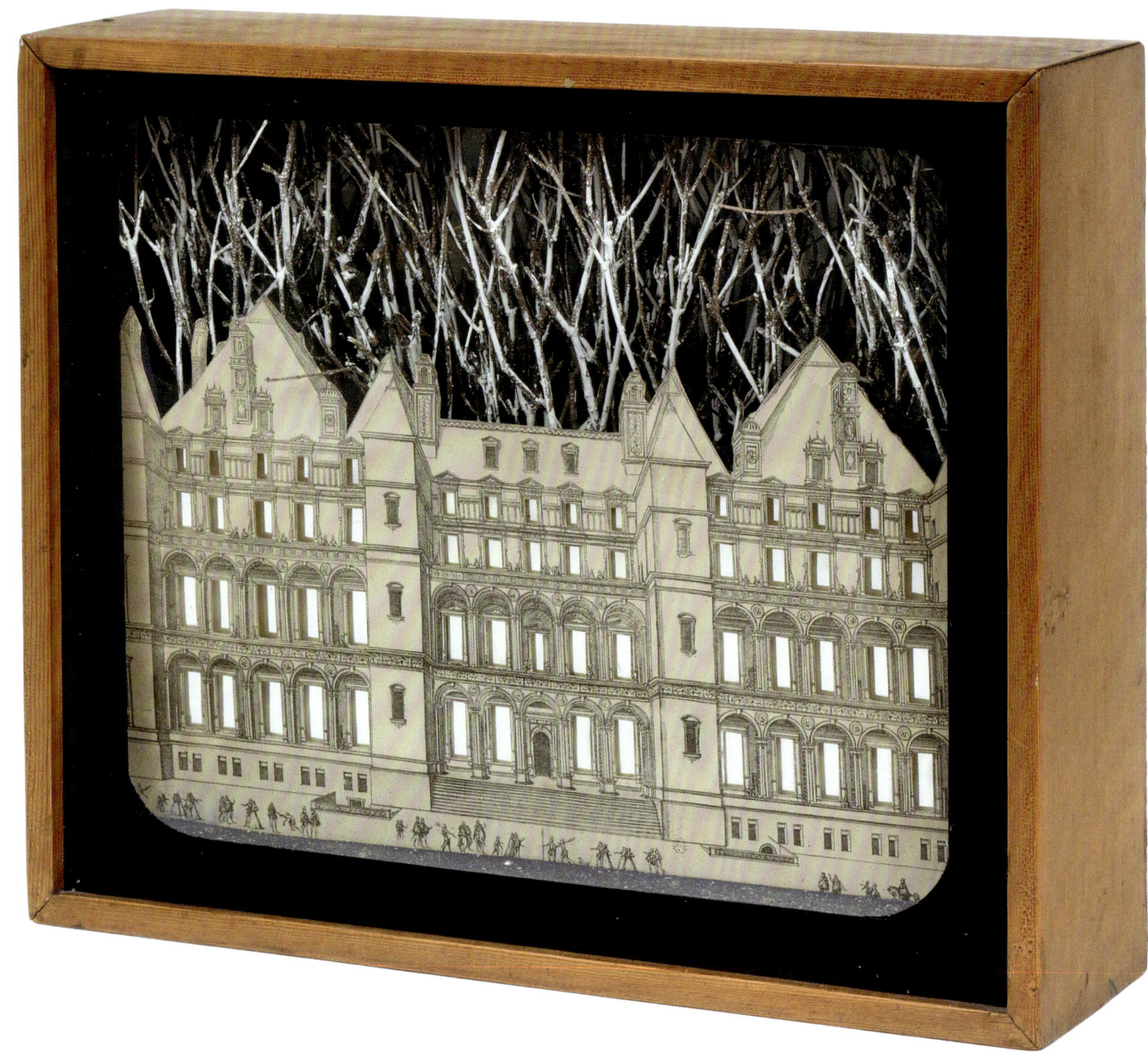

FIG. 4.30 Joseph Cornell, *Setting for a Fairy Tale*, 1942. Box construction, 11 9/16 × 14 3/8 × 3 7/8 inches. Peggy Guggenheim Collection, Venice.

Bacall's gaze points us to the entrance of another world. The ball ushers us through an enchanted world of cityscapes and cinema, of "tropical skies" and fantasy. But eventually it must come to rest. Like all moments of enchantment, this one is fleeting, lasting as long as it takes for the ball to zig-zag down the metal ramps. Cornell's description of the box encapsulates the artist's oft-stated ambition of capturing experience in a single work. And yet in its very structure the work admits that the presence it seeks to hold—possess—can only be experienced for a moment. Perhaps Cornell was learning to let go.

EMPTY STAGES

In 1942, Cornell began a series of boxes modeled on stage sets. *Setting for a Fairy Tale* (1942), the first work in the series, grapples with the subject that motivated his engagement with ballet: the dialectic of absence and presence. These boxes feature a photostat reproduction of Jacques Androuet du Cerceau's engraving of Le Château de Boulogne, dit Madrid, a sixteenth-century castle built in the Bois Du Boulogne (fig. 4.30).[69] This spectacular French chateau has a flat, frontal aspect, as if it were etched onto a stage backdrop. Twigs brushed with white paint, a forest silvered with snow, rise behind the building's facade, which towers over a frieze of tiny figures. Their small size suggests that they are illustrations drawn onto a theatrical set rather than actors. The stage is empty.

The absent body at the center of *Setting for a Fairy Tale* belongs to the dancer Tamara Toumanova (fig. 4.31). Toumanova and Cornell were introduced by Pavel Tchelitchew in 1940, just months after he began *Portrait of Ondine*.[70] One of Count de Basil's "baby ballerinas" who toured the United States a part of his revival of the Ballets Russes, Toumanova danced the title role in *Aurora's Wedding*, a condensed version of Diaghilev's version of Tchaikovsky's classic ballet *Sleeping Beauty*, on which this box is modeled.[71] With its frozen palace surrounded by dense branches, *Setting for a Fairy Tale* evokes the moment when Aurora is fast asleep within a castle surrounded by thorny brambles, awaiting the kiss of her prince. Although we do not see her, the box's invocation of this specific moment in the tale suggests that Toumanova herself lies behind the box's glass facade, recalling the glass coffin in which Aurora is encased like a relic inside a reliquary.

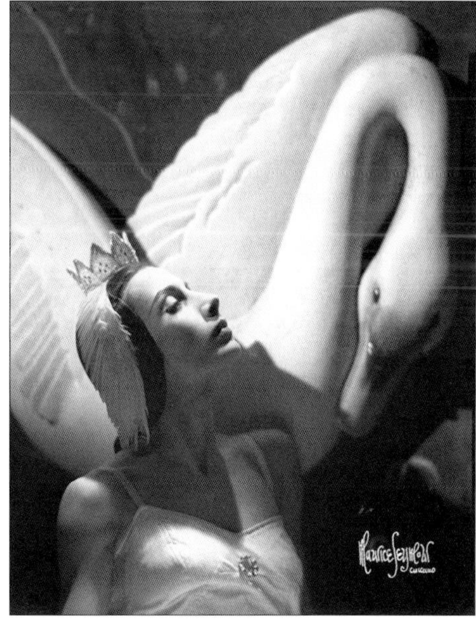

FIG. 4.31 Maurice Seymour, *Tamara Toumanova as Odette in Swan Lake*, 1948. Collection of the artist.

At their first meeting, Toumanova must have seemed like a physical manifestation of Romantic ballet's continuity into the present moment, embodying that which Cornell hoped to achieve in his work. Toumanova experienced their relationship differently. As she recalled, “The moment someone liked me as a real human being, Cornell would become anxious. He wanted me to fly in space all the time, onstage and off.”[72] Toumanova’s statement indicates Cornell’s difficulty in accepting that his beloved enchantresses were real women, and the toll this idealization exacted upon them. To allow Toumanova to fly required him to freeze her into an image of his own fashioning.

Perhaps this is why so many of Cornell’s works devoted to ballet dancers are reliquaries. Lined with faded blue velvet and crowned with an engraving of its titular nineteenth-century dancer, *Homage to the Romantic Ballet (for the Sylphide, Lucile Grahn)* (1945, fig. 4.32) holds scraps of cloth, bits of dried flowers, beads, and glitter. A thin wash of white paint clings to its wooden exterior, lending the work an air of antique patination. Nestled among the beads and tulle is a pair of real, tissue-thin butterfly wings, mounted on wood backings painted the same periwinkle as the box. Glistening with iridescence and shot through with delicate veins of

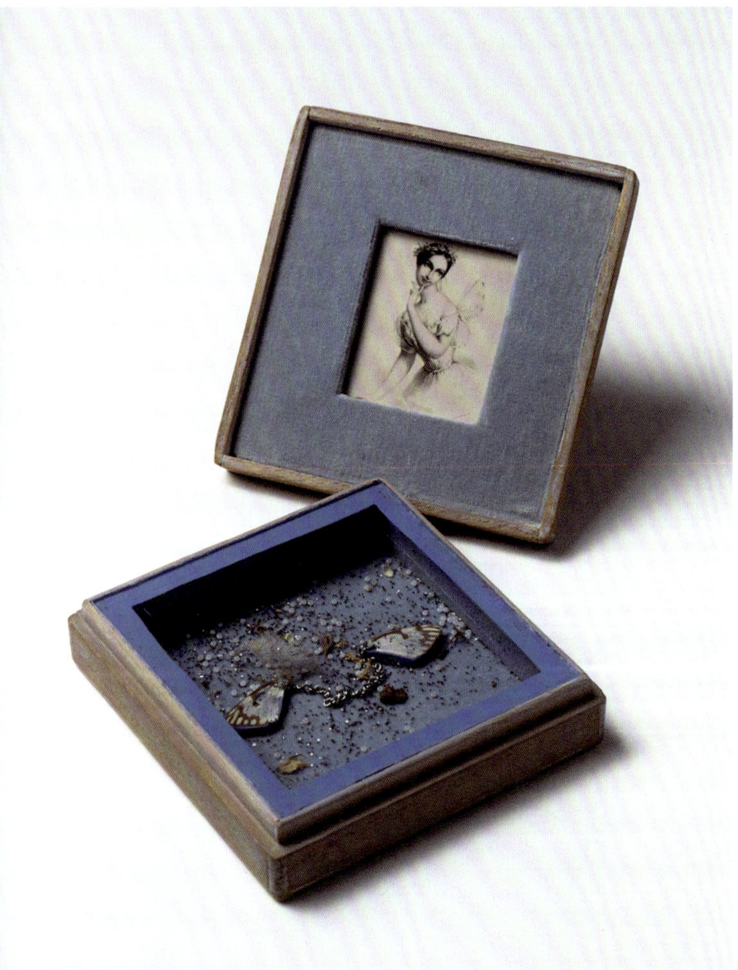

FIG. 4.32 Joseph Cornell, *Homage to the Romantic Ballet (for the Sylphide, Lucile Grahn)*, 1945. Painted wood box, glass pane, velvet, photostat, beads, glitter, potpourri, tulle, and butterfly wings, 1⅜ × 4½ × 4⅝ inches. Menil Collection, Houston, TX, bequest of Jermayne MacAgy.

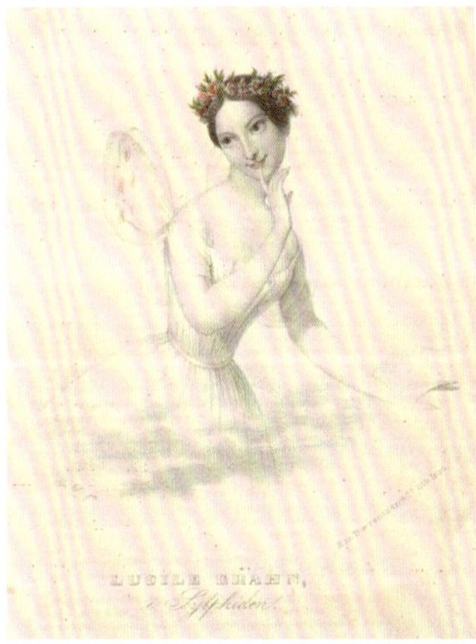

FIG. 4.33 *Lucile Grahn in Costume of La Sylphide*, 1836. Jerome Robbins Dance Division, New York Public Library.

fawn and cream, this macabre addition references the eponymous figure gracing the lid's interior, the dancer Lucile Grahn clad in the winged costume of the ethereal Sylphide.[73]

La Sylphide debuted at the Royal Danish Theater in 1836 with Grahn in the title role.[74] Grahn's Sylphide is an air spirit who bewitches a young man, convincing him to abandon his bride on their wedding day (fig. 4.33). This enchanting apparition remains out of his grasp, until out of desperation, he binds her with a spell that finally allows him to embrace her. At this first touch, the Sylphide's wings fall off, killing her. Such is the violence of trying to grasp what is ultimately a fantasy. In Cornell's box, these fictional wings are transfigured into actual insect wings, ripped from its thorax and pierced by a shining metal chain, underscoring the story's violence. For Plato's Socrates, "The function of a wing is to take what is heavy and raise it up into the region above, where the gods dwell," and yet in Cornell's box the wings assume the opposite function.[75] Against the artist's hope that they would elicit the airy escape of enchantment, here the disembodied wings instead symbolize the fatal violence of masculine possession.

Stage, box, reliquary: *A Swan Lake for Tamara Toumanova: Homage to the Romantic Ballet* (1946, fig. 4.34) is all three. Cornell created the work after seeing Toumanova dance the title role in *Swan Lake* at the Lewisohn Stadium in Harlem.[76] The work shows a swan nestled in a velvet case, which has been placed in a second box like a diamond in a jewel case. Creamy satin, snowy feathers, and mirrors line the exterior box, whose dark frame is augmented by a blue border echoing the hue of the inner case. Its midnight tint—silent film's signal for night—suggests that this is the moment in the ballet before Odette's metamorphosis from swan to human. As in *Setting for a Fairy Tale*, Cornell has chosen to show the instant before the enchantress's transformation. Yet unlike its empty antecedent, here Toumanova's presence is evoked with white feathers plucked from her Swan Queen costume. A label affixed to the back of the box verifies their provenance (fig. 4.35):

> Bordered by feather-
> flowers into which
> have drifted wisps
> from a white crown
> which once graced
> the raven tresses
> of the Queen Swan.

Below, Cornell adds another label attesting to the poem's veracity: "An actual wisp or two of a white feather from the head-piece worn by Toumanova in 'Swan Lake' mingles with the larger ones bordering the box." The labels serve a parallel function to the gold and gems that adorn reliquaries, precious additions that authenticate the holy nature of their contents (fig. 4.36).[77] And like relics, the feathers indexically evoke presence while also acknowledging the absence of the central figure. The simultaneity of presence and absence is further

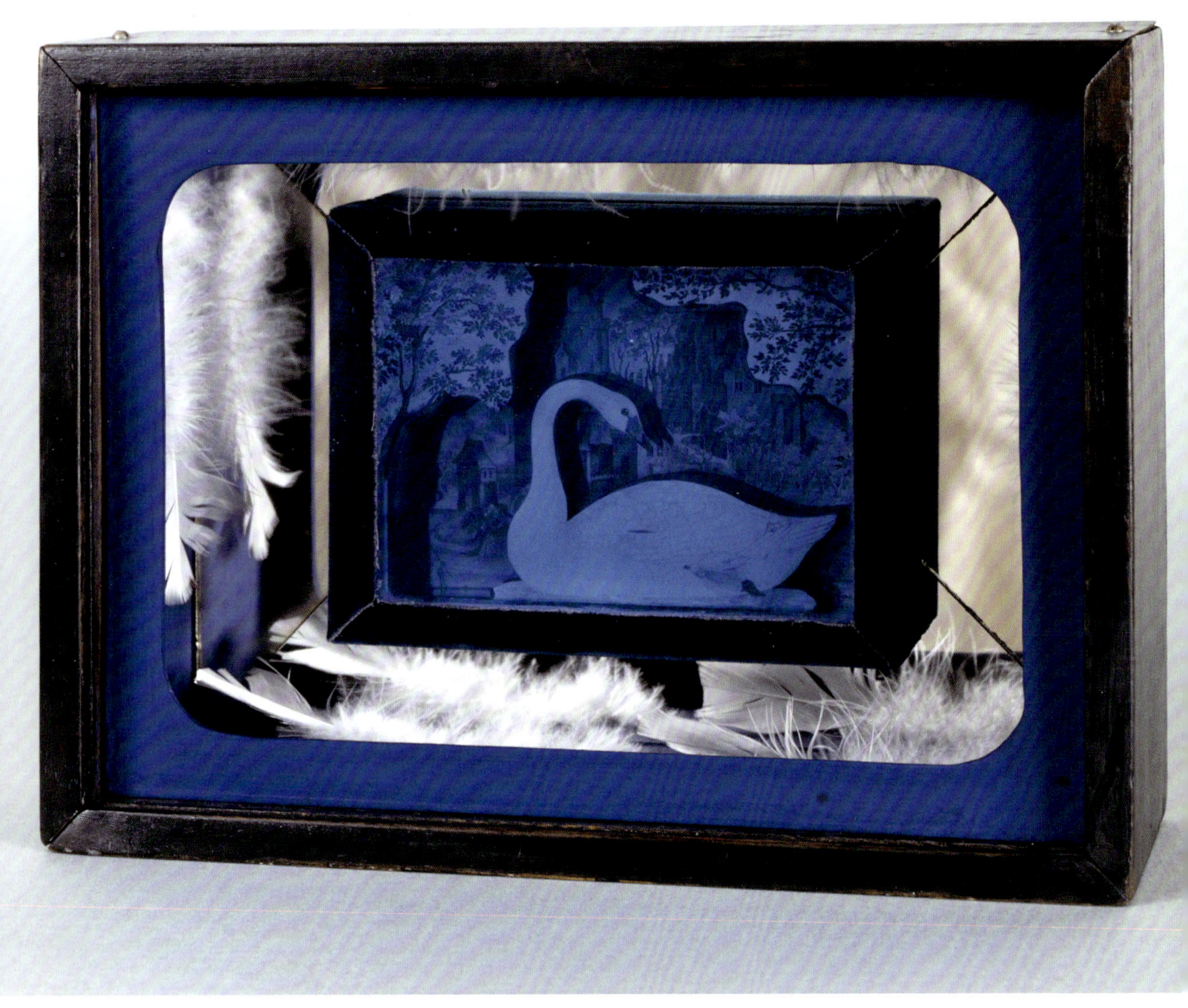

FIG. 4.34 Joseph Cornell, *A Swan Lake for Tamara Toumanova: Homage to the Romantic Ballet*, 1946. Glass, paint, wood, photostats, mirrors, paperboard, feathers, velvet, and rhinestones, 9 1/2 × 13 × 4 inches. Menil Collection, Houston, TX, gift of Alexander Iolas.

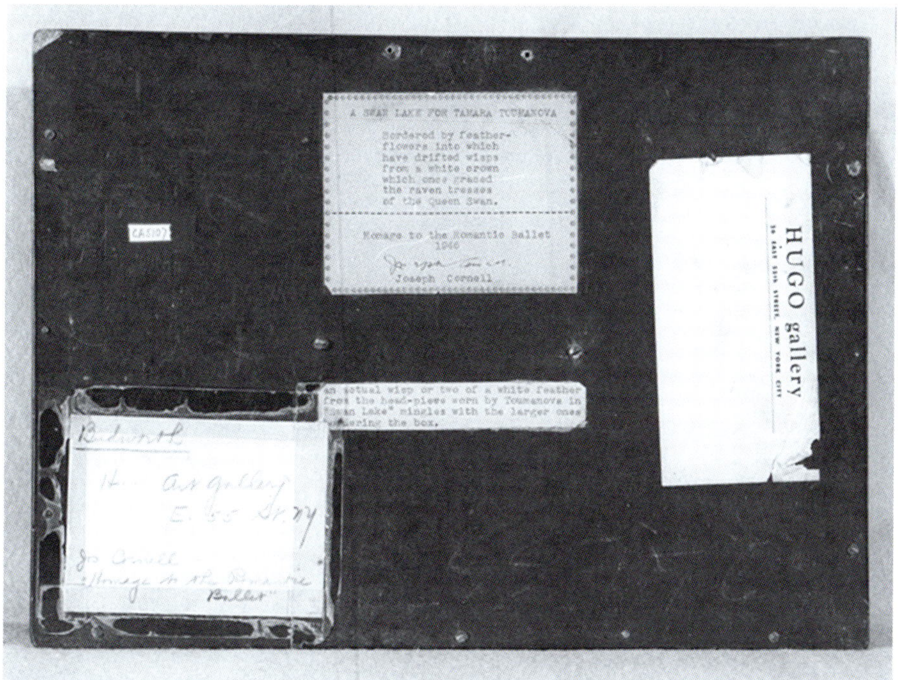

FIG. 4.35 Joseph Cornell, *A Swan Lake for Tamara Toumanova: Homage to the Romantic Ballet* (verso).

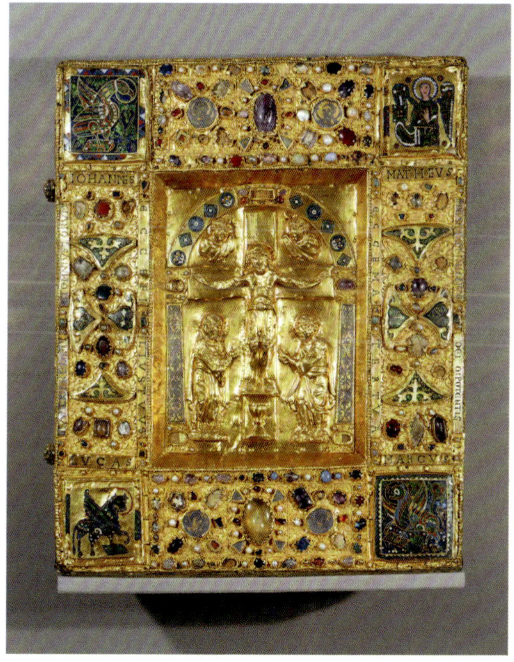

FIG. 4.36 Reliquary box with the resurrection of Christ and symbols of the evangelists, first half of the eleventh century. Gold, cloisonné enamel, niello, and cabochons over wood, 15 1/4 × 12 1/2 inches. Musée du Louvre, Paris.

complicated by the fact that the box's central figure is at once Odette and Toumanova, character and role. The shining rhinestone affixed the swan's tail extends this figurative chain, recalling the paste jewels that encrusted Toumanova's costumes as well as nineteenth-century dancer Anna Pavlova, who as legend has it, was the first dancer to adorn her tutus with gems.[78] Odette, Toumanova, Pavlova: Cornell's box evokes the presence and absence of all three. Just as the mirrors that line the box both multiply and dematerialize the feathers, this single shining spot at once conjures these women while also acknowledging the impossibility of their physical presence. In this, *A Swan Lake for Tamara Toumanova* at once traffics in the objectifying idealization that characterized Cornell's engagement with women, while also gesturing at the impossibility of his possessive desire.

Cornell was not the only artist creating empty stages during the 1940s. Jackson Pollock's iconic *Full Fathom Five* (1947) indexes the artist's movement in threads of black and marine paint, its thick, encrusted surface at once evoking and withholding the artist's presence (fig. 4.37). If Pollock's body created these marks, the now-dried canvas also points to his physical departure from the scene. Pollock's "so-called dance of dripping, slashing, squeezing, daubing," as Allan Kaprow famously described his process, renders the painter's body both present and absent.[79] The painting's title, an abbreviated line from Ariel's Song in *The Tempest*, augments this effect. Ariel's Song is the promise of the lost body of Ferdinand's father, whose bones have been turned to coral and eyes to pearls. Yet this is no simple disappearance: "Nothing of him that doth fade / But doth suffer a sea-change / Into something rich and strange."[80] In Pollock's canvas, the body of the artist is not simply absent but transfigured into the "rich and strange" surface of the painting. Like a relic, it offers both presence and absence. And like Cornell, Pollock casts the world of theater, a world in which fictive stories are enacted with real bodies, as the site of this transformation.

Philosopher Stanley Cavell describes the effects of theater's particular imbrication of fictional and real in his essay "The Avoidance of Love: A Reading of *King Lear*."[81] Watching a tragedy such as *King Lear*, we become aware of our inability to intervene in the scene in front of us. We are faced with the fundamental separateness of the world on stage from our own world, our fundamental difference from the characters in front of us.[82] Similarly, in *Setting for a Fairy Tale*, Cornell calls attention to the scene's status as a stage set. Its black border recalls a proscenium arch, transforming box into portal. Literally meaning "in front of the stage," the proscenium arch was originally designed to physically demarcate the boundary between the space of the audience and the space of the stage.[83] In Cornell's box, as in Cavell's model of theater, the frame of the stage keeps the audience at arm's length, locking its fantastical scene behind a border of glass and paint.

Cavell finds deep ethical lessons in theater's model of object relations. The essay begins with a description of the event that initiates King Lear's tragedy: his demand that his daughters proclaim their love for him, and his youngest daughter Cordelia's refusal to do so. The "avoidance of love" described by Cavell is not Cordelia's but Lear's: Lear's demand to his daughters is in fact a renunciation of love. For real love is never a command but an acknowledgment of one's own desire, one's need *to be loved*, and this is "a claim upon [Lear] he cannot face."[84] Cordelia's refusal to participate in Lear's deformation of love is love's truest possible expression: heedless of the consequences, she withdraws from the game because its rules guarantee failure.[85] Her fateful line, "love and be silent," is whispered as an aside, an utterance to herself.

For Cavell, the lesson of both Cordelia's refusal and of theater is "my separateness from what is happening to them; that I am I, and here." He continues, "It is only in this perception of them as separate from me that I make them present. That I make them *other*, and face them." Theater creates a radical disidentification that forces us to acknowledge our inability to intervene in the action before us. We are Cordelia, and our only choice is to love, and be silent. Such an acknowledgment is no mere quietism but a recognition of difference that is the basis

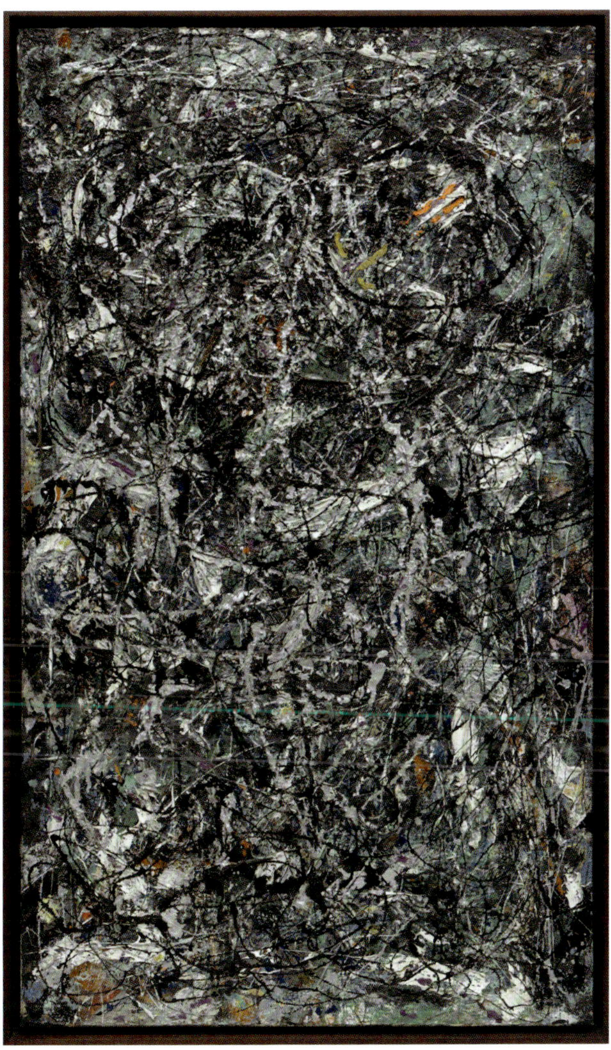

FIG. 4.37 Jackson Pollock, *Full Fathom Five*, 1947. Oil on canvas with nails, tacks, buttons, key, coins, cigarettes, matches, etc., $50\,^{7}/_{8} \times 30\,^{1}/_{8}$ inches. Museum of Modern Art, New York.

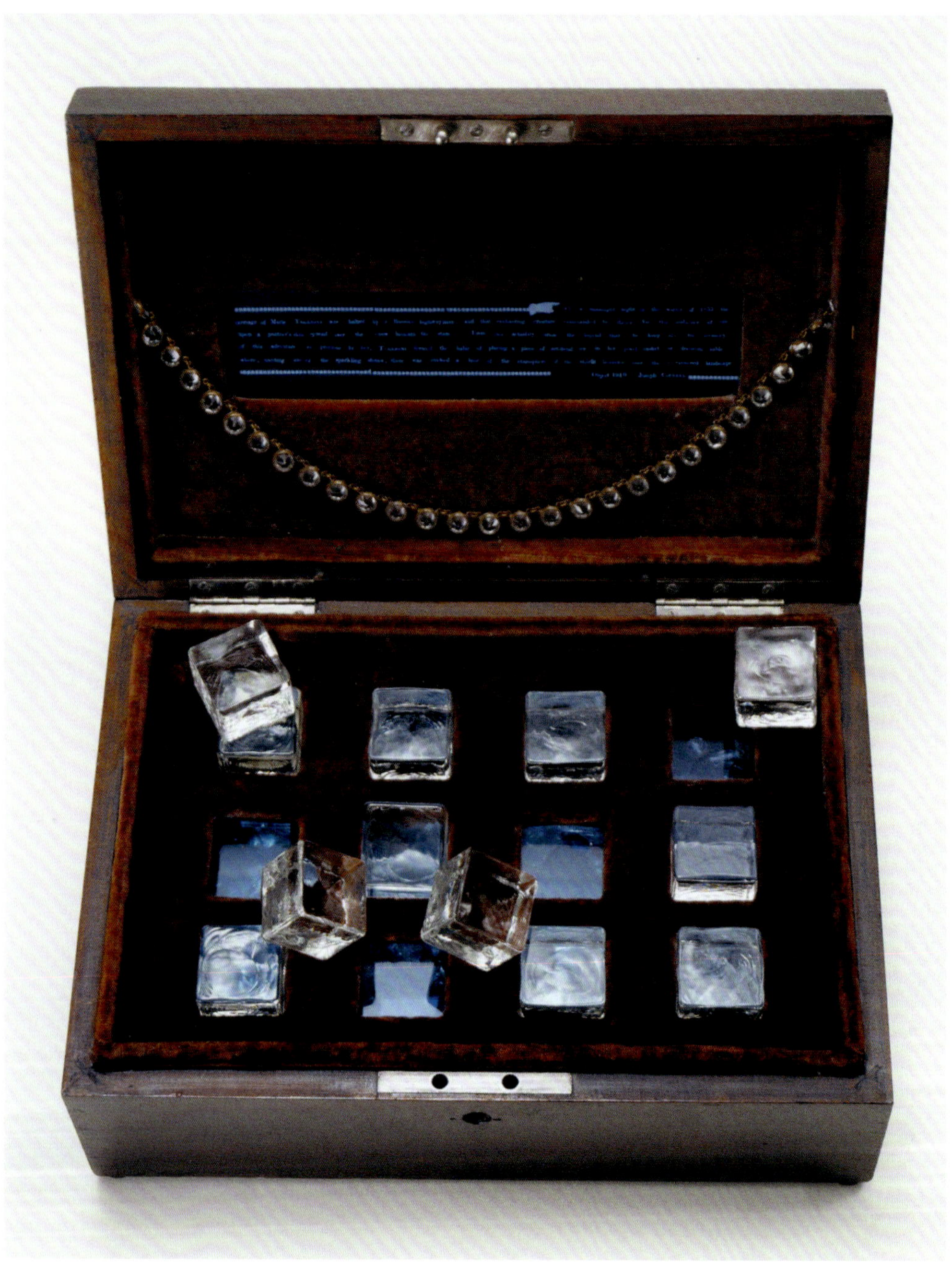

FIG. 4.38 Joseph Cornell, *Taglioni's Jewel Casket*, 1940. Wood box covered with velvet containing glass cubes resting in slots on blue glass, glass necklace, jewelry fragments, and glass chips, $4\frac{3}{4} \times 11\frac{7}{8} \times 8\frac{1}{4}$ inches. Museum of Modern Art, New York.

for true collectivity: "I am in awe before the fact that I cannot do and suffer what it is another's to do and suffer, then I confirm the final fact of our separateness. And that is the unity of our condition."[86]

With *Setting for a Fairy Tale,* Cornell similarly acknowledges the impossibility of conjuring presence. The work attempts to evoke enchantment without seeking to possess it. Unlike *Portrait of Ondine,* it does not presume to offer us an experience of Toumanova's presence but rather places us in the position of *King Lear*'s audience. Peering inside, we expect to observe a dancer, a dramatic moment, but are instead confronted with our own reflection, an image of our spectatorship. We watch ourselves watching, observers of this frozen tableaux, its mirrored windows reflecting nothing but our apartness from the world within. And in this way we are brought into the box. If *A Swan Lake for Tamara Toumanova* shows a moment of frozen stillness before transformation, the swan in the box is also Mallarmé's famous swan who, attempting flight, finds "the horror of the soil where the feathers are caught" in the hardened surface of an icy lake, here figured as reflective mirrors.[87] As viewers, we are powerless to stop Odette's transformation or to free her, a powerlessness thematized by Cornell's decision to encase the swan in a velvet container and seal the entire composition away in another box. The glittering glass that closes these boxes at once reflects us into the scene and prevents us from touching it. Love, and be silent: this is our only option. But our withdrawal from action is no withdrawal from the world. By watching theater, by looking at art, perhaps we may acknowledge the claim others make upon us.

Consider once again Cornell's *Taglioni's Jewel Casket* of 1940 (fig. 4.38). As discussed in the preface, this work gives form to a private, fleeting memory, allowing us to feel, as Cornell once wrote of Ondine, how a past event "may still be real and significant to us today." Artificial ice cubes sit alongside a string of paste jewels, not opposites but equals, glass objects that transcend their physical form by crystalizing light into shimmer. Under our gaze these objects become repositories of flickering, shifting sparkle, thematizing Cornell's concern with material and ephemeral experience. This alchemical change from glass to diamond, from common to precious, finds a corollary in Taglioni's performance for the bandit, which turns criminal transgression into an enchanted event set under "starlit heavens over the ice-covered landscape." Concealed beneath the layer of ice cubes, and tinted blue by a transparent barrier, shards of glass remind us of the crime that engendered this scene.

In the story that accompanies *Taglioni's Jewel Casket,* dance—art—forecloses the potential violence of Taglioni's encounter with the robber. Perhaps the story is embellished; perhaps it never occurred; no matter. What matters is that here, Cornell does not seek to give us Marie Taglioni's presence but to share a memory that was hers and now becomes ours. There is no ownership of this memory, for it is as impossible to possess as it is for an ice cube to endure the heat of the hand that holds it. Yet the impossible is made possible, and ice becomes permanent as diamonds. Here, spectatorship is neither intervention nor abstention, but participation. To look is to acknowledge Taglioni's distance from us, and attempt to share in her experience. This experience inheres not in some transcendental realm but in velvet, glass, and wood. Perhaps this was the only form enchantment could take at this moment.

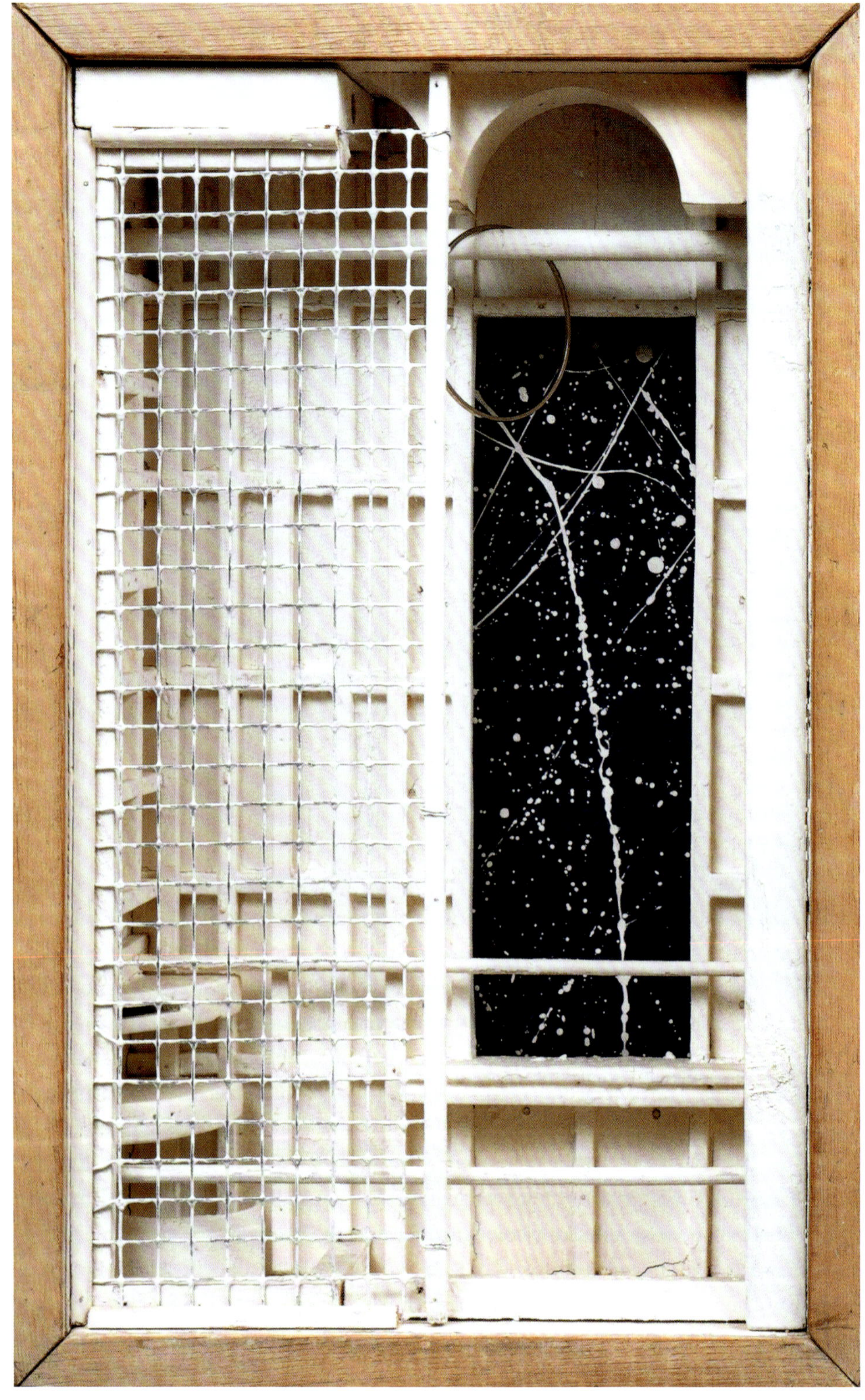

FIG. 5.2 Joseph Cornell, *Observatory: Corona Borealis Casement*, 1950. Box construction, 18 1/8 × 11 13/16 × 5 1/2 inches. Collection of Robert Bergman, Chicago.

A vertical window opens onto a rectangle of dark blue speckled with white paint, evoking bright stars in the night sky, and unmistakably, the paintings of Jackson Pollock (fig. 5.3). Although Cornell had been splattering his boxes with paint since the 1930s, the work's creation at this moment of close contact with Abstract Expressionism offers strong circumstantial evidence that the artist conceived of it in dialogue with the movement. The window's edges allow Cornell to compress Abstract Expressionism into a small box, as if viewing a painting from within a room, while also implying an infinite expanse *outward*, beyond the confines of the window. Siskind's own *Chicago 206* (1953, fig. 5.4) relies on a similar compositional conceit.

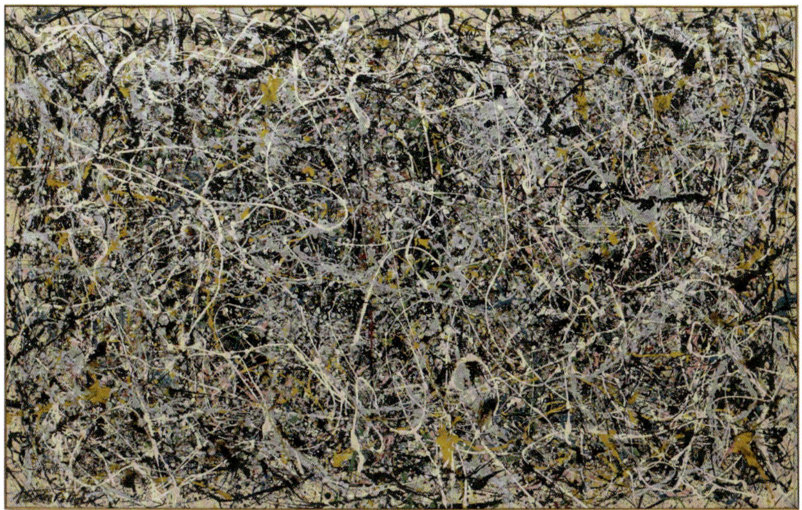

FIG. 5.3 Jackson Pollock, *Number 1, 1949*, 1949. Enamel and metallic paint on canvas, 63 × 102½ inches. Museum of Contemporary Art, Los Angeles; Rita and Taft Schreiber Collection, given in loving memory of her husband, Taft Schreiber, by Rita Schreiber.

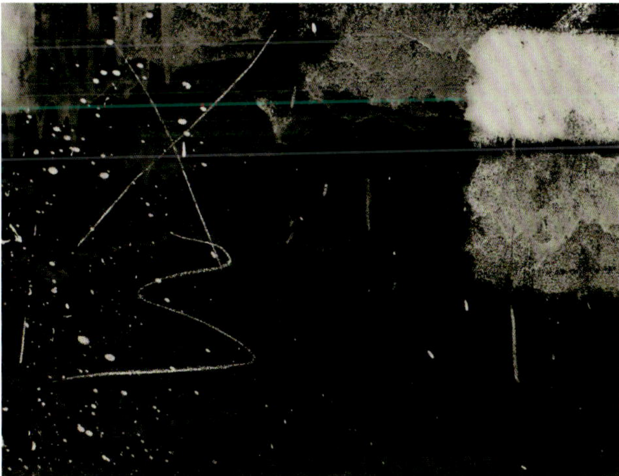

FIG. 5.4 Aaron Siskind, *Chicago 206*, 1953 (printed ca. 1980). Gelatin silver print, 16½ × 22³⁄₁₆ inches. Rhode Island School of Design, Providence.

A black wall ornamented with floating rectangles, paint splatters, and chalklike sgraffito invokes Mark Rothko and Pollock, while Siskind's slice-of-life cropping implies the wall's continuation beyond the frame. Both Siskind and Cornell use a frame—the camera, the box—to stage a juxtaposition between the seen and the unseen, of that which is inside the frame, and that stretch of canvas, of wall, of world that exists beyond its confines.

Cornell shared this preoccupation with scale with several artists in the *Ninth Street Exhibition*. As Barnett Newman famously stated, "size doesn't count. It's scale that counts. It's human scale that counts, and the only way you can achieve human scale is by content."[3] Poet Frank O'Hara likewise described Pollock's canvases in scalar terms, writing, "The scale of painting became that of the painter's body, not the image of a body, and the setting for the scale, which would include all referents, would be the canvas surface itself."[4] And as dance critic Edwin Denby wrote of the late 1940s art milieu, "At the time we all talked a great deal about scale in New York, and about the difference of instinctive scale in signs, painted color, clothes, gestures, everyday expressions between Europe and America. We were happy to be in a city the beauty of which was unknown, uncozy, and not small scale."[5] At this moment, scale allowed artists to take stock of the relationships among art and the body, paint and gesture, Europe and America. Despite their divergent views of how to evoke scale (or more precisely, which terms to put into relation with each other), O'Hara, Newman, and Denby all saw scale as a way of answering the postwar moment's most pressing issue: the relationship of a work of art to the world.

As Susan Stewart has observed, questions of scale often arise in the aftermath of war. At such moments, the classical opposition of epic and lyric is intensified. Stewart describes the distinction between these genres as a matter of scale: if the first is a grandiloquent speech in a stadium, the latter is the whisper into a lover's ear. Epic is "the genre characterizing an archaic social order, an order organized hierarchically and maintained through warfare against what was barbaric, or outside its boundaries."[6] Epic's grand, abstract narratives match the scale of war, which stages conflicts among nations, cultures, and even continents. Think of Pollock's mural-scaled canvases, which as Serge Guilbaut has shown, were put to epic *use* during the Cold War years.[7] By contrast, lyric is the form of reparation and civilian life, "bound up with the pastoral and domestic worlds to which war is counter."[8] Artists and poets turn to the lyric at such moments to counter the epic scale of war. Yet such ambitions are often misunderstood: "It is in the aftermath of war," Stewart writes, "that we find lyric poetry especially at odds with epic ambitions," for at such moments, the intimacy of lyric begins to appear insignificant in the face of larger-scale problems.[9] Stewart's trenchant observations elucidate scale's broader stakes during the late 1940s. In the aftermath of a war of unprecedented reach, a war of world scale, where should artists and poets position themselves?

Cornell's postwar boxes grapple with this question. These works stage a contest between the expansive and the intimate, the infinite sky and the rooms from which we observe its breadth. Although these works appear airy and expansive in comparison with his earlier cluttered boxes, they constitute a scaling down of Cornell's artistic ambitions. If his previous work had attempted to materialize the enchantment of the past, of nature, of the mythic tales of cinema and ballet, then by the early 1950s such ambitions began to appear untenable. In these works, enchantment emerges instead from the interpersonal and domestic, from rooms rather than skies. Perhaps the only way to approach enchantment at such moments is from the ground where one stands.

LYRIC RELATIONALITY

In 1946, Cornell began to explore this new sense of scale with a series he called *Aviary*. He began the series after seeing birds in a pet store window in Maspeth, Long Island. These "magic windows of yesterday," as he described them, were filled "with white and / tropical plumage / the kind of revelation symptomatic of city / wanderings in another era."[10] As poet Mina Loy wrote of these works, "It was a long aesthetic itinerary from Brancusi's Golden Bird to Cornell's Aviary." She continues, "The first is the purest abstraction I have ever seen; the latter the purest enticement of the abstract into the objective."[11] The artist's notes confirm Loy's assessment, describing their tenor as "clean & abstract / 'lived in' mussy aspect," an effect he achieved by applying layers of paint over paste and baking the entire structure in an oven.[12] The resulting boxes are airy and weathered rather than pristine and sterile, dissolving the crystalline clarity and precise structure of the *Medici Slot Machine* into the space of the box.

Cornell's *Aviary* series constitutes an explicit investigation of lyric, the poetic form that takes first-person experience as its basis.[13] The association of birds and lyric poetry is long and distinguished, dating back to the classical period.[14] "A poet is a nightingale," writes Shelley in "Defense of Poetry," "who sits in darkness and sings to cheer its own solitude with sweet sounds."[15] Like birds, poets communicate in song. The delicacy and evanescence of their trills, and of the creatures themselves, offer a fitting metaphor for poetic verse. Birds are also vehicles of connection. Bestowed with the power of flight, they bridge vast distances.

Cockatoo: Keepsake Parakeet (1949–53, fig. 5.5) exemplifies Cornell's lyric experiment. The work's daffodil-and-cream-crested inhabitant resides in a space double the height of the sumptuous velvet interior of an earlier avian box, *A Swan Lake for Tamara Toumanova*.[16] The box contains just three elements: a thin white bar, a now-familiar spiral watch spring, and a cockatoo who gazes up at its curled form. Opening the drawer underneath the main chamber reveals a wealth of paper ephemera, including colorful wrappers, images of stars, an excerpt from the sheet music of the Meyerbeer's Fantasia for "Les Huguenots," and an 1851 letter written in Vienna to a woman living in Dresden (figs. 5.6, 5.7). It is as if Cornell had gathered all his usual working materials and squirreled them away in a secret compartment rather than pasting them to the box. Anchored to the work's ceiling by its tip, the watch spring quivers and shimmers at the slightest touch, as responsive to our presence as the reflective glass that seals the structure. The work invites the viewer to create her own associations from the keepsakes

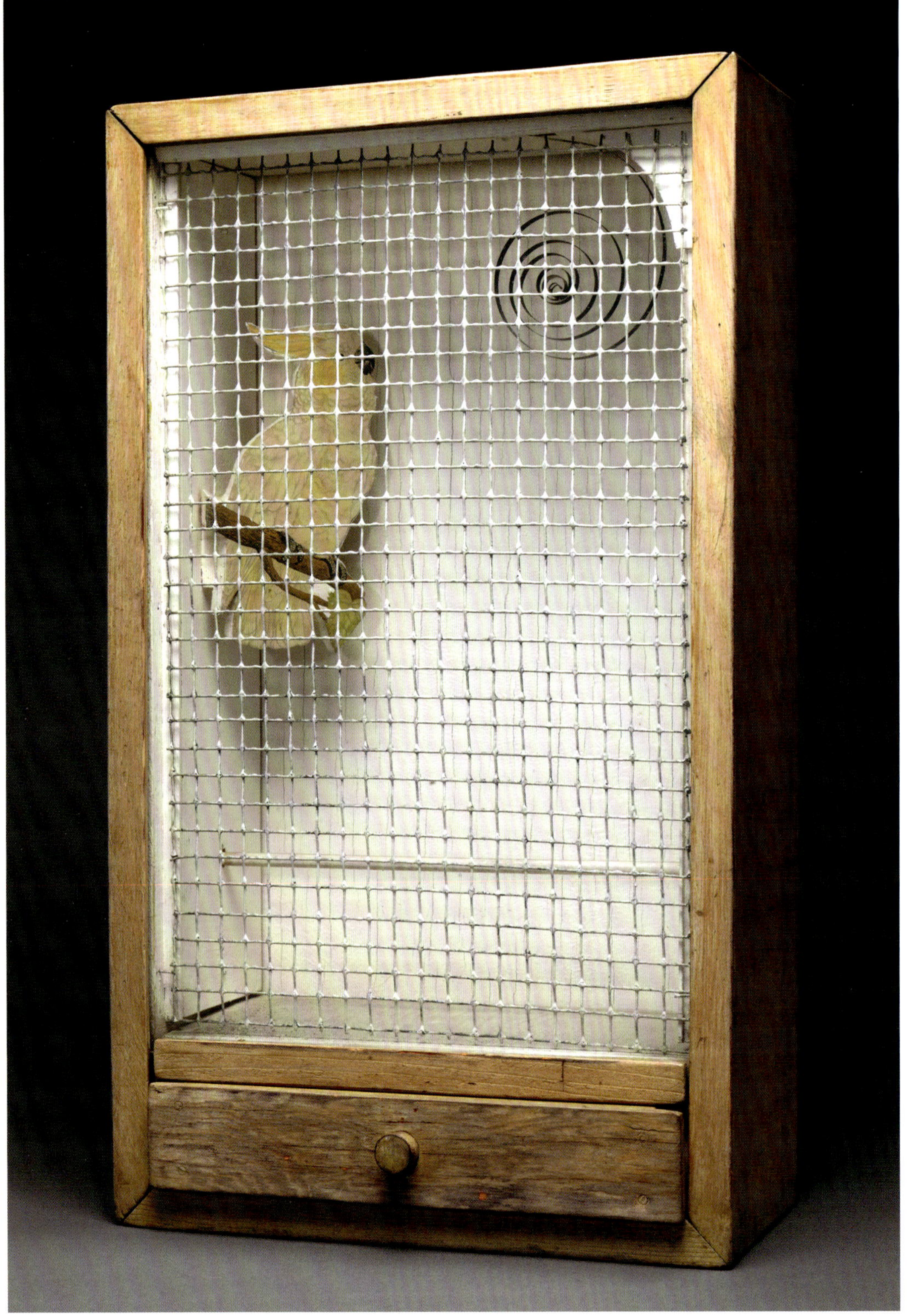

FIG. 5.5 Joseph Cornell, *Cockatoo: Keepsake Parakeet*, 1949–53. Box construction, 20¼ × 12 × 5 inches. Smithsonian American Art Museum, Washington, DC; gift of Donald Windham.

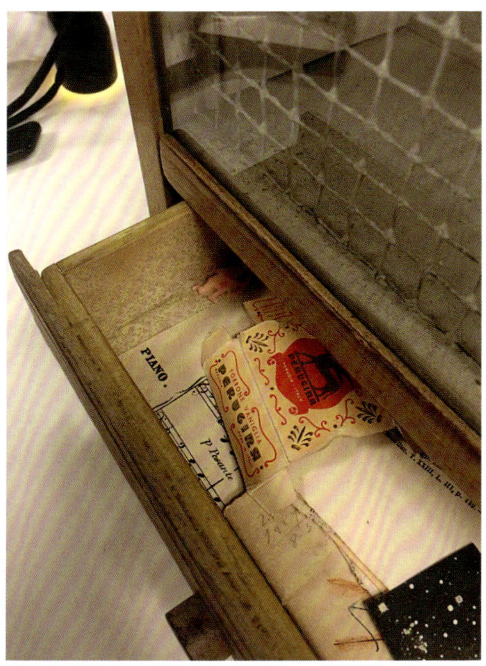

FIG. 5.6 Detail of *Cockatoo: Keepsake Parakeet*, showing the inside of the drawer.

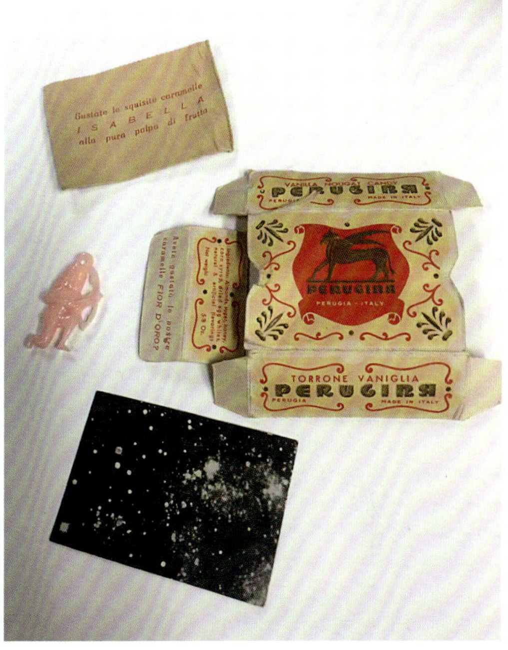

FIG. 5.7 Detail of *Cockatoo: Keepsake Parakeet*, showing selected items from inside the drawer.

The same might be said of the *Aviary*'s invocation of sound. As we are reminded in countless poems, birds are miraculous creatures endowed with voices of pure song. Cornell's research dossiers on nineteenth-century opera singers Maria Malibran and Giuditta Pasta are filled with images and descriptions of birds, connecting their songs to the honeyed bel canto melodies of these great divas.[20] Cornell also incorporated music boxes into at least two of his *Aviary* works, placing them within glass-fronted compartments to make visible the golden gears within (fig. 5.10). As with the loose balls and corks, the music box extends an invitation to handle, to hold and wind, an invitation also issued by the structures of many *Avairy* boxes, whose hinges and latches transform their glass fronts into doors. These works invite activation, prompting us to imagine their contents quivering, their gears turning, and the melody emanating forth from their interiors.

Samuel Taylor Coleridge's "The Nightingale: A Conversational Poem," first published in *Lyrical Ballads*, is perhaps the most famous example of lyric poetry's association with birds. In one verse, he describes an overgrown grove filled with nightingales:

> They answer and provoke each other's songs—
> With skirmish and capricious passagings,
> And murmurs musical and swift jug jug
> And one low piping sound more sweet than all—
> Stirring the air with such an harmony,
> That should you close your eyes, you might almost
> Forget it was not day! On moonlight bushes,
> Whose dewy leafits are but half disclos'd,
> You may perchance behold them on the twigs,
> Their bright, bright eyes, their eyes both bright and full,
> Glistning, while many a glow-worm in the shade
> Lights up her love torch.[21]

"Murmurs musical" layered over "swift jug jug" and "low piping" create a dense thicket of birdsong, weaving together different forms of communication. The "conversational" of the poem's title refers to the poet's address to the reader, his encounter with nightingales, and the encounter he asks his reader to imagine. Coleridge's words invite an act of imagination, for so beautiful are the nightingales' songs that we close our eyes and "forget it was not day!" The darkness of our closed eyes gives way to an image of birds, "their bright, bright eyes, their eyes both bright and full." Within the space of imagination, the reader visualizes these beings and sees the "bright, bright eyes" of those sending forth their voices into void. Like Coleridge's poem, Cornell's *Aviary* boxes imagine our presence, calling on us to activate them, to give life to their inhabitants.

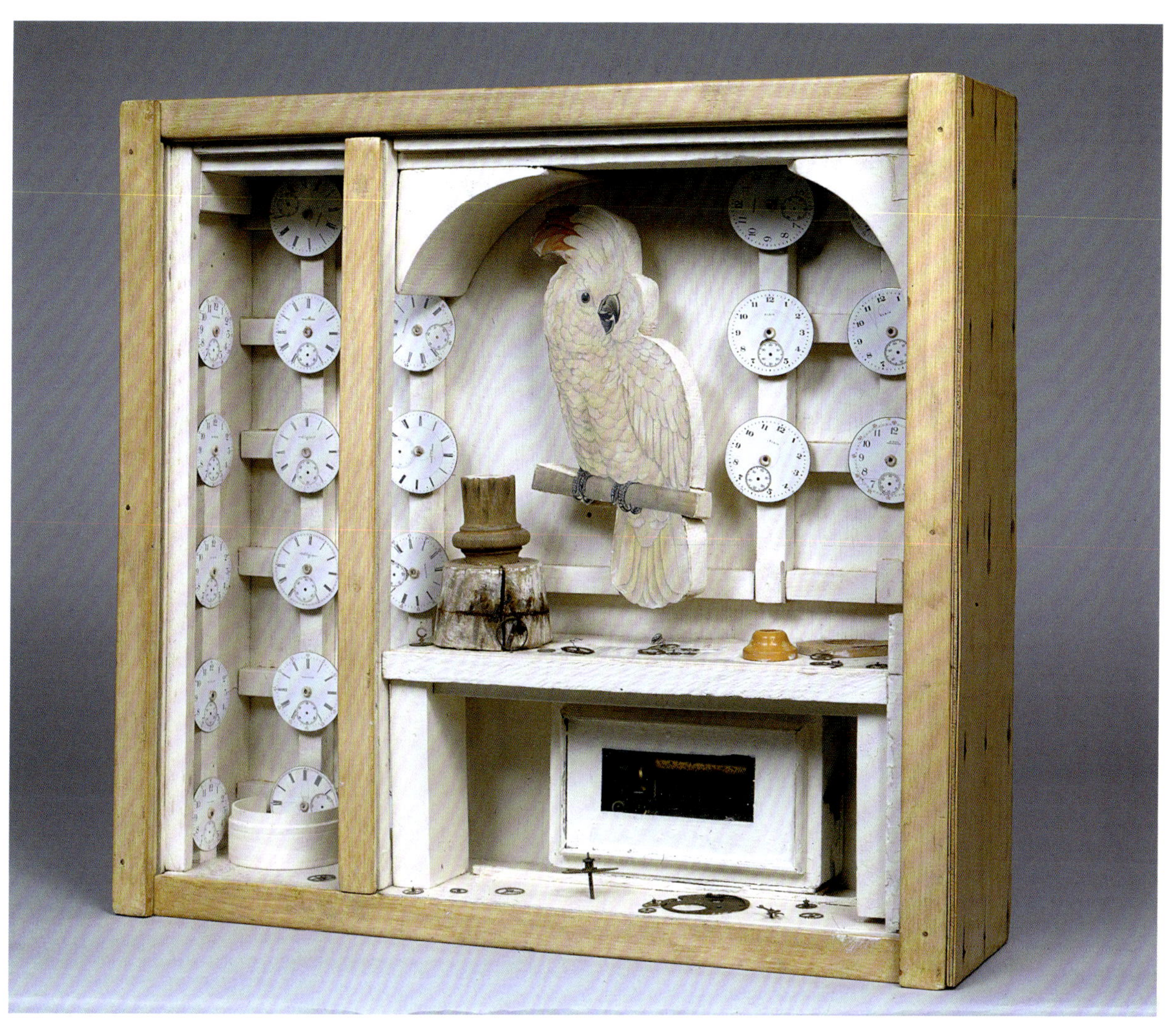

FIG. 5.10 Joseph Cornell, *Untitled (Cockatoo with Watch Faces)*, ca. 1949. Box construction with inoperative music box, 16¼ × 17 × 4⁷⁄₁₆ inches. Private collection.

SCALING AMBITION

Although Cornell's work appeared physically out of joint with the large paintings of the moment, his presence at Charles Egan Gallery suggests a more complicated story. Along with Betty Parsons Gallery, Charles Egan was one of the primary hubs of Abstract Expressionism during the early 1950s. Cornell came to show at Egan through his participation in the informal Abstract Expressionist social group known as "The Club," a coterie of artists who met regularly for lectures and courses in an airy loft at 39 East Eighth Street.[22] As art historian Valerie Hellstein has shown, The Club was engaged with metaphysical questions, staging lectures on vitalism and Zen Buddhism.[23] Harold Rosenberg's essay "Tenth Street: A Geography of Modern Art" describes Cornell's participation in this milieu:

> When the artists' "Club" was still on Eighth Street, Joseph Cornell, fabricator of dreaming cabinets, showed there an early silent film named *The Automatic Moving Company*. An express van without a driver pulls up in front of a brownstone, the rear doors open and pieces of furniture come out. They skitter in file across the sidewalk and shimmy up the steps. Inside the house the pieces arrange themselves room by room in conventional order. All except a small tabouret or end-table, which provides the comedy by wandering around in the orderly shuffle vainly trying to find a place. Whenever it is about to come to rest, an armchair beats it to the spot or it is shoved out of the way by a sofa or a piano. At the end, when everything else has settled down, the little table jigs to an uneasy stop.[24]

Looking back on these years, Cornell concluded that the time he showed at Charles Egan Gallery, spanning the years 1949–53, was the only period he felt he "really belonged."[25] Rosenberg's account confirms Cornell's sense of belonging. To this point, his exhibitions at Egan were met with praise, with Willem de Kooning writing to Cornell to express his admiration of *Aviary*, and critic Thomas Hess declaring their superiority over Cornell's "older, velours-lined jobs."[26] Although the group admired Cornell and shared his interest in the metaphysical dimensions of art, they also regarded him as a curiosity. Gallerist Ileana Sonnabend recalled the audience "laughed" at the artist during one of his presentations.[27] And during another presentation, Robert Motherwell offhandedly referred to Cornell as shy, a slight that began to fracture their close friendship.[28]

Although Cornell showed alongside the artists of The Club, this period also marked a point of divergence between the artist and his peers. While painters such as Pollock shared Cornell's preoccupation with questions of scale and lyric, their aims were different. As T. J. Clark writes:

> It seems that I cannot quite abandon the equation of Art with lyric. Or rather—to shift from an expression of personal preference to a proposal about history—I do not believe that *modernism* can ever quite escape from such an equation. By "lyric" I mean the illusion in an artwork of a singular voice or viewpoint, uninterrupted, absolute, laying

> claim to a world of its own. I mean those metaphors of agency, mastery, and self-centeredness that enforce our acceptance of the work as the expression of a single subject. This impulse is ineradicable, alas, however hard one strand of modernism may have worked, time after time, to undo or make fun of it. Lyric cannot be expunged by modernism, only repressed. Which is not to say that I have no sympathy with the wish to do the expunging. For lyric in our time is deeply ludicrous. The deep ludicrousness of lyric is Abstract Expressionism's subject, to which it returns like a tongue to a loosening tooth.[29]

Lyric was both the mode to which Modernism aspired, and that which it sought to vanquish. Clark explains his sympathy for those who would seek to eradicate lyric by pointing to the genre's alignment with modernity's valorization of the individual subject, the source of what he describes as Abstract Expressionism's "petty bourgeois vulgarity."[30] This understanding of lyric sees it as upholding the myth of the heroic individual artist, with its connotations of "agency, mastery, and self-centeredness." Clark's assessment is echoed by period critics. Thomas Hess's review of the *Ninth Street Exhibition* described Abstract Expressionism as a "shift from aesthetics to ethics; the picture was no longer supposed to be Beautiful, but True—an accurate representation or equivalence of the artist's interior sensation and experience."[31] In the realm of literary criticism, New Critics such as John Crowe Ransom took issue with the idea that subjective experience was the only source of "Truth." The New Critics embarked on a project of what Virginia Jackson has described as "lyric alienation," seeking to vanquish lyric's emphasis on subjectivity in favor of pure formalism, whose presumed objectivity would allow poetry to take on universal meaning.[32] As Ransom wrote, "the work of literature, in so far as it is valuable, approximates a real apprehension and communication of a particular kind of objective truth."[33]

As literary critic Jonathan Culler has observed, "One of the central features of the lyric is the tension between enchantment and disenchantment, or between the presumption to involve the universe in one's desires and doubts about the efficacy of such poetic acts."[34] Culler's observation nuances the alignment of lyric with individualism by recasting the genre as a site where questions about the efficacy of individual agency and action are posed. The lyric's turn inward inevitably raises questions about art's social efficacy, about its ability to affect the world around it. Cornell asked himself similar questions, copying the words of journalist Sydney J. Harris in a 1951 diary entry: "The modern school of introspective artists feeds upon its own ego, & there is no nourishment in this.... No man is big enough to comprise his own universe.... It is not that our artists can't say things well, but they have nothing worth saying outside the constricted area of their own personality. By losing contact with the outside world, they have also lost the only source of inner strength."[35]

Despite this critique, Cornell did not reject the lyric form but instead explored the genre's relational connotations.[36] While his *Aviary* works were likewise concerned with questions of agency and mastery, they sought to relinquish rather than consolidate individual control.

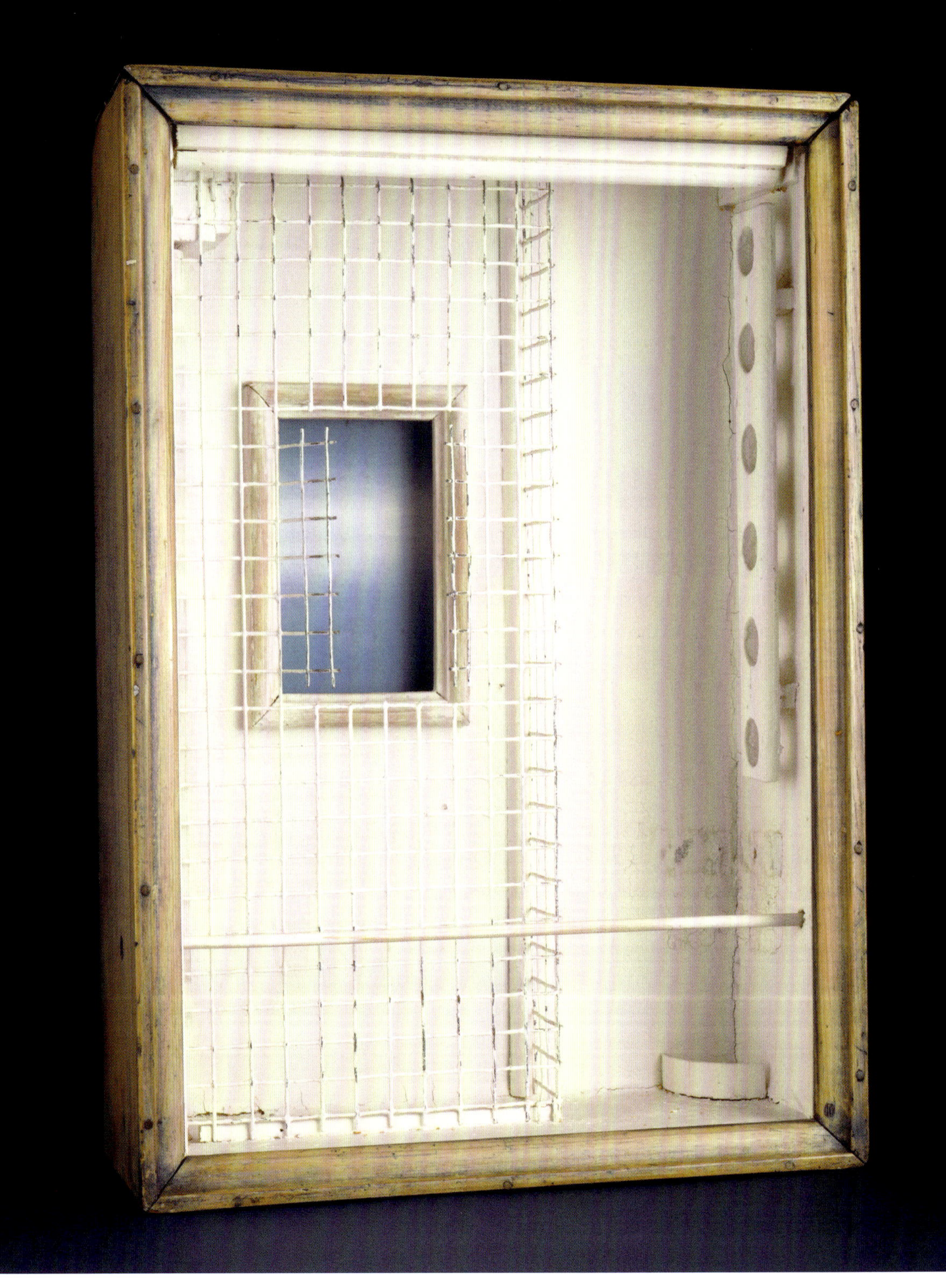

FIG. 5.15 Joseph Cornell, *Toward the Blue Peninsula (For Emily Dickinson)*, ca. 1953. Box construction, 14½ × 10¼ × 5½ inches. Long View Legacy LLC., Washington DC.

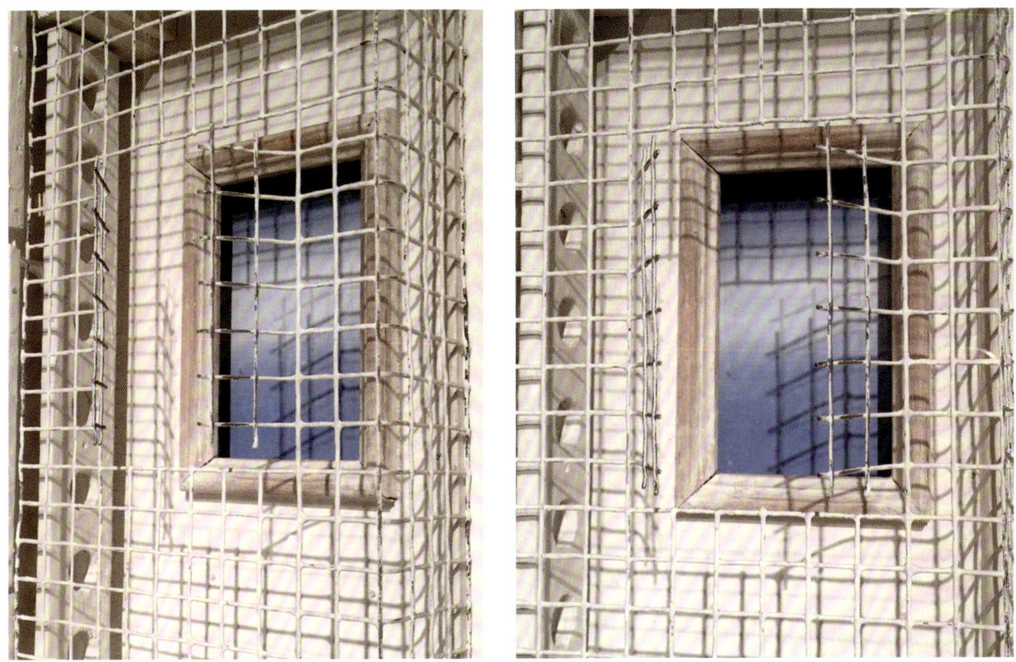

FIGS. 5.16 – 5.17 Details of *Toward the Blue Peninsula (For Emily Dickinson)*.

Dickinson's poem connects hope and suffering. The subject of the line "Ordained to Suffering–" is ambiguous: hope itself may be ordained to suffering, or it may intrude on the place ordained to suffering.[49] The poem thus offers hope as at once a form of suffering and that which may breach its tenacious grasp. With this, the implicit question of the second stanza—should one strive toward "my Blue Peninsula"?—comes into focus. To do so would be to perish, although perhaps this obliteration is due to pleasure, "of Delight." Better, perhaps—less painful, to be sure—to remain firmly in sight of land. Cornell's box materializes Dickinson's blue peninsula as an open window, and his box matches her concise diction with formal austerity. The space around the window is enclosed behind a panel of white mesh. Cuts in the wire create a second window, whose panels open toward the viewer (figs. 5.16, 5.17). The box's multiple nested and breached structures confuse the distinction between interior and exterior, entrance and exit. Are we meant to imaginatively move through the clouds in front of us, or has something been released into our space through the break in the mesh? Either is equally plausible, and the slippage between enclosure and escape suggests Cornell's intimate understanding of Dickinson's poetry.

Cornell began his intensive engagement with Dickinson in 1950, when he checked out Rebecca Patterson's controversial biography of the poet from the Flushing Public Library.[50] Patterson's book was among the first to explore Dickinson's intimate and possibly queer relationship with Kate Scott Turner, her sister's friend. Patterson reads many poems through the lens of Dickinson's desire for Turner, proposing, for example, "To Emily the South represented love and escape from irrational puritan restraint. . . . The 'blue peninsula' of Emily's poetry is a complex symbol deriving from her dreams of Italy."[51] Cornell identified deeply with this account of Dickinson's desire, wondering in a diary entry, "In E.D.'s foreign places, 'Italy' etc. is there a similar clue in her ecstatic 'voyaging' through endless encounters with old engravings, photographs, books, Baedekers, varia, etc.?"[52] Cornell connects the desire represented by Dickinson's blue peninsula to her evocation of faraway places from her home in Massachusetts, and compares this to his own "ecstatic 'voyaging.' " In this, the artist seems to intuit literary critic Diana Fuss's observation that poet's deliberate self-enclosure was a condition of possibility. As Fuss reminds us, Dickinson wrote most of her poems while gazing out her bedroom window. She notes that "Dickinson lyricizes space, recreating in the domestic interior the very condition of poetic address and response."[53] This observation might be extended to Cornell's box. By opening Dickinson's dwelling onto the blue peninsula, a space of ecstatic delight and danger, Cornell places the transcendence she seeks within a room. Freedom emerges from enclosure. The work constitutes Cornell's most explicit meditation on the power of the lyric and the intimacy that can be achieved by scaling ambition down to a single life. "A room," Cornell noted in 1949, "could be a compensation for the ephemerality of a career."[54]

POETIC VISION

In 1951, poet Wallace Stevens delivered a speech on "The Relations between Poetry and Painting" at the Museum of Modern Art. He declared:

> The paramount relation between poetry and painting today, between modern man and modern art, is simply this: that in an age in which disbelief is so profoundly prevalent or, if not disbelief, indifference to questions of belief, poetry and painting, and the arts in general, are, in their measure, a compensation for what has been lost. Men feel that the imagination is the next greatest power to faith: the reigning prince. Consequently their interest in the imagination and its work is to be regarded not as a phase of humanism but as a vital self-assertion in a world in which nothing but the self remains, if that remains.[55]

Stevens describes nothing less than the triumph of disenchantment at midcentury. Anticipating theories of art's "sacralization," he casts the imagination as a "compensation" for this profound condition of disbelief. Stevens goes on to describe the source of poetry and painting's imaginative capacities, or their enduring "mystical aesthetic," as their ability to transfigure reality.[56] Poetry and painting "sa[y] and establ[ish] that all things . . . are one and that it is only through reality, in which they are reflected or, it may be, joined together, that we can reach them."[57] Poetry and painting create connections from the fragments of "reality," offering a sense of holism, of belief, in a world "in which nothing but the self remains, if that remains." Wallace's account elucidates Cornell's continued purchase during the 1950s. At this moment of pervasive disbelief, some poets and painters sought to reconfigure the fragments of a meaningless world into a fantasy of connection and meaning. As we have seen, this was the overarching concern of Cornell's practice. Accordingly, at this moment his work became a vital resource for a generation of poets and experimental filmmakers who were searching for a way to achieve that which Stevens described.

Cornell's work found particular purchase among the coterie of poets known as the "New York school."[58] John Bernard Myers, formerly the managing editor of *View*, coined this designation in an attempt to connect poets and painters. Myers's sensitivity to the links between poetry and art was no doubt indebted to his prior work with Ford and Tyler. After meeting the wealthy Tibor de Nagy at a performance of the New York City Ballet, Myers convinced him to begin a gallery and install himself as director. Tibor de Nagy Gallery opened on Fifty-Third Street in 1950 and quickly became a key venue for poets and painters, including many Second Generation Abstract Expressionists.[59] Given the gallery's genesis in the worlds of ballet and poetry, it is fitting that Cornell was Myers's first choice for an inaugural exhibition.[60]

Just a year prior, the fledgling poet John Ashbery arrived in New York City, where he saw Cornell's *Aviary* exhibition at Egan. Ashbery had first encountered Cornell's work as a teenager while perusing a catalogue for *Fantastic Art, Dada, Surrealism*. Upon seeing *Soap Bubble Set* (1936), the poet recalled his astonishment that ordinary objects such as "marbles, and toy birds" could be made to seem "dazzling."[61] Ashbery's 1950 "Meditations of a Parrot" suggests the lessons he drew from Cornell. Loosely based on a childhood memory, the poem is composed of fragmentary images, at once quotidian and indelible: "blue cornflakes in a white bowl," "the rocks and the thimble," "Robin Hood!"[62] Cornell showed Ashbery that even what the poet described as his "dim, dopey" life could become the substance of art.[63] As Angus Fletcher has observed of Ashbery: "To make a great poetry from quotidian events is no mean trick."[64]

Cornell's example helps clarify the resources Ashbery and other New York school poets found in Surrealism.[65] Upon seeing *Soap Bubble Set*'s "dazzling" array of bric-a-brac, Ashbery recalled, "I realized I wanted to be a Surrealist, or rather that I already was one."[66] Like Ford and Tyler, Cornell's distinctive approach to Surrealism offered Ashbery a model for adopting the movement's use of everyday objects, while avoiding the totalizing (and homophobic) strictures of its founder. Departing from the movement's orthodox European formulation, Ashbery described the work of the New York school poets as practicing Surrealism "in the second, open sense."[67] Following Cornell, Ashbery found in Surrealism a means of transforming the everyday into the matter of poetry, while remaining sensitive to the world's enchantment.[68] As he wrote in a later review, "That this climate—marvelous or terrible, depending on how you react to the idea that anything can happen—can exist is largely due to Cornell. We all live in his enchanted forest."[69]

Frank O'Hara lived in an altogether different enchanted forest, one populated by soda pop, spectacles, and yogurt. "Having a coke with you," he writes, "is even more fun that going to San Sebastian, Irún, Hendaye, Biarritz, Bayonne." Art's grand proclamations pale in comparison to such quotidian pleasures: "and the portrait show seems to have no faces in it at all, just paint."[70] In 1955, O'Hara wrote a poem about Cornell, which he specified be "print[ed] like boxes."[71]

> Into a sweeping meticulously-
> detailed disaster the violet
> light pours. It's not a sky,
> it's a room. And in the open
> field a glass of absinthe is
> fluttering its song of India.
> Prairie winds circle mosques.
>
> You are always a little too
> young to understand. He is
> bored with his sense of the
> past, the artist. Out of the
> prescient rock in his heart
> he has spread a land without
> flowers of near distances.[72]

The poem is dense with dramatic plays of scale. A single absinthe glass sits in a vast field. This little vessel opens onto the vaster distances of India and the prairies. The decadent lyricism of this first "box" gives way to plain, straightforward language in the second. The artist's heart contains a "prescient rock," a phrase that combines the mystical and the material. From this rock springs "a land without / flowers of near distances." The word "distances" has two meanings: far, as in "distant," and the physical space between two places. The seemingly paradoxical phrase "near distances" thus means both far and proximate.[73] Cornell's work likewise brings the far near and makes the near far. With this poem, Cornell's lessons for New York school poetry become evident. It is only through proximity that we may grasp the enchanted violet light of the first passage; it is only in the near reality of daily life that enchantment may be reached.

In 1955, the year of O'Hara's poem, Cornell began another project dedicated to Emily Dickinson. One afternoon, Cornell called Stan Brakhage out of the blue to suggest "we spend the afternoon preserving 'the world of this house,' its environs."[74] The house was a grand Victorian in Flushing that was slated for demolition. Filmed by Brakhage following spoken direction from Cornell, *Centuries of June* (1955, fig. 5.18) opens with a series of shots that lovingly trace the house's horizontal and vertical spans and its elaborate wooden porch railing. Subsequent shots from inside the house show a distant view framed by windows, transforming open space into picturesque landscape compositions. The camera seems directed by the house's architecture, as if to overlay the structure's perspective on the world around it, lyricizing space as in Dickinson's poems and Cornell's boxes.

Like Rudy Burckhardt, Brakhage met Cornell through Parker Tyler.[75] As P. Adams Sitney has noted, Brakhage's collaboration with Cornell marked a turning point for the filmmaker.

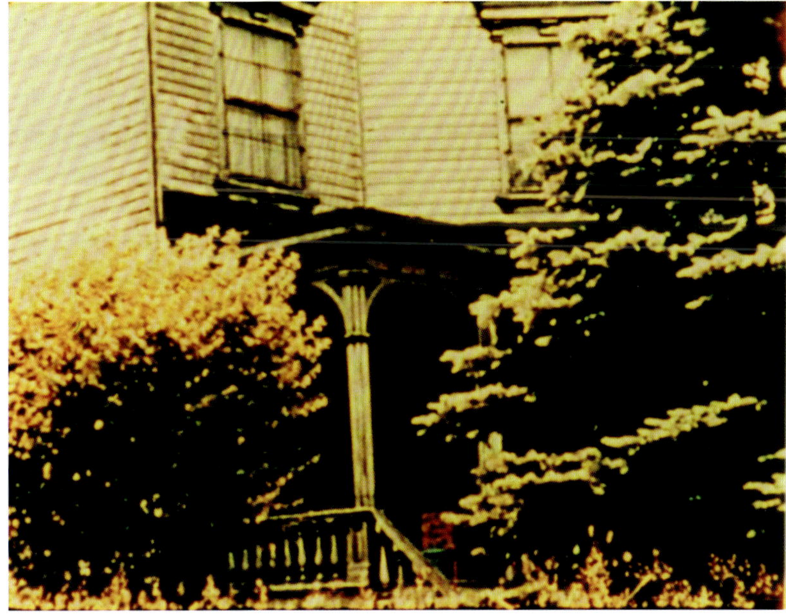

FIG. 5.18 Film still from *Centuries of June* (Joseph Cornell and Stan Brakhage, 1955). Austrian Film Museum.

EPILOGUE

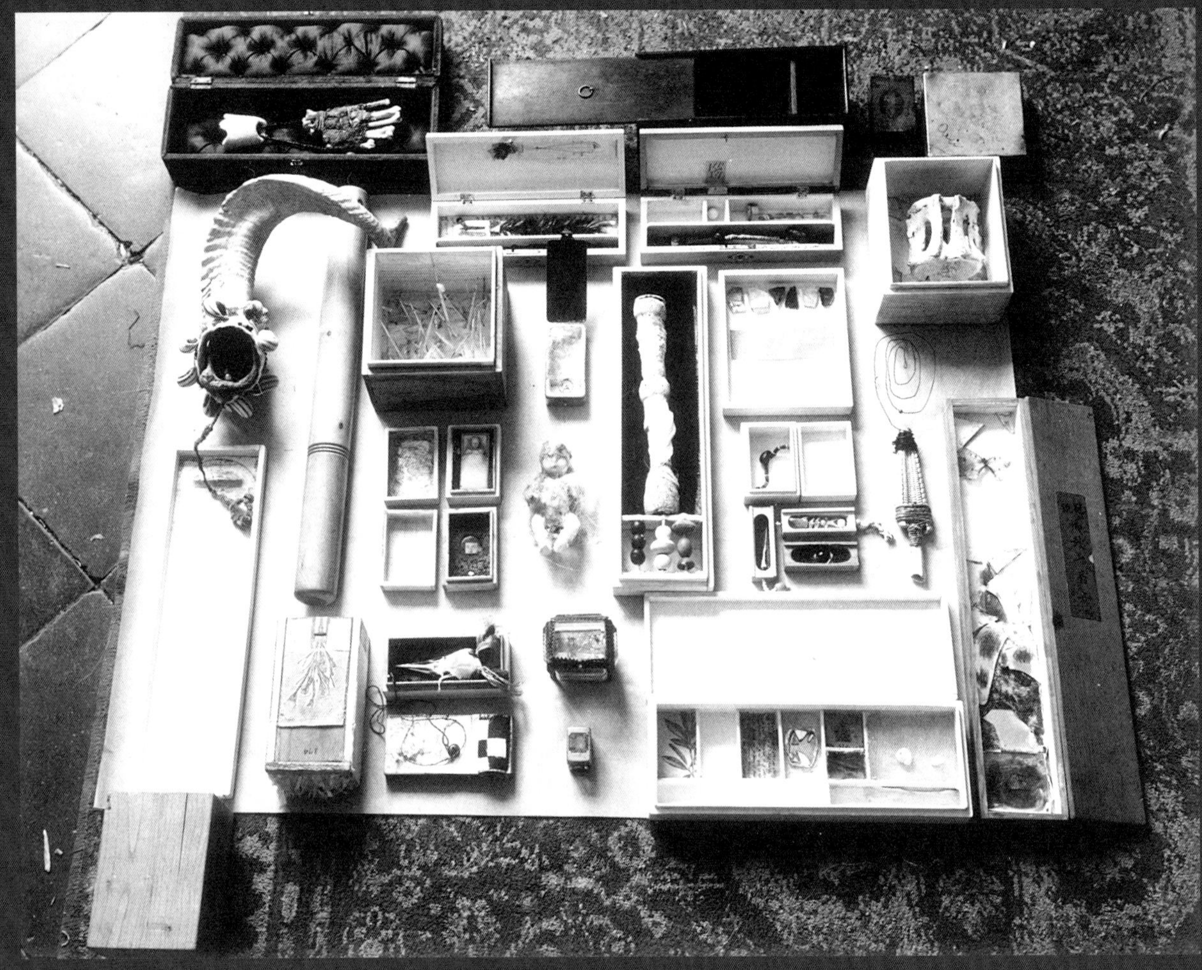

FIG. 6.1 Robert Rauschenberg, *Untitled (Scatole Personali)*, 1953. Gelatin silver print, 2¼ × 2¼ inches. Robert Rauschenberg Foundation, New York.

Some Varieties of Enchantment

A gem to be extracted
often tactile
from ordinary things.

Joseph Cornell, undated note

The end is the beginning. Although Cornell continued to make art until his death in 1972, rather than covering the remainder of his career, this epilogue instead considers three artists who engaged Cornell's enchantment. Robert Rauschenberg, Betye Saar, and Carolee Schneemann turned to the humble detritus of everyday life, building their work from found objects, scraps of paper, bits of metal, and shards of glass. Although they shared Cornell's care for the quotidian, all three found his "white magic" too ideal, too removed from the turmoil and pain of daily life, too terrified of the body. Each brought Cornell down to earth, transfiguring his enchantment into work that was alternately fierce, funky, and sacrilegious. These younger artists were unafraid of enchantment's occult registers and channeled its power to their own ends. Their example suggests enchantment's continued purchase on the aesthetic and social dimensions of artistic practice in the postwar era, while also suggesting that there are resources to be found in the past, however imperfect or compromised the past may be. The resources they found in Cornell helped them reimagine the world in which they lived as a world that has yet to come.

In December 1949, Cornell's *Aviary* exhibition opened at Charles Egan Gallery. Perhaps these boxes arrived at the gallery in the car of Robert Rauschenberg, who, as the only employee of Egan with a driver's license, was often tasked with driving to Utopia Parkway to pick up Cornell's work.[1] Three years later, Rauschenberg accompanied Cy Twombly on a now-legendary trip through Europe and North Africa.[2] Two bodies of work made by Rauschenberg during this trip grapple with Cornell's example. Fragments of bone, glass, driftwood, feathers, seashells, and clippings from botanical diagrams nestle in small containers in his *Scatole Personali* (*Personal Boxes*, ca. 1952) (fig. 6.1), thirty of which are arranged on a table like pieces of a jigsaw puzzle in a 1953 photograph. As Rauschenberg explained, he picked these particular objects "for either of two reasons: the richness of their past: like bone, hair, faded cloth and photos, broken fixtures, feathers, sticks, rocks, string, and rope; or for their vivid abstract reality: like mirrors, bells, watch parts, bugs, fringe, pearls, glass, and shells."[3] They were chosen, in other words, for their power. The *Scatole Personali* pictured at front center of the 1953 photograph holds a faux pearl suspended from frayed string (fig. 6.2). Mica rubbed into the box's sides glitters in the light, a constructed halo that imparts the paste gem with an aura of authenticity. That this work belonged to Twombly, Rauschenberg's companion and lover during this sojourn, underscores its talismanic power.[4]

With the *Scatole Personali,* Rauschenberg at once engaged with and departed from Cornell's example. As the artist explained to Deborah Solomon, "The only difference between me and Cornell is that he put his work behind glass, and mine is out in the world."[5] Cornell's boxes impart their contents with an internal syntax, a structure that transforms them into self-contained worlds. But as Rauschenberg's statement suggests, the younger artist instead perceived the box as a structure of enclosure.[6] Rauschenberg was not alone in his assessment. In 1961, MoMA included fourteen Cornell boxes in the exhibition *The Art of Assemblage*. Installed in a hallway coated in dark paint and illuminated by dramatic spotlights, each box is concentrated down to a single fetishistic unit, forming a stark contrast to the unruly, thrusting shapes displayed in the exhibition's airy main galleries (figs. 6.3, 6.4). This physical separation echoed the exhibition catalogue's description of Cornell's work as "lost illusions sheltered along with pristine innocence and pure naïveté of childhood."[7] Rather than its presumed naïveté, Rauschenberg took issue with Cornell's deployment of what he saw as frames. The frame was precisely that which Rauschenberg wished to break free of in his work, asking pointedly at the *Art of Assemblage* symposium, "Excuse me—was any art ever designed for frames?"[8] Although Cornell used materials drawn from "factories, the street, the household, the hardware store, the dump," to quote Allan Kaprow's gloss of assemblage, his boxes appeared too close to the hermetic presentation of fine art for Rauschenberg's taste.[9]

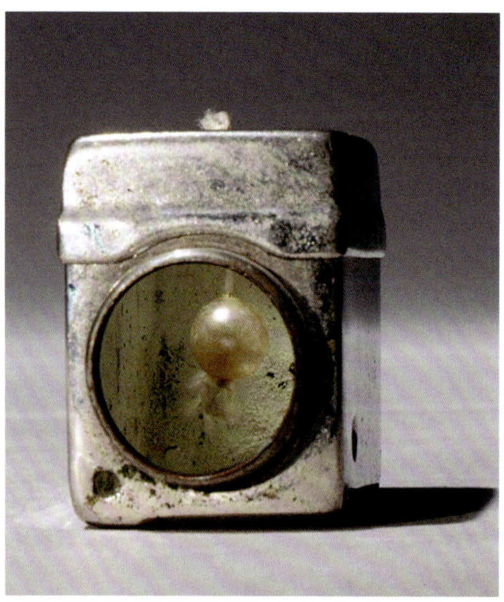

FIG. 6.2 Robert Rauschenberg, *Untitled (Scatole)*, ca. 1952. Assemblage—lidded box, with mica, pearl, and thread, 1 × 1 × 2 inches. Robert Rauschenberg Foundation, New York.

Yet as Rauschenberg would discover in Italy, the frames of Cornell's boxes served an additional purpose. As their title suggests, Rauschenberg's *Feticci Personali (Personal Fetishes)* channel the logic of the fetish. Composed of rocks, shells, and unraveled rope, the *Feticci Personali* emit a sense of uncanny embodiment.[10] A photograph of Rauschenberg bent over one of the *Feticci Personali* shows the artist unravelling tightly

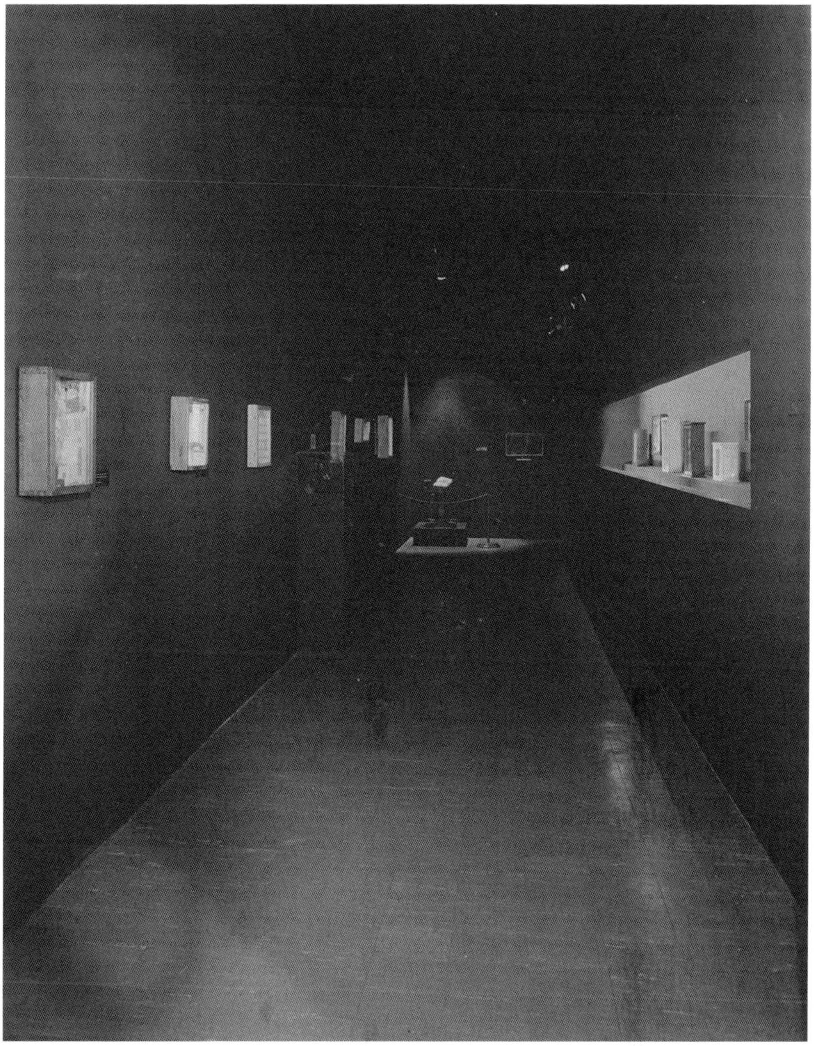

FIG. 6.3 Installation view of *The Art of Assemblage*, October 4–November 12, 1961, showing the Joseph Cornell section. Photographic Archives, Museum of Modern Art, New York.

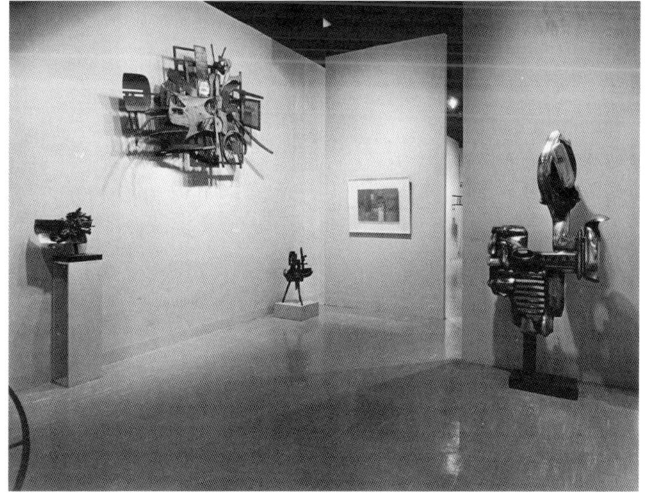

FIG. 6.4 Installation view of *The Art of Assemblage*, October 4–November 12, 1961. Photographic Archives, Museum of Modern Art, New York.

Cornell would have described the effect of the *Feticci Personali* as "black magic." Unlike "white magic," which flows from a divine source, Cornell understood black magic as the enchantment that erupts from the unruly, enigmatic forces of nature, the body, and materials themselves. The fetish, as Kaprow notes, also has a curious relationship to the frame. Fetishes "do not function on or in their field as images within a space, that is, the object–ground relationship is not present"; rather they channel "the 'aura' of the image; it is in fact the equivalent of a *mandorla* or a halo."[13] Unlike relics, whose containers signal their synecdochic relationship with an absent body, the fetish does not require a frame, for a halo of auratic power emanates from the object itself. Cornell, as we saw in chapter 2, turned to boxes in part to contain this unruly power. By locking individual objects into a syntax, the box format prevents its contents from taking on the uncanniness described by the Surrealists, and exemplified by the *Feticci Personali*. In eliminating the box, Rauschenberg inadvertently channeled what Kaprow described as the fetish's "aura," and that which Cornell attempted to control. This effect may have been too much for Rauschenberg to endure. Before leaving Rome, he threw the *Feticci Personali* into the River Arno.[14]

This anecdote would seem to encapsulate the postwar era's hostility toward enchantment. Seeking an alternative to the "bourgeois principles of autonomous art and expressive artist" represented by the New York school, postwar artists sought to disenchant art by "push[ing] the arbitrariness of the sign to the point of dissolution."[15] Art—and its connotations of universality, autonomy, and the subject—became merely material, simply another object in the world. This was the source of assemblage's critical potential.[16] The fate of the *Feticci Personali* suggests that this move to disenchantment was more fraught than previous commentators have allowed. Although scholars have attributed Rauschenberg's decision to destroy them to a single negative review, subsequent works such as *Talisman* (1958, fig. 6.8) suggest that the artist continued to puzzle over the effects of these earlier works.

Created the same year he began his ethereal *Dante Drawings*, *Talisman* disperses images of soaring birds, racing greyhounds, and misty landscapes into a panoply of decontextualized letters and symbols. The painting's title wonders about the emblematic power of its contents, a question also posed by the work's composition. The canvas is overlaid with passages of thick black paint, isolating each image from its neighbor while also placing them in a single chromatic field—at once separating and connecting them. The photograph showing a baseball player and umpire is placed alongside a picture of a hand with a folded thumb. This hand could be a catcher's signal to the unseen pitcher, or the umpire's ball count; yet seen alone, hovering in a field of black, the palm takes on the aspect of an occult symbol. Is it a sign of failure, or does it shape the path of the speeding white ball evoked by the stroke of white paint above? Might the creases that mark the palm offer a map to an unknown future? *Talisman* leaves these possibilities open. The seasoned wood panel dividing the canvas is punctuated by a cutout that holds a single silvered jar, whose suspension and shining sides recall the *Scatole Personali* owned by Twombly. But peering inside, we see not a paste pearl but a black substance "of a decidedly scatological character."[17] *Talisman* oscillates between sacred and profane, between the shining jar's promise of a magical potion and the shit that it appears to hold. Perhaps the oft-remarked upon indeterminacy of Rauschenberg's work is not simply the artist's eschewal of meaning but an emblem of his agnostic posture between magic and base materialism, of his desire for enchantment and his justifiable suspicion of its effects.

The tension between belief and disbelief, and the desire for a way out of this binary, can also be discerned in the many artists who turned to occultism and Eastern mysticism during this period. They included the vaunted avant-garde composer John Cage, whose interest in emptiness emerged from his study of Zen Buddhism and famously inspired Rauschenberg's *White Paintings* of 1951. The period interest in alternative forms of spirituality and belief were in fact a central aspect of *The Art of Assemblage*. Tracing a lineage from Symbolist poetry to assemblage, curator William C. Seitz observes in the exhibition catalogue, "Every work of art is an incarnation: an investment of matter with spirit.... It is difficult for minds nurtured by

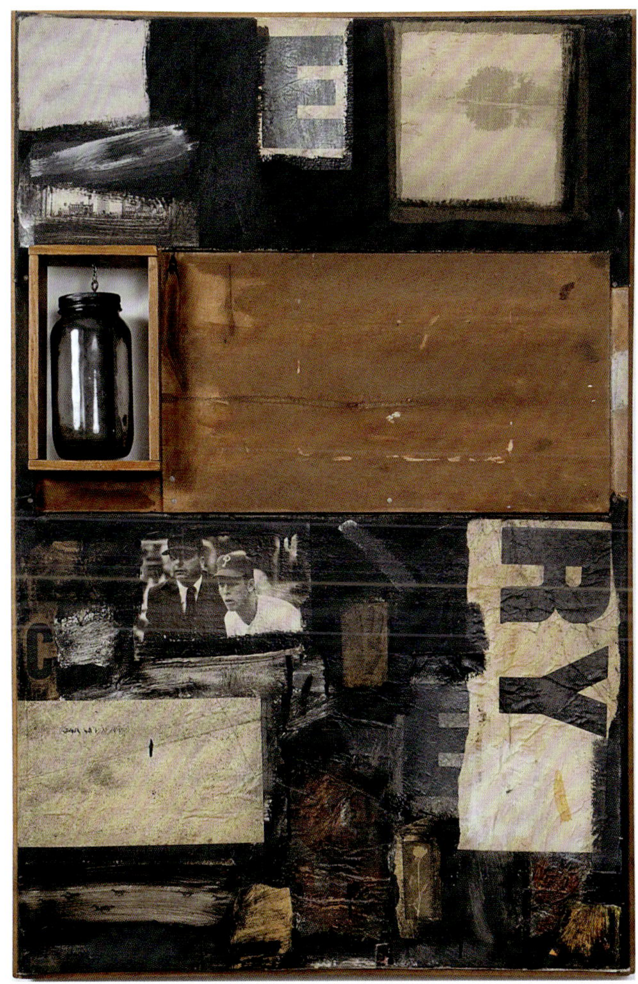

FIG. 6.8 Robert Rauschenberg, *Talisman*, 1958. Mixed media—oil, paper, printed paper, printed reproductions, wood, glass jar on metal chain and fabric on canvas, 42 1/8 × 28 × 4 1/2 inches. Des Moines Art Center, Des Moines, IA; purchased with funds from the Coffin Fine Arts Trust; Nathan Emory Coffin.

skepticism, materialism, and pragmatism to grant the existence of immaterial realties.... It was the poets, working with less physical and more immediately responsive materials than the painters and sculptors, who, cherubim and seraphim fluttering in celestial light, responded most rapidly and directly to the spirit of the times."[18]

In describing poetry as the locus of this investigation, Seitz indirectly invokes the Beat's intense period interest in alternative realms of experience.[19] He continues, "Assemblage has become, temporarily at least, the language for impatient, hypercritical, and anarchistic young artists.... The vernacular repertoire includes beat Zen and hot rods, mescalin experiences and faded flowers, photographic bumps and grinds, the *poubelle* (i.e., trash can), juke boxes, and hydrogen explosions."[20] Seitz's litany of youth-culture paraphernalia positions assemblage as the art of the counterculture, or *Art in the Age of Aquarius*, as he would title a later book.[21] Seitz's words show postwar art's continued engagement with enchantment within postwar art, albeit in forms Cornell would have likely dismissed. During the 1960s and '70s, many artists turned to the "black magic" of occultism, mysticism, and Surrealism as part of a broader antiestablishment ethos, discerning enchantment's implicit critique of rationality, materialism, and the normative social order.

BLACK MAGIC

In 1967, Betye Saar visited *An Exhibition of Works by Joseph Cornell* at the Pasadena Art Museum (figs. 6.9, 6.10). Soon after, she began to fashion her own boxes, and along with them her own theory of enchantment. *Omen* (1967, fig. 6.11), among the earliest of Saar's box constructions, contains a metronome pendulum, an astrological diagram, and a vintage photograph. The children in this picture are partially obscured by a black blur, the ghostly trace Saar's own hand photocopied onto a transparent sheet and affixed to the box's glass front. This floating hand recalls Saar's earlier *View from the Palmist's Window* (1966, fig. 6.12), which draws from the Roma iconography of palmistry.[22] Black rivulets flow into astrological symbols across the yellow palm of this earlier work. *Omen* flips the appendage in *View from the Palmist's Window*. To look into *Omen* is to seek the promise of a future foretold but to encounter its opposite. Although Saar appears to offer the omen of her palm to the figures inside, mirror shards at right reflect the reverse of what they see: the back of her hand. What we would seek, Saar seems to suggest, is right there on the surface.

The blackness of this photocopied hand is more a texture than a color, an intricate pattern of lines reproduced onto a transparent support. If palmistry seeks to divine an unknown future from such lines, *Omen* locates equivalent totems on the surface of its objects: the rust coating the metronome, the yellowing of the photograph, the decay of the mirror's silver backing. Patina is the physical trace of an object's life, an index of temperature and humidity, a material accretion of the care or neglect it received during its lifetime. As Kellie Jones has observed, "We might also think about as patina as love, an over-the-top display and coating that wraps an object."[23] Jones writes that the intimacy invited by Cornell's small-scale works "led to the emergence of [Saar's] own voice in the language of objects."[24] In Saar's box, the surfaces of objects are as powerful as the lines on a palm, at once an inheritance and the product of a lived

FIGS. 6.9 – 6.10
Installation views of *An Exhibition of Works by Joseph Cornell*, December 27, 1966–February 11, 1967. Pasadena Art Museum, Pasadena, CA.

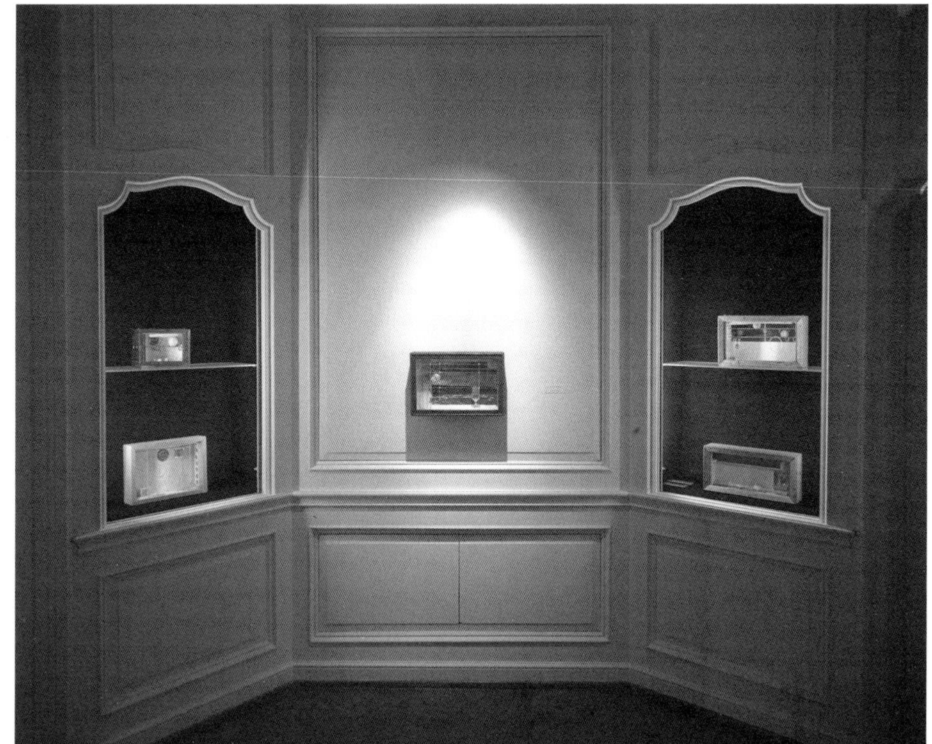

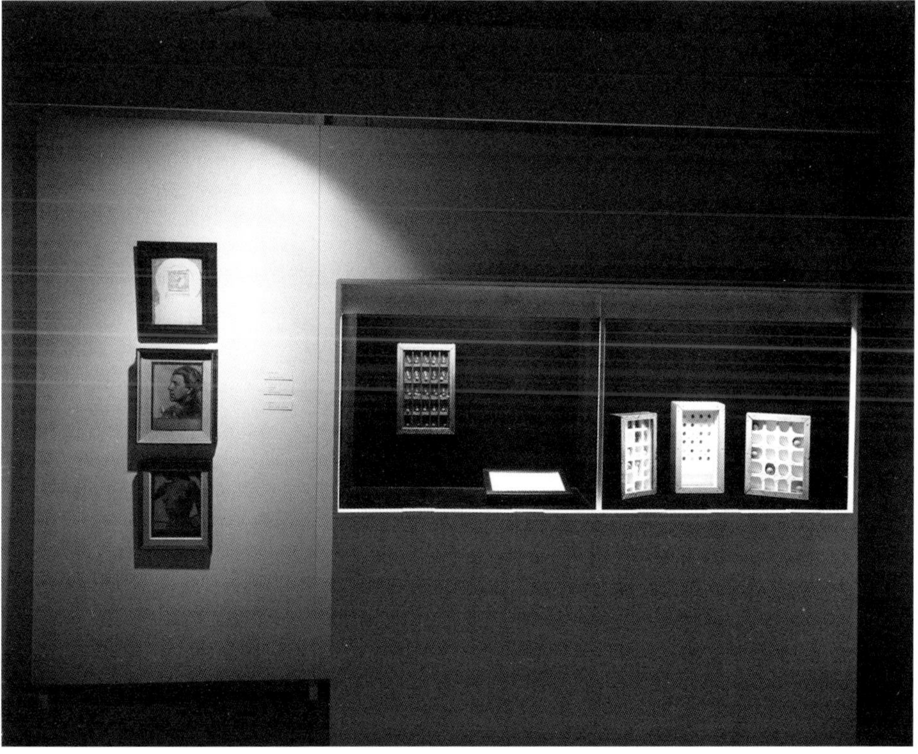

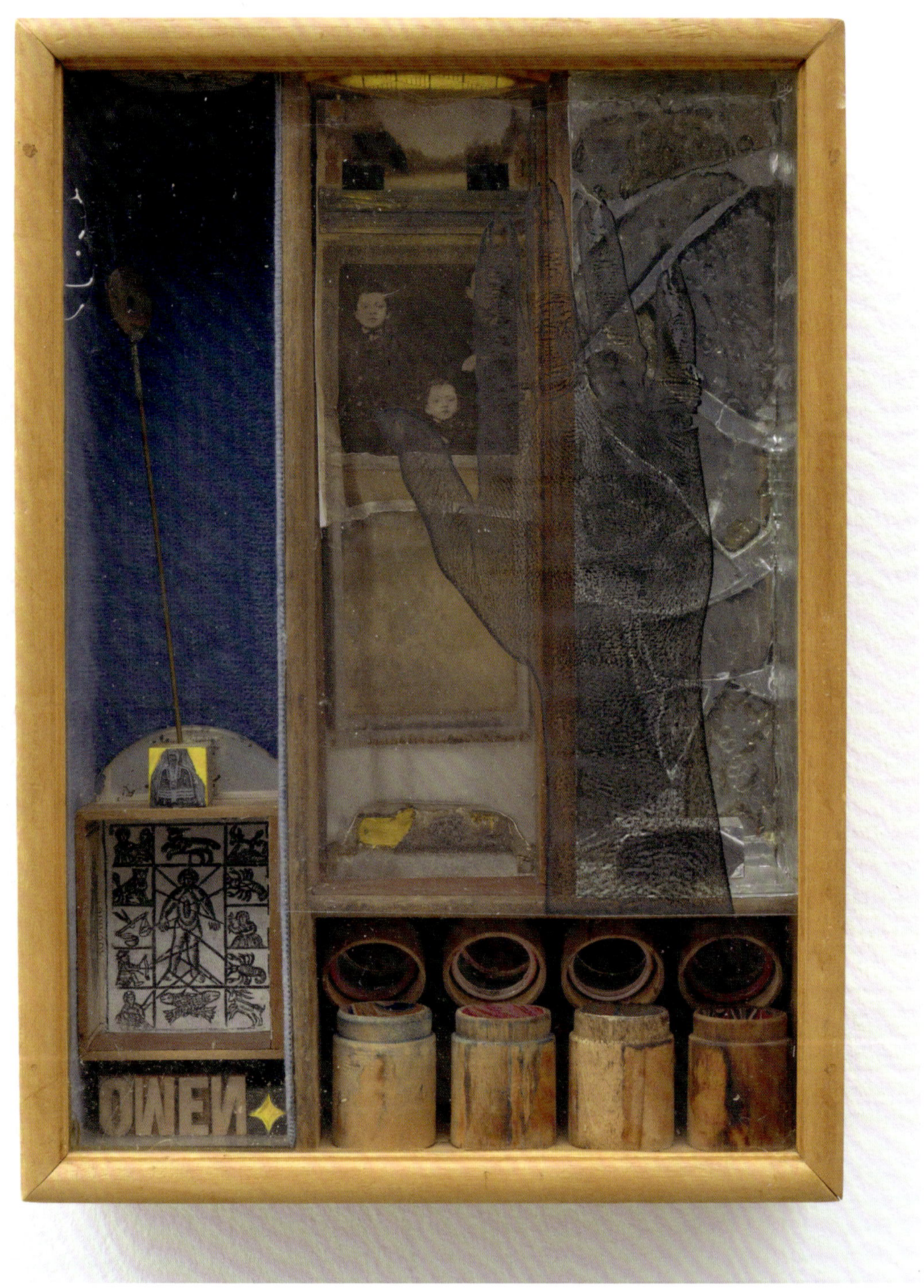

FIG. 6.11 Betye Saar, *Omen*, 1967. Mixed-media assemblage, 12 3/4 × 9 3/4 × 3 inches. Collection of Faith and Richard Flam.

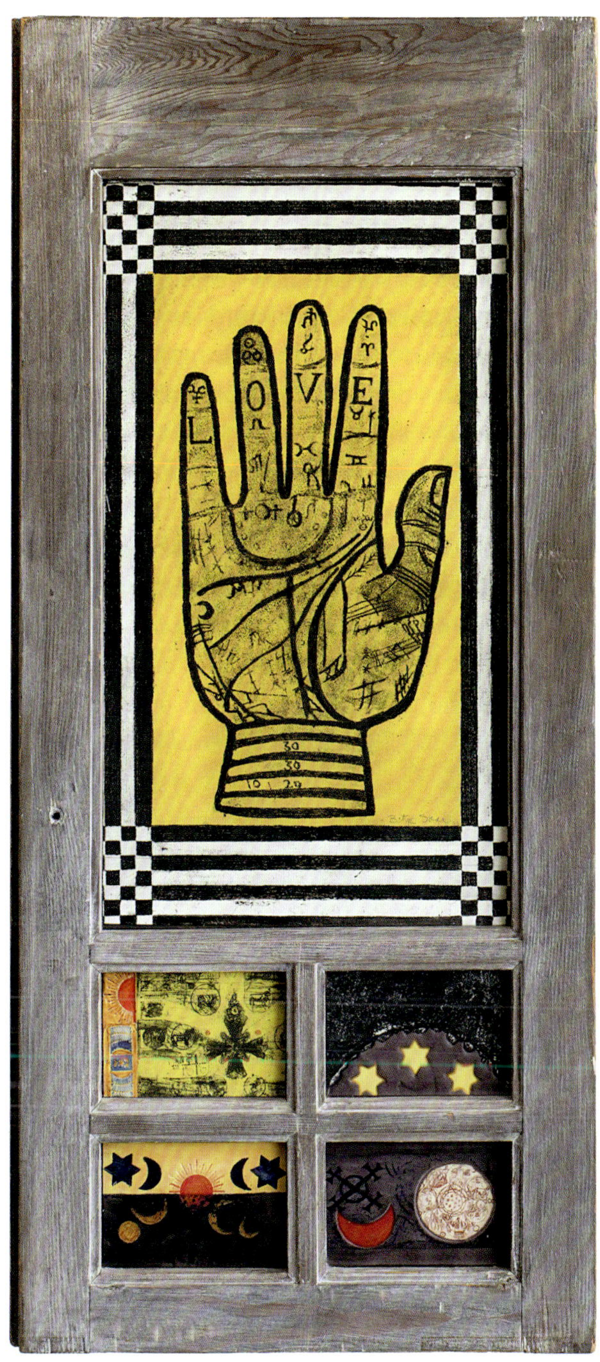

FIG. 6.12 Betye Saar, *View from the Palmist's Window*, 1966. Assemblage of color and intaglio etchings and wood window frame, $33\frac{3}{4} \times 15\frac{1}{8} \times 1\frac{1}{16}$ inches. Collection of halley k harrisburg and Michael Rosenfeld, New York.

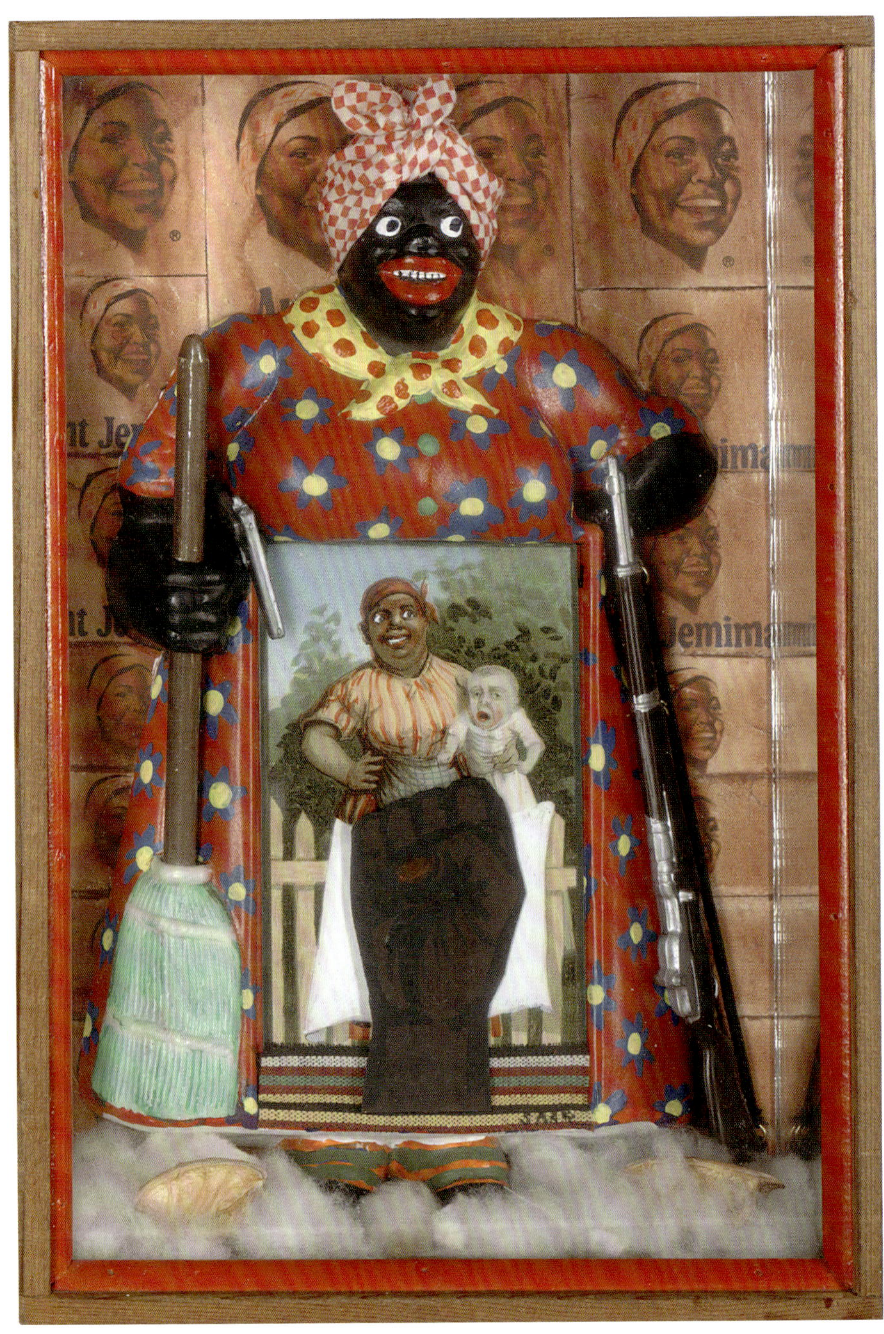

FIG. 6.15 Betye Saar, *The Liberation of Aunt Jemima*, 1972. Mixed-media assemblage, $11\frac{3}{4} \times 8 \times 2\frac{3}{4}$ inches. Collection of Berkeley Art Museum and Pacific Film Archive, Berkeley, CA; purchased with t he aid of funds from the National Endowment for the Arts (selected by the Committee for the Acquisition of Afro-American Art).

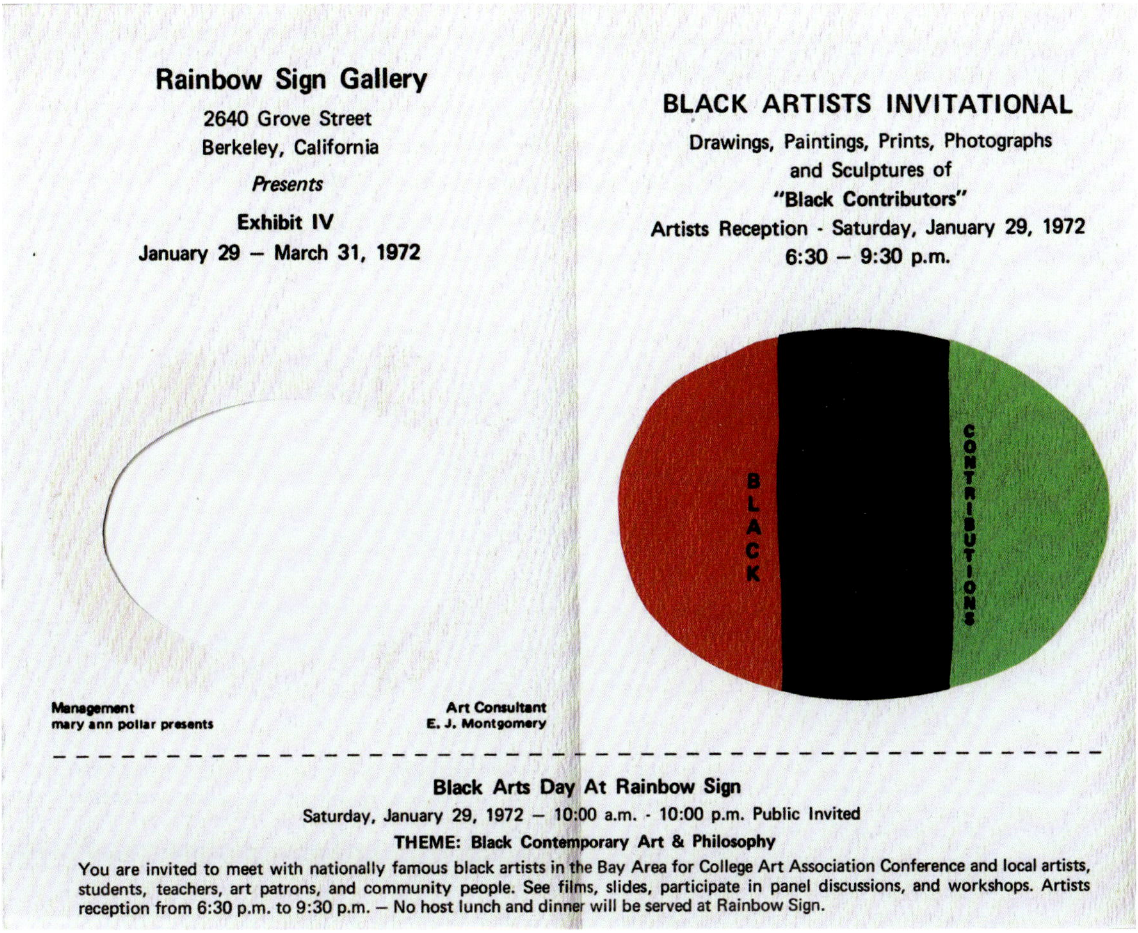

Rainbow Sign Gallery
2640 Grove Street
Berkeley, California
Presents
Exhibit IV
January 29 – March 31, 1972

Management
mary ann pollar presents

Art Consultant
E. J. Montgomery

BLACK ARTISTS INVITATIONAL
Drawings, Paintings, Prints, Photographs
and Sculptures of
"Black Contributors"
Artists Reception - Saturday, January 29, 1972
6:30 – 9:30 p.m.

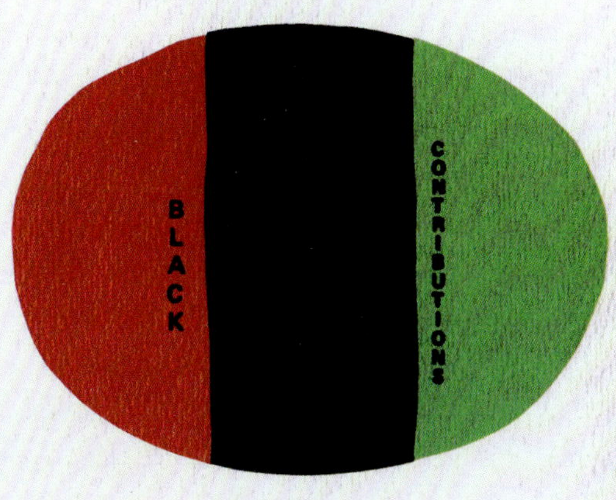

Black Arts Day At Rainbow Sign
Saturday, January 29, 1972 – 10:00 a.m. - 10:00 p.m. Public Invited
THEME: Black Contemporary Art & Philosophy
You are invited to meet with nationally famous black artists in the Bay Area for College Art Association Conference and local artists, students, teachers, art patrons, and community people. See films, slides, participate in panel discussions, and workshops. Artists reception from 6:30 p.m. to 9:30 p.m. – No host lunch and dinner will be served at Rainbow Sign.

FIG. 6.16 Invitation to artists' reception for *Black Contributors* exhibition. Card designed by E. J. Montgomery, Rainbow Sign Archive, courtesy of Odette Pollar.

bound up in the pain of memory. Its recontextualized central figure is both a charm against forgetting and an acknowledgment of the pain of collective memory. This pain is the source of the figure's power, that which allows her to expand beyond herself. Like *Black Girl's Window*, this work deploys enchantment's occult strains to suggest that there are ways of being in the world apart from those that have been imposed upon us.

WHAT REMAINS

Around 1956, Carolee Schneemann contacted Joseph Cornell at the suggestion of Stan Brakhage. She arrived at Cornell's home on Utopia Parkway wearing a modest dress and ballet slippers, a costume suggested by the other young women hired to assist the artist during the last decades of his life.[41] Cornell, she recalled, preferred that his female assistants assume an "innocent guise."[42] Although she was an ardent and outspoken feminist, Schneemann forgave the artist for his idealizing objectification. While she recognized the troublesome dimensions of their interactions, she also found in them a curious sense of freedom.[43] Entering into his world meant leaving "the terribel [*sic*] exigencies and orders of corrupt civilization," and spending hours pondering "the slowest gesture and the thinnest glass shining mica in a paving stone." These experiences made a deep impression on the young artist. To be with Cornell, she noted, was to be "enchanted in a banal ordinary daioy [*sic*] sort of way."[44]

Schneemann's early gestural paintings evidence her sensitivity to the enchantment of the ordinary. In *Secret Garden* (1956, fig. 6.17) loosely striated layers of green, chartreuse, white, and fuchsia surround a dense thicket of pink and purple brushstrokes. It is as if the chromatic intensity of the garden has dissolved flowers and trees into a swirling mass of flesh, pushing and pulling, condensing and dissipating substance into energy. In contrast to the male Abstract Expressionists she described as the "Art Stud Club," Schneemann's kinetic paintings channel and orchestrate the energy of the landscape, allowing her to become, as she described it, "a part of nature."[45] She credited Cornell for helping her experience these forces: "It was by his example that I first experienced a shaping humility and devotion—a preparedness to let an inner voice speak—prescient, timeless, beyond will, determination, or 'personality.' "[46]

Schneemann also intuited there were forces Cornell would not touch. The artist, she recalled, lived in "a great terror of his sexuality," a repression that she understood as "a source of immense, creative, suppressed exploration."[47] Schneemann seemed determined to unleash all that Cornell wished to repress. *Ice Box* (1963, fig. 6.18) looks like a Cornell box after a car crash. Twisted steel weaves among chaotic splashes of paint, twigs, and other detritus, while broken glass dangles from the box's frame. The work's wrecked, interpenetrating forms subject the structured order of Cornell's carefully cultivated enchantment to the unruly, destructive forces of the outside world. Schneemann makes this idea explicit in her *Controlled Burning* series (1963–64, fig. 6.19). Hinged boxes packed with fragments of glass, mirrors, paint, and cloth are doused with turpentine and touched with a lit match before the lid is closed. Schneemann's procedure relinquishes control over the creative process to the fire, which burns until the box's limited oxygen runs out.

FIG. 6.17 Carolee Schneemann, *Secret Garden*, 1956. Oil on canvas, 25 × 23¼ × 1⅜ inches. Estate of Carolee Schneemann.

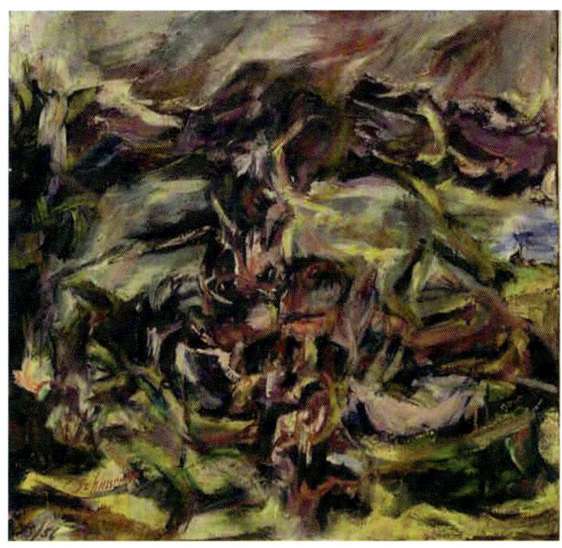

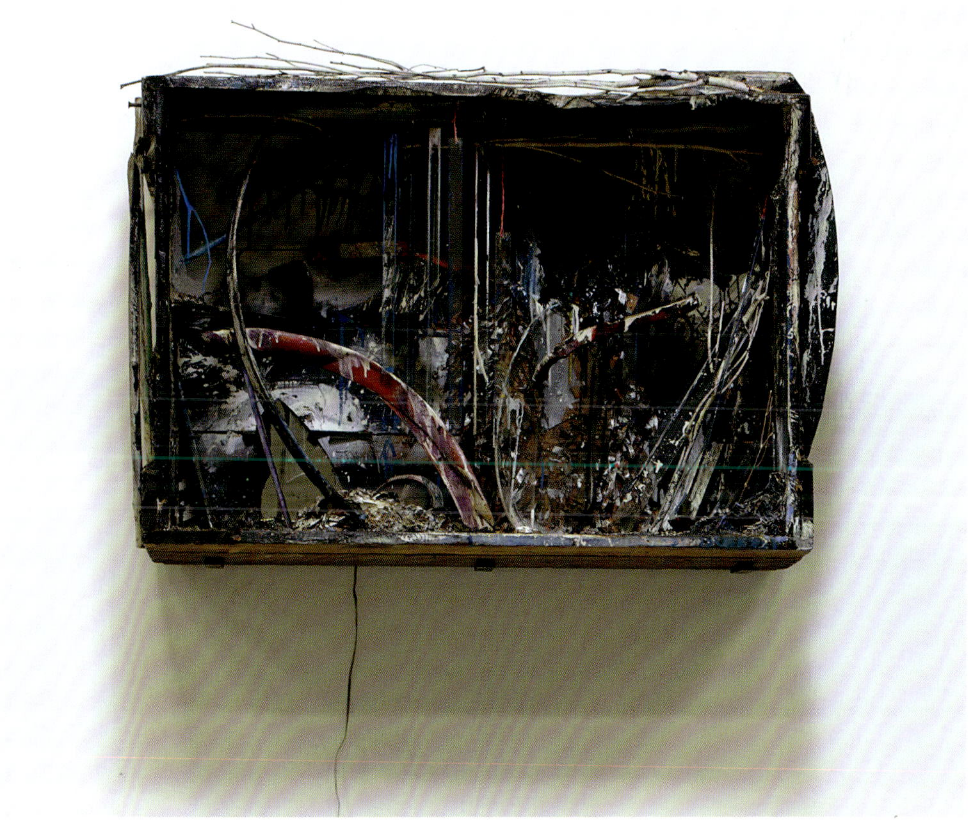

FIG. 6.18 Carolee Schneemann, *Ice Box*, 1963. Construction in wooden box—paint, mirrors, glass, motorized fan, twigs, 27 × 40 × 18 inches. Estate of Carolee Schneemann.

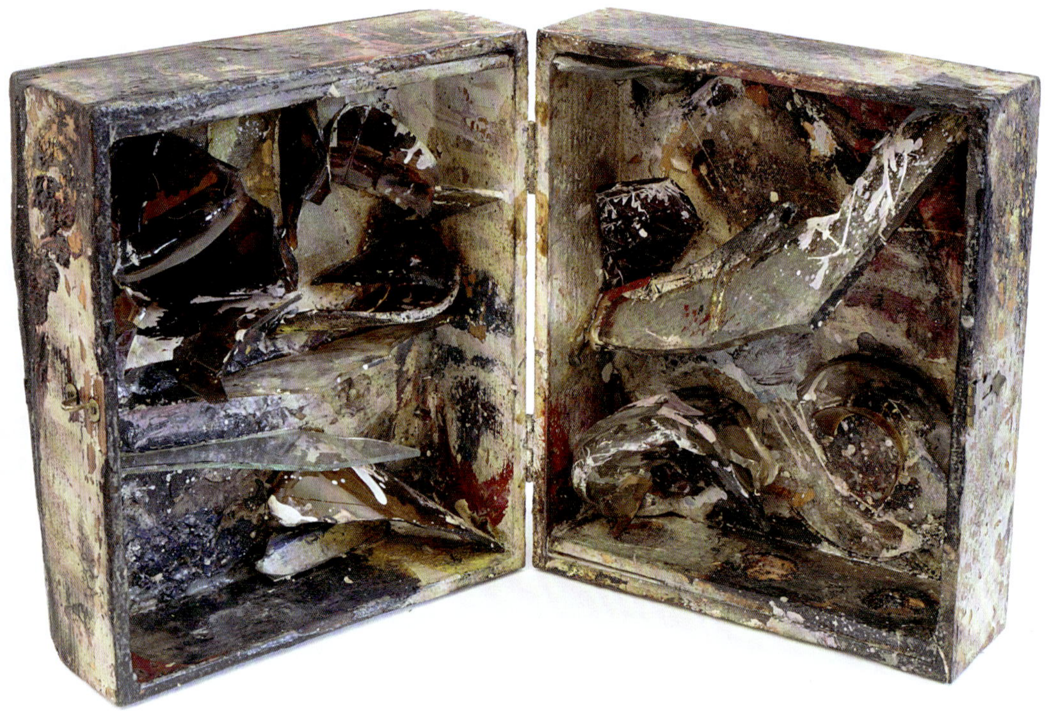

FIG. 6.19 Carolee Schneemann, *Fire-Controlled Burning: Darker Companion*, 1962. Burnt wooden box—glass, mirrors, paint, $15\frac{3}{4} \times 9\frac{1}{4} \times 2\frac{1}{2}$ inches. Estate of Carolee Schneemann.

Performances such as *Eye Body: 36 Transformative Actions for Camera* (1963, fig. 6.20) expand these boxes into rooms. To create this work, she filled a loft with glass, mirrors, paint, tarps, ropes, and trash. Her body merged into these materials as she manipulated them, a ritual she described as a "trance-like state" in which the body "may remain erotic, sexual, desired, desiring," but also "votive: marked, written over in a text of stroke and gesture discovered by my creative female will."[48] In working *among* materials rather than *with* them, Schneemann sought to abnegate the "idealized (mostly male) mythology of the 'abstract self' or the 'invented self.' . . . Another kind of glorification falsification where . . . you retain power and distancing over the situation."[49] Rather than the masterful individualism implied by such

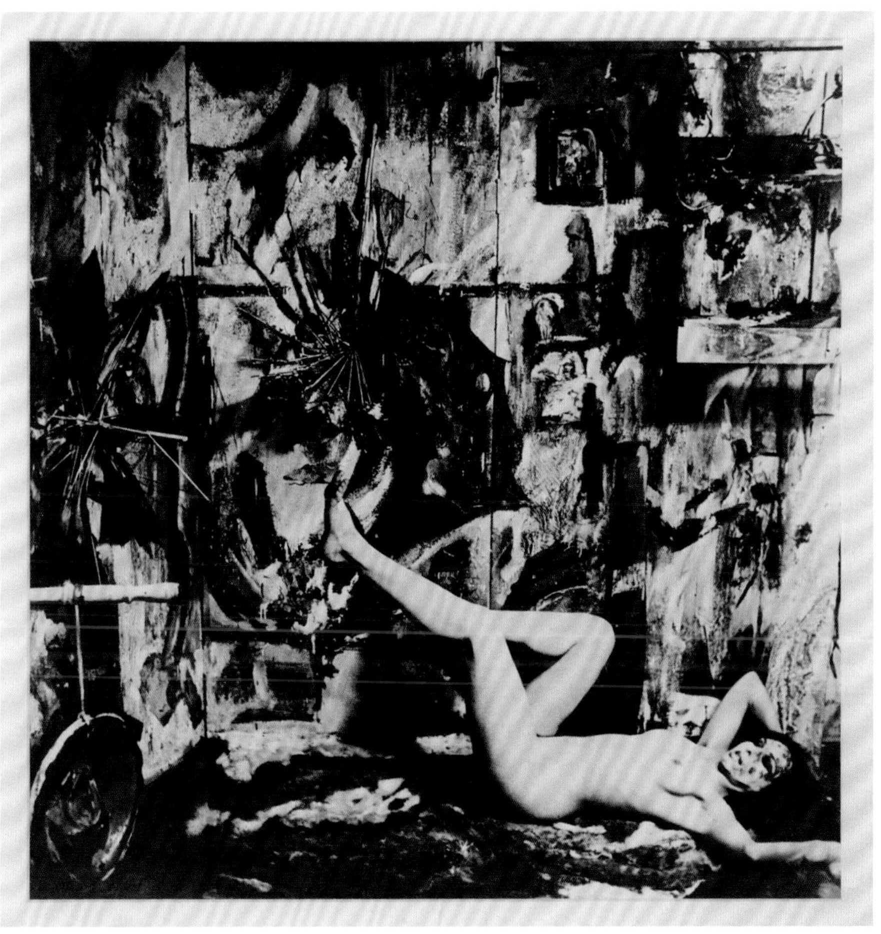

FIG. 6.20 Carolee Schneemann, *Eye Body: 36 Transformative Actions for Camera (Eye Body #1)*, 1963. Silver print, 19 × 23 inches. Estate of Carolee Schneemann.

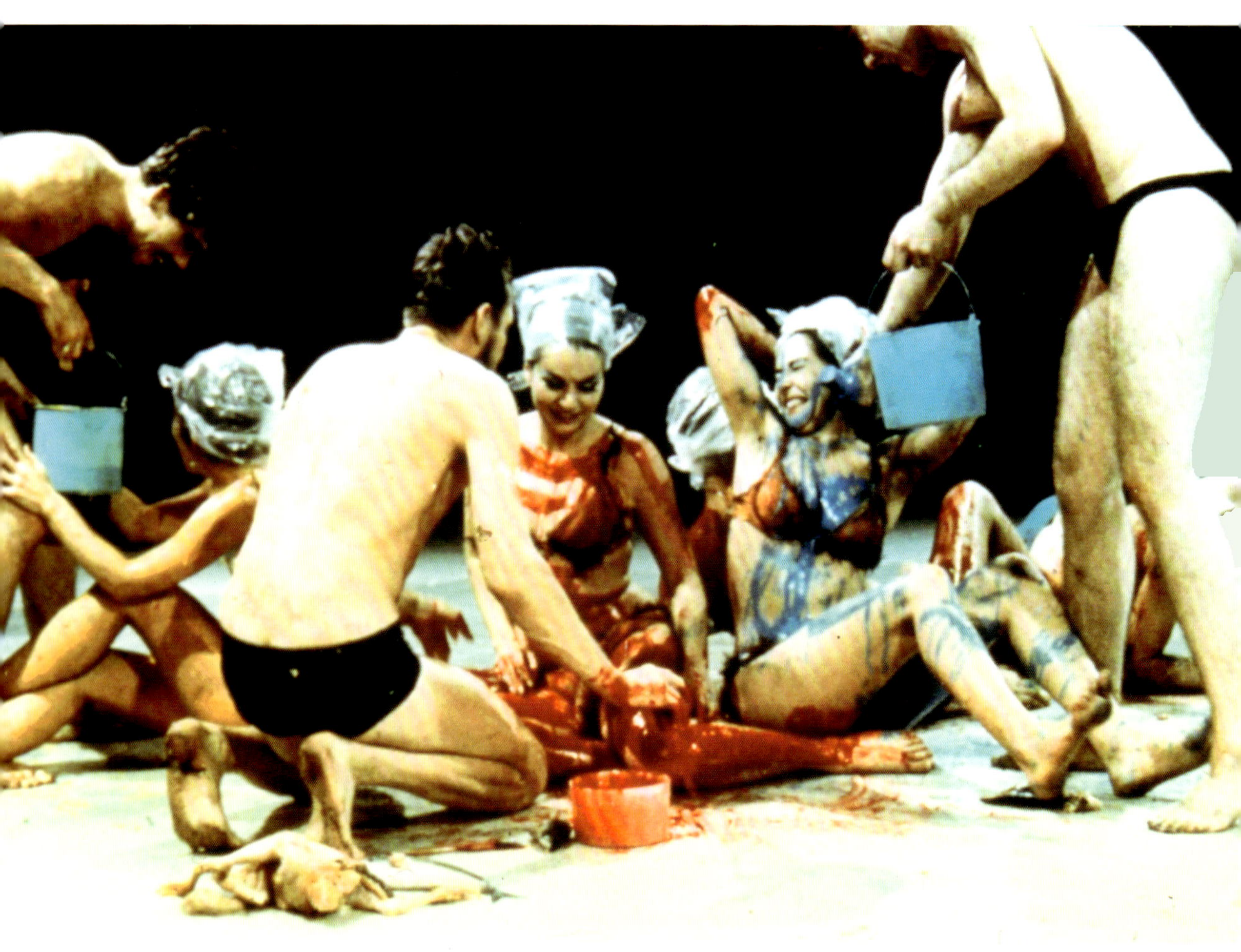

FIG. 6.21 Carolee Schneemann, *Meat Joy*, 1964. Performance. Estate of Carolee Schneemann.

a procedure, Schneemann's body at once responds to and orchestrates the world around it, a feminist rejoinder to the masculinist impulse of control. This ecstatic excess is pushed to an even higher key in *Meat Joy* (1964, fig. 6.21). In the orgiastic tumbling of bodies amidst raw fish, chicken, sausages, and paint, Schneemann locates an energy that was at once "sensual, cosmic, joyous, repellent."[50] As in *Eye Body*, Schneemann's Dionysian enchantment arises from the erotic energy of the body and the sensuous power of the materials themselves, rather than from an ideal external force. When Schneemann told Cornell about *Meat Joy*, she withheld the exact details of the performance, fearing they would upset him.[51]

But eventually she did tell him. On March 20, 1976, she performed a work she described as "another sort of box for and about Joseph Cornell" at the Anthology Film Archives, in New York. She called the performance *Moon in a Tree: A Friendship and Artifacts of Joseph Cornell*, a phrase that came to her in a dream.[52] Art historian Joanna Roche has noted that the tree evokes the quince tree in the backyard of Cornell's home, as well as Cornell himself.[53] Schneemann is the moon.

Carolee Schneemann steps onto a dark stage (figs. 6.22, 6.23). She wears a modest vintage dress and ballet flats, the same costume she donned to visit Cornell. She takes a seat in one of two empty chairs. She sips pink lemonade spiked with vodka, the drink Cornell served her during her visits (albeit without the alcohol). Three screens, projected images from three separate slide carousels, form the stage's backdrop. The left screen shows images of Schneemann's life and work, while the one at right shows Cornell's work. In the middle, Schneemann projects selections from their decade-long correspondence. The performance begins with the click of an advancing slide. An early painting by Schneemann appears with a photograph of Cornell. Click. The artist's typed directions to his home ("walk up one half block to Gertz Dept. store"), flanked by a photograph of Schneemann and Cornell, and Cornell's box *Grand Hotel Bon Port* (figs. 6.24, 6.25). As she advances the slides, Schneemann reads excerpts from their letters and offers personal anecdotes and observations. Click. Click. Click. A photograph of *Eye Body* appears next to *Untitled (Butterfly Habitat)* (ca. 1940) (figs. 6.26, 6.27). And soon thereafter, Schneemann pointedly shows an image of *Meat Joy* alongside a scene from Cornell's *Angel* (figs. 6.28, 6.29). The raw flesh and erotic intensity of the performance embodies all that is repressed in Cornell's austere stone figure, while also, perhaps, suggesting their connection.

The performance was Schneemann's way of saying all that remained unsaid between them. It was also a gift. Through the intermediary of their correspondence and Schneemann's voice, works that would seem diametrically opposed in tenor and aim come into contact. The slide projectors create a montage, in which the connections and disjunctures among Cornell's and Schneemann's work emerge. Meat and stone, bodies and sculpture, profane and sacred flow together yet remain apart. The montage extends to the realms of the living and the dead, for Schneemann sits across from an empty chair, reserved for Cornell. She feels the audience slip away. She begins to speak directly to him. He is at once present and absent. She enters

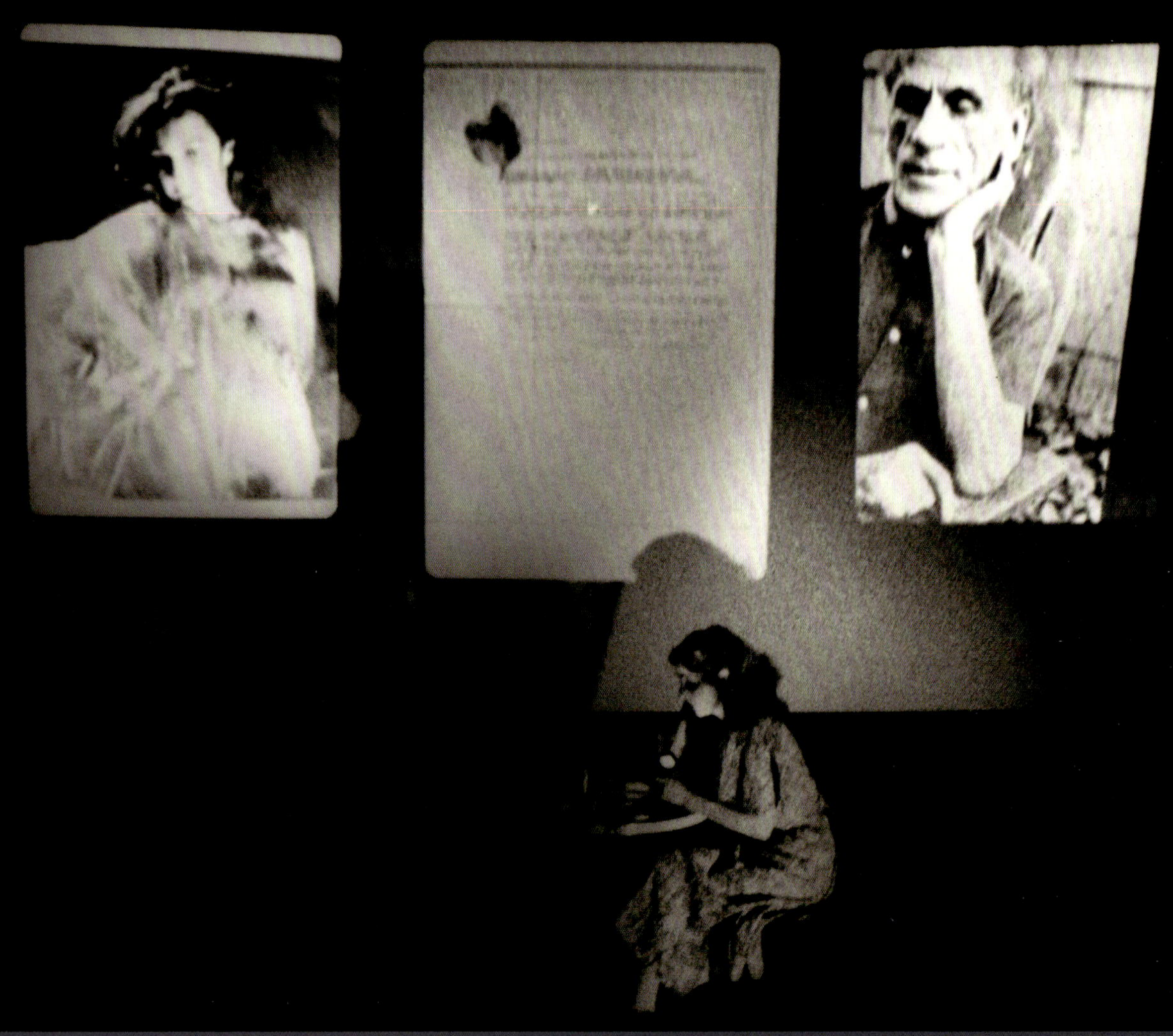

FIG. 6.22 Carolee Schneemann, *Moon in a Tree: A Friendship and Artifacts of Joseph Cornell*, Walker Art Center, January 23, 1979. Carolee Schneemann Papers, Department of Special Collections and University Archives, Stanford University.

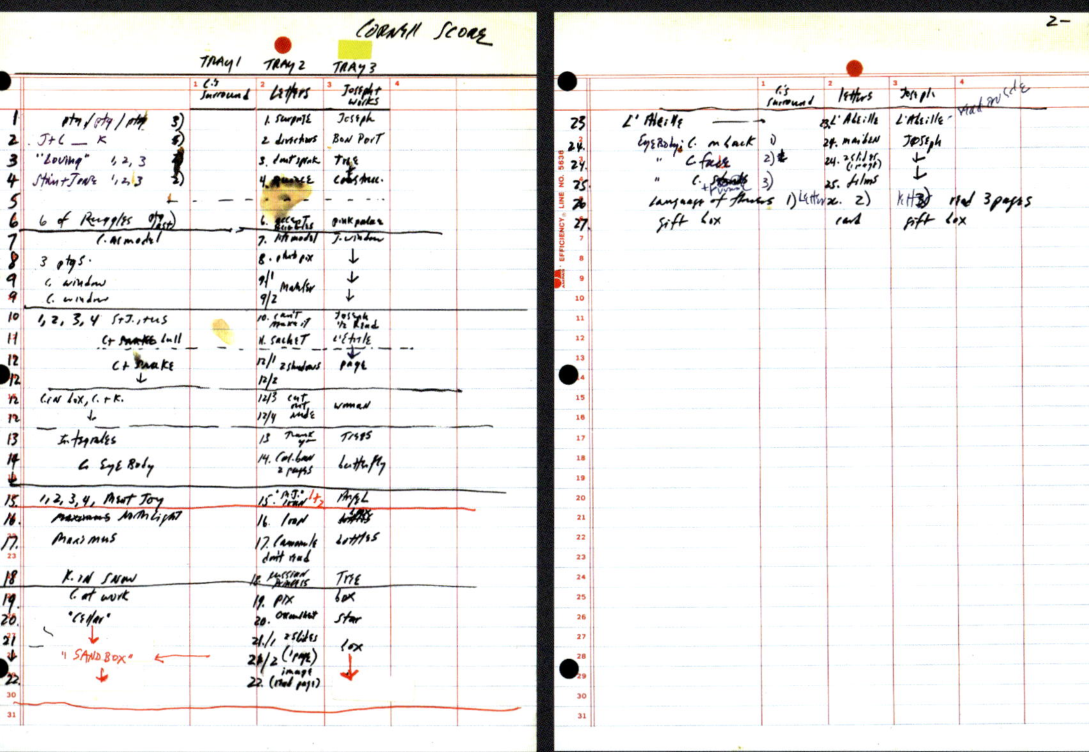

FIG. 6.23 Carolee Schneemann, performance score for *Moon in a Tree: A Friendship and Artifacts of Joseph Cornell*. Carolee Schneemann Papers, Department of Special Collections and University Archives, Stanford University.

3708 Utopia Parkway
Flushing 58. NY.
Tel/ - Fl.8-9099.

Dear Miss Schneemann,

Here are the directions promised over the phone yesterday morning in the event that things work out for next Tuesday morning. In the event that you do not call we'll be looking forward to a visit.

I hope we have such an evenly tempered day as today with its overtone of early autumn and that you might be interested in helping me overtake some "memories" of a certain one of 11 years ago that is receding too fast into the realm of legend. I do not have the gift of Novalis to help me hold fast such an experience and I think you might be interested in the means that I am using in the attempt. In the three dimensional an Uccello idea suddenly came to life with more freshness than I usually run into after hot, hectic days. I am "dedicating" the intervening work on this box to you.

late
last
night

Sincerely yours,

Joseph Cornell

Take Main St-Flushing train at Grand Central Station level lower than regular lines (Lexington Ave.)

Ride to end of line - Flushing, Main St.

Walk up one half block to Gertz Dept. store - cross street & take Bayside West bus (avoid Bayside and Bayside Avenue)

Get off at 172 St. & walk in direction of bus one block to Utopia Pkwy - turn right and walk half block to 3708

FIG. 6.24 Joseph Cornell, directions to Utopia Parkway for Carolee Schneemann. Carolee Schneemann Papers, Department of Special Collections and University Archives, Stanford University.

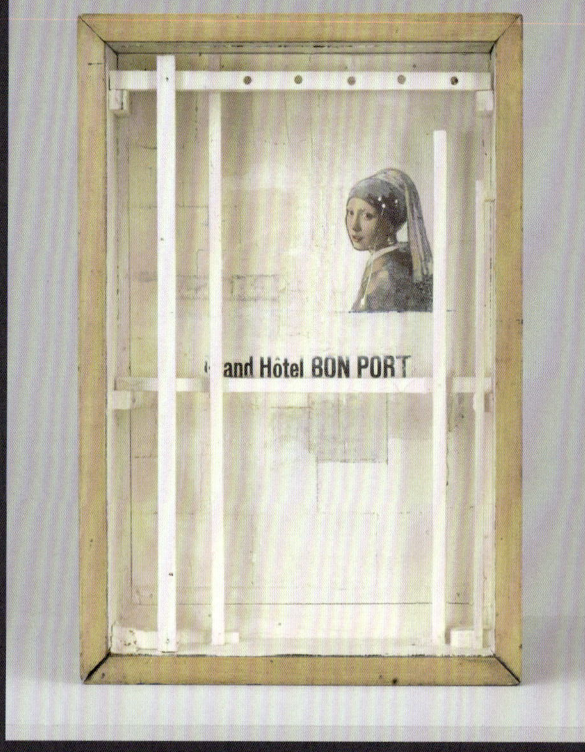

FIG. 6.25 Joseph Cornell, *Grand Hotel Bon Port*, 1952. Painted wood, paper, photolithographs on paper, glass, colored pencil, and metal hardware, 19 × 13 × 3¾ inches. Whitney Museum of American Art, New York; gift of Lindy and Edwin A. Bergman.

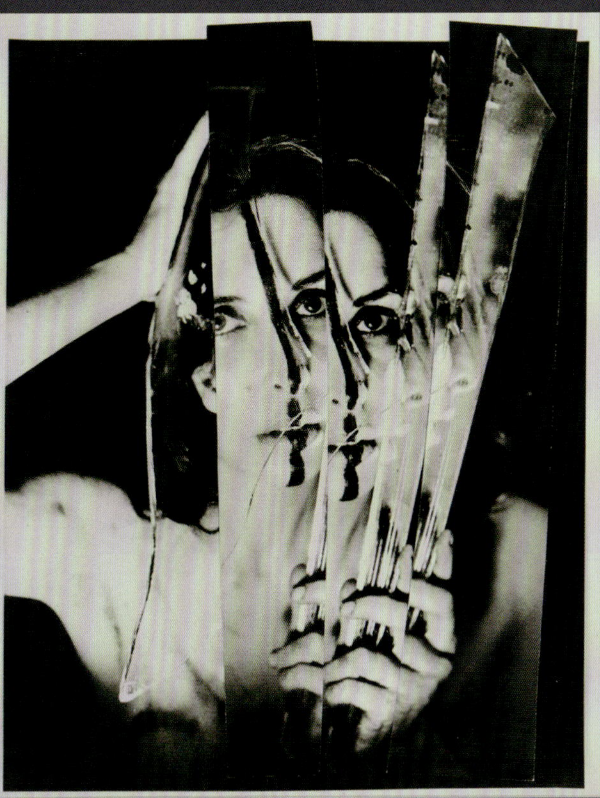

FIG. 6.26 Carolee Schneemann, *Eye Body: 36 Transformative Actions for Camera (Eye Body #11)*, 1963. Silver print, 19 × 23 inches.

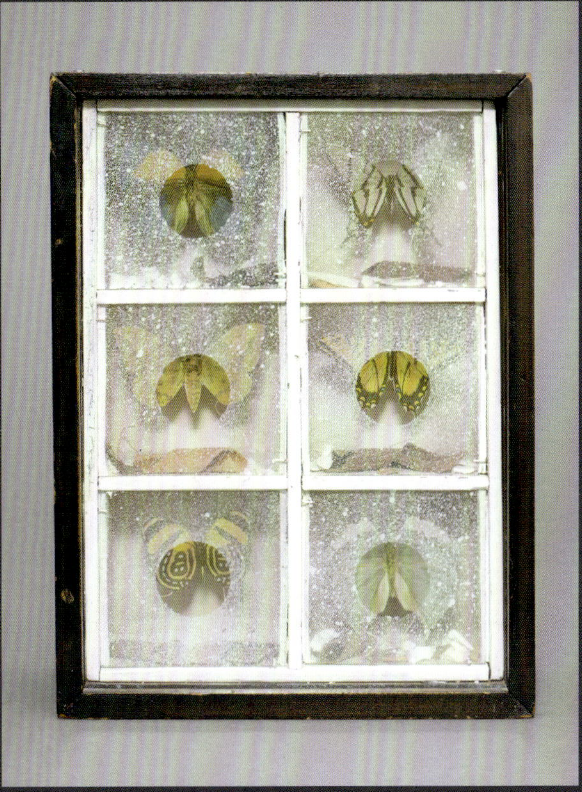

FIG. 6.27 Joseph Cornell, *Untitled (Butterfly Habitat)*, ca. 1940. Box construction with painted glass, 12 × 9⅛ × 3⅛ inches. Art Institute of Chicago, Lindy and Edwin Bergman Joseph Cornell Collection.

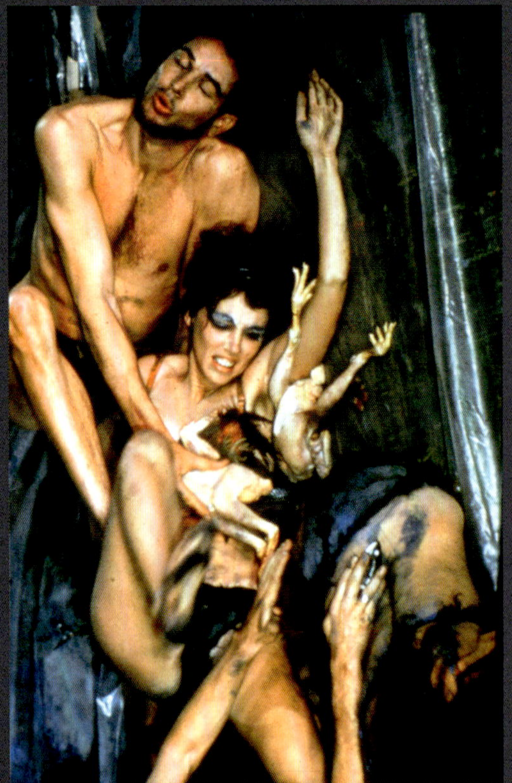

FIG. 6.28 Carolee Schneemann, *Meat Joy*, 1964.

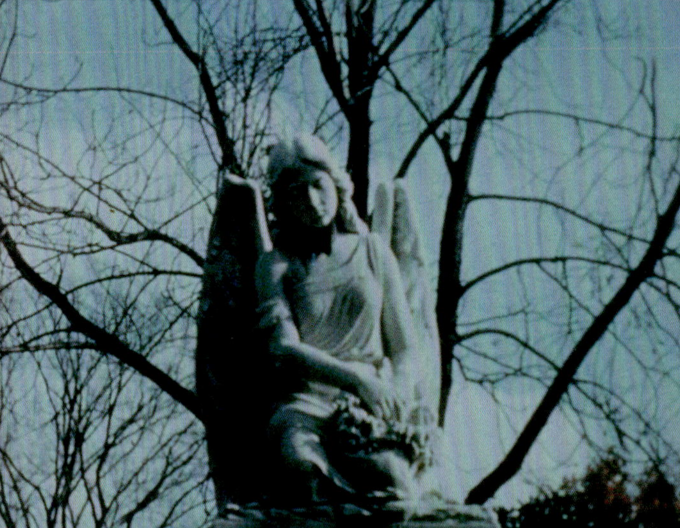

FIG. 6.29 Film still from *Angel* (Joseph Cornell, 1957). Austrian Film Museum.

Cornell's world for the last time but finally brings her full self into it. "I understood I might contribute to an enchantment," she wrote, "and was myself inspired by Joseph's deep connection to the gift of creating vision: the subtle immediacy of things observed and resonant for his 'visioning' state, his rich metaphoric erudition."[54] In the end the artists shared a conviction in the specialness of the everyday and the importance of looking and feeling deeply.

In a recent remembrance of Schneemann, writer Maggie Nelson poses two questions first asked by Fred Moten and Stefano Harney: "What do we have that we want to keep?" and "What do we not have that we need?" Nelson finds the answer to both questions in this statement from Schneemann, written when she was eighteen: "That is all, (all?!) I want—reënchantment. It is something I must do myself."[55]

What do we want to keep? What do we not have that we need? And to these I would add another question: What do we have that we *do not* need? Schneemann and Saar did not need Cornell's desire for control, order, and preservation, and his limited vision of women. But they kept his deep appreciation for the power of the quotidian and his knowledge that there are many ways of being in the world. I too want to keep these things. Cornell has shown me a richer, more complicated version of some stories I thought I knew. He also told me some stories I had never heard before, and others he likely did not intend to share. He taught me about the magic of figuration, and its ability to conjure worlds from humble things. In a certain light, with some imagination, chips of glass can become diamonds. And in his work, I recognized the pain of realizing that no one can fully grasp another's experience of the world. I find these lessons beautiful and meaningful, so I choose to keep them. I also choose to keep the wisdom that certain things cannot be explained in instrumental terms. And above all, I choose to keep the knowledge that meaning resides in the world around us, rather than in some distant realm. The smallest things are often the most consequential. Perhaps enchantment is not some lost cosmic unity, some long-departed force, but simply a recognition of that which has been with us all along.

NOTES

PREFACE: THE GREAT AND THE SMALL

Epigraph: George Eliot, *Middlemarch: A Study of Provincial Life* (Hertfordshire, UK: Wordsworth Editions, 2000), 10.

1 André Masson, *Battle of Fishes* (1926), Museum of Modern Art, 260.1937; Joan Miró, *Object* (1936), Museum of Modern Art, 940.1965.a-c.

2 Deborah Solomon, *Utopia Parkway* (Boston: MFA Publications, 1997).

3 These important revisionist texts include Kirsten Hoving, *Joseph Cornell and Astronomy: A Case for the Stars* (Princeton, NJ: Princeton University Press, 2009); Jodi Hauptman, *Joseph Cornell: Stargazing in the Cinema* (New Haven, CT: Yale University Press, 1999); Analisa Leppanen-Guerra, *Children's Stories and "Child-Time" in the Works of Joseph Cornell and the Transatlantic Avant-Garde* (Surrey, UK: Ashgate, 2011); Jason Edwards and Stephanie Taylor, eds., *Joseph Cornell: Opening the Box* (Bern: Peter Lang, 2007); Matthew Affron and Sylvie Ramond, eds., *Joseph Cornell et les surréalistes à New York* (Paris: Hazan; Lyon: Musée des beaux-arts de Lyon, 2014); Sarah Lea, ed., *Joseph Cornell: Wanderlust* (London: Royal Academy of Art, 2015); Mary Claire McKinley, *Birds of a Feather: Joseph Cornell's Homage to Juan Gris* (New York: Metropolitan Museum of Art, 2018).

4 The phrase "disenchantment of the world" first appeared in "Science as Vocation," Max Weber's 1918 speech at Munich University. The text was published in 1919 by Duncker & Humblodt, Munich, and later as "Wissenschaft als Beruf," *Gesammelte Aufsätze zur Wissenschaftslehre* (Tübingen, 1922), 524–55. See H. H. Gerth and C. Wright Mills, trans. and ed., *From Max Weber: Essays in Sociology* (New York: Oxford University Press, 1946), 129–56.

5 Throughout this book, my use of the term "Enlightenment" denotes a philosophical understanding of knowledge as residing in empirical fact (positivism), the material world (materialism), or human reason (rationalism), rather than a metaphysical, magical, or divine source. My understanding of the relationship between Enlightenment philosophy and enchantment is indebted to Jason Ā. Josephson-Storm's "philosophical archeology of this conception of modernity, the one that identifies the modern with the Enlightenment and the end of magic, the domination of nature, and the extirpation of spirits." Josephson-Storm, *The Myth of Disenchantment: Magic, Modernity, and the Birth of the Human Sciences* (Chicago: University of Chicago Press, 2017), 11.

6 T. J. Clark, *Farewell to an Idea: Episodes from a History of Modernism* (New Haven, CT: Yale University Press, 2000), 7.

7 Rosalind Krauss, "Grids," *October* 9 (Summer 1979): 12.

8 Olivia Laing, "Joseph Cornell: How the Reclusive Artist Conquered the Art World—from His Mum's Basement," *Guardian*, July 25, 2015, https://www.theguardian.com/artanddesign/2015/jul/25/joseph-cornell-wanderlust-royal-academy-exhibition-london.

9 Cornell objects to this characterization in a 1954 letter to Motherwell, writing "I'm not as withdrawn as you've sometimes thought;—have turned myself inside out & back again since receiving your article early last summer—coming to the realization that whatever I have to offer is an extremely difficult item to put out in the open such as speakers in your "Subjects of the Artist" soirées." Joseph Cornell to Robert Motherwell, March 30, 1954, I.A.35.9.48230, Robert Motherwell Papers, Dedalus Foundation Archives, Brooklyn, New York. The "article" Cornell refers to is Robert Motherwell, "Robert Motherwell on Joseph Cornell," unpublished essay for a catalogue for a proposed 1953 exhibition on Cornell at the Walker Art Center; reprinted in Mary Ann Caws, *Joseph Cornell's Theater of the Mind: Selected Diaries, Letters, and Files* (New York: Thames and Hudson, 1993), 13–16.

10 Cornell, quoted in Lea, *Joseph Cornell*, 260.

11 Jane Bennett, *The Enchantment of Modern Life: Attachments, Crossings, Ethics* (Princeton, NJ: Princeton University Press, 2001), 3.

12 Stanley Cavell, *In Quest of the Ordinary: Lines of Skepticism and Romanticism* (Chicago: University of Chicago Press, 1988), 4.

13 Joseph Cornell, diary entry, May 1, 1947, series 3: Diaries, box 6, folder 4, Joseph Cornell Papers, Archives of American Art, Smithsonian Institution, Washington, DC (hereafter AAA).

14 Eve Sedgwick, "Paranoid Reading and Reparative Reading, or You're So Paranoid, You Probably Think This Essay Is about You," in *Touching Feeling: Affect, Pedagogy, and Performativity* (Durham, NC: Duke University Press, 2003), 150–51.

15 As Richard Meyer writes of Walter Benjamin, "And he was arguing for a scholarly method that would include 'an esteem for the insignificant'—an esteem for anonymous works and overlooked details, for the obscure and for the non-canonical." Meyer, "At Home in Marginal Domains," *Documents* 18 (2000): 19–32; reprinted in Catherine Lord and Richard Meyer, *Art & Queer Culture* (New York: Phaidon Press, 2013), 358.

16 Hal Foster, *The Return of the Real: The Avant-Garde at the End of the Century* (Cambridge, MA: MIT Press, 1996), 4.

INTRODUCTION: ENCHANTMENTS

Epigraph: Walter Benjamin, "Goethe's Elective Affinities" (first published in *Neue Deutsche Beiträge*, 1924–25), trans. Stanley Corngold; reprinted in Marcus Bullock and Michael W. Jennings, eds., *Walter Benjamin: Selected Writings Volume 1, 1913–1926* (Cambridge, MA: Belknap Press of Harvard University Press, 1996), 356.

1 Joseph Cornell, diary entry, August 9, 1947, series 3: Diaries, box 6, folder 4, Joseph Cornell Papers, Archives of American Art, Smithsonian Institution, Washington, DC (hereafter AAA).

2 *Brancusi* was held at the Brummer Gallery from November 17 to December 15, 1926. Lynda Roscoe Hartigan was the first to mention Cornell's visit to this exhibition in *Joseph Cornell: Navigating the Imagination* (Salem, MA: Peabody Essex Museum, 2007), 29. The sculpture on view at Brummer in 1926 is currently owned by the Art Institute of Chicago. I am grateful to Yechen Zhao for his assistance in identifying this cast.

3 Dawn Ades, *Surrealist Art: The Lindy and Edwin Bergman Collection at the AIC* (Chicago: Art Institute of Chicago, 1997), 84.

4 Fairfield Porter, "Joseph Cornell," *Art and Literature* 8 (Spring 1966): 120–30.

5 To this point, the *Oxford English Dictionary* defines "enchantment" as "1. The action or process of enchanting, or of employing magic or sorcery. 2. Alluring or overpowering charm; enraptured condition; (delusive) appearance of beauty." (*OED Online*, Oxford University Press, https://www.oed.com/view/Entry/61664?redirectedFrom=enchantment&).

6 William Shakespeare, *Macbeth* (New York: Bantam Classic, 2005), 111.

7 As David Morgan writes, "Therefore, operating with both in hand, enchantment and disenchantment, broadens the capacity for explaining events and provides a powerful means of social control when wielded by authorities or institutions, but also as strategies for overturning the grip of authority." Morgan, "Enchantment, Disenchantment, Re-enchantment," in *Re-enchantment*, ed. James Elkins and David Morgan (New York: Routledge, 2009), 13.

8 As Josephson-Storm wisely cautions, "Power—both liberating and dominating, *potential* and *potestas*—can be actualized by way of enchantment or disenchantment. Ideologies cloak themselves in both." Jason Ā. Josephson-Storm, *The Myth of Disenchantment: Magic, Modernity, and the Birth of the Human Sciences* (Chicago: University of Chicago Press, 2017), 315.

9 Quoted in Dore Ashton, *A Joseph Cornell Album* (New York: Viking Press, 1974), 56.

10 William James, *The Varieties of Religious Experience: A Study in Human Nature* (New York: Barnes & Noble Classics, 2004), 328.

11 James, *The Varieties of Religious Experience*, 328.

12 Branka Arsić, *Bird Relics: Grief and Vitalism in Thoreau* (Cambridge, MA: Harvard University Press, 2016), 4.

13 The foundational account of the noncontradictory principle of truth can be found in Aristotle's *Metaphysics*. He writes, "For he who says that everything is true makes even the statement contrary to his own true, and therefore his own not true (for the contrary statement denies that it is true), while he who says everything is false makes himself also false." Aristotle, *Metaphysics*, trans. W. D. Ross, bk. 4, pt. 8, available online at http://classics.mit.edu/Aristotle/metaphysics.4.iv.html.

14 To this point, Rachael DeLue and Robin Veder have productively explored topics including Swedendborgian mysticism, the kinesthetic energy of line, and intersubjective communication in the history of American art. By demonstrating the philosophical richness of American modernists, their work complicates the entrenched narrative of early-twentieth-century American art as characterized by self-reflexive attempts to define a national character. Rachael Ziady DeLue, *George Inness and the Science of Landscape* (Chicago: University of Chicago Press, 2008); Rachael Ziady DeLue, *Arthur Dove: Always Connect* (Chicago: University of Chicago Press, 2016); Robin Veder, *The Living Line: Modern Art and the Economy of Energy* (Hanover, NH: Dartmouth College Press, 2015).

15 Arsić, *Bird Relics*, 3.

16 Michael Moon, *A Small Boy and Others: Imitation and Initiation in American Culture from Henry James to Andy Warhol* (Durham, NC: Duke University Press, 1998), 146.

17 Charles Taylor, *A Secular Age* (Cambridge, MA: Belknap Press of Harvard University Press, 2007), 19.

18 Sandra Leonard Starr's slim exhibition catalogue was the first extensive consideration of Cornell's metaphysical convictions. Recent work on Cornell and Christian Science include essays by Richard Vine and Erika Doss, Kirsten Hoving's detailed account of Christian Science's approach to astronomy, and Lindsay Blair's book on the artist's "search for the self." Although this book is indebted to these examples, its approach considers Christian Science as an epistemological structure that shaped Cornell's worldview rather than a set of principles he sought to illustrate. Starr, *Joseph Cornell: Art and Metaphysics* (New York: Castelli, Feigen, Corcoran, 1982); Kirsten Hoving, *Joseph Cornell and Astronomy: A Case for the Stars* (Princeton, NJ: Princeton University Press, 2009); Lindsay Blair, *Joseph Cornell's Vision of Spiritual Order* (London: Reaktion Books, 1998), 20; Richard Vine, "Eterniday: Cornell's Christian Science 'Metaphysique,'" in *Joseph Cornell: Shadowplay Eterniday*, ed. Lynda Roscoe Hartigan (New York: Thames & Hudson, 2003), 36–49; Erika Doss, "Joseph Cornell and Christian Science," in *Joseph Cornell: Opening the Box*, ed. Jason Edwards and Stephanie Taylor (Bern: Peter Lang, 2007), 113–27.

19 In this, I follow the example of philosopher Charles Taylor's *A Secular Age*,

whose "explorations of the history of thinking about God, religious institutions, the natural and social order, and the person . . . [d]emonstrate how intertwined different dimensions of historical transformation have been." Michael Warner, Jonathan VanAntwerpen, Craig Calhoun, eds., *Varieties of Secularism in a Secular Age* (Cambridge, MA: Harvard University Press, 2010), 9.

20 This book draws on D. W. Winnicott's description of experience as an intermediary zone between the subjective inner world and the material external world: "The third part of the life of a human being, a part that we cannot ignore, is an intermediate area of *experiencing*, to which inner reality and external life both contribute. It is an area that is not challenged, because no claim is made on its behalf except that it shall exist as a resting-place for the individual engaged in the perpetual human task of keeping inner and outer reality separate yet interrelated." Winnicott, "Transitional Objects and Transitional Phenomena," in *Playing and Reality* (London: Routledge Classics, 2009), 3.

21 This account is indebted to Lynda Roscoe Hartigan's decades of meticulous research on the artist. Her findings are summarized in *Joseph Cornell: Navigating the Imagination.*

22 See Deborah Solomon, *Utopia Parkway* (Boston: MFA Publications, 1997), 19–31, for a detailed consideration of Cornell's coursework and activities at Phillips Andover.

23 The textile mill Cornell worked at during the summer was owned by George Kunhardt, his father's former employer. Paul Cummings, "Interview of Elizabeth Cornell Benton, 21 April 1976," Oral History Interviews, Archives of American Art, Smithsonian Institution Washington, DC.

24 Cornell found this job through his father's friend, who had worked with him under Kunhardt. Cummings, "Interview of Elizabeth Cornell Benton, 21 April 1976."

25 Joseph Cornell, diary entry, March–April 1957, series 3: Diaries, box 7, folder 2, Joseph Cornell Papers, AAA.

26 Mary Baker Eddy, *Prose Works Other Than Science and Health with Key to the Scriptures* (Boston: First Church of Christ, the Scientist, 1925), 365; in box 60, Joseph Cornell Study Center, Smithsonian American Art Museum, Washington, DC.

27 For a detailed account of Cornell's conversion, see Cummings, "Interview of Elizabeth Cornell Benton, 21 April 1976."

28 Mary Baker Eddy, *Science and Health with Key to the Scriptures* (Boston: Christian Science Board of Directors, 1994), 129. For scholarly perspectives on the movement, see Stephen Gottschalk, *The Emergence of Christian Science in American Religious Life* (Berkeley: University of California Press, 1973); Rennie Schoepflin, *Christian Science on Trial: Religious Healing in America* (Baltimore, MD: Johns Hopkins University Press, 2002).

29 Eddy, *Science and Health with Key to the Scriptures*, 2.

30 Eddy, *Science and Health with Key to the Scriptures*, 587.

31 Eddy, *Science and Health with Key to the Scriptures*, 70.

32 James, *The Varieties of Religious Experience*, 101. As John B. Willis, coeditor of the *Christian Science Journal* noted, "The divine immanence is thus defined in Christian Science not as Spirit working in and through its opposite matter, but as the continuous manifestation of omnipresent Mind in all its vast domain." Willis, "Editor's Table," *Christian Science Journal* 29, no. 1 (April 1911): 198–99.

33 Josephson-Storm, *The Myth of Disenchantment*, 3.

34 As Eddy writes, "The belief that the universe, including man, is governed in general by material laws . . . belittles omnipotent wisdom, and gives to matter the precedence over Spirit." Eddy, *Science and Health with Key to the Scriptures*, 83.

35 Joseph Leo Koerner, *The Reformation of the Image* (Chicago: University of Chicago Press, 2004), 104.

36 Thomas Crow, *No Idols: The Missing Theology of Art* (Sydney: Power Publications, 2017), 9.

37 William Pietz, "The Problem of the Fetish I," *RES: Anthropology and Aesthetics* 9 (1985): 7.

38 See DeLue, *George Inness and the Science of Landscape*, and Veder, *The Living Line.*

39 Eddy, *Science and Health with Key to the Scriptures*, 72.

40 Christian Science is stringent in tolerating moments of doubt, categorizing them as mere mental mistakes by its practitioners. To this point, commentators have noted the parallels between Christian Science's ethos of individualism and the capitalistic logic of self-actualization. Chris Lehmann, *The Money Cult: Capitalism, Christianity, and the Unmaking of the American Dream* (Brooklyn, NY: Melville House Publishing, 2016). The most famous critique of Christian Science remains Mark Twain's biting satire of the religion. Mark Twain, *Christian Science* (New York: Harper & Brothers, 1907).

41 Carolee Schneemann, "Undated Note," in "Moon in a Tree (Cornell)," box 16, folder 78, Carolee Schneemann Papers, Department of Special Collections and University Archives, Stanford University.

42 Erich Auerbach, "On Rousseau's Place in History," reprinted in *Time, History, and Literature: Selected Essays of Erich Auerbach*, ed. James I. Porter, trans. Jane O. Newman (Princeton, NJ: Princeton University Press, 2014), 246.

43 Auerbach, "On Rousseau's Place in History," 246.

44 Mina Loy, "Brancusi's Golden Bird," in *The Dial Anthology* (Chicago: Jansen, McClurg, 1880–1929), 506–9.

45 Bissera Pentcheva has explored the relevance of chiasm to Christian art. As she writes, "Chiasm in literature operates through repetition of a word or phrase in a mirroring structure that establishes a frame arranged centripetally, around a center. As a result, the structure focuses attention on the center, which, in a chiasm occupying several lines, embodies the main idea, understood as premeditated action, a counsel, or a promise." Bissera V. Pentcheva, *Hagia Sophia: Sound, Space, and Spirit in Byzantium* (University Park: Pennsylvania State University Press, 2017), 85.

46 Ashley Lazevnick, "Impossible Descriptions in Mina Loy and Constantin Brancusi's Golden Bird," *Word & Image* 29, no. 2 (2013): 192–202.

47 I would like to thank Jamie Parra for this insightful observation.

48 Loy's "As if" fits with what religious studies scholar David Morgan has described as the "enchantment of make-believe," which he defines as "[e]nchantment that focuses on a work of art or an artifice that does not compel belief, but asks the reader or viewer to pretend or act 'as if' the story or painting were true." David Morgan, *Images at Work: The Material Culture of Enchantment*

(Oxford: Oxford University Press, 2018), 37.

49 Robert Slifkin, *Out of Time: Philip Guston and the Refiguration of Postwar American Art* (Berkeley: University of California Press, 2013), 10.

50 Slifkin, *Out of Time*, 6.

51 Erich Auerbach, *Dante: Poet of the Secular World*, trans. Ralph Manheim (New York: New York Review Books Classics, 2007), 175. In his introduction to a recent collection of Auerbach's essays, James I. Porter notes that the translation of "irdischen Welt" as "Secular World" is in fact inaccurate. He writes, "Of concern to Auerbach in this study is not the world as a secular entity, but the earthly character of the world in its experiential particularity, vividness, and proximity to life." Thus, Porter suggests that the English title of this book be translated as *Dante: Poet of the Earthly World*. James Porter, "Introduction," in *Selected Essays of Erich Auerbach: Time, History, and Literature*, ed. James I. Porter, trans. Jane O. Newman (Princeton, NJ: Princeton University Press, 2014), xviii.

52 Erich Auerbach, "Figura," in *Scenes from the Drama of European Literature*, trans. Ralph Manheim (Minneapolis: University of Minnesota Press, 1952). Quoted in Erich Auerbach, *Mimesis: The Representation of Reality in Western Literature*, trans. Willard Trask (Princeton, NJ: Princeton University Press, 2003), 11.

53 Auerbach, "Figura," in *Mimesis*, 11. Literary theorist Joshua Landy puts it this way: "[Figurative language] implies in its very form . . . [t]hat everything visible and audible and sensible merely serves as a possible symbol for something higher, something intangible, something spiritual." Landy, *How to Do Things with Fictions* (Oxford: Oxford University Press, 2012), 59.

54 Auerbach, "Figura," in *Scenes from the Drama of European Literature*, 72.

55 Auerbach, "Figura," in *Scenes from the Drama of European Literature*, 72.

56 Auerbach, "Figura," in *Scenes from the Drama of European Literature*, 68.

57 Auerbach, *Dante: Poet of the Secular World*, 67.

58 Porter, "Joseph Cornell."

59 Max Weber, "Science as Vocation," reprinted in H. H. Gerth and C. Wright Mills, trans. and ed., *From Max Weber: Essays in Sociology* (New York: Oxford University Press, 1946), 139.

60 Weber, "Science as Vocation," 144.

61 As Weber writes, "One need no longer have recourse to magical means in order to master or implore the spirits, as did the savage, for whom such mysterious powers existed." Weber's use of the term "savage" points to the centrality of discourses of irrationality to colonialism. Weber, "Science as Vocation," 139.

62 See Jane Bennett, *The Enchantment of Modern Life: Attachments, Crossings, Ethics* (Princeton, NJ: Princeton University Press, 2001); James Elkins and David Morgan, eds., *Re-enchantment*; Landy, *How to Do Things with Fictions*; Michael Saler, "Modernity and Enchantment: A Historiographic Review," *American Historical Review* 111, no. 3 (2006): 692–716; Michael Saler, *As If: Modern Enchantment and the Literary Prehistory of Virtual Reality* (Oxford: Oxford University Press, 2012).

63 Joshua Landy and Michael Saler, eds., *The Re-enchantment of the World: Secular Magic in a Rational Age* (Stanford, CA: Stanford University Press, 2009).

64 Sally Promey, "The 'Return' of Religion in the Scholarship of American Art," *Art Bulletin* 85, no. 3 (2003): 584.

65 Warner, VanAntwerpen, and Calhoun, *Varieties of Secularism in a Secular Age*, 7.

66 Taylor, *A Secular Age*, 548. Saba Mahmoud offers a trenchant critique of Taylor's text, and particularly his notion of the "buffered self," asking how Western-Christian subjectivity is "linked with its non-Western others." Mahmood, "Can Secularism Be Otherwise?," in *Varieties of Secularism in a Secular Age*, ed. Warner, VanAntwerpen, and Calhoun, 289. See also Talal Asad, *Formations of the Secular: Christianity, Islam, Modernity* (Stanford, CA: Stanford University Press, 2003).

67 Joseph Cornell, diary entry, July 10, 1948, series 3: Diaries, box 6, folder 5, Joseph Cornell Papers, AAA.

68 Morgan, *Images at Work*, 7.

69 Bruno Latour, *We Have Never Been Modern*, trans. Catherine Porter (Cambridge, MA: Harvard University Press, 1993), 35. Jane Bennett, who followed her investigation into the enchantment of nature with *Vibrant Matter: A Political Ecology of Things*, one of the touchstones of the field of new materialism, provides a concrete link between these intellectual projects. Bennett describes her choice of the term "enchantment" as a means of "contest[ing] the near monopoly over that term held by teleological perspectives, both of the traditional theological sort described by Voltaire and the New Age varieties in which some sort of divinity remains indispensable to enchantment." Bennett, *The Enchantment of Modern Life*, 10–11. See also Bennett, *Vibrant Matter: A Political Ecology of Things* (Durham, NC: Duke University Press, 2010).

70 Bruno Latour, *Reassembling the Social: An Introduction to Actor-Network-Theory* (Oxford: Oxford University Press, 2005).

71 For important critiques of new materialism's reframing of established Indigenous ontologies as Western critical theory, see Dana Luciano, "Sacred Theories of Earth: Matters of Spirit in William and Elizabeth Denton's *The Soul of Things*," *American Literature* 86, no. 4 (2014): 713–36; Elizabeth A. Povinelli, *Geontologies: A Requiem to Late Liberalism* (Durham, NC: Duke University Press, 2016).

72 Josephson-Storm, *The Myth of Disenchantment*, 3.

73 Peter Gordon observes that aesthetics remains an open question in Taylor's work, writing "Taylor grants that many moderns will seek out something *like* the sacred by opening themselves to great works of art. But he is reluctant to admit that such examples should count as genuine transcendence, since an experience of aesthetic transfiguration, no matter how profound, does not require our surpassing the human-natural matrix." Gordon, "The Place of the Sacred in the Absence of God: Charles Taylor's 'A Secular Age,'" *Journal of the History of Ideas* 69, no. 4 (October 2008): 671.

74 Alfred Gell, "The Technology of Enchantment and the Enchantment of Technology," in Jeremy Coote (ed.), *Anthropology, Art, and Aesthetics* (Oxford: Clarendon Press, 1994), 40–41.

75 Hans Belting, *Likeness and Presence: A History of the Image before the Era of Art*, trans. Edmund Jephcott (Chicago: University of Chicago Press, 1994).

76 Jeffrey Hamburger, "Hans Belting's 'Bild und Kult: eine Geschichte des

Bildes vor dem Zeitalter der Kunst 1990,' " *Burlington Magazine* 153, no. 1294 (January 2011): 42.

77 Walter Benjamin, "The Work of Art in the Age of Its Technological Reproducibility, Second Version," in *The Work of Art in the Age of Its Technological Reproducibility, and Other Writings on Media*, ed. Michael W. Jennings, Brigid Doherty, and Thomas Y. Levin, trans. Edmund Jephcott, Rodney Livingstone, Howard Eiland, et al. (Cambridge, MA: Harvard University Press, 2008), 25.

78 Benjamin, "The Work of Art in the Age of Its Technological Reproducibility, Second Version," 25.

79 As the editors note in their introduction to this essay, "It is not just that auratic art, with its ritually certified representational strategies, poses no threat to the dominant class, but that the sense of authenticity, authority, and permanence projected by the auratic work of art represents an important cultural substantiation of the claims to power of the dominant class." "The Production, Reproduction, and Reception of the Work of Art," in *The Work of Art in the Age of Its Technological Reproducibility, and Other Writings on Media*, 15.

80 In this book, I approach Modernism not as a singular hegemonic movement, but as a set of inchoate responses to the shifting historical conditions of the late nineteenth and twentieth centuries. In this, my work follows Douglas Mao and Rebecca Walkowitz's invaluable volume, *Bad Modernisms*, which describes new Modernist studies as moving toward "a pluralism or fusion of theoretical commitments, as well as a heightened attention to continuities and intersections across the boundaries of artistic media, to collaborations and influences across national and linguistic borders, and (especially) to the relationship between individual works of art and the larger cultures in which they emerged." Mao and Walkowitz, eds., "Introduction: Modernisms Bad and New," in *Bad Modernisms* (Durham, NC: Duke University Press, 2010), 2.

81 Lisa Florman, *Concerning the Spiritual and the Concrete in Kandinsky's Art* (Stanford, CA: Stanford University Press, 2014), 1.

82 Jennifer L. Roberts, *Mirror-Travels: Robert Smithson and History* (New Haven, CT: Yale University Press, 2004), 6.

83 For representative examples of this line of inquiry, see Rosalind Krauss, *The Originality of the Avant-Garde and Other Modernist Myths* (Cambridge, MA: MIT Press, 1985); Hal Foster, *The Return of the Real: The Avant-Garde at the End of the Century* (Cambridge, MA: MIT Press, 1996), 71–77.

84 Sylvia Wynter, "Unsettling the Coloniality of Being/Power/Truth/Freedom: Towards the Human, after Man, Overrepresentation—An Argument," *CR: The New Centennial Review* 3, no. 3 (2003): 257–337. As Michel Foucault wisely writes, "But that does not mean one has to be 'for' or 'against' the Enlightenment. It even means precisely that one has to refuse everything that might present itself in the form of a simplistic and authoritarian alternative: you either accept the Enlightenment and remain within the tradition of its rationalism (this is considered a positive term by some and used by others, on the contrary, as a reproach); or else you criticize the Enlightenment and then try to escape from its principles of rationality (which may be seen once again as good or bad). And we do not break free of this blackmail by introducing 'dialectical' nuances while seeking to determine what good and bad elements there may have been in the Enlightenment." Michel Foucault, "What Is Enlightenment?," in *The Foucault Reader*, ed. Paul Rabinow (New York: Pantheon Books, 1984), 42.

85 Roberts, *Mirror-Travels*, 9.

86 Clement Greenberg, "Avant-Garde and Kitsch" (1939), reprinted in *The Collected Essays and Criticism, Volume 1: Perceptions and Judgments, 1939–1944*, ed. John O'Brian (Chicago: University of Chicago Press, 1986), 10.

87 Thomas Crow, "Modernism and Mass Culture in the Visual Arts," in *Modern Art in the Common Culture* (New Haven, CT: Yale University Press, 1996), 9–11.

88 Mark Greif, *The Age of the Crisis of Man: Fiction and Thought in America, 1933–1973* (Princeton, NJ: Princeton University Press, 2015), 22.

89 As they write, "For enlightenment is totalitarian as only a system can be. Its untruth does not lie in the analytical method, the reduction to elements, the decomposition through reflection, as its Romantic enemies had maintained from the first, but in its assumption that the trial is prejudged." Theodor Adorno and Max Horkheimer, *Dialectic of Enlightenment*, trans. Edmund Jephcott (Stanford, CA: Stanford University Press, 2002), 18. See also Josephson-Storm, *The Myth of Disenchantment*, 9.

90 Adorno and Horkheimer, *Dialectic of Enlightenment*, 18.

91 Max Horkheimer, "Preface," Theodor Adorno, Else Frenkel-Brunswik, Daniel J. Levinson, R. Nevitt Sanford (London: Verso, 2019), LXXI.

92 Émile Durkheim, *The Elementary Forms of Religious Life* (New York: Free Press, 1995), 226. For a relevant recent consideration of Durkheim's theory of collective effervescence and its relationship to the consolidation of authority and collective action, see William Mazzarella, *The Mana of Mass Society* (Chicago: University of Chicago Press, 2017).

93 Mary D. Sheriff's recent book on enchantment in eighteenth-century France offers an incisive discussion of the term's entanglement with colonialist fantasies of domination and possession. Sheriff, *Enchanted Islands: Picturing the Allure of Conquest in Eighteenth-Century France* (Chicago: University of Chicago Press, 2018).

94 William Pietz, "The Problem of the Fetish I," *RES: Anthropology and Aesthetics* 9 (1985): 5–17; William Pietz, "The Problem of the Fetish II: The Origin of the Fetish," *RES: Anthropology and Aesthetics* 13 (1987): 23–45; Paul Johnson, ed., "Toward an Atlantic Genealogy of 'Sprit Possession,' " in *Spirited Things: The Work of "Possession" in Afro-Atlantic Religions* (Chicago: University of Chicago Press, 2014).

95 The question of Cornell's sexuality remains fraught. The accounts of his asexuality come from the women he worked with late in life. For example, in a recent documentary, Yayoi Kusama divulged, "he didn't like sex and I didn't like sex. So we didn't have sex." Carolee Schneemann likewise described him as "asexual." Heather Lenz, *Kusama—Infinity* (Magnolia Pictures, 2018); Carolee Schneemann, "Undated Document," box 16, folder 5, "Moon in a Tree (Cornell)" [B/N #78] ca. 1972, doc. 12, Carolee Schneemann Papers, Department of Special Collections and University Archives, Stanford University.

96 Cornell, quoted in Blair, *Joseph Cornell's Vision of Spiritual Order*, 56–57.

97 Joseph Cornell, "8-7-69," Notes on Art Work and "Rationale," box 1, folder 21, Joseph Cornell Papers, AAA.

CHAPTER ONE: PARTS OF A WORLD

Epigraphs: Ralph Waldo Emerson, "Nature," in *The Selected Writings of Ralph Waldo Emerson*, ed. William H. Gilman (New York: Signet Classics, 1965), 188. Erich Auerbach, "On the Anniversary Celebration of Dante," in *Selected Essays of Erich Auerbach: Time, History, and Literature*, ed. James I. Porter, trans. Jane O. Newman (Princeton, NJ: Princeton University Press, 2014), 122.

1 Julien Levy, *Memoir of an Art Gallery* (New York: G. P. Putnam's Sons, 1977), 76–77. For excellent scholarly considerations of Levy, see Peter Barberie and Katherine Ware, *Dreaming in Black and White: Photography at the Julien Levy Gallery* (Philadelphia: Philadelphia Museum of Art; New Haven, CT: Yale University Press, 2006); and Lisa Jacobs and Ingrid Schaffner, eds., *Julien Levy: Portrait of an Art Gallery* (Cambridge, MA: MIT Press, 1998).

2 As many sources have noted, Levy's lively account of his meeting with Cornell contains factual inaccuracies. The exact timeline of events leading to Cornell's sale of collages to Levy is therefore difficult to determine with any specificity. According to Levy, Cornell had visited the gallery before introducing himself on November 11. In an interview with Walter Hopps, Levy also states that Cornell visited him while he was unpacking works for *Surréalisme* before returning to present him with the collages. Levy, *Memoir of an Art Gallery*, 76–77; Julien Levy, "Interview by Lynda Hartigan and Walter Hopps, July 17, 1976," series 2: Subject files, box 32, folder 15, Julien Levy Gallery Records, Philadelphia Museum of Art Archives.

3 Walt Whitman, *Leaves of Grass* (Philadelphia: David McKay, 1900), 399, at Joseph Cornell Study Center, Smithsonian American Art Museum.

4 Michael Moon has argued that Whitman's grouping of poems into "clusters" or "annexes" over several editions of *Leaves of Grass* was a way for the poet to signal the interconnectedness of the political, the sexual, and the literary. Michael Moon, *Disseminating Whitman: Revision and Corporeality in "Leaves of Grass"* (Cambridge, MA: Harvard University Press, 1991).

5 The Oxford English Dictionary defines "dead reckoning" as "the estimation of a ship's position from the distance run by the log and the courses steered by the compass, with corrections for current, leeway, etc. but without astronomical observations," explicating the maritime implications of Whitman's use of the term "reckoning"; https://www.oed.com/view/Entry/47680?redirectedFrom=dead+reckoning#eid.

6 Deborah Solomon, *Utopia Parkway* (Boston: MFA Publications, 1997), 58.

7 The only extended consideration of Cornell's activities during the 1920s are Solomon's *Utopia Parkway* and Lynda Roscoe Hartigan's essay "When Does an Artist Become an Artist?," in *Joseph Cornell: Navigating the Imagination* (Salem, MA: Peabody Essex Museum, 2007), 14–92.

8 Kenneth Baker, "What Went Wrong?," *Connoisseur* 185 (September 1987): 173, quoted in Kate Stanley, "Unrarified Air: Alfred Stieglitz and the Modernism of Equivalence," *Modernism/Modernity* 26, no. 1 (January 2019): 206.

9 Joseph Cornell, diary entry, November 11, 1967, series 3: Diaries, box 8, folder 60, Joseph Cornell Papers, Archives of American Art, Smithsonian Institution, Washington, DC (hereafter AAA).

10 Joseph Cornell, diary entry, August 3, 1947, series 3: Diaries, box 6, folder 4, Joseph Cornell Papers, AAA.

11 Joseph Cornell, quoted in Hartigan, *Joseph Cornell: Navigating the Imagination*, 20.

12 For an excellent account of this milieu, see Marvin Mondlin and Roy Meador, *Book Row: An Anecdotal and Pictorial History of the Antiquarian Book Trade* (New York: Carroll & Graf, 2003).

13 William Whitman Company's offices were located at 25 Madison Avenue, at Twenty-Fourth Street. The Sign of the Sparrow was just two avenues away, at 42 Lexington Avenue (at Twenty-Fourth Street).

14 Cornell was encouraged to write this reflection by Parker Tyler, a good friend and the editor of *View* magazine, where Cornell considered publishing the text. Tyler suggested he write it during a period of what Cornell described as "frustration from my commercial work." The relationship between Cornell's art work and his "commercial" graphic design will be addressed in subsequent chapters. Joseph Cornell, diary entry, November 26, 1948, series 3: Diaries, box 6, folder 5, Joseph Cornell Papers, AAA.

15 Cornell was correct in describing the store's proprietor, Alfred F. Goldsmith, as "tops in the first edition field." Goldsmith worked in the paper business before opening The Sign of the Sparrow in 1918, and in addition to being a noted Whitman expert, was also widely beloved for his financial generosity, especially during the Great Depression. See John T. Winterich, *Alfred F. Goldsmith: An Appreciation* (New York: Swann Auction Galleries, 1947), reprinted in *Publishers Weekly*, November 22, 1947.

16 Edmund Wilson, *The American Earthquake: A Documentary of the Twenties and Thirties* (New York: Octagon Books, 1971), 82.

17 Hartigan, *Joseph Cornell: Navigating the Imagination*, 21.

18 Joseph Cornell, diary entry, August 11, 1952, series 3: Diaries, box 6, folder 14, Joseph Cornell Papers, AAA.

19 This book is currently held in private hands and is not available to researchers. Hartigan provides a partial inventory in her essay "When Does an Artist Become an Artist?" in *Joseph Cornell: Navigating the Imagination*, 36–38.

20 I am grateful to Owen Thomas of the *Christian Science Monitor* for fielding my inquiries about the history and ethos of the paper's Home Forum section.

21 "Songs of Innocence: Poetry for Children and Poetry about Children," *Christian Science Monitor*, February 4, 1915, 15; "Magic Casements," *Christian Science Monitor*, January 26, 1927, 11; "Night Butterflies," *Christian Science Monitor*, July 12, 1926, 7.

22 "Insight into Poetry's Essential Nature," *Christian Science Monitor*, June 19, 1926, 9.

23 "Insight into Poetry's Essential Nature," *Christian Science Monitor*, June 19, 1926, 9; excerpted from Henry Newbolt, *The Tide of Time in English Poetry* (London: Thomas Nelson, 1925).

24 Quoted in Hartigan, "When Does an Artist Become an Artist?," in *Joseph Cornell: Navigating the Imagination*, 36.

25 Stewart, *On Longing: Narratives of the Miniature, the Gigantic, the Souvenir, the Collection* (Durham, NC: Duke University Press, 1993), 156.

26 Dore Ashton, *A Joseph Cornell Album* (New York: Viking Press, 1974), 18. See also Ségolène Le Men, "The Book-Boxes of Joseph Cornell: A Romantic Art?," in *Joseph Cornell and Surrealism*, 278–84.

27 David Morgan, "Enchantment, Disenchantment, Re-enchantment," in *Re-enchantment*, ed. James Elkins and David Morgan (New York: Routledge, 2009), 4.

28 M. H. Abrams's influential book *The Mirror and the Lamp* helped establish Romanticism's association with inwardness and heroic individualism. Abrams describes Romantic poetry as a lamp, emanating beams of expressive light from the author's "inward eye." As Abrams writes, "Poetry is the overflow, utterance, or projection of the thought and feelings of the poet; or else (in the chief variant formulation) poetry is defined in terms of the imaginative process which modifies and synthesizes the images, thoughts, and feelings of the poet." Abrams, *The Mirror and the Lamp: Romantic Theory and the Critical Tradition* (Oxford: Oxford University Press, 1971), 21–22.

29 Théophile Gautier, *The Works of Théophile Gautier*, vol. 16: *A History of Romanticism: The Progress of French Poetry since 1830*, ed. and trans. Frederick C. de Sumichrast (Cambridge: Cambridge University Press, 1902). Gautier's book included mentions of Saint-Pierre's star-crossed lovers Paul and Virginie, the French city of Dijon, and Ludwig of Bavaria, all of which would become subjects of Cornell's work. In addition to this book, Cornell's library contained ten works by Gautier and seven by Nerval upon the artist's death.

30 Gautier, *A History of Romanticism*, 123.

31 Gautier, *A History of Romanticism*, 120.

32 Gautier, *A History of Romanticism*, 123.

33 Janine Mileaf has discussed Cornell's invitation of the physical manipulation of his objects, and particularly his boxes filled with sand, in *Please Touch: Dada and Surrealist Objects after the Readymade* (Hanover, NH: Dartmouth College Press, 2010).

34 Nicholas Halmi, "Romanticism, the Temporalization of History, and the Historicization of Form," *Modern Language Quarterly* 74, no. 3 (September 2013): 363.

35 Erich Auerbach, *Scenes from the Drama of European Literature*, trans. Ralph Manheim (Minneapolis: University of Minnesota Press, 1952), 72.

36 The letter in Cornell's box slightly alters More's original text, which reads: "Fountain of Being! teach us to devote / To Thee each purpose, action, word, and thought! Thy grace our hope, thy love our only boat, / Be all distinctions in the Christian loft! / Be this in ev'ry fate our wish alone, / Almighty, Wise and Good, Thy will be done!" Hannah More, *Search after Happiness: A Pastoral Drama* (London: T. Cadell, junior, and W. Davis, 1800), 58.

37 John Donne, *The Complete Poetry and Selected Prose of John Donne*, ed. Charles M. Coffin (New York: Modern Library, 2001), 14.

38 Cleanth Brooks, *The Well Wrought Urn: Studies in the Structure of Poetry* (Boston: Houghton Mifflin Harcourt, 1947), 14.

39 Brooks, *The Well Wrought Urn*, 3.

40 Mary Ann Caws, ed., *Joseph Cornell's Theater of the Mind: Selected Diaries, Letters, and Files* (New York: Thames and Hudson, 1993), 109.

41 Novalis, *Novalis: Philosophical Writings*, trans. Margaret Mahony Stoljar (Albany: State University of New York Press, 1997), 60.

42 Gautier, *A History of Romanticism*, 102.

43 John Bernard Myers, *Tracking the Marvelous: A Life in the New York Art World* (New York: Random House, 1983), 73.

44 Stéphane Mallarmé, "The Crisis in Poetry," in *Mallarmé: Selected Prose Poems, Essays, and Letters*, trans. Bradford Cook (Baltimore, MD: Johns Hopkins Press, 1965), 40.

45 Richard Cándida Smith, *Mallarmé's Children: Symbolism and the Renewal of Experience* (Berkeley: University of California Press, 1999).

46 Wanda Corn, *The Great American Thing: Modern Art and National Identity, 1915–1931* (Berkeley: University of California Press, 1999), 7–16.

47 Joseph Cornell, draft of a letter to James Huth, July 20, 1953, series 3: Diaries, box 6, folder 20, Joseph Cornell Papers, AAA. As Cornell observed, Symbolism's introduction to the United States was partly due to the popular critic James Gibbons Huneker, who died the year Cornell arrived in New York City. Huneker was a popular critic who wrote about art, music, literature, and theater for a range of publications including *Harper's Bazar, Harper's Weekly*, and *Scribner's* between 1880 and 1910. Cornell likely first encountered Huneker's work through his two-volume autobiography, *Steeplejack*, described by one critic as "an arsenal of epigrams, an Odyssey of psychic and physical adventures, a symphony of gossip, a violent purge for sentimentalists." See Arnold T. Schwab, *James Gibbons Huneker: Critic of the Seven Arts* (Stanford, CA: Stanford University Press, 1963), 95, 282–83.

48 Marilyn Kushner and Kimberly Orcutt, eds., *The Armory Show at 100: Modernism and Revolution* (New York: New-York Historical Society, 2013), as well as the excellent Web resource, The Armory Show at 100, http://armory.nyhistory.org/opening.

49 "Walter Pach's Notes from a Conversation with Odilon Redon, December 1912," series 1: Armory Show Records, box 1, folder 82, Walt Kuhn Papers, AAA. For a recent consideration of Redon's influence in the United States, see Alicia J. D. Cooper, "Odilon Redon in America" (master's thesis, Hunter College, 2013).

50 "Odilon Redon," *The Sun* (New York), March 30, 1913, 15. See also "International Exhibition," *Evening Post* (New York), February 20, 1913, 9.

51 Walter Pach, *Odilon Redon* (New York: Association of American Painters and Sculptors, 1913), 9. This pamphlet was published for distribution at the International Exhibition of Modern Art, colloquially known as the Armory Show. See also Walter Pach, "The Significance of Redon," *The Dial: A Fortnightly* 66, no. 784 (February 22, 1919): 191–93.

52 Paul Rosenfeld, "The Authors and Politics," *Scribner's Magazine* 93 (May 1933): 318.

53 The first mention of André Mellerio's monograph on Redon comes in a diary entry dated August 3, 1947, in which Cornell describes the "transcendent experience similar to the purchase of "Odilon Redon"—the Fleury [*sic*] edition." Here Cornell refers to André Mellerio, *Odilon Redon, peintre, dessinateur et graveur* (Paris: H. Floury, 1923). Cornell also made reference to Redon's *A soi-même journal (1867–1915), notes sur la vie, l'art et les artistes* (1922) in 1926, the same year he saw seven of the painter's

works in the *Memorial Exhibition of Representative Works Selected from the John Quinn Collection*, held at the New York Art Center on January 17, 1926. Joseph Cornell, diary entry, August 3, 1947, series 3: Diaries, box 6, folder 4, Joseph Cornell Papers, AAA.

54 Joseph Cornell, diary entry, September 9, 1952, series 3: Diaries, box 6, folder 15, Joseph Cornell Papers, AAA. The quotation continues: "What should music be called (of a type cherished by Redon and Hartley) if he ever had a chance to hear the work of this little known composer)—friend of Redon, Mallarmé, etc.—an "extension" at least of the mood above, an unexpected delightful 'recapturing' in addition to the joy of discovery of this work . . ."

55 Joseph Cornell, diary entry, September 9, 1952, series 3: Diaries, box 6, folder 15, Joseph Cornell Papers, AAA.

56 The term "correspondence" was also a central term in the theology of Swedish mystic Emanuel Swedenborg, which was influential with nineteenth- and twentieth-century American artists and writers. Cornell's use of the term was indebted instead to French Symbolist art and poetry.

57 Odilon Redon, quoted in Jodi Hauptman, *Beyond the Visible: The Art of Odilon Redon* (New York: Museum of Modern Art, 2005), 83.

58 The availability of *Journal d'Agriculture Pratique* as both a facsimile edition and CD-ROM is due to the efforts of Analisa Leppanen-Guerra and Dickran Tashjian. See their book *Joseph Cornell's Manual of Marvels* (New York: Thames and Hudson, 2012).

59 Jason Francisco, *The Steerage and Alfred Stieglitz* (Berkeley: University of California Press, 2012), 87. I am grateful to Elyse Nelson for her assistance in deciphering the original French text.

60 Kaja Silverman, *The Miracle of Analogy, or The History of Photography* (Stanford, CA: Stanford University Press, 2015), 11.

61 Rosalind Krauss, "Stieglitz/ "Equivalents," *October* 11 (Winter 1979): 129–40; Kristina Wilson, "The Intimate Gallery and the *Equivalents*: Spirituality in the 1920s Work of Stieglitz," *Art Bulletin* 75, no. 4 (December 2003): 746–68. These two essays are representative of what critic Kate Stanley has described as the "modernist semiotics of absence" and the "transcendentalist idealist" positions taken by readers of his work. Stanley, "Unrarefied Air," 186.

62 As Stieglitz wrote, "Through clouds [I wanted] to put down my philosophy of life—to show that my photographs were not due to subject matter—not to special trees, or faces, or interiors, to special privileges—clouds were there for everyone—no tax as yet on them—free." Alfred Stieglitz, "How I Came to Photograph Clouds," *Amateur Photographer and Photography* 56, no. 1819 (1923): 255.

63 Analisa Leppanen-Guerra, " 'To the Immortal Geniuses': Joseph Cornell's *Agriculture* Book—Object as Homage," in Leppanen-Guerra and Tashjian, eds., *Joseph Cornell's Manual of Marvels*. (New York: Thames and Hudson, 2012).

64 Paul Cummings, "Interview of Elizabeth Cornell Benton, 21 April 1976," Oral History Interviews, Archives of American Art, Smithsonian Institution Washington, DC. Cornell's use of montage is paralleled by the work of Walter Benjamin, who described the method of his seminal *Arcades Project* as a form of "literary montage." Walter Benjamin, *The Arcades Project*, ed. Rolf Tiedemann, trans. Howard Eiland and Kevin McLaughlin (Cambridge, MA: Belknap Press of Harvard University Press, 2002), 460.

65 His use of the term began in 1932, with his brochure design for Julien Levy Gallery's 1932 *Surréalisme* exhibition that includes the heading "Montages by Joseph Cornell."

66 Joseph Cornell, diary entry, March 21, 1960, series 3: Diaries, box 7, folder 29, Joseph Cornell Papers, AAA.

67 Hartigan, *Joseph Cornell: Navigating the Imagination*, 23–24. Cornell's residence in the outer boroughs also afforded him access to numerous film productions and sound stages, where he watched legendary directors such as D. W. Griffith direct films while amassing an extensive collection of film stills and sixteen-millimeter prints. By 1939, Cornell began writing to friends such as Charles Henri Ford and James Thrall Soby to ask them to purchase his films, or help him lend them out. According to Annette Michelson, by the end of his life Cornell's collection encompassed over fifteen thousand film stills and production shots. Cornell's collection of film prints is now in the collection of the Anthology Film Archives in New York City.

68 Carl Theodor Dreyer, "Realized Mysticism in *The Passion of Joan of Arc*," Criterion Collection, November 9, 1999, https://www.criterion.com/current/posts/69-realized-mysticism-in-the-passion-of-joan-of-arc.

69 Joseph Cornell, "Monsieur Phot," in *Surréalisme*, ed. Julien Levy (New York: Black Sun Press, 1936), 77–88.

70 Sergei Eisenstein, "A Dialectic Approach to Film Form," in *Film Theory and Criticism: Introductory Readings*, ed. Gerald Mast, Marshall Cohen, and Leo Braudy (New York: Oxford University Press, 1992), 138–54.

71 Pavle Levi, *Cinema by Other Means* (Oxford: Oxford University Press, 2012), 143.

72 Matthew Affron and Sylvie Ramond, eds., *Joseph Cornell and Surrealism* (Charlottesville, VA: Fralin Museum of Art, 2015; distributed by Penn State University Press), 111.

73 Rachael Z. DeLue, *Arthur Dove: Always Connect* (Chicago: University of Chicago Press, 2016), 201.

74 Stanley, "Unrarified Air," 195. Both Celeste Connor and Wanda Corn have argued that the period turn to Transcendentalism signaled an ambition to create a distinctly democratic, and therefore "American" art. Celeste Connor, *Democratic Visions: Art and Theory of the Stieglitz Circle, 1924–1934* (Berkeley: University of California Press, 2001); Corn, *The Great American Thing*.

75 Wilson, "The Intimate Gallery and the *Equivalents*," 748.

76 Waldo Frank, *Our America* (New York: Boni and Liveright, 1919), 203, 205, 206.

77 Frank, *Our America*, 184.

78 Frank, *Our America*, 221.

79 My discussion of Transcendentalism as a means of defeating individualism departs from T. J. Jackson Lears's influential discussion of antimodernism in American culture. As Lears writes of the turn to spirituality in the early twentieth century, "As belief in the supernatural wavered, the loss of conscious selfhood might become simply another route to self-fulfillment. Seeking authentic experience in their own inner lives, many antimodernists joined devotees of mind cure in sentimentalizing unconscious impulse. Depriving instinct of its darker dimensions, they exacerbated the weightlessness they had set out to escape. Even as they rejected older forms of

rationalization, they promoted a new and subtler rationalization of the inner life. And most important: they remained imprisoned in the problematic self. Lacking firm religious or ethical commitments, antimodern dissenters became immersed in endless self-absorption—the 'morbid introspection' they had longed to transcend." Lears's account glosses over the political dimensions of antimodernism, such as the relationship between Symbolism and anarchism, as exemplified by both the *Seven Arts* group and the important critic Randolph Bourne. T. J. Jackson Lears, *No Place of Grace: Antimodernism and the Transformation of American Culture, 1880–1920* (Chicago: University of Chicago Press, 1983), 302. See also Edward Abrahams, *The Lyrical Left: Randolph Bourne, Alfred Stieglitz, and the Origins of Cultural Radicalism in America* (Charlottesville: University Press of Virginia, 1986.

80 As Weber writes, "*Today's* capitalist economic order is a monstrous cosmos, into which the individual is born and which in practice is for him, at least as an individual, simply a given, an immutable shell, in which he is obliged to live." Max Weber, *The Protestant Ethic and the "Spirit" of Capitalism* (first published in German in 1903; translated to English in 1930), ed. and trans. Peter Baehr and Gordon C. Wells (New York: Penguin Books, 2002), 13.

81 Cummings, "Interview of Elizabeth Cornell Benton, 21 April 1976."

82 Joseph Cornell, letter to Julien Levy, October 23, 1960, series 1: Correspondence, box 7, folder 4, Julien Levy Gallery Records, Philadelphia Museum of Art.

83 Comte de Lautréamont, *Lautréamont's "Maldoror,"* trans. Alexis Lykiard (New York: Thomas Y. Cromwell, 1972), 177.

84 When and where Cornell first saw work by Max Ernst remains a question in Cornell scholarship. The question is difficult to answer because Cornell likely saw Ernst's collage novel *La femme 100 têtes* (1929) rather than a proper exhibition of his work. Cornell stated in a letter to Levy that he first saw Ernst's work at John Becker Gallery, but there is no evidence of an exhibition of Surrealism or collage before November 1931. Interestingly, John Becker Gallery was at this point loosely partnered with the Society of Contemporary Art at Harvard, and presented several of its exhibitions in New York, including the landmark Bauhaus show in 1930. After consulting the gallery's limited archives, I have not been able to determine whether it ever showed or sold any work by Ernst. A copy of *La femme 100 têtes* is currently in the Joseph Cornell Study Center, but letters in the book from Max Ernst to Julien Levy, and from Levy to Cornell indicate that it was sent to Levy on the occasion of *Surréalisme*, and then given to Cornell by Levy. Joseph Cornell, letter to Julien Levy, August 21, 1959, series 1: Correspondence, box 7, folder 4, Julien Levy Gallery Records, Philadelphia Museum of Art Archives. I consulted Joseph Cornell's copy of *La femme 100 têtes* at the Joseph Cornell Study Center.

85 Gavin Parkinson, *Enchanted Ground: André Breton, Modernism, and the Surrealist Appraisal of Fin-de-Siècle Painting* (London: Bloomsbury Visual Arts, 2018), 23.

86 Hal Foster, *Compulsive Beauty* (Cambridge, MA: MIT Press, 1995), 19.

87 Foster, *Compulsive Beauty*, 33.

88 Tom Gunning, "Hand and Eye: Excavating a New Technology of the Image in the Victorian Era," *Victorian Studies* 54, no. 3 (Spring 2012): 495–516. Jonathan Crary has described the instability of the thaumatropic image as paving the way for modernity's distributed subjectivity or phantasmagoric image world. Crary, *Techniques of the Observer: On Vision and Modernity in the Nineteenth Century* (Cambridge, MA: MIT Press, 1992).

89 Julien Levy, introduction to *Surrealism* (New York: Black Sun Press, 1936), 5. The title of the book dropped the "é" from the original exhibition name.

90 Paul Sachs was instrumental in shaping this identity for Harvard's Fine Arts Department. Sachs himself had turned away from his role as the scion of the banking titan Goldman Sachs, and he promised his pupils a similar freedom. In trying to convince Levy of the merits of a major in fine arts, Sachs opined, "Whatever you pick at Harvard is really unimportant to your career. It's an opportunity for you to study and you will find, with your background, that the fine arts courses are very small, have a very small enrollment. An English course, if you happened to have gotten a good mark, you would be in it with hundreds and hundreds of youngsters who were going to be stockbrokers eventually, and wanted to be well read, and read novels, and have some conversation." Here, Sachs proposes a new metric of ambition and success, one premised on intellectual growth and humanistic education rather than material accumulation. Julien Levy, "Interview with Paul Cummings, May 30, 1978," Oral History Interviews, microfilm reel 398, AAA.

91 For a detailed discussion of this group, see Steven Watson, "Julien Levy: Exhibitionist and Harvard Modernist," in Jacobs and Schaffner, eds., *Julien Levy: Portrait of an Art Gallery*, 80–95.

92 Julien Levy, "Art to Me Is Almost a Religion," *Harvard Magazine* 82, no. 1 (September–October 1979). I consulted this article in the Julien Levy Gallery Records, Philadelphia Museum of Art Archives.

93 Watson, "Julien Levy: Exhibitionist and Harvard Modernist," 78.

94 Levy, *Memoir of an Art Gallery*, 11.

95 Levy originally intended for the gallery to specialize in photography but found it difficult to sell. Julien Levy, "Art to Me Is Almost a Religion"; Peter Lloyd, *Photographs by Henri Cartier-Bresson and an Exhibition of Anti-Graphic Photography*, exh. cat. (New York: Julien Levy Gallery, September 25–October 16, 1933).

96 Julien Levy and Chick Austin both began working on an exhibition of Surrealism separately between 1929 and 1930. At some point they realized the other was working on the same project and collaborated on several aspects of the project. Levy claimed credit for initiating the show in his memoirs, but Eugene Gaddis has nuanced the picture, demonstrating both men's importance to the exhibition. Eugene Gaddis, *Magician of the Modern: Chick Austin and the Transformation of the Arts in America* (New York: Knopf, 2000).

97 Austin's efforts to ease the Connecticut audience into avant-garde art can be seen in an unsigned article, which he published in the *Hartford Times* in 1931. The article draws a parallel between avant-garde art and fashion, noting, "Fashion in art is very much like fashion in dress. Most of our clothes are bought with the idea of ultimately discarding

them and few indeed with the idea that they will ultimately be acquired by museums, yet we do not hesitate to dress in fashion because we fear the next year the mode will alter." Anonymous [Chick Austin], "The Newer Super-Realism," *Hartford Times*, November 7, 1931. I consulted a transcript of this article with a note on authorship in Chick Austin Papers, Wadsworth Atheneum Archives, Hartford, CT. See also Gaddis, *Magician of the Modern*, 155–67 for a detailed consideration of the exhibition and its reception in Hartford.

98 Last-minute additions to the show included a seventeenth-century anamorphic portrait owned by Alfred Barr Jr. and his wife that transformed from a landscape to a head depending on its orientation. *Surréalisme* also featured a number of collages by Max Ernst and was supplemented by a collection of Surrealist texts and magazines, including Aragon's "Le Peinture au Défi." Although these materials were not listed on the checklist of the exhibition, a letter from James Thrall Soby to Levy indicates that these texts, along with copies of Max Ernst's *La femme 100 têtes* were available for purchase at the exhibition. An invoice from Levy to Austin also indicates that Levy sent copies of these texts, including the Aragon catalogue, to Hartford so they could be sold to visitors. Thrall Soby, letter to Julien Levy, December 30, 1931, series 1: Correspondence, box 24, folder 12, Julien Levy Gallery Records, Philadelphia Museum of Art Archives; Julien Levy, undated invoice to Chick Austin, series 7: Audio/visual materials, box 46, folder 1–4, Julien Levy Gallery Records, Philadelphia Museum of Art Archives.

99 Shop clerk Frances "Peaches" Heenan married real estate mogul Edward "Daddy" Browning in 1926, when she was just sixteen and he was fifty-two. Their marriage lasted six months and ended in a sensational divorce trial that included accusations of perversity, infidelity, and abuse. Although their separation was granted, the court eventually ruled that Peaches was not entitled to any alimony. Dan P. Lee, "Peaches: Who's Your Daddy," *New York Magazine*, April 1, 2012.

100 Charles Desmarais, "Julien Levy: Surrealist Author, Dealer, and Collector," *Afterimage* (January 1977): 729–32. I consulted this article in the Julien Levy Gallery Records, Philadelphia Museum of Art Archives.

101 Matthew Josephson, "The Superrealists," *New Republic* 69, no. 896 (February 3, 1932): 321–22.

102 Thomas Crow, "Modernism and Mass Culture in the Visual Arts," *Modern Art in the Common Culture* (New Haven, CT: Yale University Press, 1996), 36.

103 André Breton, "Manifesto of Surrealism" (1924), *Manifestoes of Surrealism*, trans. Richard Seaver and Helen R. Lane (Ann Arbor: University of Michigan, 1972), 26.

104 Breton, "Manifesto of Surrealism" (1924), 31.

105 Edward Alden Jewell, "A Bewildering Exhibition," *New York Times*, January 13, 1932, 27.

106 The checklist for *Surréalisme* lists Cornell's contribution to the exhibition as "Montages" and "Potpourri (Glass Bell)." According to an interview with Julien Levy conducted by Walter Hopps and Lynda Roscoe Hartigan, "the Cornells I had in my Surrealist show were a couple of collages, the sewing machine one and one of a boat with I think a spider web, a little tiny one.... And the ball and book that [Alfred] Barr bought (for himself) and that's all, the boat collage, that were in the show." The two montages Levy refers to are undoubtedly *Untitled (Schooner)*, 1931, and *Untitled*, 1931. The boat object is now lost but was recorded in a series of portraits taken by Lee Miller of Cornell in 1933. The inclusion of both these montages, as well as the boat object can be verified by Edward Alden Jewell's review of the exhibition for the *New York Times*, which mentions these three works by name. I have not been able to identify the "ball and book" that Levy says Barr purchased. Levy, "Interview by Lynda Hartigan and Walter Hopps, July 17 1976"; Jewell, "A Bewildering Exhibition," *New York Times*, January 13, 1932, 27. Jewell also wrote two other articles about the exhibition. See Edward Alden Jewell, "One View of 'Surrealisme,'" *New York Times*, February 1, 1932, 21; and Edward Alden Jewell, "From Fantin-Latour to Surrealisme," *New York Times*, January 17, 1932, 12.

107 For more on the relationship between poetry and Surrealism, see the pioneering work of Mary Ann Caws, especially *The Poetry of Dada and Surrealism: Aragon, Breton, Tzara, Eluard, Desnos* (Princeton, NJ: Princeton University Press, 1966).

108 Joseph Cornell, *Glass Bell, Minotaure* 10 (Winter 1937): 34.

109 Alan Filreis, *Modernism from Left to Right: Wallace Stevens, the Thirties, and Literary Radicalism* (New York: Cambridge University Press, 1994), 2.

110 Edmund Wilson, *Axel's Castle: A Study in the Imaginative Literature of 1870–1930* (New York: C. Scribner's Sons, 1931), 266.

111 Wilson, *Axel's Castle*, 293.

CHAPTER TWO: UNIVERSE TO COSMOS

Epigraph: Guilielmus Hesius, *Emblemata sacra de fide, spe, charitate* (Antwerp, 1636), 88–90. Quoted in David R. Smith, "Vermeer and Iconoclasm," *Zeitschrift für Kunstgeschichte* 74, no. 2 (2011): 200.

1 Joseph Cornell, draft of a letter to James Huth, July 20, 1953, series 3: Diaries, box 6, folder 20, Joseph Cornell Papers, Archives of American Art, Smithsonian Institution, Washington, DC (hereafter AAA).

2 I refer to this work as *Soap Bubble Set* because Cornell used this title in correspondence to Alfred Barr. Joseph Cornell, letter to Alfred Barr, November 9, 1936, folder 55.2: *Fantastic Art, Dada, Surrealism*: United States Correspondence: A–H, Museum of Modern Art Exhibition Records, New York.

3 The map of the moon that serves as *Soap Bubble Set*'s focal point was drawn from Camille Flammarion's nineteenth-century book *Astronomie populaire*. See Danielle Chaperon, *Camille Flammarion: Entre astronomie et littérature* (Paris: Imago, 1998).

4 Joseph Cornell, quoted in Dore Ashton, *A Joseph Cornell Album* (New York: Viking Press, 1974), 110.

5 Don Duco, curator of Amsterdam's Clay Pipe Museum, has identified this pipe as a late-nineteenth-century or early-twentieth-century copy of a popular type of Dutch clay pipe. I am grateful to Mr. Duco for his generosity during our conversation at the Clay Pipe Museum.

6 Charles Taylor, *A Secular Age* (Cambridge, MA: Belknap Press of Harvard University Press, 2007), 59.

7 Max Weber, "Science as Vocation," reprinted in H. H. Gerth and C. Wright Mills, trans. and ed., *From Max Weber: Essays in Sociology* (New York: Oxford University Press, 1946), 142.

8 Deborah Solomon, *Utopia Parkway* (Boston: MFA Publications, 1997), 79.

9 Kirsten Hoving, *Joseph Cornell and Astronomy: A Case for the Stars* (Princeton, NJ: Princeton University Press, 2009), 30–34.

10 Bonnie Costello, *Planets on Tables: Poetry, Still Life, and the Turning World* (Ithaca, NY: Cornell University Press, 2008), 122.

11 Eva Del Soldato, "Natural Philosophy in the Renaissance," *The Stanford Encyclopedia of Philosophy*, ed. Edward N. Zalta, https://plato.stanford.edu/archives/sum2019/entries/natphil-ren, last modified April 8, 2019.

12 For example, Cornell made special note of the essay "Of Truth" in an abridged volume of Bacon's writings, which describes the intense difficulty of discerning and bringing truth to light. Sir Francis Bacon, *Bacon's Essays*, ed. Guy Montgomery (New York: Macmillan, 1930), 2. As Stephen Gaukroger has noted, "Natural philosophy, for Bacon as for his contemporaries, was a theology about nature understood as a creation of a Christian God, whether it took its models from Plato, Aristotle, Democritus, or the Stoics, just as much as ethics was about Christian happiness, whatever its classical models." Gaukroger, *Francis Bacon and the Transformation of Early-Modern Philosophy* (Cambridge: Cambridge University Press, 2004), 77.

13 Mary Baker Eddy, *Science and Health with Key to the Scriptures* (Boston: Christian Science Board of Directors, 1994), 121.

14 Michel Foucault, *The Order of Things: An Archeology of the Human Sciences* (New York: Vintage Books, 1994), 21.

15 Metropolitan Museum of Art, "The Creation of the World and the Expulsion from Paradise (1445)," Heilbrunn Timeline of Art History, https://www.metmuseum.org/toah/works-of-art/1975.1.31.

16 Foucault, *The Order of Things*, 21.

17 Quoted in Smith, "Vermeer and Iconoclasm," 200. For more on this painting, see Daniel Arasse, "Vermeer's Private Allegories," *Studies in the History of Art* 55, Symposium Papers 33: Vermeer Studies (1998): 340–49; E. De Jongh, "Pearls of Virtue and Pearls of Vice," *Simiolus: Netherlands Quarterly for the History of Art* 8, no. 2 (1975–76): 69–79.

18 Smith, "Vermeer and Iconoclasm," 200.

19 György E. Szönyi, "The 'Emblematic' as a Way of Thinking and Seeing in Renaissance Culture," *e-Colloquia*, 1, no. 1 (2003): 4, https://ecolloquia.btk.ppke.hu/index.php/2003/leader.

20 Szönyi, "The 'Emblematic' as a Way of Thinking and Seeing in Renaissance Culture," 4. As Peter M. Daly has noted, the question of whether the *vraisemblable* means the emblem is a "natural sign," connoting an "intrinsic" affinity, or "conventional" sign, suggesting a culturally constructed sense of truth, has led to the emblem's importance to considerations of poststructuralist theory. Daly, *Literature in Light of the Emblem* (Toronto: University of Toronto Press, 1998), 71.

21 Smith, "Vermeer and Iconoclasm," 200.

22 Thomas Crow, *No Idols: The Missing Theology of Art* (Sydney: Power Publications, 2017), 15–32.

23 Crow, *No Idols*, 15–32.

24 Quoted in De Jongh. "Pearls of Virtue," 73–74.

25 Gilbert Seldes, *The Years of the Locust, America, 1929–1932* (Boston: Little, Brown, 1933).

26 Franklin D. Roosevelt, "First Inaugural Address," in *The Roosevelt Reader: Selected Speeches, Messages, Press Conferences, and Letters of Franklin D. Roosevelt*, ed. Basil Rauch (New York: Rinehart, 1957), 92–93.

27 Edmund Wilson, "The Literary Consequences of the Crash" (March 23, 1932), in *The Shores of Light: A Literary Chronicle of the Twenties and Thirties* (New York: Farrar, Straus & Young, 1952), 498.

28 My characterization of the art of the 1930s as concerned with artistic populism and accessibility rather than a search for an essential "American" art follows the example of scholars such as Lauren Kroiz, whose insightful recent book discusses the importance of pedagogy and citizenship to the art of this decade. Kroiz, *Cultivating Citizens: The Regional Work of Art in the New Deal Era* (Oakland: University of California Press, 2018).

29 Wallace Stevens, *The Necessary Angel: Essays on Reality and Imagination* (New York: Vintage Books, 1951), 20.

30 Michael Denning, *The Cultural Front: The Laboring of American Culture in the Twentieth Century* (London: Verso, 1996).

31 Cécile Whiting provides an excellent account of these debates in *Antifascism in American Art* (New Haven, CT: Yale University Press, 1989).

32 For a detailed account of Dewey's relevance to period debates over the formation of a "public art," see John X. Christ, "Stuart Davies as Public Artist: American Painting and the Reconstruction of the Public Sphere," *Oxford Art Journal* 37, no. 1 (March 2014): 65–82.

33 John Dewey, *The Public and Its Problems: An Essay in Political Inquiry* (University Park: Pennsylvania State University Press, 2012), 154.

34 Dewey, *The Public and Its Problems*, 155.

35 William Empson, *Some Versions of Pastoral* (New York: New Directions, 1974), 16.

36 This idea serves as the basis of Empson's theory of pastoralism, which he posits as an alternative to proletarian literature. See also Thomas Crow's "The Simple Life: Pastoralism and the Persistence of Genre in Recent Art," in *Modern Art in the Common Culture* (New Haven, CT: Yale University Press, 1996), 173–211.

37 Quoted in Suzanne Hudson, *Robert Ryman: Used Paint* (Cambridge, MA: MIT Press, 2009), 37.

38 According to Russell Lynes, the women hoped to create a venue for modern art comparable to the Tate Gallery in London or the Musée Luxembourg in Paris. Lynes, *Good Old Modern: An Intimate Portrait of the Museum of Modern Art* (New York: Athenaeum, 1973), 13.

39 Quoted in Andrew Hemingway, *Artists on the Left: American Arts and the Communist Movement, 1926–1956* (New Haven, CT: Yale University Press, 2002), 81.

40 Carol Duncan and Alan Wallach, "The Museum of Modern Art as Late Capitalist Ritual: An Iconographic Analysis," *Marxist Perspectives* 1 (Winter 1978): 28–51. Beginning with Sybil Kantor's indispensable volume, scholars have nuanced this view of Barr as a strident ideologue. See Sybil Gordon Kantor, *Alfred H. Barr, Jr., and the Intellectual Origins of the Museum of Modern Art* (Cambridge, MA: MIT Press, 2002); see also Richard Meyer, *What*

Was Contemporary Art? (Cambridge, MA: MIT Press, 2013); Thomas Crow, *The Long March of Pop: Art, Music, and Design, 1930–1995* (New Haven, CT: Yale University Press, 2015); and Leah Dickerman, "An Introduction to Jere Abbott's Russian Diary 1927–1928," *October* 145 (Summer 2013): 115–24; A. Joan Saab, *For the Millions: American Art and Culture between the Wars* (Philadelphia: University of Pennsylvania Press, 2004); Kristina Wilson, *The Modern Eye: Stieglitz, MoMA, and the Art of the Exhibition, 1925–1934* (New Haven, CT: Yale University Press, 2009); Jennifer Jane Marshall, *Machine Art, 1934* (Chicago: University of Chicago Press, 2012); and Sandra Zalman, *Consuming Surrealism in American Culture: Dissident Modernism* (New York: Routledge, 2016).

41 Quoted in Kantor, *Alfred H. Barr, Jr.*, 309.

42 As Isadora Anderson Helfgott has noted, "In the 1930s, ties between the art world and consumer culture were more incident than defined, and the populist vision of many artists, art administrators, and critics had more transformative social implications." Helfgott, *Framing the Audience: Art and the Politics of Culture in the United States, 1929–45* (Philadelphia: Temple University Press, 2015), 4.

43 Saab, *For the Millions*, 86.

44 Marshall, *Machine Art*, xxii–xxiii.

45 Alfred Barr to Dwight MacDonald, quoted in Kantor, *Alfred H. Barr, Jr.*, 309.

46 Ralph Ellison, "Going to the Territory," in *The Collected Essays of Ralph Ellison*, ed. John Callahan (New York: Modern Library, 1995), 602, 612.

47 Erich Auerbach, *Dante: Poet of the Secular World*, trans. Ralph Manheim (New York: New York Review Books Classics, 2007), 77.

48 Alfred Barr, *Fantastic Art, Dada, Surrealism* (New York: Museum of Modern Art, 1936), 7. The five shows in this series were *Cubism and Abstract Art*, MoMA Exhibition No. 46, March 2–April 19, 1936, https://www.moma.org/calendar/exhibitions/2748?locale=en; *Fantastic Art, Dada, Surrealism*, MoMA Exhibition No. 55, December 7, 1936-January 17, 1937, https://www.moma.org/calendar/exhibitions/2823?locale=en; *Masters of Popular Painting: Modern Primitives of Europe and America*, MoMA Exhibition No. 76, April 27–July 24, 1938, https://www.moma.org/calendar/exhibitions/2090?locale=en; *Americans 1943: Realists and Magic-Realists*, MoMA Exhibition No. 217, February 10–March 21, 1943, https://www.moma.org/calendar/exhibitions/2854?locale=en; and *Romantic Painting in America*, MoMA Exhibition No. 246, November 17, 1943–February 6, 1944, https://www.moma.org/calendar/exhibitions/2903?locale=en.

49 The exhibition checklist included the subject headings "Artists and Works of Art," "Art of Children," "Art of the Insane," "Folk Art," "Commercial and Journalistic Art," "Miscellaneous Objects and Pictures of a Surrealist Character," "Scientific Objects," Fantastic Architecture," and "Films." Alfred Barr, *Fantastic Art, Dada, Surrealism*, 246–88.

50 Barr, *Fantastic Art, Dada, Surrealism*, 220. Barr's description of Cornell as "self-taught" is an early use of the phrase. Cornell would later describe himself as "self-taught" in his unsuccessful 1945 application for a Guggenheim Fellowship. "Self-taught" would become a codified term to describe "folk" artists with the publication of Sidney Janis's *They Taught Themselves: American Primitive Painters of the 20th Century* (New York: Dial Press, 1942); Joseph Cornell, application for a Guggenheim grant, September 12, 1945, Archives of the Guggenheim Memorial Foundation, New York.

51 For an excellent recent genealogy of the various terms used to designate "folk" artists, see Lynne Cooke's essay "Boundary Trouble: Navigating the Margin and the Mainstream," in *Outliers and American Vanguard Art*, ed. Lynne Cooke (Washington DC: National Gallery of Art, 2018), 2–30. My use of the terms "folk" and "self-taught" in this book follows the convention of period sources, approaching them as historically contingent rather than ontological classifications.

52 According to Cahill, the other candidate for the job was James Johnson Sweeney, whom the board rejected for being too difficult. See Holger Cahill, interview with Joan Pring, series 1: Biographical Material and Personal Papers, reel 5282, frames 245–47, Holger Cahill Papers, AAA.

53 Cahill, quoted in Michael Gold, "Two Critics in a Bar-Room," *Liberator* 4, no. 9 (September 1921): 28. In this article, the ardent radical praised Cahill's proletarian pedigree, noting, "He hoboed and dug ditches and sweated in the Kansas harvest fields, he had washed dishes, rebelling at his own worthlessness, and swaggered in the fire zone and at political rallies with a newspaper reporter's badge."

54 Before arriving at MoMA, Cahill curated *American Primitives* (1929) and *American Folk Sculpture* (1931) at the Newark Museum, which was then under the directorship of Progressive reformer John Cotton Dana. Together with Edith Halpert, and Berthe Kroll Goldsmith, Cahill also cofounded the American Folk Art Gallery in 1929. It was in this capacity that he first met Abby Aldrich Rockefeller, who purchased $21,000 of folk art from the gallery in 1931. For more on John Cotton Dana and the Newark Museum, see Carol G. Duncan, *A Matter of Class: John Cotton Dana, Progressive Reform, and the Newark Museum* (New York: Periscope, 2010); John Michael Vlach, "Holger Cahill as Folklorist," *Journal of American Folklore* 98, no. 388 (April–June 1985): 148–62. Recent scholarship on Cahill and folk art include Kathleen Jentleson, "'Not as Rewarding as the North': Holger Cahill's Southern Folk Art Expedition," Archives of American Art Graduate Essay Prize, 2013, http://www.aaa.si.edu/essay/katherine-jentleson%22%20%5Cl%20%22_ftn22. See also Jillian Russo, "From the Ground Up: Holger Cahill and the Promotion of American Art" (PhD diss., CUNY Graduate Center, 2011). See also Rebecca Shaynkin, *Edith Halpert, the Downtown Gallery, and the Rise of American Art* (New Haven, CT: Yale University Press; New York: The Jewish Museum, 2019).

55 Holger Cahill, *American Folk Art: The Art of the Common Man in America, 1750–1900* (New York: Museum of Modern Art, 1932), 6.

56 Malcolm Cowley, *The Dream of the Golden Mountains: Remembering the 1930s* (New York: Viking, 1964), 37.

57 Cahill, *American Folk Art*, 27.

58 Cahill's tendency to compare folk art with children's art was present as early as 1930. As he noted in a 1930 radio speech, "One of the characteristi[cs] of folk art is that it goes straight to the essentials. It is like the art of children. It is naive, but it has great vitality. It is highly individual and often original

expression." Holger Cahill, "American Folk Art Radio Talk, November 1930," series 4: Writings, Lectures and Speeches, reel 5290, frame 1148, Holger Cahill Papers, AAA.

59 Lawrence W. Levine, *Highbrow/ Lowbrow: The Emergence of Cultural Hierarchy in America* (Cambridge, MA: Harvard University Press, 1988), 132; see also George Lipsitz, *Time Passages: Collective Memory and American Popular Culture* (Minneapolis: University of Minnesota Press, 1990).

60 See also Marci Kwon, "Folk Surrealism," *The Modern in the Making: MoMA and the Modern Experiment 1929–1949*, ed. Austin Porter and Sandra Zalman (New York: Bloomsbury, 2020).

61 Barr, *Fantastic Art, Dada, Surrealism*, 12.

62 Barr, *Fantastic Art, Dada, Surrealism*, 8, 9. Quite predictably, this framing drew the ire of André Breton and Paul Éluard, who implored Barr to hew more closely to their published theories, to no avail. See Sandra Zalman, "Vernacular as Vanguard: Alfred Barr, Salvador Dalí, and the U.S. Reception of Surrealism in the 1930s," *Journal of Surrealism and the Americas* 1 (2007): 46.

63 "The Surrealists," *Harper's Bazaar* 56, no. 2689 (November 1936): 62.

64 "The Surrealists," 126.

65 André Breton, "Manifesto of Surrealism" (1924), *Manifestoes of Surrealism*, trans. Richard Seaver and Helen R. Lane (Ann Arbor: University of Michigan, 1972), 16; *The Objects of Joseph Cornell*, Julien Levy Gallery (November 26–December 30, 1932). *New York Times* critic Edward Alden Jewell wrote of Cornell's work "These objects prove to be amusingly clever bibelots for the Christmas season—'toys for adults,' and maybe, for children of the present day, who it may be supposed, are growing up with an innate appreciation of surrealism." Jewell, "Art in Review: Picasso's Illustrations of Balzac Book Are Held Less Felicitous Than Work for Ovid Volume," *New York Times*, December 1, 1932, 19.

66 Cornell, letter to Alfred Barr, November 9, 1936, folder 55.2: *Fantastic Art, Dada, Surrealism*: United States Correspondence: A–H, Museum of Modern Art Exhibition Records.

67 The full quotation is as follows: "I haven't time for a long letter to answer about Dali [*sic*]. I don't really think it is up my alley. You would want his magic tied in the surrealism, but both kinds don't appeal to me together. I have never liked the kind of black magic that Dali, Breton etc. go in for—It's always seemed cheap to me. I've always liked stage magic as white magic—remember Houdini and Thurston well and saw them many times. The kind of magic I like in surrealism is also white magic for a long time I've been trying to do things to which the word 'magic' cannot be applied." Joseph Cornell, letter to Charles Henri Ford, September 25, 1940, series 1: Correspondence, box 1, folder 4, Charles Henri Ford Papers, Getty Research Institute, Los Angeles.

68 According to Barr's catalogue, Hoisington's drawing was titled "A God of War Shooting Arrows to Protect the People." Alfred Barr, *Fantastic Art, Dada, Surrealism*, 283.

69 To this point, Cornell offered Barr his phone number at Traphagen in advance of the exhibition, noting, "Although this is an emergency number for me the few calls that would come in preparatory to the Surrealist exhibition would be perfectly alright." Solomon, *Utopia Parkway*, 83.

70 As Solomon notes, this was a quarter of the pay he received while working at Whitman.

71 Barr, *Fantastic Art, Dada, Surrealism*, 283.

72 Joseph Cornell, letter to Wadsworth Atheneum, July 5, 1938, Joseph Cornell Papers, Wadsworth Atheneum Archives, Hartford, CT.

73 Rosalind Krauss, "Grids," *October* 9 (Summer 1979): 59.

74 Krauss, "Grids," 54–55.

75 Krauss, "Grids," 62. Krauss's article illustrates Cornell's *Nouveaux Contes de Fées* (1948), although she does not discuss it. Krauss's caption for this image (in both its original 1979 publication in *October* and its reprinting in *The Originality of the Avant-Garde*), lists its title as *Nouveaux Contes de Fées (Poison Box)*, but she provides no explanation for the curious subtitle.

76 Cornell, letter to Alfred Barr, November 9, 1936, folder 55.2: *Fantastic Art, Dada, Surrealism*: United States Correspondence: A–H, Museum of Modern Art Exhibition Records.

77 Lorraine Daston and Katherine Park, *Wonders and the Order of Nature, 1150–1750* (New York: Zone Books, 2001), 260.

78 Daston and Park, *Wonders and the Order of Nature*, 291.

79 Lynda Roscoe Hartigan, *Joseph Cornell: Navigating the Imagination* (Salem, MA: Peabody Essex Museum, 2007), 60. This work is currently inaccessible in a private collection. My analysis is informed by Hartigan's careful cataloguing of its contents.

80 Stephen Greenblatt explicates the colonialist underpinnings of the idea of "wonders" and "marvels" in *Marvelous Possessions: The Wonder of the New World* (Chicago: University of Chicago Press, 1991).

81 Mark Doty, *Still Life with Oysters and Lemon* (Boston: Beacon Press, 2001), 36.

82 Craven quoted in Lynes, *Good Old Modern*, 145.

83 Katherine Dreier, letter to Alfred Barr, February 27, 1937, folder 55.2: *Fantastic Art, Dada, Surrealism*: United States Correspondence: A–H, Museum of Modern Art Exhibition Records. Zalman's excellent *Consuming Surrealism in American Culture* provides an expanded account of this incident and expands the present chapter's concern with Surrealism at MoMA through the 1939 World's Fair.

84 Alfred Barr, letter to Katherine Dreier, folder 55.2: *Fantastic Art, Dada, Surrealism*: United States Correspondence: A–H, Museum of Modern Art Exhibition Records.

85 Emily Genauer, "The Fur-Lined Museum," *Harper's Magazine* 189, no. 1130 (July 1944): 130. "Joe Milone's Shoe Shine Stand," ran from December 22, 1942 to January 10, 1943 at the Museum of Modern Art. See Crow, *The Long March of Pop*, 3–4.

86 Genauer, "The Fur-Lined Museum," 130.

87 Genauer, "The Fur-Lined Museum," 130.

88 Crow, *Modern Art in the Common Culture*, 36.

89 Thomas Crow, "The Absconded Subject of Pop," *RES: Anthropology and Aesthetics* 55/56 (Spring–Autumn 2009): 5–20.

90 For discussions of Surrealism's reception in the United States, see Ellen Adams, "After the Rain: Surrealism and the Post–World War II Avant-Garde, 1940–1950" (PhD diss., New York University, 2007); Isabelle Dervaux, ed., *Surrealism USA* (New York: National Academy Museum, 2005); Angela Miller, " 'With Eyes Wide Open': The Americanization Surrealism," in *Caught by Politics: Hitler Exiles and American Visual Culture*, ed. Sabine Eckmann

and Lutz Kepnick (New York: Palgrave Macmillan, 2007); Martica Sawin, *Surrealism in Exile and the Beginning of the New York School* (Cambridge, MA: MIT Press, 1995); and Dickran Tashjian, *A Boatload of Madmen: Surrealism and the American Avant-Garde, 1920–1950* (New York: Thames and Hudson, 2001).

91 Clement Greenberg, "Avant-Garde and Kitsch" (1939), reprinted in *The Collected Essays and Criticism, Volume 1: Perceptions and Judgments, 1939–1944*, ed. John O'Brian (Chicago: University of Chicago Press, 1986), 34–49. For more on Greenberg's art theory, and especially its relationship to Marxist politics, see T. J. Clark, "Clement Greenberg's Theory of Art," *Critical Inquiry* 9, no. 1 (September 1982): 139–56; Caroline A. Jones, *Eyesight Alone: Clement Greenberg's Modernism and the Bureaucratization of the Senses* (Chicago: University of Chicago Press, 2005); Fred Orton and Griselda Pollock, *Avant-Gardes and Partisans Reviewed* (Manchester, UK: Manchester University Press, 1996); Susan Noyes Platt, *Art and Politics in the 1930s: Modernism, Marxism, Americanism; A History of Cultural Activism during the Depression Years* (New York: Midmarch Arts Press, 1999).

92 Robert Slifkin, *Out of Time: Philip Guston and the Refiguration of Postwar American Art* (Berkeley: University of California Press, 2013), 14–16.

93 For more on American fears of propaganda at midcentury, see Fred Turner, *The Democratic Surround: Multimedia and American Liberalism from World War II to the Psychedelic Sixties* (Chicago: University of Chicago Press, 2013).

94 Clement Greenberg, letter to Dwight Macdonald, February 6, 1939, series 3: Manuscripts, box 24, folder 8, Clement Greenberg Papers, Getty Research Institute. This letter, with Macdonald's encouragement, evolved into "Avant-Garde and Kitsch."

95 Eugene Lyons, *The Red Decade: The Stalinist Penetration of America* (Indianapolis: Bobbs-Merrill, 1941), 16.

96 Charles Postel, *The Populist Vision* (Oxford: Oxford University Press, 2009); Brian Vick, "The Origins of German Volk: Cultural Purity and National Identity in Nineteenth-Century Germany," *German Studies Review* 26, no. 2 (May 2003): 241–56.

97 Daston and Park, *Wonders and the Order of Nature*, 14–15.

98 Daston and Park, *Wonders and the Order of Nature*, 343.

99 Taylor, *A Secular Age*, 85–87.

100 Taylor, *A Secular Age*, 86.

101 Clement Greenberg, "Review of Joint Exhibition of Joseph Cornell and Laurence Vail," in *The Collected Essays and Criticism, Volume 1: Perceptions and Judgments, 1939–1944*, ed. John O'Brian (Chicago: University of Chicago Press, 1988), 131.

102 Randall K. Van Schepen, "From the Form of Spirit to the Spirit of Form," in *Re-enchantment*, ed. James Elkins and David Morgan (New York: Routledge, 2009), 47–68.

103 Greenberg, "Review of Joint Exhibition of Joseph Cornell and Laurence Vail," 132.

104 Joseph Cornell, diary Entry, December 8, 1948, series 3: Diaries, box 6, folder 5, Joseph Cornell Papers, AAA.

105 Helleu quoted in Sam Roberts, *Grand Central: How a Train Station Transformed America* (New York: Hatchette Book Group, 2013).

106 Hoving, *Joesph Cornell and Astronomy*, 12.

107 Matthew Hunter, *Wicked Intelligence: Visual Art and the Science of Experiment in Restoration London* (Chicago: University of Chicago Press, 2013), 59.

108 This reading is indebted to Kirsten Hoving's perceptive description of another collage in this series. See Hoving, *Joseph Cornell and Astronomy*, 14.

109 Joshua Landy, *How to Do Things with Fictions* (Oxford: Oxford University Press, 2012), 81–82.

110 John Robert Christianson, *On Tycho's Island: Tycho Brahe, Science, and Culture in the Sixteenth Century* (Cambridge: Cambridge University Press, 2003), 17.

CHAPTER THREE: FOLK INTO MYTH

Epigraph: Virgil, *The Aeneid*, trans. David Ferry (Chicago: University of Chicago Press, 2017), 175.

1 Joseph Cornell, ed., "Clowns, Elephants and Ballerinas," special issue, *Dance Index* 5, no. 6 (June 1946).

2 Cornell saw *Le cirque* during the 1924 exhibition of John Quinn's collection at the Brooklyn Museum. He wrote of the exhibition, "In a single room one glimpsed the SLEEPING GYPSY of Rousseau, LE CIRQUE of Seurat, the largest Picasso of MOTHER & CHILD I have ever seen, Derain's best known WINDOW-STILL-LIFE, and others." Joseph Cornell, draft of a letter to James Huth, July 20, 1953, series 3: Diaries, box 6, folder 20, Joseph Cornell Papers, Archives of American Art, Smithsonian Institution, Washington, DC (hereafter AAA).

3 The credit for Cornell's cover reads, "Arranged by Joseph Cornell from the painting 'Le Cirque' by Seurat, in the Louvre. (Photographed by Larry Colwell)." *Dance Index* 5, no. 6 (June 1946): 135.

4 Joseph Cornell, "Clowns, Elephants and Ballerinas," 136.

5 Cornell noted Harpo Marx's importance to the genesis of this issue in a 1945 diary entry. Joseph Cornell, diary entry, 1945, box 6, folder 2, Joseph Cornell Papers, AAA.

6 My use of the word "queer" throughout this chapter follows Richard Meyer's explication of the term as it applied to Lincoln Kirstein. As he writes, "For him, being 'queer' did not mean simply having sex with other men, or, for that matter, with both men and women. It involved a broader departure from convention—and from normative binary relations both heterosexual and homosexual—that included a range of intimate possibilities. In Kirstein's day, 'queer' also carried its original connotation of peculiar, eccentric, or otherwise impossible to assimilate to the norm. For Kirstein, 'queer' in that sense of 'peculiar,' was often seen as a positive attribute rather than a problem to be regretted or corrected." Meyer, "Threesomes: Lincoln Kirstein's Queer Arithmetic," in *Lincoln Kirstein's Modern*, ed. Samantha Friedman and Jodi Hauptman (New York: Museum of Modern Art, 2019), 99–100. See also George Chauncey, *Gay New York* (New York: Basic Books, 1993).

7 These long-neglected figures have been the subject of renewed art historical attention in recent years. Important work includes Friedman and Hauptman, *Lincoln Kirstein's Modern*; Jarred Earnest, ed., *The Young and Evil: Queer Modernism in New York: 1930–1944* (New York: David Zwirner Books, 2020); Nick Mauss, *Transmissions* (New York: Whitney Museum of American Art, 2020); Tirza True Latimer, *Eccentric Modernisms: Making Differences in the*

History of American Art (Berkeley: University of California Press, 2016); and a forthcoming book on the Kirstein Circle by Angela Miller. Literary scholar Ellen Levy's book considers this milieu, Cornell included, as well as the links among art, poetry, ballet, and Surrealism. In Levy's book, midcentury American culture is defined by a Greenbergian "struggle between the arts." My account suggests that questions of medium specificity were less urgent to the artistic production of the period than the social exigencies placed on all culture at this moment. Levy, *Criminal Ingenuity: Moore, Cornell, Ashbery, and the Struggle between the Arts* (Oxford: Oxford University Press, 2011).

8 Cornell owned several of these texts, including Cyril Beaumont, *Complete Book of Ballets: A Guide to the Principal Ballets of the Nineteenth and Twentieth Centuries* (London: Putnam, 1955); Cyril Beaumont, *The Romantic Ballet as Seen by Theophile Gautier* (London: C. W. Beaumont, 1947); Cyril Beaumont and Sacheverell Sitwell, *The Romantic Ballet in Lithographs of the Time* (London: Faber and Faber, 1938); Théophile Gautier, *The Works of Théophile Gautier*, vol. 16: *A History of Romanticism: The Progress of French Poetry since 1830*, ed. and trans. Frederick C. de Sumichrast (Cambridge: Cambridge University Press, 1902). Joseph Cornell Study Center, Smithsonian Museum of American Art.

9 The first session of the School of American Ballet was held in January 1934. According to Kirstein, "Balanchine had the walls [of the studio] painted a gray-blue he remembered from the Imperial School." The two men chose the school's first home, at 637 Madison Avenue, because it was the site of Isadora Duncan's former studio. Lincoln Kirstein, *Thirty Years: Lincoln Kirstein's The New York City Ballet* (New York: Knopf, 1978), 33–35.

10 According to Kirstein biographer Martin Duberman, "The football team noisily arrived smack in the middle of Dollar's elegant Promenade and proceeded to whistle and cheer whenever a male dancer touched a female one." Duberman, *The Worlds of Lincoln Kirstein* (Evanston, IL: Northwestern University Press, 2008), 337, 346.

11 As with discussions of the interwar vogue for folk, the present understanding of ballet's emergence in the United States is often attributed to a nationalistic desire to create a truly "American" art. This understanding was in fact present in contemporaneous reception of ballet. For example, critic John Martin was vocal in his calls for an "American" ballet. Although Kirstein used this rhetoric, his nationalism was fundamentally concerned with questions of audience: "These efforts of our American Age of Iron were considered as individual initial solutions of our immediate personal problems.... Yet many audiences and local folk who had never been able to see ballet before, liked them. They wanted more of them. And these audiences formed the basic nucleus of the mass public for the popular future of ballet in America." Lincoln Kirstein, *Blast at the Ballet* (1937), in *Ballet: Bias and Belief, "Three Pamphlets Collected" and Other Dance Writings of Lincoln Kirstein*, ed. Lincoln Kirstein (New York: Dance Horizons, 1983), 194.

12 Kirstein, *Blast at the Ballet*, 192.

13 As Lincoln Kirstein wrote in 1937, "Our plans include works based on the subject matter, if not the actual plots used by Melville, Hawthorne, Mark Twain, Whitman, Henry James, Stephen Crane, Hart Crane, Thomas Beer, or James Farrell; folk or popular material that is comprehensible to all of us whether we've read these particular writers, or have ourselves had experiences on this continent which they have already recognized. Our treatment, we hope, is moral rather than rhetorical, although there is plenty of work to be done along this line. By moral, I do not mean ethical. By moral, I mean having some connection with the manners and behavior of men and women with whom we are familiar, as directly or indirectly displayed in theatrical settings which have a real, not a rhetorical or decorative relevance to ourselves." Lincoln Kirstein, *Blast at the Ballet*, 202. Lisa C. Arkin and Marian Smith, "National Dance in the Romantic Ballet," in *Rethinking the Sylph: New Perspectives on the Romantic Ballet*, ed. Lynn Garafola (Hanover, NH: University Press of New England, 1997), 46.

14 Lincoln Kirstein, "About Billy the Kid" (1938), in Kirstein, *Ballet: Bias, and Belief*, 73–76. The comment on Eugene Loring can be found in Jennifer Homans, *Apollo's Angels: A History of Ballet* (New York: Random House, 2010), 461.

15 Lynn Garafola, "Lincoln Kirstein, Modern Dance, and the Left: The Genesis of an American Ballet," *Journal of the Society of Dance Research* 23, no. 1 (Summer 2005): 18–35; James Steichen, *Balanchine and Kirstein's American Enterprise* (Oxford: Oxford University Press, 2018).

16 Lincoln Kirstein, *Three Pamphlets Collected: Blast at Ballet, 1937; Ballet Alphabet, 1939; What Ballet Is All About* (New York: Dance Horizons, 1967), 192.

17 An article about *Dance Index*'s debut noted its "scholarly" tone, as well as the fact that it contained no advertisements. M. L., "New *Dance Index* Out," *Christian Science Monitor*, February 4, 1942, 15.

18 The Joseph Cornell Study Center holds several programs of ballets that Cornell likely attended, including Col. W. de Basil's Ballets Russes de Monte-Carlo (4th American Season, 1936–37); Original Ballet Russe (Season 1940–41, 6th American Tour); The Ballet Theatre (1st Transcontinental Tour). Joseph Cornell Study Center, Smithsonian American Art Museum.

19 The *Dance Index* covers designed by Cornell are: "Hommage à Isadora," *Dance Index* 1, no. 1 (January 1942); "The Parker Sisters," *Dance Index* 1, no. 2 (February 1942); "Untitled" (strips from an original hand-colored 35 mm print in Cornell's possession of Loïe Fuller's *Fire Dance*), *Dance Index* 1, no. 3 (March 1942); "Denishawn," *Dance Index* 1, no. 6 (June 1942); "Portrait of Allen Dodworth (1847)," *Dance Index* 2, no. 4 (April 1943); "European Dance Teachers in the United States" (reading left to right from the top are George Balanchine, Bronislava Nijinska, Michel Fokine, Mary Wigman, Louis Chalif, Adolph Bolm, Elizabeth Menzeli, Rosina Galli, Stefano Mascagno, Enrico Cecchetti, Malvina Cavallazzi, and A. I. Papanti), *Dance Index* 3, nos. 4–6 (April–June 1944); "Le Quatuor dansé à Londres par: Taglioni, Charlotte Grisi, Cerrito et Fanny Elsler," *Dance Index* 3, nos. 7–8 (July–August 1944); "Three or Four Graces," *Dance Index* 3, nos. 9–11 (September–November 1944); "A Catalogue of Dance Films," *Dance Index* 4, no. 5 (May 1945); "George Washington Smith" (Cornell rearranged five of Smith's partners: Annetta Galletti, Louise Lamoureux, Ermesilda Diana, Kate Penoyer, and Josephine de Rosa, on Smith's choreographic notations), *Dance Index* 4, nos. 6–8 (June–August 1945);

"Hans Christian Andersen," *Dance Index* 4, no. 9 (September 1945); "Ballet in Britain, 1934–1944" (scene from the Sadler Wells 1943 revival of *Swan Lake*), *Dance Index* 4, no. 10 (October 1945); "Clowns, Elephants and Ballerinas" (arranged from *Le cirque* by Seurat), *Dance Index* 5, no. 6 (June 1946); and "Americana Romantic Ballet (cartouche proscenium of music-titles for Mlle Ellsler in the *Cachuca*), *Dance Index* 6, no. 9 (September 1947). Cornell's special issues (included in the above) are: "Le Quatuor dansé à Londres par: Taglioni, Charlotte Grisi, Cerrito et Fanny Elsler," "Hans Christian Andersen," "Clowns, Elephants and Ballerinas," and "Americana Romantic Ballet."

20 In a letter to Lincoln Kirstein that accompanied a bill for his services, Cornell detailed the labor entailed by his work for the magazine, as well as his history of compensation: "The first four covers at ten dollars apiece for DANCE INDEX were done with the intention that some of the simpler ones involving less work in research and layout would come my way, something which was overlooked. Per the "Pas de Quatre" number [special issue] I was paid seventy-five dollars and for the 'Andersen' fifty dollars, in each case (as with the current Circus number) the covers not being charged. The work involved in covers even at the subsequently established price of twenty dollars (plus cents due to my complicated way of working makes it practically an honorary affair, and I drew these details to your attention should they against my all ever services to DANCE INDEX deserve some kind of retroactive compensation." Kirstein responded by sending Cornell an additional check. Joseph Cornell, letter to Lincoln Kirstein, July 2, 1946, box 3, folder 54, Lincoln Kirstein Papers, Jerome Robbins Dance Division, New York Public Library.

21 Joseph Cornell, letter to Lincoln Kirstein, August 11, 1946, box 3, folder 54, Lincoln Kirstein Papers, Jerome Robbins Dance Division, New York Public Library.

22 Homans, *Apollo's Angels*, xxii. I am grateful to Jennifer for her generosity in our many conversations about the history of ballet.

23 Lincoln Kirstein, "Comment," in "Clowns, Elephants and Ballerinas," ed. Joseph Cornell, *Dance Index* 5, no. 6 (June 1946): 135.

24 Kirstein's regard for Cornell can also be seen in his recommendation letter for the artist's unsuccessful Guggenheim grant application. He writes, "I have known Cornell for many years and observed his work with increasing interest. His albums, or monographs as he calls them, amount to a new kind of pictorial lyricism, like a fairy tale. A single example may not be readily comprehensible but, because of his continuous inspiration and obstinate integrity, his work has come to be very impressive." Lincoln Kirstein, recommendation letter for Joseph Cornell's 1945 Guggenheim grant application, September 24, 1945, Archives of the Guggenheim Memorial Foundation, New York.

25 Kirsten, quoted in Duberman, *The Worlds of Lincoln Kirstein*, 346.

26 The full quotation follows: "A Soviet writer digging into the neglected fields of Romantic Ballet to me is NEWS— the Perrot, I mean. Makes me feel less 'escapist' in my work." Joseph Cornell to Donald Windham, January 20, 1946, box 9, Donald Windham and Sandy Campbell Papers, Beinecke Rare Book and Manuscript Library, Yale University.

27 Irving Howe, quoted in George Amberg, *Ballet in America: The Emergence of an American Art* (New York: Dell, Sloan, and Pearce, 1949), 66.

28 Balanchine took his company to Hollywood in the summer of 1937 and mounted two ballets for *The Goldwyn Follies*. Other film productions he worked on included *On Your Toes* (1939), *I Was an Adventuress* (1940), and *Star Spangled Rhythm* (1942).

29 Marianne Moore, "Ballet des Elephants," in "Clowns, Elephants and Ballerinas," *Dance Index* 5, no. 6 (June 1946): 148.

30 Lincoln Kirstein, "Comment," in "Clowns, Elephants and Ballerinas," 135.

31 Marianne Moore, "Ballet des Elephants," 148.

32 Peta Tait, *Fighting Nature: Traveling Menageries, Animal Acts and War Shows* (Sydney: Sydney University Press, 2016), 47.

33 That *Fantasia* debuted at almost the same moment as the opening of MoMA's Dance Archives did not escape notice, especially because curator Paul Magriel actively sought to collect material from Disney. A *New York Herald Tribune* article about the film noted, "The great figures of the dance world are represented in the newly opened dance archives at the Museum of Modern Art, and among those great figures is Walt Disney." "Disney to Feature Ballet in Next Film, 'Fantasia,'" *New York Herald Tribune*, March 10, 1940.

34 Joseph Cornell, "Clowns, Elephants and Ballerinas," 136.

35 Joseph Cornell, "Clowns, Elephants and Ballerinas," 136.

36 Baird Hastings, Paul Magriel, and Lincoln Kirstein, "Foreword," *Dance Index* 1, no. 1 (January 1942): 3.

37 Baird Hastings, Paul Magriel, and Lincoln Kirstein, "Foreword," *Dance Index* 1, no. 1 (January 1942): 3.

38 Cornell clearly saw this cover as a distinct work of art. He wrote to Donald Windham to nuance his use of the term "montage" to describe his *Dance Index* work: "First, to confirm notation on my layout requesting you not to call the cover for the Chaffee article a 'montage' one. This has been done, although with the best of intentions, too many times. The only real 'montage' one was the first (the Duncan). Cover by J.C. is good enough." Joseph Cornell, postcard to Donald Windham, September 2 (illegible), 1944, box 9, Donald Windham and Sandy Campbell Papers, Beinecke Rare Book and Manuscript Library.

39 E. H. Gombrich, *Aby Warburg: An Intellectual Biography* (London: Warburg Institute, 1970), 105–27.

40 Gombrich writes, "Warburg attended one of [Duncan's] performances and commented ironically on her bare feet and 'holy expression.'" In another passage, Gombrich notes, "The loose garments of the 'Nympha' may or may not have impressed Lorenzo d'Medici's contemporaries in the same way as Isadora Duncan's daring costume impressed Warburg." Gombrich, *Aby Warburg*, 110n1, 320. I am grateful to Shawon Kinew for our discussions of Warburg.

41 Earnest, *The Young and Evil*; Mauss, *Transmissions*; Richard Meyer, *Outlaw Representation: Censorship and Homosexuality in Twentieth-Century American Art* (New York: Beacon Press, 2002), 291n55.

42 Meyer, "Threesomes," 99–100.

43 Anatole Chujoy, *The New York City Ballet: The First Twenty Years* (New York: Alfred A. Knopf, 1953), 147–48.

44 "May, 1945: Trier, Germany. Bumped

into Lew Christensen. He's in Graves Registration. . . . We touched on plans for what could be done in the ballet; he doubts if he will dance again." After the war, Christensen would go on to serve as ballet master in Ballet Society and, eventually, the San Francisco Ballet. Kirstein, *Thirty Years*, 88.

45 Lynn Garafola, "Lincoln Kirstein: Man of the People," in *Lincoln Kirstein's Modern*, ed. Samantha Friedman and Jodi Hauptman (New York: Museum of Modern Art, 2019), 31.

46 Lincoln Kirstein, preface to *Choreography by George Balanchine: A Catalogue of Works* (New York: Viking, 1984), 14.

47 Suzanne Ramljak, ed., *Elie Nadelman: Classical Folk* (New York: American Federation of the Arts, 2001).

48 Lincoln Kirstein, *Elie Nadelman* (New York: Eakins Press, 1973), 236.

49 Some have claimed that the enlargement of these works was commissioned by Johnson, who along with John Burgee designed the New York State Theater building (now the David H. Koch Theater). Barbara Haskell cites the Nadelman Estate Papers in attributing the posthumous casting of Nadelman's late works, including the Lincoln Center figures, to Kirstein. Barbara Haskell, *Elie Nadelman: Sculptor of Modern Life* (New York: Whitney Museum of American Art, 2003), 211n.192.

50 *Through the Big End of the Opera Glass*, Julien Levy Gallery, December 7, 1943.

51 Edward Alden Jewell, "Modernism," *New York Times*, December 12, 1943, X8.

52 Analisa Leppanen-Guerra, "Immortal Dancers: Joseph Cornell's Pacifism during the Second World War," in *Dance, American Art, 1830–1960*, ed. Jane Dini (New York: Metropolitan Museum of Art, 2016), 265–77.

53 Joseph Cornell, "Comment," *Dance Index* 4, no. 9 (September 1945): 139.

54 Sandra Leonard Starr, *Joseph Cornell and the Ballet* (New York: Castelli, Feigen, Corcoran, 1983), 41.

55 For more on Andersen's paper-cutouts, see Erik Dal, *Christine's Picture Book: Hans Christian Andersen and Grandfather Drewsen* (New York: Holt, Rinehart, and Winston, 1984); Jakob Stougaard-Nielsen, "The Fairy Tale and the Periodical: Hans Christian Andersen's Scrapbooks," *Book History* 16, no. 1 (January 1, 2013): 132–54.

56 Cornell, "Comment," *Dance Index* 4, no. 9 (September 1945): 139.

57 For more on *View* and its relationship to Surrealism, see Dickran Tashjian, *A Boatload of Madmen: Surrealism and the American Avant-Garde, 1920–1950* (New York: Thames and Hudson, 2001), 176–201.

58 According to Myers, Cornell lent several of his boxes to Ford and Tyler to decorate *View*'s offices. John Bernard Myers, *Tracking the Marvelous: A Life in the New York Art World* (New York: Random House, 1983), 20–27.

59 Joseph Cornell, letter to Charles Henri Ford, January 14, 1940, series 1: Correspondence, box 1, folder 4, Charles Henri Ford Papers, Getty Research Institute, Los Angeles.

60 Quoted in Mary Ann Caws, ed., *Joseph Cornell's Theater of the Mind: Selected Diaries, Letters, and Files* (New York: Thames and Hudson, 1993), 91.

61 Charles Henri Ford, *The Overturned Lake* (New York: Little Man Press, 1941), inscribed to Joseph Cornell, November 27, 1941; Parker Tyler, *The Metaphor in the Jungle: And Other Poems* (Prairie City, IL: Press of James A. Decker, 1941), inscribed to Joseph Cornell, January 18, 1941. Both in box 46, Joseph Cornell Study Center, Smithsonian American Art Museum.

62 For an extended discussion of Cornell's relationship with André Breton, see Matthew Affron and Sylvie Ramond, eds., *Joseph Cornell and Surrealism* (Charlottesville, VA: Fralin Museum of Art, 2015; distributed by Penn State University Press), 104–21.

63 Parker Tyler, letter to Charles Henri Ford, series 1: Correspondence, box 2, folder 176, Charles Henri Ford Papers, Beinecke Rare Book and Manuscript Library.

64 Charles Henri Ford, letter to Parker Tyler, series 2: Correspondence, box 15, folder 3, Charles Henri Ford Papers, Henry Ransom Center, University of Texas; quoted in Tashjian, *A Boatload of Madmen*, 171.

65 Meyers, *Tracking the Marvelous*, 27.

66 For a detailed account of *View*'s early history, see Catrina Neiman, "Introduction," in *View: Parade of the Avant-Garde; An Anthology of View Magazine*, ed. Charles Henri Ford (New York: Thunder's Mouth Press, 1991), xi–xvi.

67 Ira Cohen, "Charles Henri Ford: An Interview," in *Gay Sunshine Interviews*, ed. Winston Leyland (San Francisco: Gay Sunshine Press, 1978), 1:35–65.

68 Latimer, *Eccentric Modernisms*, 7.

69 Latimer, *Eccentric Modernisms*, 81.

70 Jean-Pierre Vernant, *Myth and Society in Ancient Greece* (New York: Zone Books, 1990), 203.

71 Vernant, *Myth and Society in Ancient Greece*, 260.

72 Vernant, *Myth and Society in Ancient Greece*, 221.

73 Charles Henri Ford and Parker Tyler, *The Young and the Evil* (New York: Masquerade Books, 1996), 11.

74 Sam See, *Queer Natures, Queer Mythologies*, ed. Christopher Looby and Michael North (New York: Fordham University Press, 2020), 196.

75 Sam See, "Making Modernism: New Queer Mythology in *The Young and Evil*," *English Literary History* 76, no. 4 (Winter 2009): 1074.

76 See, "Making Modernism," 1074.

77 Parker Tyler, *Magic and Myth of the Movies* (New York: Holt, 1947), xxiii.

78 Tyler, *Magic and Myth of the Movies*, 83; "What Is Your Element?," with montages by Joseph Cornell, *Harper's Bazaar* 75, no. 2786 (August 1942): 88–89.

79 Tyler, *Magic and Myth of the Movies*, xix.

80 Michael Leja, *Reframing Abstract Expressionism: Subjectivity and Painting in the 1940s* (New Haven, CT: Yale University Press, 1993).

81 Published in 1890, the book offers a syncretic theory of myth, drawing from contemporaneous anthropological work, Greek myths, and most scandalously at the time, Christianity. For Frazier, the golden bough and the Sacred Grove of Nemi in Italy, offer a foundational "monomyth" that can be threaded through the tales collected in the enormous volume. Mary Beard, "Frazier, Leach, and Virgil: The Popularity (and Unpopularity) of the *Golden Bough*," *Comparative Studies in Society and History* 34, no. 2 (April 1992): 203–24; Jewel Spears Brooker, "The Case of Missing Abstraction: Eliot, Frazier, and Modernism," *Massachusetts Review* 25, no. 4 (Winter 1984): 539–52.

82 Tyler, *Magic and Myth of the Movies*, xx–xxi, ix.

83 Tyler, *Magic and Myth of the Movies*, xx.

84 Parker Tyler, "Symbolism, Myth, and Film Form," unpublished remarks for the Friday Forum series "Symbolism, Myth,

and Film," April 13, 1956, at the Creative Film Foundation. Charles Boultenhouse and Parker Tyler Papers, 14.9, New York Public Library, New York.

85 Parker Tyler, *Exhibition of Objects (Biblioquet)* (New York: Julien Levy Gallery, 1939).

86 For an extended discussion of this work, see Starr, *Joseph Cornell: Art and Metaphysics*, 38–49.

87 Pavle Levi, *Cinema by Other Means* (Oxford: Oxford University Press, 2012), xiii.

88 Joseph Cornell, quoted in Lindsay Blair, *Joseph Cornell's Vision of Spiritual Order* (London: Reaction Books, 1998), 59–60.

89 Lincoln Kirstein, "Introduction," *American Realists and Magic Realists* (New York: Museum of Modern Art, 1943), 7.

90 Kirstein, quoted in Ann Reynolds, "No Strangers," in *The Young and Evil: Queer Modernism in New York, 1930–1955*, ed. Jarrett Earnest (New York: David Zwirner Books, 2019), 34.

91 Guglielmi quoted in Whitney Museum of American Art, https://whitney.org/collection/works/1776.

92 Joseph Cornell working materials, Joseph Cornell Study Center, Smithsonian Museum of American Art.

93 Kirsten Hoving, *Joseph Cornell and Astronomy: A Case for the Stars* (Princeton, NJ: Princeton University Press, 2009), 102–6.

94 Linnaeus Banks, ed., *Blondin: His Life and Performances* (New York: Routledge, Warne, and Routledge, 1862).

95 Parker Tyler, "Americana Fantastica," *View* 2, no. 4 (January 1943): 5.

96 Hoving, *Joseph Cornell and Astronomy*, 102–6.

97 Joseph Cornell, letter to Charles Henri Ford, July 27, 1940, series 1: Correspondence, box 1, folder 4, Charles Henri Ford Papers, Getty Research Institute.

98 Angela Miller, "Vibrant Matter: The Countermodern World of Pavel Tchelitchew," *Art Bulletin* 102, no. 2 (May 2020): 121–45.

99 Pavel Tchelitchew, quoted in Parker Tyler, *The Divine Comedy of Pavel Tchelitchew: A Biography* (New York: Fleet Publishing, 1967), 387.

100 Walter D. Ward, *Mirage of the Saracen: Christians and Nomads in the Sinai Peninsula in Late Antiquity* (Berkeley: University of California Press, 2014), 30.

101 For more on de Bry, see Michael Gaudio, *Engraving the Savage* (Minneapolis: University of Minnesota Press, 2008).

102 Theodor Adorno and Max Horkheimer, *Dialectic of Enlightenment*, trans. Edmund Jephcott (Stanford, CA: Stanford University Press, 2002), xvii.

103 Adorno and Horkheimer, *Dialectic of Enlightenment*, 14. See also Roland Barthes, "Myth Today," in *Mythologies*, trans. Annette Lavers (New York: Hill and Wang, 1984), 26; Benjamin H. D. Buchloh, "Beuys: The Twilight of the Idol, Preliminary Notes for a Critique," in *Joseph Beuys: Mapping the Legacy*, ed. Gene Ray (Sarasota, FL: Ringling Museum, 2001), 203.

104 Adorno elaborates on this point in his writings on astrology and occultism. Theodor Adorno, *The Stars down to Earth and Other Essays on the Irrational in Culture*, ed. Stephen Crook (London: Routledge Classics, 2002).

105 Ernst Cassirer, *The Myth of the State* (New Haven, CT: Yale University Press, 1961), 284–85.

106 For a detailed account of this feud, see Lena Hoff, *Nicolas Calas and the Challenge of Surrealism* (Chicago: University of Chicago Press, 2014), 210.

107 Calas's critique of Greenberg, one of the earliest responses to this canonical essay, implies that the critic was forced to create a justification for *Partisan Review*'s championing of abstraction. He writes, "I well understand that *Partisan Review* is forced to back abstract art—it is in fact the only consistent point in its policy—but it is a pity the editors cannot do it in a more straightforward way. Perhaps then it would not be Mr. Greenberg who would write articles on abstract art, because otherwise how are we to explain that this critic paints pictures that are the exact opposite of what abstract painting should be? . . . In a previous article published last fall in *Partisan Review*, Mr. Greenberg developed an interesting idea on the opposition between avant-garde and kitsch. In the light of this theory we could call Dwight Macdonald's political essays as a kitsch expression of political avant-garde and Mr. Greenberg's new Laocoon, a kitsch statuette. May I suggest that it would be a good idea if *Partisan Review* stopped making such mistakes about art and turned into a monthly supplement of the *Commonwealth*, where no doubt its jesuit methods would be appreciated at their just value by all concerned and especially by T. S. Eliot? Mr. Greenberg's non-abstract paintings, although not good enough to interest the New Laocoon, could then be miraculously transformed into works of art through holy blessing." Nicolas Calas, "View Listens," *View* 1, no. 2 (October 1940): 1, 5.

108 Clement Greenberg, "The Renaissance of the Little Mag: Review of *Accent, Diogenes, Experimental Review, Vice Versa*, and *View*," in *The Collected Essays and Criticism*, vol. 1: *Perceptions and Judgments, 1939–1944*, ed. John O'Brian (Chicago: University of Chicago Press, 1986), 42–47; Philip Rahv, "The Cult of Experience in American Writing," *Partisan Review* 7, no. 6 (November–December 1940): 412–24.

109 Greenberg, "The Renaissance of the Little Mag," 43.

110 Adorno and Horkheimer, *Dialectic of Enlightenment*, xvii.

111 Webb Keane, *Christian Moderns: Freedom and Fetish in the Mission Encounter* (Berkeley: University of California Press, 2007), 53.

112 Charles Henri Ford and Parker Tyler, "Point of View: An Editorial," *View* 1, no. 3 (April 1943): 5. Here Ford and Tyler situate their work with *View* in relation to the political imperatives of the past two decades, writing, "In the twenties and thirties the two main themes of inspiration were the unconscious and the masses. The genuine artist, the pure poet, the authentic composer, according to his political inclinations, believed either that his mission consisted in expressing the depressing feelings of the masses or in giving form to his own dream. Today, in the fearful tragedy mankind is experiencing, we must ask the question if it has not become necessary to focus our attention upon other aspects of the artistic problem."

113 P. Adams Sitney, *The Cinema of Poetry* (Oxford: Oxford University Press, 2015).

114 Parker Tyler, *Underground Film: A Critical History* (New York: Grove Press, 1970).

115 Joseph Cornell, diary entry, November–December 1957, box 7, folder 5, Joseph Cornell Papers, AAA.

116 Tony Kushner, *Angels in America: A Gay Fantasia on National Themes* (New York: Theater Communications Group, 2014), 289.

117 Joseph Cornell, letter to Charles Henri Ford, November 19, 1957, series 1: Correspondence, box 1, folder 10, Charles Henri Ford Papers, Getty Research Institute.

118 Cornell, quoted in Deborah Solomon, *Utopia Parkway* (Boston: MFA Publications, 1997), 247.

CHAPTER FOUR: ENCHANTRESSES

Epigraph: William Shakespeare, *King Lear*, ed. K. Muir (Cambridge, MA: Harvard University Press, 1952), I.1.61.

1 Joseph Cornell, "(Windows and Fanny Cerrito,) Discovery—New York City 1940, January 4, 1944, Revised July 8, 1944," series 3: Diaries, box 6, folder 1, Joseph Cornell Papers, Archives of American Art, Smithsonian Institution, Washington, DC (hereafter AAA).

2 Although Cornell's discovery of the print took place in the summer of 1940, he did not record it in his diary until the mid-1940s and continued to revise his account for various exhibitions of the portfolio—for example, a document titled "Discovery—New York City 1940," which is annotated to indicate that it was recorded on January 4, 1944, and revised "after visit to Miss M.[arianne] Moore" on July 8, 1944. According to a note made on what is likely an earlier version of this account (which had been crossed out), the revisions were made in favor of making the account seem less "factual." Joseph Cornell, "(Windows and Fanny Cerrito,) Discovery—New York City 1940, January 4, 1944, Revised July 8, 1944," series 3: Diaries, box 6, folder 1, Joseph Cornell Papers, AAA.

3 Sandra Leonard Starr was the first to identify this print. Her catalogue on Cornell's relationship to the ballet remains the most extensive consideration of the artist's ballet works. Sandra Leonard Starr, *Joseph Cornell and the Ballet* (New York: Castelli, Feigen, Corcoran, 1983).

4 Quoted in Mary Ann Caws, ed., *Joseph Cornell's Theater of the Mind: Selected Diaries, Letters, and Files* (New York: Thames and Hudson, 1993), 104.

5 Théophile Gautier, "Opéra: *Gemma*," in *Gautier on Dance*, ed. and trans. Ivor Guest (London: Dance Books, 1986), 267.

6 Quoted in Starr, *Joseph Cornell and the Ballet*, 20.

7 Mary D. Sheriff, *Enchanted Islands: Picturing the Allure of Conquest in Eighteenth-Century France* (Chicago: University of Chicago Press, 2018), 2.

8 Jodi Hauptman, *Joseph Cornell: Stargazing in the Cinema* (New Haven, CT: Yale University Press, 1999); Michael Moon, *A Small Boy and Others: Imitation and Initiation in American Culture from Henry James to Andy Warhol* (Durham, NC: Duke University Press, 1998).

9 Caws, *Joseph Cornell's Theater of the Mind*, 34.

10 David Morgan, *Images at Work: The Material Culture of Enchantment* (Oxford: Oxford University Press, 2018), 33.

11 Morgan, *Images at Work*, 18.

12 Joseph Cornell, series 3: Diaries, box 6, folder 1, Joseph Cornell Papers, AAA. Joseph Cornell, "'Ondine (Cerrito)' Portfolio," series 4: Source material, box 25, folders 1–2, Joseph Cornell Papers, AAA. See also Joseph Cornell, *Portrait of Ondine*, 1940, mixed media: paperboard, cardboard, paint, prints, maps . . . , 6.4 × 27.3 × 32.4 cm, Washington DC, Smithsonian American Art Museum, https://americanart.si.edu/artwork/portrait-ondine-5649.

13 Starr, *Joseph Cornell and the Ballet*, 20. Cornell reproduces de Chirico's *The Evil Genius of a King* (spring–summer 1914), and captions it with an altered title of de Chirico painting, *Playthings of the Prince* (1915), which he renders as "Toys of a Prince." Both works are in the collection of the Museum of Modern Art. I am grateful to Beth Gianfagna for alerting me to this.

14 Starr, *Joseph Cornell and the Ballet*, 29.

15 Quoted in Caws, *Joseph Cornell's Theater of the Mind*, 104.

16 For a full consideration of Cornell's compilation and organization of these dossiers, see Lindsay Blair, *Joseph Cornell's Vision of Spiritual Order* (London: Reaktion Books, 1998), 23–28. See also Janine Mileaf, *Please Touch: Dada and Surrealist Objects after the Readymade* (Hanover, NH: Dartmouth College Press, 2010), 169–77; Joanna Roche, "Joseph Cornell's Garden Center 44: The Poetics of Memory," in *Joseph Cornell: Opening the Box*, ed. Jason Edwards and Stephanie Taylor (Bern: Peter Lang, 2007), 189–204; and Hauptman, *Stargazing the Cinema*, 22.

17 Hauptman, *Stargazing the Cinema*, 22–23.

18 Quoted in Hauptman, *Stargazing the Cinema*, 24.

19 Joseph Cornell, letter to Jermayne MacAgy, June 5, 1947, box 4, folder 4, Jermayne MacAgy Papers, Menil Archives, Houston, TX.

20 Sharon Kim, *Literary Epiphany in the Novel, 1850–1950: Constellations of the Soul* (New York: Palgrave Macmillan, 2012), 7, 8. I am indebted to Michaela Bronstein for pointing me to this literature.

21 Quoted in Caws, *Joseph Cornell's Theater of the Mind*, 104.

22 Lisa C. Arkin and Marian Smith, "National Dance in the Romantic Ballet," in *Rethinking the Sylph: New Perspectives on the Romantic Ballet*, ed. Lynn Garafola (Hanover, NH: University Press of New England, 1997), 46. See also Sally Banes and Nöel Carroll, "Marriage and the Inhuman: *La Sylphide*'s Narratives of Domesticity and Community," in Garafola, *Rethinking the Sylph*, 91–106.

23 Cornell, "(Windows and Fanny Cerrito,) Discovery—New York City 1940, January 4, 1944, Revised July 8, 1944."

24 Joseph Cornell, "Portrait of Ondine (Fanny Cerrito)," series 4: Source material, box 16, folder 46, Joseph Cornell Papers, AAA.

25 Starr, *Joseph Cornell and the Ballet*, 20.

26 Cornell, "'Ondine (Cerrito)' Portfolio," series 4: Source material, box 25, folder 1, Joseph Cornell papers, AAA.

27 According to an internal museum document, "An institution founded in Paris in 1929 known as the Archives Internationales de la Danse was the model on which the present Museum of Modern Art Dance Archives has been founded. . . . Taken altogether the Archives is a well balanced body of dance material and compares favorably with major collections here and abroad. Of course since Paris and Milano were for so many years the center of theatrical dance activity it is natural that there are housed in the several libraries of these cities some of the great original documents pertaining to ballet. Especially rich in dance related material is the great Rondel collection and the Bibliothèque d' l'Arsenal. Unfortunately here as in most European libraries there are no suitable working catalogues hence it is only with great diligence and patience that one can weed out the magnificence of their treasures. The same holds true

for the Bibliothèque de l'Opéra and the Bibliothèque Nationale." "Undated, Unsigned Memo," box 3, folder 42, Dance Archives, Museum of Modern Art Archives. For more on Rolf de Maré and ballet as a popular art, see Inge Baxmann, Clair Rousier, and Patricia Veroli, *Les Archives Internationales de la Danse 1931–1952* (Paris: Centre National de la Danse, 2006). See also "The Dance Archives," *Bulletin of the Museum of Modern Art* 8, no. 3 (March 1941): 3–11.

28 This same report goes on to detail the founding collection of the Dance Archives, which included over 2,000 books, 1,631 prints, 1,212 photographs, 238 stereoscopes, and "thousands" of programs, clippings, and other materials. " 'Purpose,' and 'Resources' in 'Museum of Modern Art Dance Archives,' " box 3, folder 42, Dance Archives, Museum of Modern Art Archives.

29 "Activities: Six Months Ending April 30, 1940," box 3, folder 42, Dance Archives, Museum of Modern Art Archives.

30 John Martin, "The Dance: New Archives," *New York Times*, March 10, 1940, 153.

31 These prints were lent by George Chaffee, who was a soloist for the Metropolitan Opera Ballet Company and a well-known scholar and collector of Romantic ballet prints. Garafola, "Introduction," in *Rethinking the Sylph*, 1–2.

32 Lincoln Kirstein, "Comment," *Dance Index* 3, nos. 7, 8 (July, August 1944): 103. Cornell confirmed the association of his ballet work and the Dance Archives in a later letter to Kirstein, in which he wrote, "In thinking about this I have suddenly experienced the old enthusiasms originally experienced with the beginning of the Archives and the magazine." Joseph Cornell, letter to Lincoln Kirstein, April 19, 1949, box 3, folder 54, Lincoln Kirstein Papers, Jerome Robbins Dance Division, New York Public Library.

33 Susan Davidson, "Marcel Duchamp / Joseph Cornell Chronology," in *Joseph Cornell / Marcel Duchamp... in Resonance*, ed. Anne d'Harnoncourt and Anne Temkin (Philadelphia: Philadelphia Museum of Art, 1998), 280.

34 Davidson's chronology dates this commission to July 31, 1942. Davidson, "Marcel Duchamp / Joseph Cornell Chronology," 283.

35 d'Harnoncourt and Temkin, *Joseph Cornell / Marcel Duchamp... in Resonance*, 304.

36 Donald Windham, "Joseph Cornell and His Audience: The Reward of the Puzzle," series 1, box 10, Donald Windham and Sandy Campbell Papers, Beinecke Rare Book and Manuscript Library, Yale University.

37 As he wrote to Donald Windham, "I'm hoping the Chagall color falls thru. I'm still loyal to the humble garb of D.I. and think of what color did to the last issue of VIEW." Joseph Cornell to Donald Windham, October 19, 1945, box 9, Donald Windham and Sandy Campbell Papers, YCAL MSS 424, Beinecke Rare Book and Manuscript Library.

38 Cornell was employed at Allied Control Company from March 1943 to January 1944 and was paid 55 cents an hour. Deborah Solomon, *Utopia Parkway* (Boston: MFA Publications, 1997), 148.

39 Paul Cummings, "Interview of Elizabeth Cornell Benton, 21 April 1976," Oral History Interviews, Archives of American Art, Smithsonian Institution, Washington, DC.

40 "Group Insurance for Company," *New York Times*, August 19, 1943, 29.

41 According to Susan Davidson, in March 1942, Duchamp advised Peggy Guggenheim to purchase three works by Cornell, including Cornell's *Fortune Telling Parrot* (ca. 1937–38). Davidson, "Marcel Duchamp / Joseph Cornell Chronology," 283.

42 Joseph Cornell, "Summer 1943," series 4: Source material, box 18, folder 16, Joseph Cornell Papers, AAA.

43 Joseph Cornell, "Summer 1943," series 4: Source material, box 18, folder 16, Joseph Cornell Papers, AAA.

44 Joseph Cornell, "Summer 1943," series 4: Source material, box 18, folder 16, Joseph Cornell Papers, AAA.

45 Joseph Cornell, "Note, September 1, 1943," series 4: Source material, box 18, folder 16, Joseph Cornell Papers, AAA.

46 Donald Windham, "Speech at Joseph Cornell Memorial Service, January 15, 1973," series 1, box 10, Donald Windham and Sandy Campbell Papers, Beinecke Rare Book and Manuscript Library.

47 The exhibitions were *Portrait of Ondine: Dance and Theatre Design*, Museum of Modern Art, November 28, 1945–February 17, 1946, https://www.moma.org/calendar/exhibitions/3183?locale=en; *The Romantic Museum: Portraits of Women, Constructions, and Arrangements by Joseph Cornell*, Hugo Gallery, December 1946; *Portrait of Ondine*, One-Wall Gallery, November 1–15, 1956. The MoMA show also included works by Giorgio de Chirico, Eugene Berman, Pavel Tchelitchew, Eugene Bérard, and André Masson, which Cornell arranged into an exhibition "so small that the entire display is contained within a large shadow box." "Press Release: Museum of Modern Art to Open Two Small Exhibitions in Auditorium Gallery," folder 301.2: *Portrait of Ondine: Dance and Theatre Design*: Press Release and Correspondence, Museum of Modern Art Exhibition Records, New York.

48 Joseph Cornell, letter to Donald Windham, October 19, 1945, series 1, box 9, Donald Windham and Sandy Campbell Papers, Beinecke Rare Book and Manuscript Library. By the time he exhibited *Portrait of Ondine* at the One-Wall Gallery at Wittenborn Bookstore, Cornell had given up the idea of an inexpensive publication and instead tried to create something more along the lines of a luxury edition, as suggested by his letter to Jermayne MacAgy suggesting "the tentative price for a double set of [*Portrait of Ondine*] prints (100) $100–150." Joseph Cornell, letter to Jermayne MacAgy, April 8, 1956, box 4, folder 4, Jermayne MacAgy Papers, Menil Archives, Houston, TX.

49 Joseph Cornell, application for a Guggenheim grant, September 12, 1945, Archives of the Guggenheim Memorial Foundation, New York.

50 Quoted in Hauptman, *Stargazing the Cinema*, 24.

51 Cornell, quoted in Caws, *Joseph Cornell's Theater of the Mind*, 95.

52 Joseph Cornell, "Enchanted Wanderer: Excerpt from a Journey Album of Hedy Lamarr," *View* 1, nos. 9–10 (December 1941–January 1942): 3.

53 Erwin Panofsky, "Style and Medium in the Motion Pictures," in *Film Theory and Criticism*, ed. Gerald Mast and Marshall Cohen (New York: Oxford University Press, 1985), 224. Originally published as "On Movies," *Bulletin of the Department of Art and Archaeology of Princeton University* (June 1936): 5–15. According to Thomas Levin, Panofsky came to write about cinema at the encouragement of Iris Barry, the founding curator of MoMA's film department. Levin, "Iconology at the Movies: Panofsky's

Film Theory," *Yale Journal of Criticism* 9, no. 1 (1996): 27–55.

54 Benjamin is critical of Gance's approach as trying to recover cinema's cult value. He writes, "But the difficulties which photography caused for traditional aesthetics were child's play compared to those presented by film. Hence the obtuse and hyperbolic character of early film theory. Abel Gance, for instance, compares film to hieroglyphs: 'By a remarkable regression, we are transported back to the expressive level of the Egyptians.... Pictorial language has not matured, because our eyes are not yet adapted to it. There is not yet enough respect, not enough *cult*, for what it expresses.'" Walter Benjamin, *The Work of Art in the Age of Its Technological Reproducibility, and Other Writings on Media* (Cambridge, MA: Harvard University Press, 2008), 28–29.

55 Cedric Belfrage, quoted in Scott Eyman, *The Speed of Sound: Hollywood and the Talkie Revolution, 1926–1930* (New York: Simon and Schuster, 1997), 378.

56 The film has been the subject of extensive debate by scholars, who have argued for its status as a portrait of its star, the story of an eclipse, or a series of disjunctive fragments. See Hauptman, *Stargazing the Cinema*, 85–115; and Kirsten Hoving, *Joseph Cornell and Astronomy: A Case for the Stars* (Princeton, NJ: Princeton University Press, 2009), 57–67. For the most thorough account of Cornell's films, see also P. Adams Sitney, "The Cinematic Gaze of Joseph Cornell," in *Joseph Cornell*, ed. Kynaston McShine (New York: Museum of Modern Art, 1980).

57 Annette Michelson, "*Rose Hobart* and *Monsieur Phot*: Early Films from Utopia Parkway," *Artforum* 11, no. 10 (June 1973): 49.

58 Cornell, "Enchanted Wanderer," 3.

59 Cornell, "Enchanted Wanderer," 3.

60 T. J. Clark, *Heaven on Earth: Painting and the Life to Come* (London: Thames and Hudson, 2018), 11.

61 Lucy Poate Stebbins and Richard Poate Stebbins, *The Enchanted Wanderer: The Life of Carl Maria Von Weber* (New York: G. P. Putnam's Sons, 1940).

62 Hauptman, *Stargazing the Cinema*, 7.

63 Sandra Leonard Starr, *Joseph Cornell: Art and Metaphysics* (New York: Castelli, Feigen, Corcoran, 1982), 38–49.

64 Joseph Cornell, "Women Painters" (undated), series 4: Source material, box 17, folder 24, Publishing Project, "Women Painters," 1855, 1948–53, Joseph Cornell Papers, AAA.

65 Joseph Cornell, "Sofonisba Anguissola" (undated), series 4: Source material, box 17, folder 24, Publishing Project, "Women Painters," 1855, 1948–53, Joseph Cornell Papers, AAA.

66 Quoted in Joanna Roche, "Performing Memory in Moon in a Tree: Carolee Schneemann Recollects Joseph Cornell," *Art Journal* 60, no. 4 (Winter 2001): 13.

67 Quoted in Hauptman, *Stargazing the Cinema*, 15.

68 Quoted in Hauptman, *Stargazing the Cinema*, 74, 76.

69 Elizabeth C. Childs, "Setting for a Fairy Tale," Guggenheim Collection, http://www.guggenheim.org/new-york/collections/collection-online/artwork/903.

70 Childs, "Setting for a Fairy Tale."

71 *Aurora's Wedding*, with Toumanova in the title role, ran from 1940 to 1941 at the State Theater of New York. Jerome Robbins Dance Division, New York Public Library, "Aurora's wedding [excerpts]," New York Public Library Digital Collections, http://digitalcollections.nypl.org/items/ca999cd0-e35e-0130-8168-3c075448cc4b.

72 Quoted in Starr, *Joseph Cornell and the Ballet*, 68.

73 The first version of *La Sylphide* opened on March 12, 1832, at the Académie Royale de Musique in Paris, with Marie Taglioni in the title role. The production is widely seen as inaugurating the Romantic ballet in Paris, and subsequently became an international sensation. Staged four years later, August Bournonville's version of *La Sylphide* utilized a new score by H. S. Løvenskoild. Another notable version, titled *Les Sylphides* was staged in Paris in 1909 by Mikhail Fokine for the Ballets Russes. Susan An, "*La Sylphide*," in *The International Encyclopedia of Dance*, ed. Selma Jeanne Cohen (London: Oxford University Press, 2005).

74 This version was choreographed by August Bournonville, with music by Herman Severin Løvenskoild.

75 Socrates, quoted in Plato, *Phaedrus*, trans. Walter Hamilton (New York: Penguin Books, 1973), 51.

76 Solomon, *Utopia Parkway*, 122.

77 Cynthia Hahn, *The Reliquary Effect: Enshrining the Sacred Object* (London: Reaktion Books, 2017).

78 Starr, *Joseph Cornell and the Ballet*, 59–70.

79 Allan Kaprow, "The Legacy of Jackson Pollock," in *Essays on the Blurring of Art and Life*, ed. Jeff Kelley (Berkeley: University of California Press, 1983), 3–4.

80 William Shakespeare, *The Tempest* (New York: Penguin Books, 1999), 1.2.399–401.

81 Stanley Cavell, "The Avoidance of Love: A Reading of *King Lear*," in *Must We Mean What We Say? A Book of Essays* (Cambridge: Cambridge University Press, 2002). For a consideration of Cavell's essay and its relevance to the artistic and political valences of "action" in the postwar period, see Robert Slifkin, "The Tragic Image: Action Painting Refigured," *Oxford Art Journal* 34, no. 2 (June 2011): 227–46. Although "The Avoidance of Love" postdates the time period addressed in this chapter, its genesis in Cavell's friendships with art historian Michael Fried and especially literary critic Paul Alpers suggests that the essay can be read as a continuation of literary and artistic questions that first arose in the 1940s. Cavell and Fried were both members of the Harvard Society of Fellows in the 1960s. Cavell's initial reading of *King Lear* is structured as a response to Paul Alpers's article "King Lear and the Theory of the Sight Pattern," and he later adds a discussion of scapegoats, Jesus Christ, and William Empson in response to "a detailed and very useful set of comments on an earlier draft of this essay" by Alpers. Cavell, "The Avoidance of Love," 272, 303.

82 My understanding of Cavell's approach to character is indebted to Jamie Parra, "Prisoners of Style: Slavery, Ethics, and the Lives of American Literary Characters" (PhD diss., Columbia University, 2015).

83 Gay McCauley, *Space in Performance: Making Meaning in the Theater* (Ann Arbor: University of Michigan Press, 1999), 77–78.

84 Cavell, "The Avoidance of Love," 290.

85 Cavell's approach to disidentification is grounded in his larger philosophical project considering the status of skepticism in Kantian epistemology. As he writes later, "This is why we think skepticism must mean that we cannot know the world exists, and hence that perhaps there isn't one (a conclusion some

profess to admire and others to fear). Whereas what skepticism suggests is that since we cannot know the world exists, its presentness to us cannot be a function of knowing. The world is to be *accepted*; as the presentness of other minds is not known, but acknowledged." Cavell, "The Avoidance of Love," 324. For a discussion of skepticism and the status of knowledge, see Cavell, "Knowing and Acknowledging," in *Must We Say What We Mean?*, 238–66. This essay ends with the following line, which is crucial to understanding Cavell's reading of *Lear*: "To know you are in pain is to acknowledge it, or to withhold the acknowledgment.—I know your pain the way you do."

86 Cavell, "The Avoidance of Love," 338–39.

87 Stéphane Mallarmé, "Le Vierge, le vivace . . . ," quoted in Mary Ann Caws, "Mallarmé's Progeny," in *Mallarmé in the Twentieth Century*, ed. Robert Greer Cohn (Madison, NJ: Fairleigh Dickinson University Press, 1998), 86–91. Caws was the first scholar to note the comparison between this poem and Cornell's work, and to investigate the artist's engagement with Symbolist poetry.

CHAPTER FIVE: ROOMS AND SKIES

Epigraph: William Wordsworth, "To the Cuckoo," in *William Wordsworth*, ed. Geoffrey Durrant (Cambridge: Cambridge University Press, 1969), 28.

1 *Ninth Street Exhibition of Paintings and Sculpture*, May 21–June 10, 1951, 60 East Ninth Street, New York. Marika Herskovic, ed., *New York School Abstract Expressionists: Artists Choice by Artists; A Complete Documentation of the New York Painting and Sculpture Annuals, 1951–57* (Franklin Lakes, NJ: New York School Press, 2000), 36. For a detailed account of the planning of the *Ninth Street Exhibition*, see Bruce Altshuler, *The Avant-Garde in Exhibition: New Art in the 20th Century* (New York: Harry N. Abrams, 1994), 156–73.

2 Scale, which Jennifer Roberts describes as "a comparative relationship between two or more extents or quantities," has become an important site of art historical inquiry in recent years. See Andrew James Hamilton, *Scale and the Incas* (Princeton, NJ: Princeton University Press, 2018); Joan Kee and Emanuele Lugli, "To Scale," *Art History* 38, no. 2 (April 2015); Jennifer Roberts, ed., *Scale* (Chicago: Terra Foundations Essay, 2016), 15.

3 Barnett Newman, quoted in Wouter Davidts, "'As Pointless as a Yard Rule': Barnett Newman and the Scale of Art," in Roberts, *Scale*, 149.

4 Frank O'Hara, "Jackson Pollock," in *Art Chronicles: 1954–1966* (New York: George Braziller, 1974), 34–35.

5 Edwin Denby, *Dancers, Buildings, and People in the Streets* (New York: Horizon Press, 1965), 262.

6 Susan Stewart, *Poetry and the Fate of the Senses* (Chicago: University of Chicago Press, 2002), 296.

7 Serge Guilbaut, *How New York Stole the Idea of Modern Art*, trans. Arthur Goldhammer (Chicago: University of Chicago Press, 1983).

8 Stewart, *Poetry and the Fate of the Senses*, 304.

9 Stewart, *Poetry and the Fate of the Senses*, 309.

10 Quoted in Dawn Ades, "The Transcendental Surrealism of Joseph Cornell," in *Joseph Cornell*, ed. Kynaston McShine (New York: Museum of Modern Art, 1980), 37.

11 Mina Loy, "Phenomenon in American Art (typescript), November 25, 1950," series 9: Writings about Cornell, box 19, folder 12, Joseph Cornell Papers, Archives of American Art, Smithsonian Institution, Washington, DC (hereafter AAA)

12 Joseph Cornell, "AVIARY," series 4: Source material, box 12, folder 24, Joseph Cornell Papers, AAA.

13 Virginia Jackson and Yopie Prins, "General Introduction," in *The Lyric Theory Reader: A Critical Anthology* (Baltimore MD: Johns Hopkins University Press, 2014), 3.

14 Frank Doggett, "Romanticism's Singing Bird," *Studies in English Literature, 1500–1900* 14, no. 4 (Autumn 1974): 547–61.

15 Percy Bysshe Shelley, *A Defense of Poetry* (Indianapolis: Bobbs-Merrill, 1904), 30.

16 Joseph Cornell, *Cockatoo: Keepsake Parakeet*, 1949–53, wooden cutout, paper, spring, and found objects in a glass-fronted wood box, 20¼ × 12 × 5 in. (51.4 × 30.5 × 12.7 cm), Smithsonian American Art Museum, Washington, DC. Joseph Cornell, *A Swan Lake for Tamara Toumanova (Homage to the Romantic Ballet)*, 1946, painted wood, glass pane, photostats on wood, blue glass, mirrors, painted paperboard, printed matter, feathers, velvet, and rhinestones, 9½ × 13 × 4 in. (24.1 × 33 × 10.2 cm), Menil Collection, Houston, TX. Cornell himself compared the *Aviary* series with his ballet works in a 1952 diary entry, writing of the former, "Toumanova SWAN relates of course to an entirely different realm with a flavor (connotation) here of more than the footlights—into the mysterious world of the sylphide tradition—the Xmas tree ornaments with a more familiar connotation—all of the above not competing with the conventional display of oils or sculpture, but offered as a way of approaching a subject esthetically but not too far removed from available channels to the spectator." Joseph Cornell, diary entry, September 10, 1952, series 3: Diaries, box 6, folder 15, Joseph Cornell Papers, AAA.

17 According to Sarah Lea, Cornell "conceived the exhibition as a total experience for visitors. . . . The works were arranged in a brightly lit room at different heights, their display and collective presence enhancing the sense of animation common to the individual works." Lea, ed., *Joseph Cornell: Wanderlust* (London: Royal Academy of Art, 2015), 186.

18 Mina Loy, "Phenomenon in American Art (typescript), November 25, 1950," series 9: Writings about Cornell, box 19, folder 12, Joseph Cornell Papers, AAA.

19 Joseph Cornell, "AVIARY," Series 4: Source material, box 12, folder 24, Joseph Cornell Papers, AAA.

20 Jennifer Mundy, "An 'Overflowing, a Richness & Poetry': Joseph Cornell's Planet Set and Giuditta Pasta," *Tate Papers* 1 (Spring 2004): http://www.tate.org.uk/download/file/fid/7230.

21 Samuel Taylor Coleridge, "The Nightingale: A Conversational Poem, Written in April, 1798," in Coleridge and William Wordsworth, *Lyrical Ballads, with a Few Other Poems* (London: J & A Arch, 1798), 66–67.

22 Valerie Hellstein, "Ground the Social Aesthetics of Abstract Expressionism: A New Intellectual History of the Club" (PhD diss., Stony Brook University, 2010).

23 Valerie Hellstein, "The Cage-iness of Abstract Expressionism," *American Art* 28, no. 1 (Spring 2014): 56–77.

24 Harold Rosenberg, "Tenth Street: A

Geography of Modern Art," in *Discovering the Present: Three Decades in Art, Culture, and Politics* (Chicago: University of Chicago Press, 1972), 108. The film *The Automatic Moving Company* was created in 1912 by Romeo Bosetti and Émile Cohl and is considered one of the earliest stop-motion animation films.

25 Joseph Cornell, quoted in Dore Ashton, *A Joseph Cornell Album* (New York: Viking Press, 1974), 82. Cornell was the subject of three solo exhibitions at Egan Gallery: *Aviary by Joseph Cornell*, Charles Egan Gallery, December 7, 1949–January 7, 1950; *Night Songs and Other New Work—1950 by Joseph Cornell*, Charles Egan Gallery, December 1, 1950–January 13, 1951; and *Night Voyage by Joseph Cornell*, Charles Egan Gallery, February 10–March 28, 1953.

26 Thomas B. Hess, "Joseph Cornell," *ARTnews* 48, no. 9 (January 1950): 45.

27 Deborah Solomon, *Utopia Parkway* (Boston: MFA Publications, 1997), 202.

28 Solomon, *Utopia Parkway*, 220–21. Motherwell described his friendship with Cornell in the late 1940s and early 1950s in a 1981 letter, writing, "In those days I was an ardent admirer of his, as was Matta, who introduced me to him and was surprised that the Surrealist exiles in New York did not make more of him." Robert Motherwell, letter to Jim Cohen and Arthur Greenberg, July 26, 1981, Robert Motherwell Papers, XV.15.1, Dedalus Foundation, New York.

29 T. J. Clark, *Farewell to an Idea: Episodes from a History of Modernism* (New Haven, CT: Yale University Press, 2000), 401.

30 Clark, *Farewell to an Idea*, 376–78.

31 Hess, quoted in Altshuler, *The Avant-Garde in Exhibition*, 162.

32 Virginia Jackson, *Dickinson's Misery: A Theory of Lyric Reading* (Princeton, NJ: Princeton University Press, 2005), 92.

33 John Crowe Ransom, quoted in Jackson, *Dickinson's Misery*, 93.

34 Jonathan Culler, *Theory of the Lyric* (Cambridge, MA: Harvard University Press, 2015), 229–30.

35 Joseph Cornell, diary entry, copied October 18–19, 1951, series 3: Diaries, box 6, folder 10, Joseph Cornell Papers, AAA.

36 As Culler writes of the familiar association of lyric with artistic subjectivity, "This conception of the lyric, as representation of subjective experience, while widely disseminated and influential, no longer has great currency in the academic world. It has been replaced by a variant which treats the lyric not as mimesis of the experience of the poet but as a representation of the action of a fictional speaker: in this account, the lyric is spoken by a persona, whose situation and motivation one needs to reconstruct." Culler, *Theory of the Lyric*, 2.

37 Stewart, *Poetry and the Fate of the Senses*, 13.

38 Stewart, *Poetry and the Fate of the Senses*, 3.

39 As Stewart writes, "The flux of sense impressions has a transitive and intransitive aspect. What propels us outward will also transform us, and it is only by finding means of making sense impressions intelligible to others that we are able to situate ourselves and our own experiences." Stewart, *Poetry and the Fate of the Senses*, 3.

40 Donald Windham, *Aviary*, exh. cat. (New York: Egan Gallery, 1949).

41 Julie Haifley, "Oral History Interview with Grace Hartigan, May 10, 1979," AAA, http://www.aaa.si.edu/collections/interviews/oral-history-interview-grace-hartigan-12326.

42 Haifley, "Oral History Interview with Grace Hartigan."

43 Denby, *Dancers, Buildings, and People in the Streets*, 263–64.

44 Erika Doss, *Benton, Pollock, and the Politics of Modernism: From Regionalism to Abstract Expressionism* (Chicago: University of Chicago Press, 1991).

45 Hartigan, quoted in Robert Saltonstall Mattison, *Grace Hartigan: A Painter's World* (New York: Hudson Hills Press, 1990), 16.

46 Haifley, "Oral History Interview with Grace Hartigan."

47 Robert Slifkin, "The Tragic Image: Action Painting Refigured," *Oxford Art Journal* 34, no. 2 (June 2011): 229–30.

48 Emily Dickinson, *Selected Poems* (London: Macmillan, 1993), 55.

49 I am indebted to Jamie Parra for this observation, and for thinking with me about this poem.

50 Joseph Cornell, diary entries, November–December 1952, series 3: Diaries, box 6, folder 16, Joseph Cornell Papers, AAA.

51 Rebecca Patterson, *The Riddle of Emily Dickinson* (New York: Houghton Mifflin, 1951), 92.

52 Joseph Cornell, diary entry, October 10, 1952, series 3: Diaries, box 6, folder 15, Joseph Cornell Papers, AAA.

53 Diana Fuss, *The Sense of an Interior: Four Writers and the Rooms That Shaped Them* (New York: Routledge, 2004), 49.

54 Quoted in Solomon, *Utopia Parkway*, 187.

55 Wallace Stevens, *The Necessary Angel: Essays on Reality and Imagination* (New York: Vintage Books, 1951), 170–71.

56 Stevens, *Necessary Angel*, 173.

57 Stevens, *Necessary Angel*, 174.

58 Shaw, *Frank O'Hara: The Poetics of Coterie* (Iowa City: Iowa University Press, 2006). See also Andrew Epstein, *Beautiful Enemies: Friendship and Postwar American Poetry* (Oxford: Oxford University Press, 2006), 4; David Lehman, *The Last Avant-Garde: The Making of New York School Poets* (New York: Anchor Books, 1999).

59 For a detailed account of the early history of Tibor de Nagy Gallery, see Karen Wilkin, "The First Fifty Years," in *Tibor de Nagy Gallery: The First Fifty Years* (New York: Tibor de Nagy, 2000), 17–84. See also Douglas Crase, "A Hidden History of the Avant-Garde," in *Tibor de Nagy Gallery*, 6–29.

60 Bernard Myers, *Tracking the Marvelous: A Life in the New York Art World* (New York: Random House, 1983), 115. In fact, the gallery opened on December 14, 1951, with an exhibition of Constantino Nivola.

61 Karin Roffman, *The Songs We Know Best: John Ashbery's Early Life* (New York: Farrar, Straus and Giroux, 2017), 40–41.

62 Ashbery quoted in Roffman, *The Songs We Know Best*, 187–88.

63 Roffman, *The Songs We Know Best*, 41.

64 Angus Fletcher, *A New Theory for American Poetry: Democracy, the Environment, and the Future of Imagination* (Cambridge, MA: Harvard University Press, 2004), 82.

65 Poet Kenneth Koch, another member of the New York school milieu, boasted that he had been the only soldier in the Philippines with a subscription to *View*. Mark Ford, *Raymond Roussel and the Republic of Dreams* (Ithaca, NY: Cornell University Press, 2000), 229.

66 John Ashbery, quoted in Ellen Levy, *Criminal Ingenuity: Moore, Cornell, Ashbery, and the Struggle between the Arts* (Oxford: Oxford University Press, 2011), 133.

67 John Ashbery, *Reported Sightings: Art Chronicles 1957–1987* (New York: Knopf, 1989), 27. Ellen Levy sees Ashbery's potent phrase as addressing questions of medium specificity, modernist autonomy, and institutionalization, which she regards as the predominant concern of artists and writers during this period. Levy, *Criminal Ingenuity*, 141.

68 Ashbery, "The Heritage of Dada and Surrealism," in *Reported Sightings*.

69 Ashbery, *Reported Sightings*, 18.

70 Frank O'Hara, "Having a Coke with You," in *The Collected Works of Frank O'Hara*, ed. Donald Allen (Berkeley: University of California Press, 1995), 360.

71 O'Hara, *The Collected Works of Frank O'Hara*, 537.

72 O'Hara, "Joseph Cornell," in *The Collected Works of Frank O'Hara*, 237.

73 I am grateful to Jamie Parra for this observation.

74 Stan Brakhage, "*Centuries of June* Catalogue," The New American Cinema Group: The Film-Makers' Coop, http://film-makerscoop.com/catalogue/stan-brakhage-centuries-of-june.

75 P. Adams Sitney, *Visionary Film: The American Avant-Garde, 1943–2000* (New York: Oxford University Press, 2002), 159.

76 Sitney, *Visionary Film*, 160. Sitney extends this argument in *The Cinema of Poetry*.

77 Stan Brakhage, *Metaphors on Vision* (New York: Anthology Film Archives; Brooklyn: Light Industry, 2017), n.p.

78 Stan Brakhage, "Introduction," *Metaphors on Vision* (New York: Film Culture, 1963), n.p.

79 Cornell quoted in Jeanne Liotta, *Joseph Cornell: Films* (San Francisco: Museum of Modern Art, 2007), Programs, http://www.jeanneliotta.net/SFMOMA_Cornell.pdf.

80 Emily Dickinson, "Centuries of June," in *The Poems of Emily Dickinson*, ed. Thomas H. Johnson (Cambridge, MA: Belknap Press of Harvard University Press, 1998), 745–46.

81 *Magic of Flowers in Painting: Loan Exhibition for the Benefit of the Lenox Hill Neighborhood Association*, Wildenstein Gallery, April 13–May 15, 1954.

82 Joseph Cornell, diary entry, April 19, 1954, series 3: Diaries, box 6, folder 27, Joseph Cornell Papers, AAA.

83 Joseph Cornell, diary entry, undated, series 3: Diaries, box 6, folder 27, Joseph Cornell Papers, AAA.

84 "Art Show to Help Lenox Hill Group," *New York Times*, April 7, 1954, 39.

85 Joseph Cornell, diary entry, undated, series 3: Diaries, box 6, folder 27, Joseph Cornell Papers, AAA.

86 Quoted in Sitney, *Visionary Film*, 165.

87 Mark Toscano, "Archiving Brakhage," *Journal of Film Preservation* 72 (November 2006): 13–25.

EPILOGUE: SOME VARIETIES OF ENCHANTMENT

Epigraph: Joseph Cornell, "Undated note," box 16, folder 5: Moon in a Tree (Cornell) [B/N #78] ca. 1972, doc. 20, Carolee Schneemann Papers, Department of Special Collections and University Archives, Stanford University.

1 I am grateful to Robert Lehrman for sharing this anecdote with me. According to Walter Hopps, the parents of Susan Weil, Rauschenberg's wife, owned several of Cornell's boxes, which they displayed in their Upper West Side apartment. Walter Hopps, *Robert Rauschenberg: The Early 1950s* (Houston: Menil Collection, 1991).

2 Thomas Crow, "Southern Boys Go to Europe: Rauschenberg, Twombly, and Johns in the 1950s," in *Jasper Johns to Jeff Koons: Four Decades of Art from the Broad Collections*, ed. Stephanie Barron and Lynn Zelevansky (Los Angeles: Museum of Contemporary Art, 2002), 44–67.

3 Quoted in Crow, *The Long March of Pop*, 44.

4 For more on the exchange of gifts among this coterie of artists, see Carlos Basualdo and Erica F. Battle, eds., *Dancing Around the Bride: Cage, Cunningham, Johns, Rauschenberg, and Duchamp* (Philadelphia: Philadelphia Museum of Art, 2012).

5 Robert Rauschenberg, quoted in Deborah Solomon, "Joseph Cornell: Pioneer of Assemblage Art," Royal Academy, May 21, 2015, https://www.royalacademy.org.uk/article/joseph-cornell-shadow-boxes-assemblage-art.

6 As Walter Hopps wrote in a 1964 review of an exhibition at Dwan Gallery devoted to boxes, "A year ago, with deep conviction, a young artist explained to me that all physical existence divides into two realms: the container and the contained." Walter Hopps, "Boxes," *Art International* 8, No. 2 (March 20, 1964): 38. The original *Boxes* exhibition was held at Dwan Gallery, Los Angeles, from February 2-February 29, 1964.

7 William Chapin Seitz, *The Art of Assemblage* (New York: Museum of Modern Art, 1961), 68

8 Robert Rauschenberg, quoted in Lawrence Alloway et al., "The Art of Assemblage: A Symposium (1961)," in *Essays on Assemblage*, ed. John Elderfield (New York: Museum of Modern Art, 1992), 148.

9 Allan Kaprow, *Assemblage, Environments & Happenings* (New York: H. N. Abrams, 1966), 166.

10 William Pietz, "The Problem of the Fetish I," *RES: Anthropology and Aesthetics* 9 (1985): 5.

11 Robert Rauschenberg, "L'Obelisco, March 3–10, 1953," in Walter Hopps, *Robert Rauschenberg*, 232.

12 Kaprow, *Assemblage, Environments & Happenings*, 154.

13 Kaprow, *Assemblage, Environments & Happenings*, 163.

14 As Crow writes, "The legend has been that a hostile review after their second exhibition in Florence caused Rauschenberg to thrown nearly all of these objects into the River Arno—obeying to the letter the sarcastic instruction of the critic in question. 'It saved the packing problem,' he said at the time; but that literally throwaway remark arguably masked a deeper motivation, a panicked response to some disquiet engendered by his own creations." Thomas Crow, *The Long March of Pop: Art, Music, and Design, 1930–1995* (New Haven, CT: Yale University Press, 2015), 45.

15 Hal Foster, *The Return of the Real: The Avant-Garde at the End of the Century* (Cambridge, MA: MIT Press, 1996), 4, 78.

16 For a representative example of this line of criticism, see Branden Joseph, *Random Order: Robert Rauschenberg and the Neo-Avant-Garde* (Cambridge, MA: MIT Press, 2003).

17 "Robert Rauschenberg," *Des Moines Art Center: An Uncommon Vision* (Des Moines, IA: Des Moines Art Center, 1998).

18 Seitz, *The Art of Assemblage*, 10, 13.

19 For more on this milieu, see Sally Banes, *Greenwich Village 1963: Avant-Garde Performance and the Effervescent Body* (Durham, NC: Duke University Press, 1993).

20 Seitz, *The Art of Assemblage*, 87, 89.

21 William Chapin Seitz, *Art in the Age of Aquarius*, ed. Marla Price (Washington, DC: Smithsonian Institution Press, 1992).

22 James Christen Steward, *Betye Saar: Extending the Frozen Moment* (Berkeley: University of California Press, 2005), 15.

23 Kellie Jones, *South of Pico: African American Artists in Los Angeles in the 1960s and 70s* (Durham, NC: Duke University Press, 2017), 130.

24 Jones, *South of Pico*, 129.

25 Quoted in Susan M. Anderson, "Journey into the Sun: California Artists and Surrealism," in *On the Edge of America: California Modernist Art, 1900–1950*, ed. Paul J. Karlstrom (Berkeley: University of California Press, 1996), 181; see also Susan Elrich, ed., *Pacific Dreams: Currents of Surrealism and Fantasy in California Art, 1934–1957* (Los Angeles: Armand Hammer Museum of Art and Cultural Center, 1995).

26 Man Ray provided the connective tissue between Copley and the Surrealists, introducing him to Max Ernst and Marcel Duchamp, as well as Alexander Iolas at Hugo Gallery. William N. Copley, "CPLY: Portrait of the Artist as a Young Dealer," in *CPLY: X-RATED* (New York: Paul Kasmin Gallery, 2011).

27 Walter Hopps, "Gimme Strength: Joseph Cornell and Marcel Duchamp Remembered," in *Joseph Cornell / Marcel Duchamp . . . in Resonance*, ed. Anne d'Harnoncourt and Anne Temkin (Philadelphia: Philadelphia Museum of Art, 1998), 67.

28 Betye Saar, "Influences: Betye Saar," *Frieze*, September 27, 2016, https://frieze.com/article/influences-betye-saar.

29 Saar, "Influences: Betye Saar."

30 Quoted in Steward, *Betye Saar: Extending the Frozen Moment*, 64.

31 Quoted in Steward, *Betye Saar: Extending the Frozen Moment*, 72.

32 Jones, *South of Pico*, 108.

33 Sylvia Wynter, "Unsettling the Coloniality of Being/Power/Truth/Freedom: Towards the Human, after Man, Overrepresentation—An Argument," *CR: The New Centennial Review* 3, no. 3 (2003): 264.

34 Sylvia Wynter, "On Disenchanting Discourse: 'Minority' Literary Criticism and Beyond," *Cultural Critique* 7 (Autumn 1987): 242.

35 Richard Cándida Smith, *Utopia and Dissent: Art, Poetry, and Politics in California* (Berkeley: University of California Press, 1996).

36 Wynter herself approaches a version of this idea in her far-ranging interview with David Scott, which addresses the historical "de-godding" of the world in relation to the invention of Man, among many other topics. Near the end of the interview, Scott states, "You want—if I might put it this way, to *re-enchant* the human in humanism? What justifies this? Why not abandon humanism? Why not leave humanism in Europe?" Wynter eventually answers that what she hopes for is, "A new mode of experiencing ourselves in which every mode of being human, every form of life that has ever been enacted, is a part of us, We, a part of them." David Scott and Sylvia Wynter, "The Re-Enchantment of Humanism: An Interview with Sylvia Wynter," *Small Axe* 8 (September 2000): 195, 197.

37 Betye Saar, "Influences: Betye Saar."

38 "Invitation to Artist's Reception for 'Black Contributors,'" Berkeley Revolution digital archive, http://revolution.berkeley.edu/black-contributions/?cat=437&subcat=3.

39 Saar, quoted in Steward, *Betye Saar: Extending the Frozen Moment*, 96.

40 James Baldwin, quoted in Ashon T. Crawley, *Blackpentecostal Breath: The Aesthetics of Possibility* (New York: Fordham University Press, 2017), 75.

41 Carolee Schneemann, "Cornell at an [illegible]," box 16, folder 5: "Moon in a Tree (Cornell) [B/N #78] ca. 1972, doc. 18, Carolee Schneemann Papers, Department of Special Collections and University Archives, Stanford University.

42 Carolee Schneemann, "Interview with Robert Lehrman, April 27, 2001," 2, in box 69, folder 11, Carolee Schneemann Papers, Department of Special Collections and University Archives, Stanford University.

43 As Schneemann wrote of their relationship, "perhaps I never struggled with Joseph becaus e [*sic*] his position was as e xtreme [*sic*] as mine seemed to be/explain: there were no negociable [*sic*] social transformations; you couldn't say to Joseph, why don't you get married and settled down and he would never posit such a thing to me; if I came to him in a transfigured state, a state which emphasised [*sic*] my solitary pre-pubescent, enchanted self this condition absyraacted [*sic*] and fragmented my full life but did not do dammage [*sic*] to my integral self that is one come to Joseph as a self not as a female in r lationship [*sic*] to another man, of a female self being conventionally mythicized away from her unique self—the aspect he cherished was one totally neglected forgotten abjured by all exiisting [*sic*] cultural forms and attributes in a real woman." Carolee Schneemann, untitled essay, box 16, folder 5: "Moon in a Tree (Cornell) [B/N #78] ca. 1972, doc. 18, Carolee Schneemann Papers, Department of Special Collections and University Archives, Stanford University.

44 Carolee Schneemann, "Undated Document," box 16, folder 5: "Moon in a Tree (Cornell) [B/N #78] ca. 1972, Carolee Schneemann Papers, Department of Special Collections and University Archives, Stanford University.

45 Sabine Breitwieser, "Kinetic Painting: Carolee Schneemann's Media," in *Carolee Schneemann, Kinetic Painting* (Salzburg: Museum der Moderne, 2015), 116, 14.

46 Carolee Schneemann, "Undated Document," box 16, folder 5: "Moon in a Tree (Cornell) [B/N #78] ca. 1972, Carolee Schneemann Papers, Department of Special Collections and University Archives, Stanford University.

47 Carolee Schneemann, "Interview with Robert Lehrman, April 27, 2001," 4.

48 Carolee Schneemann, *Eye Body: 36 Transformative Actions for Camera, 1963*, in Breitwieser, *Carolee Schneemann, Kinetic Painting*, 116.

49 Schneemann quoted in Andrea Juno, *Angry Women* (New York: Juno Books, 1999), 169.

50 Carolee Schneemann, "Meat Joy," in Breitwieser, *Carolee Schneemann, Kinetic Painting*, 130.

51 Joanna Roche, "Performing Memory in Moon in a Tree: Carolee Schneemann Recollects Joseph Cornell," *Art Journal* 60, no. 4 (Winter 2001): 12.

52 Carolee Schneemann, "Undated Note," box 16, folder 5: "Moon in a Tree (Cornell) [B/N #78] ca. 1972, Carolee Schneemann Papers, Department of Special Collections and University Archives, Stanford University.

53 Roche, "Performing Memory in Moon in a Tree," 9.

54 Carolee Schneemann, "Undated Note," box 16, folder 5: "Moon in a Tree (Cornell) [B/N #78] ca. 1972, Carolee Schneemann Papers, Department of

Special Collections and University Archives, Stanford University.

55 Maggie Nelson, "The Reënchantment of Carolee Schneemann," *New Yorker,* March 15, 2019, https://www.newyorker.com/books/page-turner/the-re-enchantment-of-carolee-schneemann.

"the end

is

the beginning."

INDEX

Page numbers in *italics* refer to illustrations.

CREDITS

Addison Gallery of American Art, Phillips Academy, Andover, MA / Art Resource, NY: 5.11

Photograph by Al Giese. Courtesy of Estate of Carolee Schneemann, Galerie Lelong & Co., Hales Gallery, and P·P·O·W, New York. © Carolee Schneemann: 6.21, 6.28

Photograph by Allen Lester. Image courtesy of the John and Mable Ringling Museum of Art, Sarasota, FL: 3.11

Photograph by Allen Phillips / Wadsworth Atheneum: 2.1

Art Institute of Chicago: 5.2, 5.12

Art Institute of Chicago / Art Resource, NY: 0.1, 5.14

Art Institute of Chicago. © Joseph and Robert Cornell Foundation / VAGA at Artists Rights Society (ARS), New York: 6.27

Digital image © Art Institute of Chicago, Chicago / Licensed by SCALA / Art Resource, NY. © Joseph and Robert Cornell Foundation / VAGA at Artists Rights Society (ARS), New York: 0.3

Austrian Film Museum Collections, Vienna: 1.17, 3.39–3.42, 4.18, 4.19, 4.21, 4.23, 4.27, 5.18, 5.20–5.23, 6.29

Photograph by author: 0.5, 1.30, 1.31, 4.20, 5.6, 5.7, 5.16, 5.17

Photo Benjamin Blackwell. Courtesy of the artist and Roberts Projects, Los Angeles, CA: 6.15

Courtesy of the artist (Betye Saar) and Roberts Projects, Los Angeles, CA: 6.11

Courtesy of Estate of Carolee Schneemann, Galerie Lelong & Co., Hales Gallery, and P·P·O·W, New York. © Carolee Schneemann: 6.17–6.19

Photograph by Cathy Carver. Hirshhorn Museum and Sculpture Garden, Washington, DC: 1.1

Photograph © Christie's Images / Bridgeman Images: 1.27, 2.12

Chronicle/Alamy Stock Photo: 4.9

Photograph by Cy Twombly. © Robert Rauschenberg Foundation: 6.5

Photograph courtesy of Cynthia Nadelman. © Estate of Elie Nadelman: 3.18

Courtesy of David Rumsey Map Collection, David Rumsey Map Center, Stanford Libraries: 3.35, 3.38

Digital image courtesy of Duke University Libraries: 2.7

© Edward Owen / Art Resource, NY. © Joseph and Robert Cornell Foundation / VAGA at Artists Rights Society (ARS), New York: 5.15

Photograph by Erich Lessing / Art Resource, NY: 3.2, 4.26, 4.36

Photograph by Erró. Courtesy of Estate of Carolee Schneemann, Galerie Lelong & Co., Hales Gallery, and P·P·O·W, New York. © Carolee Schneemann: 6.20, 6.26

Photograph by Frank J. Thomas. Courtesy of Frank J. Thomas Archives: 6.9, 6.10

Photograph by George Platt Lynes. Courtesy of Estate of George Platt Lynes. Digital image by Stanford Visual Resources Center: 2.16

Photograph by Hans Namuth. Courtesy of Center for Creative Photography, University of Arizona. © 1991 Hans Namuth Estate: 1.3–1.5

Digital image courtesy of Harper's Bazaar Archive, ProQuest: 2.24, 3.27

Jerome Robbins Dance Division, New York Public Library: 4.2, 4.33

Photograph by Jerry L. Thompson: 3.20

© Joseph and Robert Cornell Foundation / VAGA at Artists Rights Society (ARS), New York: 1.8–1.13, 1.15, 1.16, 1.18, 1.29, 2.29

Digital image courtesy of Joseph Cornell Study Center, Smithsonian American Art Museum, Washington, DC: 1.2, 3.1, 3.12, 3.23–3.25, 3.31–3.34, 4.17

Digital image courtesy of Joseph Cornell Study Center, Smithsonian American Art Museum, Washington, DC. © Joseph and Robert Cornell Foundation / VAGA at Artists Rights Society (ARS), New York: 2.31, 4.4–4.8, 4.10, 4.25, 5.5

Photograph courtesy of Leo Castelli Gallery Records, Archives of American Art, Smithsonian Institution. © Virginia Museum of Fine Arts: 5.1

Digital image courtesy of Linda Hall Library, Kansas City, MO: 2.30

Photograph by Mary Evans. Courtesy of AF Archive / Everett Collection, New York: 4.24

Mashter Movie Archive / Alamy Stock Photo: 3.26

Menil Collection, Houston, TX: 4.32, 4.34, 4.35

Image © Metropolitan Museum of Art, New York: 2.5, 2.6, 2.8, 4.3, 4.22

© Metropolitan Museum of Art, New York / Art Resource, NY: 1.20

Image © Metropolitan Museum of Art. Courtesy of Estate of George Platt Lynes: 3.8, 3.16

Courtesy of Michael Rosenfeld Gallery LLC, New York: 6.12

MoMA Film Department / Art Resource, NY: 1.21–1.23

Photograph by Morris Huberland. © Photography Collection, New York Public Library: 1.6
Digital image courtesy of Museum of Contemporary Art, Los Angeles. Licensed by SCALA / Art Resource, NY: 5.3
Digital image © Museum of Modern Art, New York / Licensed by SCALA / Art Resource, NY: P.1, P.3, 1.24, 2.11, 2.14, 2.15, 4.11, 4.12, 4.38, 6.14
Digital image © Museum of Modern Art, New York / Licensed by SCALA / Art Resource, NY. © Joseph and Robert Cornell Foundation / VAGA at Artists Rights Society (ARS), New York: 4.37
Image courtesy of Museum of Performance + Design, San Francisco, CA. Courtesy of Estate of George Platt Lynes: 3.9
National Gallery of Art, Washington, DC: 5.19
National Gallery of Canada, Ottawa. © Joseph and Robert Cornell Foundation / VAGA at Artists Rights Society (ARS), New York: 5.9
Image courtesy of National Portrait Gallery, Washington, DC. Courtesy of Estate of George Platt Lynes: 3.10
Courtesy Odette Pollar and the Mary Ann Pollar Collection: 6.16
Photograph by Patrick Shyu. Courtesy of New York Transit Museum: 2.28
Photograph courtesy of Peabody Essex Museum. © Joseph and Robert Cornell Foundation / VAGA at Artists Rights Society (ARS), New York: 1.7, 2.2, 2.4, 2.18, 2.20–2.22, 3.28, 4.28, 5.10
Photograph courtesy of Peggy Guggenheim Collection, Venice. © Joseph and Robert Cornell Foundation / VAGA at Artists Rights Society (ARS), New York: 4.30
Photograph by Peter Geymayer. Wikimedia Commons: 4.1
Philadelphia Museum of Art. © Joseph and Robert Cornell Foundation / VAGA at Artists Rights Society (ARS), New York: 4.13, 4.15, 4.16
© Phillips Collection, Washington, DC: 1.14
Purchase College, State University of New York: 5.13
Photograph by Rich Sanders, Des Moines. © Joseph and Robert Cornell Foundation / VAGA at Artists Rights Society (ARS), New York: 3.21, 3.22
Photograph by Rich Sanders, Des Moines. © Robert Rauschenberg Foundation: 6.8
© Robert Rauschenberg Foundation: 6.1, 6.2, 6.6, 6.7
Photograph courtesy of Ron Seymour. © Estate of Maurice Seymour: 4.31
© Roy Export S.A.S: 3.3–3.5
Royal Collection Trust / © Her Majesty Queen Elizabeth 2019: 2.19
Photograph by R. V. Smutny: 3.17
Photograph by Seymour Rosen. Courtesy of SPACES Archives: 6.13
Photograph by Soichi Sunami. Digital image © Museum of Modern Art, New York / Licensed by SCALA / Art Resource, NY: 2.3, 2.10, 2.13, 2.23, 6.3, 6.4
Courtesy of Stanford Special Collections: 6.22–6.24
Photograph by Stanford Visual Resources Center: 0.4, 1.19, 1.26, 1.28, 2.17, 2.25, 3.6, 3.7, 3.13–3.15, 4.14, 4.29
Photograph by Thomas Griesel. Digital image © Museum of Modern Art, New York / Licensed by SCALA / Art Resource, NY: P.2
Image © Tretyakov Gallery, Moscow: 3.36
Photographer unidentified. Collection of Mark Kelman, New York: 1.25
© Virginia Museum of Fine Arts: 5.4, 5.8
Digital image courtesy of Vogue Archive, ProQuest: 2.26, 2.27
Photograph by Wurts Brothers. Digital image © The Museum of Modern Art, New York / Licensed by SCALA / Art Resource, NY: 2.9
Photograph by Yasuo Kuniyoshi. © CNAC/MNAM/Dist. RMN-Grand Palais / Art Resource, NY: 0.2
Digital image © Whitney Museum of American Art / Licensed by Scala / Art Resource, NY: 3.19, 3.30
Digital image © Whitney Museum of American Art / Licensed by SCALA / Art Resource, NY. © Joseph and Robert Cornell Foundation / VAGA at Artists Rights Society (ARS), New York: 6.25

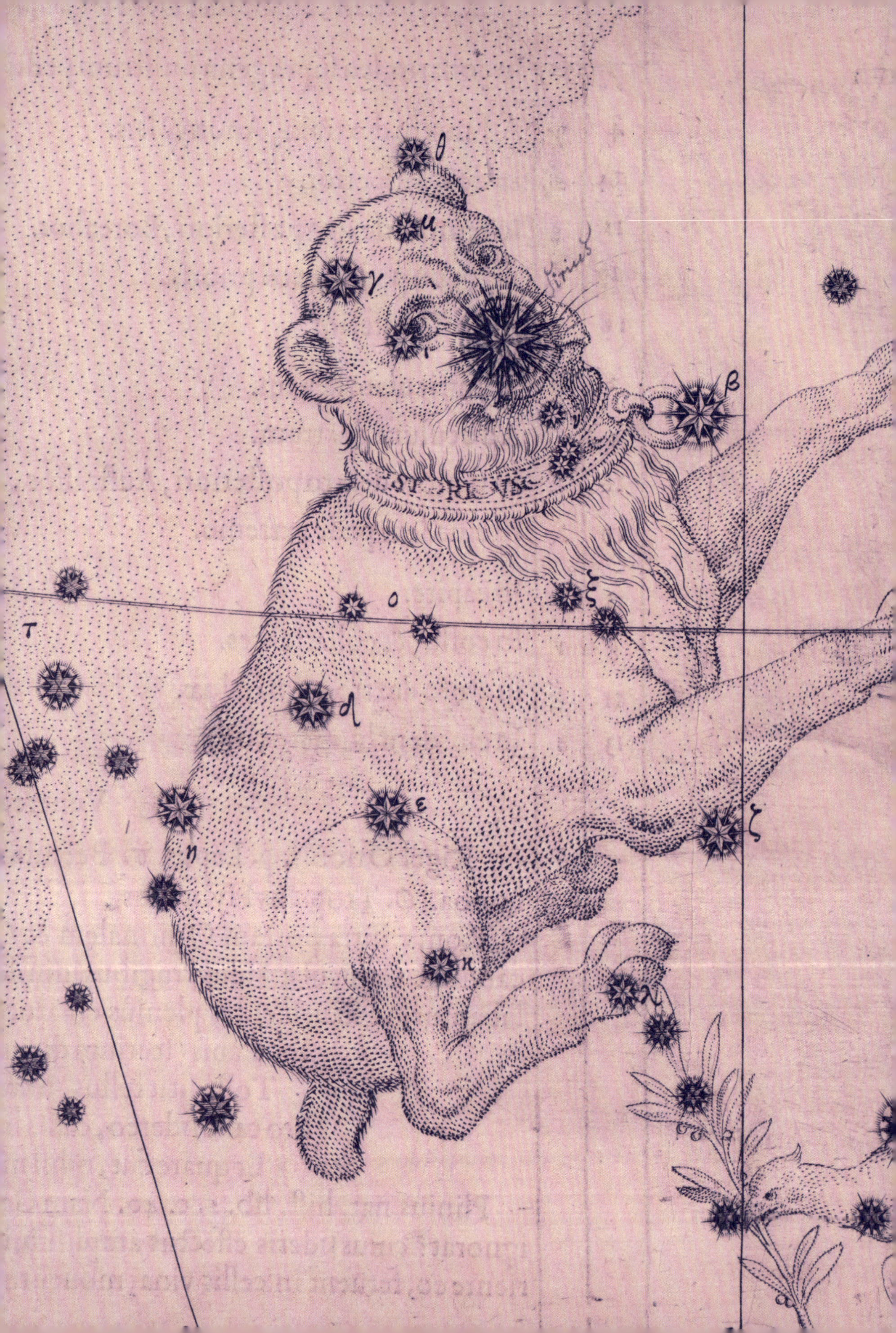
SYRIVS